Document Sets for the South
in U.S. History

Document Sets for the South in U.S. History

Richard Purday

North Georgia College

D. C. Heath and Company
Lexington, Massachusetts   Toronto

Address editorial correspondence to:

D. C. Heath
125 Spring Street
Lexington, MA 02173

Acquisitions Editor: James Miller
Developmental Editor: Sylvia Mallory
Production Editor: Rosemary Jaffe
Designer: Kenneth Hollman
Production Coordinator: Charles Dutton
Text Permissions Editor: Margaret Roll

Cover: "Alfred Graham, the first teacher of basketry at Penn School, St. Helena
           Island, South Carolina, brought the craft from Africa as a boy," 1909.
           Penn School Collection. Permission granted by Penn Center, St. Helena
           Island, South Carolina.

Published simultaneously in Canada.

Printed in the United States of America.

International Standard Book Number: 0–669–27108–X

Library of Congress Catalog Number: 90–85657

10 9 8 7 6 5 4 3 2 1

Preface

Anyone compiling a documentary history of the American South faces agonizing decisions. With such an abundance of rich primary-source material, what should be included and what should be left out? And the primary sources are indeed rich. Political figures like James Madison and John C. Calhoun have been among the nation's greatest constitutional theorists. Few Americans have made such an impact on United States history by the power of their oratory as Patrick Henry and Martin Luther King, Jr. Southerners have always prided themselves on their ability to communicate their ideas and opinions to others. They have, it has been said, a rage to explain.

Document Sets for the South in U.S. History has a dual purpose. It is intended for use by instructors who incorporate a study of the South into their survey courses of American history. It is also designed to stimulate the interest of students who wish to explore southern history further. Each document set includes questions addressing issues that have been and continue to be debated and analyzed by scholars of the region. Each document set also contains a select bibliography of secondary sources.

The astute student quickly learns that historians, despite being seekers after the truth, are rarely entirely objective either in the selection of source material for their research or in the conclusions they reach. I make no claims to impartiality. As one who is much more fascinated by dissent from than acceptance of orthodox values, I have included many documents reflecting nonconformity with prevailing attitudes and customs. It would have been easy, for example, to fill Document Set 6 with expressions of southern women's support for slavery. The search to find dissenting viewpoints was more arduous but infinitely more rewarding and, I hope, more interesting to the reader. Some of the selections in Document Set 6 appear in print for the first time. My interpretation of the course of southern history should emerge from a reading of the introductions to the document sets.

The examination of documentary material adds an extra dimension to the study of history, but a word of caution is necessary. Because most people write or speak to express opinions, often for purposes of vindicating their own actions and beliefs, students should be aware that somebody else will have articulated different and conflicting ideas on the same subject. Documents therefore rarely provide definitive answers to historical problems. Instead, they convey to the student a sense of the rich and infinite complexity of the historical process.

The first document set examines the southern colonies from the settlement at Jamestown to the establishment of the plantation system, including the introduction of black slaves from Africa to the North American continent. Document Set 2 concentrates on the southern colonies' opposition to imperial policies. It includes a rare printing of the full text of Patrick Henry's speech to the Virginia convention. The theme of Document Set 3 is the South's role in the creation of the American republic, including James Madison's brilliant defense of republican government, and southerners' subsequent concerns for the security of their section's interests. The fourth document set reveals the evolution of a new southern justification for the existence of slavery, as well as an examination of white attitudes and actions toward slaves. Document Set 5 focuses on the slaves' reaction to their bondage. Included are the views of Frederick Douglass and Nat Turner, two slaves who used very different methods to fight for their freedom. Women suffered a different brand of oppression, a stultifying conformity to the values of a male-dominated society. Documents in the sixth set present the concept of the "cult of pure womanhood" and women's opinions on themselves, their husbands, and slavery.

The role of nonslaveholders, who composed a majority of the population in the antebellum South, provides the topic for Document Set 7. Beginning with John C. Calhoun's changing attitude to the federal government and to the North, Document Set 8 traces the evolution of southern sectionalism, culminating in the decision for secession and the uncertainty that this momentous decision generated. The ninth document set looks at some of the reasons why the South lost the Civil War. Document Set 10 spotlights the hopes and expectations of the emancipated black people of the South during Reconstruction and their subsequent disillusionment with the conditions of their newly won freedom. Document Set 11 offers a glimpse of the ideology and the reality of life in the New South. The emergence and maintenance of a segregated South is the theme of Document Set 12. The advocation of extreme violence to keep blacks subservient is graphically illustrated here.

African-Americans' efforts to survive in a hostile society that refused to allow them any form of progress is the theme of Document Set 13. The social, economic, and cultural deficiencies of the South became more apparent between the world wars. Document Set 14 reveals some of those problems. A sustained challenge to the doctrine of white supremacy, which began during World War II, accelerated in the 1950s, resulting in the legal overthrow of Jim Crow in southern society by 1965. Document Set 15, outlining the methods and goals of the civil-rights movement begins with the historic 1954 Supreme Court decision that outlawed segregation in education. Document Set 16 looks as the considerable impact of modernization, both positive and negative, on the South. Despite its successes, the civil-rights movement could not erase racial prejudice from the South. Discrimination against African-Americans has decreased, but the improvement in race relations has fallen far short of the hopes and expectations of civil-rights leaders. Document Set 17 shows that issues related to race remain central to the southern experience. In the final document set, the South's ability to survive as a distinct geographical and cultural region of the nation is featured.

For their comments and advice on sections of the manuscript, I am grateful to James A. Hodges, Larry E. Hudson, Jr., Brian Murphy, Ray C. Rensi, Robert M. Weir, and Clyde N. Wilson. Marc Jason Gilbert expertly examined the page proofs. Fully aware of my lack of proficiency with computers, Vicki M. Dowdy came to my rescue many times. I appreciate the confidence of James Miller, history editor at D. C. Heath, in my ability to carry out the project, and I could not have wished for more understanding and supportive editors than Sylvia Mallory and Rosemary Jaffe. Marcia Cook Purday has always provided encouragement for all my efforts. For that and everything else, I thank her.

R. P.

Contents

Document Set 1

Patterns of Settlement, c. 1600–1740

Before a group of adventurers established the first permanent English settlement in America, at Jamestown in May 1607, English people regarded the region that would become known as the South as a promised land. Prevented by law from inheriting family estates in England, many younger sons of the aristocracy and gentry sailed across the Atlantic after Jamestown, in hopes that the availability of vast tracts of land in Virginia would satisfy their frustrated desires for wealth and power. Other English subjects, including Catholics who migrated to Maryland, left England seeking a haven from the growing intolerance of Stuart England toward religious dissenters. And to ambitious adventurers from the English West Indian island of Barbados, where land was concentrated in the hands of a few great sugar planters, Carolina—especially the lush subtropical southern part—proved an irresistible attraction. Eighty years later, Georgia, the last of the thirteen colonies, became a refuge for England's "worthy poor," whose efforts at economic advancement had been thwarted by the English goverment's fiscal policies. These policies held down wages, resulting in widespread poverty among the working classes.

For some, the dream that had lured them came true. The cultivation of tobacco in the Chesapeake Bay area and rice and indigo on the Carolina coast led to the creation of a privileged planter class that developed strong commercial ties to England. For other social groups, the colonial experience was not so fruitful. The propensity of planters to consolidate and expand their landholdings pushed many less fortunate people into the backcountry, where frontier life was often economically unrewarding and perilous. Moreover, as English settlers moved farther into the interior, they took over the ancestral lands of the native Americans (whom they called Indians) and pushed them steadily westward. Meanwhile, dark-skinned Africans, whose status in the colonies was initially unclear and imprecise, quickly became defined as slaves, who served their owners for the duration of their lives and whose offspring inherited their condition. From an early stage, the southern experience was different from that of both old England and the New England colonies farther north. In their increasing commitment to a plantation system manned by involuntary black slave labor, the people of the southern colonies clearly emulated the islands of the English West Indies in their pattern of development.

Once the English interest in North America moved beyond exploration to colonization, England's need to populate the continent became paramount. The first selection, an ode from the works of the English poet Michael Drayton, typifies the literature written in the early seventeenth century to lure people to Virginia. The harsh reality of life there was reflected in an extremely high mortality rate, as shown in the second document, an account by George Percy, one of the first colonists. Percy's initial impressions of the native Americans who inhabited the country were far from favorable, even though the Indians' help in providing food saved the survivors from sharing the grim fate of their stricken colleagues. European-Indian relations remained fairly amicable until the 1620s, when the native people's discontent, inflamed by English colonists' encroachment on their land and contempt for their culture, led to open warfare. Nearly 350 settlers died in what became known as the Massacre of 1622. The interpretation of the incident in the third document, written by Captain John Smith, the most famous of the early-seventeenth-century adventurers, did much to persuade the English that the Indians were treacherous and untrustworthy. Death by disease or by Indian attack might have been preferable to early Virginians than punishment for violations of the law. As the fourth document indicates, the Virginia Company believed that the colony could prevent breaches of conduct only by imposing strict disciplinary measures.

The fifth, sixth, and seventh documents trace the evolution of a labor system in the southern colonies. The promise of a small land grant prompted Wessell Webling, writing in document 5, to bind himself to service for three years. By mid-century, however, indentured servitude of this kind could not provide the amount of labor necessary to work the large tobacco plantations of the Chesapeake, and so tobacco growers turned increasingly to slave labor. The act passed by the Maryland General Assembly of 1664 (document 6) defines slavery as both a permanent and hereditary condition, relegating blacks transported from Africa to the lowest level of colonial society. In answer to criticism of the slave-labor system, Robert Beverley offers in document 7 one of the earliest defenses of slavery. The Chesapeake tidewater area was dominated by men like Beverley, who formed a self-conscious planter elite. Another, William Byrd, shows his contempt for the habits and customs of the backwoods people of North Carolina in the eighth document. The basis of the planters' wealth lay in the successful cultivation of tobacco, the economic importance of which is explained by George Alsop, an indentured servant, in the ninth document. Rice was the most important staple crop of South Carolina, but indigo became a valuable export in the mid-eighteenth century, thanks to the experiments of a remarkable woman, Eliza Lucas Pinckney. In the final document, a letter to her son, Pinckney remembers her first efforts at planting and cultivating indigo.

Questions for Analysis

1. In what ways did the environment shape the colonial experience in the South?

2. How did the preconceptions of Europeans affect their relationship with the native Americans?

3. To what extent was the class system of England duplicated in the southern colonies?

4. How important was the cultivation of tobacco and other staple crops in the development of colonial society?

5. Which came first: slavery or racism?

6. When and how did slavery evolve from a labor system into an integral part of the southern colonies' structure?

1. A Poet's Impressions of Virginia, 1619*

You brave Heroique minds,
Worthy your Countries Name;
   That Honour still pursue,
   Goe, and subdue,
Whilst loyt'ring Hinds
Lurke here at home, with shame.

Britans, you stay too long,
Quickly aboard bestow you,
   And with a merry Gale
   Swell your stretch'd Sayle,
With Vowes as strong,
As the Winds that blow you.

---

* Some of the spelling in this document has been modernized.

Your Course securely steere,
West and by South forth keepe,
 Rocks, Lee-shores, nor Sholes,
 When EOLUS scowles,
You need not feare,
So absolute the Deepe.

And cheerefully at Sea,
Successe you still intice,
 To get the Pearle and Gold,
 And ours to hold,
VIRGINIA,
Earth's onely Paradise.

Where Nature hath in store
Fowle, Venison, and Fish,
 And the Fruitfull'st Soyle,
 Without your Toyle,
Three Harvests more,
All greater then your Wish.

And the ambitious Vine
Crownes with his purple Masse,
 The cedar reaching hie
 To kisse the Sky
The Cypresse, Pine
And use-full Sassafras.

To whome, the gold Age
Still Natures lawes doth give,
 No other Cares that tend,
 But Them to defend
From Winters rage,
That long there doth not live.

When as the Lushious smell
Of that delicious Land,
 Above the Seas that flowes,
 The cleere Wind throwes,
Your Hearts to swell
Approaching the deare Strande.

In kenning of the Shore
(Thanks to God first given,)
 O you the happy'st men,
 Be Frolike then,
Let Cannons roare,
Frighting the wide Heaven.

And in Regions farre
Such Heroes bring yee foorth,
 As those from whom We came,
 And plant Our name,
Under that Starre
Not knowne unto our North.

And as there Plenty growes
Of Lawrell every where,
 APOLLO'S Sacred tree,
 You may it see,
A Poets Browes
To crowne, that may sing there.

Thy Voyages attend
Industrious HACKLUIT,
 Whose Reading shall inflame
 Men to seeke Fame,
And much commend
To after-Times thy Wit.

2. *George Percy on Disease and Death, 1607*

. . . Munday the two and twentieth of June, in the morning Captaine Newport in the Admirall departed from James Port for England.

Captaine Newport being gone for England, leaving us (one hundred and foure persons) verie bare and scantie of victualls, furthermore in warres and in danger of the Savages. We hoped after a supply which Captaine Newport promised within twentie weekes. But if the beginners of this action doe carefully further us, the Country being so fruitfull, it would be as great a profit to the Realme of England, as the Indies to the King of Spaine, if this River which wee have found had beene discovered in the time of warre with Spaine, it would have beene a commoditie to our Realme, and a great annoyance to our enemies. The seven and twentieth of July the King of Rapahanna, demanded a Canoa which was restored, lifted up his hand to the Sunne, which they worship as their God, besides he laid his hand on his heart, that he would be our speciall friend. It is a generall rule of these people when they swere by their God which is the Sunne, no Christian will keepe their Oath better upon this promise. These people have a great reverence to the Sunne above all other things at the rising and setting of the same, they sit downe lifting up their hands and eyes to the Sunne making a round Circle on the ground with dried Tobacco, then they began to pray making many Devillish gestures with a Hellish noise foming at the mouth, staring with their eyes, wagging their heads and hands in such a fashion and deformitie as it was monstrous to behold.

The sixt of August there died John Asbie of the bloudie Fluxe. The ninth day died George Flowre of the swelling. The tenth day died William Bruster Gentleman, of a wound given by the Savages, and was buried the eleventh day.

The fourteenth day, Jerome Alikock Ancient, died of a wound, the same day Francis Midwinter, Edward Moris Corporall died suddenly.

The fifteenth day, there died Edward Browne and Stephen Galthrope. The sixteenth day, there died Thomas Gower Gentleman. The seventeenth day, there died Thomas Mounslic. The eighteenth day, there died Robert Pennington, and John Martine Gentleman. The nineteenth day, died Drue Piggase Gentleman. The two and twentieth day of August, there died Captaine Bartholomew Gosnold one of our Councell, he was honourably buried, having all the Ordnance in the Fort shot off with many vollies of small shot.

After Captaine Gosnols death, the Councell could hardly agree by the dissention of Captaine Kendall, which afterward was committed about hainous matters which was proved against him.

The foure and twentieth day, died Edward Harington and George Walker, and were buried the same day. The sixe and twentieth day, died Kenelme Throgmortine. The seven and twentieth day died William Roods. The eight and twentieth day died Thomas Stoodie, Cape Merchant.

The fourth day of September died Thomas Jacob Sergeant. The fift day, there died Benjamin Beast. Our men were destroyed with cruell diseases as Swellings, Fluxes, Burning Fevers, and by warres, and some departed suddenly, but for the most part they died of meere famine. There were never Englishmen left in a forreigne Countrey in such miserie as wee were in this new

discovered Virginia. Wee watched every three nights lying on the bare cold ground what weather soever came warded all the next day, which brought our men to bee most feeble wretches, our food was but a small Can of Barlie sod in water to five men a day, our drinke cold water taken out of the River, which was at a floud verie salt, at a low tide full of slime and filth, which was the destruction of many of our men. Thus we lived for the space of five months in this miserable distresse, not having five able men to man our Bulwarkes upon any occasion. If it had not pleased God to have put a terrour in the Savages hearts, we had all perished by those vild and cruell Pagans, being in that weake estate as we were; our men night and day groaning in every corner of the Fort most pittifull to heare, if there were any conscience in men, it would make their harts to bleed to heare the pittiful murmurings & out-cries of our sick men without reliefe every night and day for the space of sixe weekes, some departing out of the World, many times three or foure in a night, in the morning their bodies trailed out of their Cabines like Dogges to be buried: in this sort did I see the mortalitie of divers of our people.

It pleased God, after a while, to send those people which were our mortall enemies to releeve us with victuals, as Bread, Corne, Fish, and Flesh in great plentie, which was the setting up of our feeble men, otherwise wee had all perished. Also we were frequented by divers Kings in the Countrie, bringing us store of provision to our great comfort.

The eleventh day, there was certaine Articles laid against Master Wingfield which was then President, thereupon he was not only displaced out of his President ship, but also from being of the Councell. Afterwards Captaine John Ratcliffe was chosen President.

The eighteenth day, died one Ellis Kinistone which was starved to death with cold. The same day at night, died one Richard Simmons. The nineteenth day, there died one Thomas Mouton.

William White (having lived with the Natives) reported to us of their customes in the morning by breake of day, before they eate or drinke both men, women and children, that be above tenne yeeres of age runnes into the water, there washes themselves a good while till the Sunne riseth, then offer Sacrifice to it, strewing Tobacco on the water or Land, honouring the Sunne as their God, likewise they doe at the setting of the Sunne.

3. Captain John Smith Exposes Indian "Treachery," 1622*

. . . Sir *Francis Wyat* at his arrivall [*Oct.* 1621] was advertised, he found the Countrey setled in such a firme peace, as most men there thought sure and inviolable, not onely in regard of their promises, but of a necessitie. The poore weake Salvages being every way bettered by us, and safely sheltred and defended, whereby wee might freely follow our businesse: and such was the conceit of this conceited peace, as that there was seldome or never a sword, and seldomer a peece [used], except for a Deere or Fowle; by which assurances the most plantations were placed straglingly and scatteringly, as a choice veine of rich ground invited them, and further from neighbours the better. Their houses [were] generally open to the Salvages, who were alwaies friendly fed at their tables, and lodged in their bed-chambers; which made the way plaine to effect their intents, and the conversion of the Salvages as they supposed.

Having occasion to send to *Opechankanough* about the middle of March, hee used the Messenger well, and told him he held the peace so firme, the sky should fall or he dissolved it; yet such was the treachery of those people, when they had contrived our destruction, even but two daies before the massacre, they guided our men with much kindnesse thorow the woods, and one *Browne* that lived among them to learne the language, they sent home to his Master. Yea, they borrowed our Boats to transport themselves over the River, to consult on the devillish murder that insued, and of our utter extirpation, which God of his mercy (by the meanes of one of themselves converted to Christianitie) prevented; and as well on the Friday morning that fatall day, being the two and twentieth of March [1622], as also in the evening before, as at other times they came unarmed into our houses, with Deere, Turkies, Fish, Fruits, and other provisions to sell us: yea in some places sat downe at breakfast with our people, whom immediatly with their owne tooles they slew most barbarously, not sparing either age or sex, man woman or childe; so sudden in their execution, that few or none discerned the weapon or blow that brought them to destruction. In which manner also they slew many of our people at severall works in the fileds, well knowing in what places and quarters each of our men were, in regard of their familiaritie with us, for the effecting that great master-peece of worke their conversion: and by this meanes fell that fatall morning under the bloudy and barbarous hands of that perfidious and inhumane people, three hundred forty seven men, women and children; most[l]y by their owne weapons; and not being content with their lives, they fell againe upon the dead bodies, making as well as they could a fresh murder, defacing, dragging, and mangling their dead carkases into many peeces, and carrying some parts away in derision, with base and brutish triumph.

Neither yet did these beasts spare those amongst the rest well knowne unto them, from whom they had daily received many benefits; but spightfully also massacred them without any remorse or pitie: being in this more fell then Lions and Dragons, as Histories record, which have preserved their Benefactors; such is the force of good deeds, though done to cruell beasts, to take humanitie upon them, but these miscreants put on a more unnaturall brutish-nesse then beasts, as by those instances may appeare. . . .

* Some of the spelling in this document has been modernized.

4. *The Laws of Virginia, 1610–1611*

. . . Whereas his Majesty, like himself a most zealous prince, has in his own realms a principal care of true religion and reverence to God and has always strictly commanded his generals and governors, with all his forces wheresoever, to let their ways be, like his ends, for the glory of God.

And forasmuch as no good service can be performed, or were well managed, where military discipline is not observed, and military discipline cannot be kept where the rules or chief parts thereof be not certainly set down and generally known, I have, with the advice and counsel of Sir Thomas Gates, Knight, Lieutenant-General, adhered unto the laws divine and orders politic and martial of his lordship, the same exemplified, as addition of such others as I found either the necessity of the present state of the colony to require or the infancy and weakness of the body thereof as yet able to digest, and do now publish them to all persons in the colony, that they may as well take knowledge of the laws themselves as of the penalty and punishment, which, without partiality, shall be inflicted upon the breakers of the same.

1. First, since we owe our highest and supreme duty, our greatest, and all our allegiance to him from whom all power and authority is derived and flows as from the first and only fountain, and being especial soldiers impressed in this sacred cause, we must alone expect our success from him, who is only the blesser of all good attempts, the king of kings, the commander of commanders, and lord of hosts, I do strictly command and charge all captains and officers, of what quality or nature soever, whether commanders in the field or in town or towns, forts or fortresses, to have a care that the Almighty God be duly and daily served and that they call upon their people to hear sermons, as that also they diligently frequent morning and evening prayer themselves by their own exemplar and daily life and duty herein, encouraging others thereunto, and that such who shall often and willfully absent themselves be duly punished according to the martial law in that case provided.

2. That no man speak impiously or maliciously against the holy and blessed Trinity or any of the three persons, that is to say, against God the Father, God the Son, and God the Holy Ghost, or against the known articles of the Christian faith, upon pain of death.

3. That no man blaspheme God's holy name upon pain of death, or use unlawful oaths, taking the name of God in vain, curse, or bane upon pain of severe punishment for the first offense so committed and for the second to have a bodkin thrust through his tongue; and if he continue the blaspheming of God's holy name, for the third time so offending, he shall be brought to a martial court and there receive censure of death of his offense.

4. No man shall use any traitorous words against his Majesty's person or royal authority, upon pain of death.

5. No man shall speak any word or do any act which may tend to the derision or despite of God's holy word, upon pain of death; nor shall any man unworthily demean himself unto any preacher or minister of the same, but generally hold them in all reverent regard and dutiful entreaty; otherwise he the offender shall openly be whipped three times and ask public forgiveness in the assembly of the congregation three several Sabbath days.

6. Every man and woman duly, twice a day upon the first tolling of the bell, shall upon the working days repair unto the church to hear divine service upon pain of losing his or her day's allowance for the first omission, for the second to be whipped, and for the third to be condemned to the galleys for six months. Likewise, no man or woman shall dare to violate or break the Sabbath by any gaming, public or private abroad or at home, but duly sanctify and observe the same, both himself and his family, by preparing themselves at home with private prayer that they may be the better fitted for the public, according to the commandments of God and the orders of our church. As also every man and woman shall repair in the morning to the

divine service and sermons preached upon the Sabbath day and in the afternoon to divine service and catechising, upon pain for the first fault to lose their provision and allowance for the whole week following, for the second to lose the said allowance and also to be whipped, and for the third to suffer death.

7. All preachers or ministers within this our colony or colonies shall, in the forts where they are resident, after divine service, duly preach every Sabbath day in the forenoon and catechise in the afternoon and weekly say the divine service twice every day and preach every Wednesday. Likewise, every minister where he is resident, within the same fort or fortress, towns or town, shall choose unto him four of the most religious and better disposed as well to inform of the abuses and neglects of the people in their duties and service of God, as also to the due reparation and keeping of the church handsome and fitted with all reverent observances thereunto belonging. Likewise, every minister shall keep a faithful and true record or church book of all christenings, marriages, and deaths of such our people as shall happen within their fort or fortress, towns or town, at any time, upon the burden of a neglectful conscience and upon pain of losing their entertainment.

8. He that, upon pretended malice, shall murder or take away the life of any man, shall be punished with death.

9. No man shall commit the horrible and detestable sins of sodomy, upon pain of death; and he or she that can be lawfully convict of adultery shall be punished with death. No man shall ravish or force any woman, maid, or Indian, or other, upon pain of death; and know that he or she that shall commit fornication, and evident proof made therof, for their first fault shall be whipped, for their second they shall be whipped, and for their third they shall be whipped three times a week for one month and ask public forgiveness in the assembly of the congregation.

10. No man shall be found guilty of sacrilege, which is a trespass as well committed in violating and abusing any sacred ministry, duty, or office of the church irreverently or prophanely, as by being a church robber to filch, steal, or carry away anything out of the church appertaining thereunto or unto any holy and consecrated place to the divine service of God, which no man should do upon pain of death. Likewise, he that shall rob the store of any commodities therein of what quality soever, whether provisions of victuals, or of arms, trucking stuff, apparel, linen, or woolen, hose or shoes, hats or caps, instruments or tools of steel, iron, etc., or shall rob from his fellow soldier or neighbor anything that is his, victuals, apparel, household stuff, tool, or what necessary else soever, by water or land, out of boat, house, or knapsack, shall be punished with death. . . .

. . . Every minister or preacher shall, every Sabbath day before catechising, read all these laws and ordinances publicly in the assembly of the congregation upon pain of his entertainment checked for that week. . . .

5. A Free Man Signs an Indenture, 1622*

To all to whom theise presents shall come greeting in o' Lord God everlasting.

Know yee that I *Wessell Webling* sonne of *Nicolas Webling* of *London* Brewer for & in consideration that I have bene furnished & sett out & am to bee transported unto *Virginia*, at the cost & charges of *Edward Bennett* of *London*, marchant & his associates, & for & in considera-tion that they have promised & covenanted to maintain me with sufficient meat drinke & apparell doe by these presents bind myself an apprentise unto the said *Edward Bennett* for the full terme of three yeares to begin the first [*sic.* feast] of St. *Michaell* the Archangell next after the date of these presents. And I doe promise & bind myself to doe & perform all the said terme of my aprentishippe true & faythfull service in all

* Some of the spelling in this document has been modernized.

such labours & busines as the said *Edward Bennett* or his assignes shall imploy me in, & to bee tractable & obedient as a good servant ought to bee in all such things as shalbe comaunded me by the said *Edward Bennett* or his Assignes in *Virginia*, & at the end of the said terme of three yeares the said *Edward Bennett* do promise to give unto the said apprentice an house & 50 acres of land in *Virginia* to hold to me my heires & assignes for ever, according to the custome of land there holden, & alsoe shall give to the said apprentice necessary & good apparell, & the sayd apprentice shall inhabitt & dwell uppon the said land, & shall pay yearely for the said fiftye acres of land fro & after that hee shalbe therof

possessed unto the said *Edward Bennett* the yearely rent of 50 shillings *starling* for ever & two dayes worke yearely, & to all & singuler the covenants aforesaid, one the party & behalfe of the said apprentice to bee performed & kept in manner & forme as aforesaid. The said apprentice bindeth himselfe to his said Master for these presents: In witness whereof the partyes aforesaid to these present Indentures have sett their hands & seales, the 25th of September 1622.

Signet *Ed. Bennett*

Ex' *Willm Claybourne*

6. *Maryland Legislates on Slavery for Life, 1664**

An Act Concerning Negroes & Other Slaves

Bee itt Enacted by the Right Honorable the Lord Proprietary by the advice and Consent of the upper and lower house of this present Generall Assembly That all Negroes or other slaves already within the Province And all Negroes and other slaves to bee hereafter imported into the Province shall serve Durante Vita And all Children born of any Negro or other slave shall be Slaves as their [fathers were for the terme of their lives And forasmuch as divers freeborne English women forgettfull of their free Condicon and to the disgrace of our Nation doe intermarry with Negro Slaves by which alsoe divers suites may arise touching the Issue of such woemen

and a great damage doth befall the Masters of such Negros for prevention whereof for deterring such freeborne women from such shamefull Matches Bee itt further Enacted by the Authority advice and Consent aforesaid That whatsoever free borne woman shall inter marry with any slave from and after the Last day of this present Assembly shall Serve the master of such slave dureing the life of her husband And that all the Issue of such freeborne woemen soe marryed shall be Slaves as their fathers were And Bee itt further Enacted that all the Issues of English or other freeborne woemen that have already marryed Negroes shall serve the Masters of their Parents till they be Thirty yeares of age and noe longer.

7. *Robert Beverley Defines Servants and Slaves, 1705*

···50. Their Servants, they distinguish by the Names of Slaves for Life, and Servants for a long time.

Slaves are the Negroes, and their Posterity, following the condition of the Mother, according to the Maxim, *partus sequitur ventrem*. They are

call'd Slaves, in respect of the time of their Servitude, because it is for Life.

Servants, are those which serve only for a few years, according to the time of their Indenture, or the Custom of the Country. The Custom of the Country takes place upon such as have no

---

* Some of the spelling in this document has been modernized.

Indentures. The Law in this case is, that if such Servants be under Nineteen years of Age, they must be brought into Court, to have their Age adjudged; and from the Age they are judg'd to be of, they must serve until they reach four and twenty: But if they be adjudged upwards of Nineteen, they are then only to be Servants for the term of five Years.

51. The Male-Servants, and Slaves of both Sexes, are imployed together in Tilling and Manuring the Ground, in Sowing and Planting Tobacco, Corn, & c. Some Distinction indeed is made between them in their Cloaths, and Food; but the Work of both, is no other than what the Overseers, the Freemen, and the Planters themselves do.

Sufficient Distinction is also made between the Female-Servants, and Slaves; for a White Woman is rarely or never put to work in the Ground, if she be good for any thing else: And to Discourage all Planters from using any Women so, their Law imposes the heaviest Taxes upon Female-Servants working in the Ground, while it suffers all other white Women to be absolutely exempted: Whereas on the other hand, it is a common thing to work a Woman Slave out of Doors; nor does the Law make any Distinction in her Taxes, whether her Work be Abroad, or at Home.

52. Because I have heard how strangely cruel, and severe, the Service of this Country is represented in some parts of *England*; I can't forbear affirming, that the work of their Servants, and Slaves, is no other than what every common Freeman do's. Neither is any Servant requir'd to do more in a Day, than his Overseer. And I can assure you with a great deal of Truth, that generally their Slaves are not worked near so hard, nor so many Hours in a Day, as the Husbandmen, and Day-Labourers in *England*. An Overseer is a Man, that having served his time, has acquired the Skill and Character of an experienced Planter, and is therefore intrusted with the Direction of the Servants and Slaves. . . .

8. *William Byrd Discovers "Lubberland," 1728*

. . . Surely there is no place in the World where the Inhabitants live with less Labour than in N Carolina. It approaches nearer to the Description of Lubberland than any other, by the great felicity of the Climate, the easiness of raising Provisions, and the Slothfulness of the People.

Indian Corn is of so great increase, that a little Pains will Subsist a very large Family with Bread, and then they may have meat without any pains at all, by the Help of the Low Grounds, and the great Variety of Mast that grows on the Highland. The Men, for their Parts, just like the Indians, impose all the Work upon the poor Women. They make their Wives rise out of their Beds early in the Morning, at the same time that they lye and Snore, till the Sun has run one third of his course, and disperst all the unwholesome Damps. Then, after Stretching and Yawning for half an Hour, they light their Pipes, and, under the Protection of a cloud of Smoak, venture out into the open Air; tho', if it happens to be never so little cold, they quickly return Shivering into the Chimney corner. When the weather is mild, they stand leaning with both their arms upon the corn-field fence, and gravely consider whether they had best go and take a Small Heat at the Hough: but generally find reasons to put it off till another time.

Thus they loiter away their Lives, like Solomon's sluggard, with their Arms across, and at the Winding up of the Year Scarcely have Bread to Eat.

To speak the Truth, tis a thorough Aversion to Labor that makes People file off to N Carolina, where Plenty and a Warm Sun confirm them in their Disposition to Laziness for their whole Lives. . . .

9. George Alsop on the Importance of Tobacco, 1660

. . . Tobacco is the only solid Staple Commodity of this Province: The use of it was first found out by the *Indians* many Ages agoe, and transferr'd into Christendom by that great Discoverer of *America Columbus*. It's generally made by all the Inhabitants of this Province, and between the months of *March* and *April* they sow the seed (which is much smaller then Mustard seed) in small beds and patches digg'd up and made so by art, and about *May* the Plants commonly appear green in those beds: In *June* they are transplanted from their beds, and set in little hillocks in distant rowes, dug up for the same purpose; some twice or thrice they are weeded, and succoured from their illegitimate Leaves that would be peeping out from the body of the Stalk. They top the several Plants as they find occasion in their predominating rankness: About the middle of *September* they cut the Tobacco down, and carry it into houses, (made for that purpose) to bring it to its purity: And after it has attained, by a convenient attendance upon time, to its perfection, it is then tyed up in bundles, and packt into Hogs-heads, and then laid by for the Trade.

Between *November* and *January* there arrives in this Province Shipping to the number of twenty sail and upwards all Merchant-men loaden with Commodities to Trafique and dispose of, trucking with the Planter for Silks, Hollands, Serges, and Broad-clothes, with other necessary Goods, priz'd at such and such rates as shall be judg'd on is fair and legal, for Tobacco at so much the pound, and advantage on both sides considered; the Planter for his work, and the Merchant for adventuring himself and his Commodity into so far a Country: Thus is the Trade on both sides drove on with a fair and honest *Decorum*. . . .

Tobacco is the currant Coyn of *Mary-Land*, and will sooner purchase Commodities from the Merchant, then money. . . .

10. Eliza Lucas Pinckney Relates Her Experiments with Indigo (1740s), 1785

Eliza Pinckney to Charles C. Pinckney

My dear child,

You wish me to inform you what I recollect of the introducing and culture of indigo in this country. You have heard me say I was very early fond of the vegetable world, my father was pleased with it and encouraged it, he told me the turn I had for those amusements might produce something of real and public utility, If I could bring to perfection the plants of other countries which he would procure me. Accordingly when he went to the West Indies he sent me a variety of seeds, among them the indigo. I was ignorant both of the proper season for sowing it, and the soil best adapted to it. To the best of my recollection I first try'd it in March 1741, or 1742; it was destroyed (I think by a frost). The next time in April, and it was cut down by a worm; I persevered to a third planting and succeeded, and when I informed my father it bore seed and the seed ripened, he sent a man from the Island of Monserat by the name of Cromwell who had been accustomed to making indigo there, and gave him high wages; he made some brick vats on my fathers plantation on Wappo Creek and then made the first indigo; it was very indifferent, and he made a great mistery of it, said he repented coming as he should ruin his own country by it, for my father had engaged him to let me see the whole process. I observed him as carefully as I could and informed Mr. Deveaux an old gentleman a neighbour of ours of the little knowledge I had gain'd and gave him notice when the indigo was to be beat; he saw and afterwards improved upon it, not withstanding the churlishness of Cromwell, who wished to deceive him, and threw in so large a quantity of lime water as to spoil the colour. In the year 1744 I married, and my father made Mr. Pinckney a present of all the indigo then upon the ground as the fruit of my industry. The whole was saved for seed, and your father gave part of it away in small quantities to a great number of people that year, the rest he planted the next year at Ashipo for seed, which he sold, as did some of the gentlemen to whom he had given it the year before; by this means there soon became plenty in the country. Your father gained all the information he could from the French prisoners brought in here, and used every other means of information, which he published in the Gazette for the information of the people at large.

The next year Mr. Cattle sent me a present of a couple of large plants of the wild indigo which he had just discovered. Experiments were afterwards made upon this sort, which proved to be good indigo, but it did not produce so large a quantity as the cultivated sort. I am

Your truly affectionate mother,

Eliza Pinckney

Sept. 10th, 1785.

References

1. A Poet's Impressions of Virginia, 1619
   Michael Drayton, "Ode to the Virginian Voyage," from Cyril Brett, ed., *Minor Poems of Michael Drayton* (Oxford: The Clarendon Press, 1907), pp. 70–72.

2. George Percy on Disease and Death, 1607
   George Percy, "Observations Gathered out of a Disclosure of the Plantation of the Southern Colonie in Virginia by the English, 1606," from Samual Purchas, *Hakluytus Posthumus or Purchas His Pilgrimes*, Volume XVIII (Glasgow, Scotland: James MacLehose and Sons, 1906), pp. 416–419.

3. Captain John Smith Exposes Indian "Treachery," 1622
   Edward Arber, ed., *Travels and Works of Captain John Smith*, Part II (Edinburgh, Scotland, John Grant, 1910), pp. 573–574.

4. The Laws of Virginia, 1610–1611
   "Articles, Lawes, and Orders, Divine, Politique, and Martiall for the Colony in Virginea," in William Strachey, *For the Colony in Virginea Britannia: Lawes, Divine, Morall and Martiall, Etc.* (London: Walter Barre, 1612), pp. 1–7, 19.

5. A Free Man Signs an Indenture, 1622
   "A Record of Wessell Webling His Indentures," in H. R. McIlwaine, ed., *Minutes of the Council and General Court of Colonial Virginia* (Richmond, Virginia, 1924), pp. 124–125.

6. Maryland Legislates on Slavery for Life, 1664
   Proceedings and Acts of the General Assembly of Maryland, January 1637/8–September 1664 (Baltimore: Maryland Historical Society, 1883), pp. 533–534.

7. Robert Beverley Defines Servants and Slaves, 1705
    Louis B. Wright, ed., *Robert Beverley's The History and Present State of Virginia* (Chapel Hill: University of North Carolina Press, 1947), pp. 271–272.

8. William Byrd Discovers "Lubberland," 1728
    William K. Boyd, ed., *William Byrd's Histories of the Dividing Line Betwixt Virginia and North Carolina* (Raleigh, North Carolina: The North Carolina Historical Commission, 1929), pp. 90–92.

9. George Alsop on the Importance of Tobacco, 1660
    George Alsop, *A Character of the Province of Maryland* (Baltimore: Maryland Historical Society Fund—Publication, No. 15, 1880), pp. 475–477.

10. Eliza Lucas Pinckney Relates Her Experiments with Indigo, (1740s), 1785
    "A Letter from Eliza Lucas Pinckney," in H. Roy Merrens, ed., *The Colonial South Carolina Scene: Contemporary Views, 1697–1774* (Columbia, South Carolina: University of South Carolina Press, 1977), pp. 145–146.

Further Reading

Warren Billings, John E. Selby, and Thad Tate, *Colonial Virginia: A History* (1986)

Carl Bridenbaugh, *Myths and Realities: Societies of the Colonial South* (1952)

Kenneth Coleman, *Colonial Georgia: A History* (1976)

Wesley F. Craven, *The Southern Colonies in the Seventeenth Century* (1949)

Richard B. Davis, *Intellectual Life in the Colonial South, 1585–1763*, 3 vols. (1978)

Winthrop D. Jordan, *White over Black: American Attitudes Toward the Negro, 1550–1812* (1968)

Allan Kulikoff, *Tobacco and Slaves: The Development of Southern Cultures in the Chesapeake, 1680–1800* (1986)

Aubrey C. Land, *Colonial Maryland, A History* (1981)

Hugh T. Lefler and William S. Powell, *Colonial North Carolina: A History* (1973)

Gloria L. Main, *Tobacco Colony: Life in Early Maryland, 1650–1720* (1982)

Edmund S. Morgan, *American Slavery, American Freedom: The Ordeal of Colonial Virginia* (1975)

David B. Quinn, *Set Fair for Roanoke: Voyages and Colonies, 1584–1606* (1985)

Thad W. Tate and David L. Ammerman, eds., *The Chesapeake in the Seventeenth Century: Essays on Anglo-American Society* (1979)

Clarence L. Ver Steeg, *Origins of a Southern Mosaic: Studies of Early Carolina and Georgia* (1975)

Robert M. Weir, *Colonial South Carolina: A History* (1983)

Peter Wood, *Black Majority: Negroes in South Carolina from 1670 Through the Stono Rebellion* (1974)

Document Set 2

The Colonial South and the Path to Revolution, c. 1650–1775

Commitment to the idea of independence from England did not come easily in the southern colonies. Although theirs was a heritage of dissent, colonists in the South had sound reasons for wanting the imperial-colonial connection to continue. The Carolinas and Georgia, for example, had welcomed the establishment of royal government as being less oppressive than their earlier rule by Lords Proprietors and Trustees. All along the south Atlantic seaboard, tobacco, rice, and indigo provided the basis of prosperity, and commercial and social ties with England were strong throughout the South. Plantation mansions were modeled on the architectural style of English country houses. The sons of wealthy planters attended the universities of Oxford and Cambridge and studied law at the Inns of Court. To a degree, the experience of the southern colonies was different from that of New England, where liberal charters of government made the people extremely sensitive to imperial legislation.

The tougher administrative measures and increasing restrictions on trade that England imposed after 1763 affected all the colonies. The white inhabitants of the South were acutely conscious of threats to their liberty because of the presence among them of large numbers of black slaves. Indeed, slavery had become the cornerstone of the South's social system by the mid-eighteenth century. As such, it served as a constant reminder to the colonists that the deprivation of liberty could result in their own enslavement.

Still, the prospect of revolution, while stimulating, terrified southerners because of the enormous risks it presented to the social order. Disturbances among the slaves, usually small, were nevertheless frequent, especially during periods of social turmoil. If a revolution were to occur, southerners wondered, how would the powerful Indian tribes who threatened western frontier regions react? Among the southern white population, moreover, inequities in wealth and political representation divided individuals and bred conflict between the tidewater region and the backcountry.

Torn between his duty to an imperial government demanding stricter regulation of colonial activities and the reality of living among people who resented his authority but who controlled his salary, the royal governor was the most controversial and frequently the most unpopular figure of the colonial period. As the first document shows, Virginia's governor, William Berkeley, was accused of nepotism, corruption, treachery, and murder by Nathaniel Bacon, the leader of a large group of disaffected Virginia backcountry farmers. After the English government sent an armed expedition to Virginia that successfully suppressed Bacon's Rebellion, Berkeley was recalled to England in disgrace after serving as the colony's governor for thirty-five years. Nearly a century later, North Carolina's governor, William Tryon, faced a similar problem. His advice to the ill-equipped Regulators (document 2), who had gathered strength to protest against the undemocratic nature of the colony's political and legal institutions, went unheeded, and the rebels met defeat at the Battle of Alamance Creek (1771). Slave disturbances concerned many white southerners, as is revealed in the third document, two extracts from the letterbook of the Charleston, South Carolina, merchant Robert Pringle.

Conflict in England, including a civil war in the 1640s, had long diverted the attention of the English government from North America, allowing the colonists to trade freely among themselves and with the merchants of other nations. Free trade was incompatible, however, with mercantilism, the prevailing economic theory in Europe in the seventeenth and eighteenth centuries. The Coercive Act of 1650, part of which is reprinted as the fourth document, was the first of many parliamentary measures designed to limit the colonists', commercial ambitions. Still for more than a century after the law's passage, the colonists had experienced little difficulty in evading the restrictions placed on trade. Colonial resistance became militant, however, when the British government attempted to levy new duties on the colonies in the aftermath of Great Britain's victory in 1763 over the French and Indians, which consolidated British power in North America. The passage of the Stamp Act of 1765 was instrumental in the creation of a group of radicals known as the Sons of Liberty, whose objections to imperial taxation are presented in the fifth selection. Not all colonists felt as strongly as these firebrands; in fact, many remained loyal to the mother country. The sixth document, one of numerous letters of support sent to royal governors in the late colonial period, is an example of the loyalist viewpoint in North Carolina.

Confronting imperial authority, dissatisfied colonists staged the famous Boston Tea Party to protest against the British government's efforts to make them buy English-exported tea, a favorite colonial beverage. The events following the Boston Tea Party, however, were far more important than the historic incident itself. The retaliatory measures taken by the British against the city of Boston and the people of Massachusetts held profound implications for all the colonies. The seventh selection, an entry from the diary of the wealthy Virginia planter Landon Carter, points to the need for a united effort against the British government. With war imminent, Patrick Henry, a leading revolutionary and a man of outstanding rhetorical gifts, stood up at the Second Virginia Convention to deliver one of the most famous addresses in American history. The eighth document contains the full text of Henry's speech.

Questions for Analysis

1. When did the southern colonists begin to regard themselves as Americans rather than as transplanted English people?

2. How important were the tensions between the tidewater region and the backcountry in stimulating revolutionary sentiment in the South?

3. Was slavery a significant factor in the decision for revolution in the South? Why or why not?

4. Did the British government's policies generate a sense of unity in the South during the late colonial period?

5. Which motive was more important for the revolutionaries of the South—economic self-interest or the preservation of fundamental political principles?

6. What did the southern colonists really want—reform or revolution?

1. Governor William Berkeley Is Branded a Traitor, 1676

Declaration of Nathaniel Bacon in the Name of the People of Virginia, July 30, 1676

1. For having, upon specious pretences of public works, raised great unjust taxes upon the commonalty for the advancement of private favorites and other sinister ends, but no visible effects in any measure adequate; for not having, during this long time of his government, in any measure advanced this hopeful colony either by fortifications, towns, or trade.

2. For having abused and rendered contemptible the magistrates of justice by advancing to places of judicature scandalous and ignorant favorites.

3. For having wronged his Majesty's prerogative and interest by assuming monopoly of the beaver trade and for having in it unjust gain betrayed and sold his Majesty's country and the lives of his loyal subjects to the barbarous heathen.

4. For having protected, favored, and emboldened the Indians against his Majesty's loyal subjects, never contriving, requiring, or appointing any due or proper means of satisfaction for their many invasions, robberies, and murders committed upon us.

5. For having, when the army of English was just upon the track of those Indians, who now in all places burn, spoil, murder and when we might with ease have destroyed them who then were in open hostility, for then having expressly countermanded and sent back our army by passing his word for the peaceable demeanor of the said Indians, who immediately prosecuted their evil intentions, committing horrid murders and robberies in all places, being protected by the said engagement and word past of him the said Sir William Berkeley, having ruined and laid desolate a great part of his majesty's country, and

have now drawn themselves into such obscure and remote places and are by their success so emboldened and confirmed by their confederacy so strengthened that the cries of blood are in all places, and the terror and consternation of the people so great, are now become not only a difficult but a very formidable enemy who might at first with ease have been destroyed.

6. And lately, when, upon the loud outcries of blood, the assembly had, with all care, raised and framed an army for the preventing of further mischief and safeguard of this his Majesty's colony.

7. For having, with only the privacy of some few favorites without acquainting the people, only by the alteration of a figure, forged a commission, by we know not what hand, not only without but even against the consent of the people, for the raising and effecting civil war and destruction, which being happily and without bloodshed prevented; for having the second time attempted the same, thereby calling down our forces from the defense of the frontiers and most weakly exposed places.

8. For the prevention of civil mischief and ruin amongst ourselves while the barbarous enemy in all places did invade, murder, and spoil us, his Majesty's most faithful subjects.

Of this and the aforesaid articles we accuse Sir William Berkeley as guilty of each and every one of the same, and as one who has traitorously attempted, violated, and injured his Majesty's interest here by a loss of a great part of this his colony and many of his faithful loyal subjects by him betrayed and in a barbarous and shameful manner exposed to the incursions and murder of the heathen. And we do further declare these the ensuing persons in this list to have been his wicked and pernicious councillors, confederates, aiders, and assisters against the commonalty in these our civil commotions.

Sir Henry Chichley	Richard Whitacre
Lt. Col. Christopher Wormeley	Nicholas Spencer
	Joseph Bridger
Phillip Ludwell	William Claiburne, Jr.
Robt. Beverley	Thomas Hawkins
Ri. Lee	William Sherwood
Thomas Ballard	John Page Clerke
William Cole	John Cluffe Clerk

John West, Hubert Farrell, Thomas Reade, Math. Kempe

And we do further demand that the said Sir William Berkeley with all the persons in this list be forthwith delivered up or surrender themselves within four days after the notice hereof, or otherwise we declare as follows.

That in whatsoever place, house, or ship, any of the said persons shall reside, be hid, or protected, we declare the owners, masters, or inhabitants of the said places to be confederates and traitors to the people and the estates of them is also of all the aforesaid persons to be confiscated. And this we, the commons of Virginia, do declare, desiring a firm union amongst ourselves that we may jointly and with one accord defend ourselves against the common enemy. And let not the faults of the guilty be the reproach of the innocent, or the faults or crimes of the oppressors divide and separate us who have suffered by their oppressions.

These are, therefore, in his Majesty's name, to command you forthwith to seize the persons abovementioned as traitors to the King and country and them to bring to Middle Plantation and there to secure them until further order, and, in case of opposition, if you want any further assistance you are forthwith to demand it in the name of the people in all the counties of Virginia.

Nathaniel Bacon
General by consent of the people.

William Sherwood

2. Governor William Tryon Offers the Regulators Mercy, 1771

To the People Now Assembled in Arms, Who Style Themselves Regulators

Great Alamance Camp   May 16th 1771

In Answer to your Petition, I am to acquaint you that I have ever been attentive to the true Interest of this Country, and to that of every Individual residing within it. I lament the fatal Necessity to which you have now reduced me, by withdrawing yourselves from the Mercy of the Crown, and the Laws of your Country, to require you who are Assembled as Regulators, to lay down your Arms, Surrender up the outlawed Ringleaders, and Submit yourselves to the Laws of your Country, and then rest on the lenity and Mercy of Government: By accepting these Terms in one Hour from the delivery of this Dispatch you will prevent an effusion of Blood, as you are at this time in a state of War and Rebellion against your King, your Country, and your Laws.

Wm Tryon

3. *A Merchant Worries About Slave Insurrections, 1739, 1740*

Robert Pringle to John Richards*

Charles Town, 26th September 1739

. . . I hope our Government will order Effectual methods for the taking of St. Augustine from the Spaniards which is now become a great Detriment to this Province by the Encouragement & Protection given by them to our Negroes that Run away there. An Insurrection has been made of late here in the Country by some Negroes in order to their Going there & in less than Twenty four hours they murthered in their way there between Twenty & Thirty white People & Burnt Severall houses before they were overtaken, tho' now most of the Gang are already taken or Cut to Pieces. This has happened within these Three Weeks Past. . . .

Robert Pringle to Andrew Pringle**

Charles Town, 22nd November 1740

. . . You'll please excuse this Incorrect Confus'd Scrawl, being att present very much fatigued both in body & mind having slept but very Little these three Days & three nights past, & if the fire had happen'd at the same time at night as it did in the Day a great part of us had lost our Lives in the flames. It Came so suddenly upon us as well as the great Risque we Run from an Insurrection of our Negroes which we were very apprehensive off, but all as yet Quiet by the strict Guards & watch we are oblidg'd to keep Constantly night & Day. . . .

4. *The English Government Orders Restrictions on Trade, 1650*

. . . Whereas in Virginia, and in the Islands of Barbada's, Antego, St. Christophers, Mevias, Mounsirat, Bermuda's, and divers other Islands and places in America, there hath been and are Colonies and Plantations, which were planted at the Cost, and setled by the People, and by Authority of this Nation, which are and ought to be subordinate to, and dependent upon England; and hath ever since the Planting thereof been, and ought to be subject to such Laws, Orders and Regulations as are or shall be made by the Parliament of England; And whereas divers acts of Rebellion have been committed by many persons inhabiting in Barbada's, Antego, Bermuda's and Virginia, whereby they have most Trayterously, by Force and Subtilty, usurped a Power of Government, and seized the Estates of many well-affected persons into their hands, and banished others, and have set up themselves in opposition to, and distinct from this State and Commonwealth, many of the chief Actors in, and Promoters of these Rebellions, having been

transported and carried over to the said Plantations in Foreign Ships, without leave, license or consent of the Parliament of England; the Parliament of England taking the premises into consideration, and finding themselves obliged to use all speedy, lawful and just means for the Suppression of the said Rebellion in the said Plantations, and reducing the same to fidelity and due obedience, so as all peaceable and well-affected people, who have been Robbed, Spoiled, Imprisoned or Banished through the said Treasonable practices, may be restored to the freedom of their persons, and possession of their own Lands and Goods, and due punishment inflicted upon the said Delinquents, do Declare all and every the said persons in Barbada's, Antego, Bermuda's and Virginia, that have contrived, abetted, aided or assisted those horrid Rebellions, or have since willingly joyned with them, to be notorious Robbers and Traitors, and such as by the Law of Nations are not to be permitted any maner of Commerce or Traffique with any

---

*John Richards was a London merchant.
**Andrew Pringle was a sea captain who became a merchant.

people whatsoever; and do forbid to all maner of persons, Foreigners, and others, all maner of Commerce, Traffique and Correspondency whatsoever, to be used or held with the said Rebels in the Barbada's, Bermuda's, Virginia and Antego, or either of them.

And be it Enacted by this present Parliament, and by the authority of the same, That after due publication of this Act made, to the end that none may justly pretend ignorance, it shall and may be lawful to any the Fleet or Ships sent forth or imployed by the Parliament, or any private Men of War or Ships to be allowed or approved in that behalf by the immediate Power of Parliament, or the Council of State established by Parliament, to seize, surprize and take all and all manner of Ships, Vessels and Goods, of what

nature or kinde soever, belonging to all persons whatsoever whether Foreiners or others, or of what Nation soever, that shall be found or met withal, Trading or going to Trade, or coming from Trading with the said Rebels, or in or at the said Island of Barbada's, Bermuda's, Virginia, or Antego aforesaid, or any part or parts thereof, or that shall hold any Correspondency with the said Rebels, or yield them any assistance or relief for the supporting their said Rebellion: And the same Ships and Goods so surprized, to send in to be proceeded against in the Court of Admiralty by vertue of this Act; and the Judges of that Court finding the same to be within the tenor and true meaning of this Act, to adjudge the same to be well taken, and to be good and lawful Prize. . . .

5. *The Sons of Liberty Oppose the Stamp Act, 1766*

At a meeting of a considerable number of inhabitants of the town and county of Norfolk, and others, Sons of Liberty, at the court-house of the said county, in the colony of Virginia, on Monday the 31st of March, 1766.

Having taken into consideration the evil tendency of that oppressive and unconstitutional act of Parliament commonly called the Stamp Act, and being desirous that our sentiments should be known to posterity, and recollecting that we are a part of that colony, who first, in General Assembly, openly expressed their detestation to the said act, which is pregnant with ruin, and productive of the most pernicious consequences; and unwilling to rivet the shackles of slavery and oppression on ourselves, and millions yet unborn, have unanimously come to the following resolutions:

I. Resolved, That we acknowledge our sovereign Lord King George III, to be our rightful and lawful King, and that we will at all times, to the utmost of our power and ability, support and defend his most sacred person, crown, and dignity; and will be always ready, when constitutionally called upon, to assist his Majesty

with our lives and fortunes, and defend all his just rights and prerogatives.

II. Resolved, That we will by all lawful ways and means, which Divine Providence hath put into our hands, defend ourselves in the full enjoyment of, and preserve inviolate to posterity, those inestimable privileges of all free born British subjects, of being taxed by none but Representatives of their own choosing, and of being tried only by a Jury of their own Peers; for, if we quietly submit to the execution of the said Stamp Act, all our claims to civil liberty will be lost, and we and our posterity become absolute slaves.

III. Resolved, That we will, on any future occasion, sacrifice our lives and fortunes, in concurrence with the other Sons of Liberty, in the American provinces, to defend and preserve those invaluable blessings transmitted us by our ancestors.

IV. Resolved, That whoever is concerned, directly or indirectly, in using, or causing to be used, in any way or manner whatever, within this colony, unless authorized by the General Assembly thereof, those detestable papers called the Stamps, shall be deemed, to all intents and purposes, an enemy to his country, and by the Sons of Liberty treated accordingly.

V. Resolved, That a committee be appointed to present the thanks of the Sons of Liberty to Colonel Richard Bland, for his treatise entitled "An Inquiry into the rights of the British colonies."

VI. Resolved, That a committee be appointed, who shall make publick the above resolutions, and correspond, as they shall see occasion, with the associated Sons and Friends of Liberty in the other British colonies in America.

6. Loyalists Express Support for King and Parliament, 1774

Address of the Inhabitants of Anson County to Governor Martin.

To His Excellency, Josiah Martin Esquire, Captain General, Governor, &c,

Most Excellent Governor:

Permit us, in behalf of ourselves, and many others of His Majesty's most dutiful and loyal subjects within the County of Anson, to take the earliest opportunity of addressing your Excellency, and expressing our abomination of the many outrageous attempts now forming on this side the Atlantick, against the peace and tranquility of His Majesty's Dominions in North America, and to witness to your Excellency, by this our Protest, a disapprobation and abhorence of the many lawless combinations and unwarrantable practices actually carrying on by a gross tribe of infatuated anti-Monarchists in the several Colonies in these Dominions; the baneful consequence of whose audacious contrivance can, in fine, only tend to extirpate the fundamental principles of all Government, and illegally to shake off their obedience to, and dependance upon, the imperial Crown and Parliament of Great Britain; the infection of whose pernicious example being already extended to this particular County, of which we now bear the fullest testimony.

It is with the deepest concern (though with infinite indignation) that we see in all public places and papers disagreeable votes, speeches and resolutions, said to be entered into by our sister Colonies, in the highest contempt and derogation of the superintending power of the legislative authority of Great Britain. And we further, with sorrow, behold their wanton endeavors to vilify and arraign the honour and integrity of His Majesty's most honourable Ministry and Council, tending to sow the seeds of discord and sedition, in open violation of their duty and allegiance. . . .

. . . We are truly invigorated with the warmest zeal and attachment in favour of the British Parliament, Constitution and Laws, which our forefathers gloriously struggled to establish, and which are now become the noblest birthright and inheritance of all Britannia's Sons. . . .

We are truly sensible that those invaluable blessings which we have hitherto enjoyed under His Majesty's auspicious Government, can only be secured to us by the stability of his Throne, supported and defended by the British Parliament, the only grand bulwark and guardian of our civil and religious liberties.

Duty and affection oblige us further to express our grateful acknowledgements for the inestimate blessings flowing from such a Constitution. And we do assure your Excellency that we are determined, by the assistance of Almighty God, in our respective stations, steadfastly to continue His Majesty's loyal Subjects, and to contribute all in our power for the preservation of the publick peace; so, that, by our unanimous example, we hope to discourage the desperate endeavours of a deluded multitude, and to see a misled people turn again from their atrocious offences to a proper exercise of their obedience and duty.

And we do furthermore assure your Excellency, that we shall endeavor to cultivate such sentiments in all those under our care, and to warm their breasts with a true zeal for His Majesty, and affection for his illustrious family. And may the Almighty God be pleased to direct his Councils, his Parliament, and all those in authority under him, that their endeavors may be for the advancement of piety, and the safety, honour and welfare of our Sovereign and his Kingdoms, that the malice of his enemies may be assuaged, and their evil designs confounded and defeated; so that all the world may be convinced that his sacred person, his Royal family, his Parliament, and our Country, are the special objects of Divine dispensation and Providence.

[Signed by two hundred and twenty-seven of the Inhabitants of the county of Anson.]

7. *Landon Carter Urges Intercolonial Solidarity, 1774*

Wednesday, June 8, 1774

. . . I went to Court on Monday and there I endeavoured by my Conversation to Convince the People that the case of the Bostonians was the case of all America and if they Submitted to this Arbitrary taxation begun by the Parliament all America must, and then farewell to all our Liberties. Therefore I deduced the necessity in our heartily Joining to assist Boston by every means in our Power and as a proof of what might be expected to remove this armed force against them, I shewed them the resolutions entered into by the Philadelphians, and Marylanders. . . .

I farther hinted to our own Peo[ple] that as the People of Great Britain had seemed to be quite Patient under this Arbitrary Proceeding of their Parliament, it behoved us to have as little Commerce with them as Possible; and farther to refuse to do them the service to determine their suits for their debts since they had consented to a Manifest Violation of our whole Constitution. There seemed to be an assent to all I said and I do hope that at some meeting that our two representatives will be active soon in getting together We shall all be Pretty unanimous in Associating against any Commerce or use of any of the Manufactures of Great Britain or of any Place that shall be passive in this grand affair of Liberty. And except as to what was really engaged before we got intelligence of this arbitrary Measure, which by the by was a declaration of war against Boston and through her against all America carried as it were in the fore topsails of their ships, than which no enemy could have been treated worse, I say to avoid exporting anything to Great Britain or to any place whose activity must needs be necessary to Preserve the freedom of their fellow subjects. . . .

8. *Patrick Henry Demands Liberty or Death, 1775*

Mr. President:

It is natural to man to indulge in the illusions of hope. We are apt to shut our eyes against a painful truth, and listen to the song of that siren till she transforms us into beasts. Is this the part of wise men, engaged in a great and arduous struggle for liberty? Are we disposed to be of the number of those who having eyes see not, and having ears hear not, the things which so nearly concern their temporal salvation? For my part, whatever anguish of spirit it may cost, I am willing to know the whole truth; to know the worst and to provide for it.

I have but one lamp by which my feet are guided; and that is the lamp of experience. I know of no way of judging of the future but by the past. And judging by the past, I wish to know what there has been in the conduct of the British ministry for the last ten years, to justify those hopes with which gentlemen have been pleased to solace themselves and the house? Is it that insidious smile with which our petition has been lately received? Trust it not, sir: it will prove a snare to your feet. Suffer not yourselves to be betrayed with a kiss. Ask yourselves how this gracious reception of our petition comports with those warlike preparations which cover our waters and darken our land. Are fleets and armies necessary to a work of love and reconciliation? Have we shown ourselves so unwilling to be reconciled that force must be called in to win back our love? Let us not deceive ourselves, sir. These are the implements of war and subjugation—the last arguments to which kings resort. I ask gentlemen, sir, what means this martial array, if its purpose be not to force us to submission? Can gentlemen assign any other possible motive for it? Has Britain any enemy in this quarter of the world, to call for all this accumulation of navies and armies? No, sir, she has none. They are meant for us; they can be meant for no other. They are sent over to bind and rivet upon us those chains which the British ministry have been so long forging. And what have we to oppose to them? Shall we try argument? Sir, we have been trying that for the last ten years. Have we anything new to offer upon the subject? Nothing. We have held the subject up in every light of which it is capable; but it has been all in vain. Shall we resort to entreaty and humble supplication? What terms shall we find which have not been already exhausted? Let us not, I beseech you, sir, deceive ourselves longer.

Sir, we have done everything that could be done to avert the storm which is now coming on. We have petitioned, we have remonstrated, we have supplicated, we have prostrated ourselves before the throne, and have implored its interposition to arrest the tyrannical hands of the ministry and Parliament. Our petitions have been slighted; our remonstrances have produced additional violence and insult; our supplications have been disregarded; and we have been spurned with contempt from the foot of the throne. In vain, after these things, may we indulge the fond hope of peace and reconciliation. There is no longer any room for hope. If we wish to be free, if we mean to preserve inviolate those inestimable privileges for which we have been so long contending, if we mean not basely to abandon the noble struggle in which we have been so long engaged, and which we have pledged ourselves never to abandon until the glorious object of our contest shall be obtained—we must fight! I repeat it, sir, we must fight! An appeal to arms and to the God of Hosts is all that is left us!

They tell us, sir, that we are weak—unable to cope with so formidable an adversary. But when shall we be stronger? Will it be the next week, or the next year? Will it be when we are totally disarmed, and when a British guard shall be stationed in every house? Shall we gather strength by irresolution and inaction? Shall we acquire the means of effectual resistance by lying supinely on our backs, and hugging the delusive phantom of hope until our enemies shall have bound us hand and foot? Sir, we are not weak, if we make a proper use of those means which the God of nature hath placed in our power. Three millions of people, armed in the holy cause of liberty, and in such a country as that which we possess, are invincible by any force which our enemy can send against us. Besides, sir, we shall not fight our battles alone. There is a just God who presides over the destinies of nations; and who will raise up friends to fight our battles for us. The battle, sir, is not to the strong alone; it is to the vigilant, the active, the brave. Besides, sir, we have no election. If we were base enough to desire it, it is not too late to retire from the contest. There is no retreat but in submission and slavery! Our chains are forged; their clanking may be heard on the plains of Boston! The war is inevitable—and let it come! I repeat it, sir, let it come!

It is in vain, sir, to extenuate the matter. Gentlemen may cry, Peace, peace; but there is no peace. The war is actually begun. The next gale that sweeps from the north will bring to our ears the clash of resounding arms. Our brethren are already in the field. Why stand we here idle? What is it that gentlemen wish? What would they have? If life so dear, or peace so sweet, as to be purchased at the price of chains and slavery? Forbid it, Almighty God–I know not what course others may take; but as for me, give me liberty or give me death!

References

1. Governor William Berkeley Is Branded a Traitor, 1676
   "Declaration of Nathaniel Bacon in the Name of the People of Virginia, July 30, 1676," in Keith Kavenagh, ed., *Foundations of Colonial America: A Documentary History, Southern Colonies* (New York: Chelsea House Publishers, 1973), pp. 1783–1784.

2. Governor William Tryon Offers the Regulators Mercy, 1771
   William Tryon to the Regulators, Great Alamance Camp, May 16, 1771, in William S. Powell, ed., *The Correspondence of William Tryon and Other Selected Papers*, Volume II, 1768–1818 (Raleigh, North Carolina: Division of Archives and History, 1981), pp. 738–739.

3. A Merchant Worries About Slave Insurrections, 1739, 1740
   Robert Pringle to John Richards, 26th September 1739, and Robert Pringle to Andrew Pringle, 22nd November 1740, in Walter B. Edgar, ed., *The Letterbook of Robert Pringle*, Volume I, April 2, 1737–September 25, 1742 (Columbia, South Carolina: University of South Carolina Press, 1972), pp. 135, 273.

4. The English Government Orders Restrictions on Trade, 1650
   "An Act for Prohibiting Trade with the Barbadoes, Virginia, Bermuda and Antego," in C. H. Firth and R. S. Rait, eds., *Acts and Ordinances of the Interregnum, 1642–1660*, Volume II (London: His Majesty's Stationery Office, 1911), pp. 425–429.

5. The Sons of Liberty Oppose the Stamp Act, 1766
   "Resolutions of the Sons of Liberty of the Borough and the County of Norfolk in Defiance of the Stamp Act, 31 March, 1766," in Robert L. Scribner, ed., *Revolutionary Virginia: The Road to Independence, A Documentary Record*, Volume I, *Forming Thunderclouds and the First Convention, 1763–1774*, (Charlottesville, Virginia: University Press of Virginia, 1973), pp. 46–47.

6. Loyalists Express Support for King and Parliament, 1774
   "Address of the Inhabitants of Anson County to Governor Martin," in William L. Saunders, ed., *The Colonial Records of North Carolina*, Volume IX, 1771 to 1775 (Raleigh, North Carolina: State Printers, 1890), pp. 1161–1164.

7. Landon Carter Urges Intercolonial Solidarity, 1774
   Entry for Wednesday, June 8, 1774, from Jack P. Greene, ed., *The Diary of Landon Carter of Sabine Hall, 1752–1778*, Volume II (Charlottesville, Virginia: University Press of Virginia, 1965), pp. 821–822.

8. Patrick Henry Demands Liberty or Death, 1775
   Patrick Henry, "Speech in the Virginia Convention, March 23, 1775," from Charles D. Warner, ed., *Library of the World's Best Literature, Ancient and Modern*, Volume XII (New York: R. S. Peale and J. A. Hill, 1897), pp. 7242—7244.

Further Reading

John R. Alden, *The South in the Revolution, 1763—1789* (1957)

Bernard Bailyn, *The Ideological Origins of the American Revolution* (1967)

Richard R. Beeman, *Patrick Henry: A Biography* (1975)

Ira Berlin and Ronald Hoffman, eds., *Slavery and Freedom in the Age of the American Revolution* (1978)

T. H. Breen, *Tobacco Culture: The Mentality of the Great Tidewater Planters on the Eve of Revolution* (1985)

Richard M. Brown, *The South Carolina Regulators* (1963)

Edward J. Cashin and Heard Robertson, *Augusta and the American Revolution: Events in the Georgia Back Country* (1975)

Jeffrey Crow and Larry Tise, eds., *The Southern Experience in the American Revolution* (1978)

Marc Egnal, *A Mighty Empire: The Origins of the American Revolution* (1988)

Jack P. Greene, *The Quest for Power: The Lower Houses of Assembly in the Southern Royal Colonies, 1689—1776* (1963)

Rhys Isaac, *The Transformation of Virginia, 1740—1790* (1982)

Pauline Maier, *From Resistance to Revolution: Colonial Radicals and the Development of American Opposition to Britain, 1765—1776* (1972)

Edmund S. Morgan and Helen M. Morgan, *The Stamp Act Crisis: Prologue to Revolution* (1953)

Wilcomb E. Washburn, *The Governor and the Rebel: A History of Bacon's Rebellion in Virginia* (1957)

Robert M. Weir, *"The Last of American Freemen": Studies in the Political Culture of the Colonial and Revolutionary South* (1986)

Document Set 3

The South in the New Nation, c. 1787–1825

At the same time that the American Revolution bound the states together and laid the foundation for nationhood, regional self-interest emerged. The debates at the constitutional convention in Philadelphia clearly indicate that the delegates had widely different priorities that they had to address and resolve before they could agree on the form and content of a new government for the United States.

Slavery vitally concerned the southern delegates, who were well aware that the presence of the institution stood in contradiction to the great ideals expressed in the Declaration of Independence. Slavery had expanded rapidly in the South, with the invention of the cotton gin inadvertently stimulating a growing demand for slaves. Cotton culture and slavery had spread to the interior of existing southern states and into areas that soon would become new states. In marked contrast, slavery was dying out in the North. By the end of the eighteenth century, most northern state constitutions either forbade the ownership of slaves or provided for gradual emancipation. The Northwest Ordinance of 1787 prohibited slavery in future U.S. territories north of the Ohio River. Manufacturing and industrialization gradually began to characterize northern economic development. Factory workers were free wage laborers.

The rise of political parties in the 1790s emphasized the new nation's geographical differences, with Federalist party strength coming mainly from the mercantile, manufacturing Northeast and the Republican party drawing its support from the planters and farmers of the South and the West. The erosion of support for the Federalists in the last years of the century gave the Republicans control of both the Congress and the presidency for the next quarter-century. Not only southerners but Americans more broadly continued to express dissatisfaction about the nation's course of development. Although a surge of American nationalism after the War of 1812 appeared to presage a long period of unity and harmony, it was not to be. The proposed admission of Missouri into the Union revived the debate on slavery and fractured the fragile consensus of the Era of Good Feelings, which prevailed during President James Monroe's administration.

Nothing is more remarkable about the War for Independence than the fact that the Americans achieved their triumph with an exceedingly weak, ineffective central government. The new nation that emerged from the crucible of conflict could not solve its numerous problems, however, by persisting with its existing form of government. Paradoxically, the very weakness of the Articles of Confederation endeared them to Americans who feared a return to the despotism that had led to the war in the first place. Consequently, the ratification of the new constitution that was drafted at Philadelphia in the summer of 1787 was by no means a formality. Richard Henry Lee was a leading Virginia Antifederalist, but as the first selection, an extract from a letter to Governor Edmund Randolph, suggests, his objections might be overcome if the constitution contained more safeguards against the possibility of tyranny. Accepting factionalism and self-interest as inevitable in politics, James Madison believed that the checks and balances written into the Constitution to limit the power of elected officials would minimize the effect of those tendencies.

As one of the contributors to *The Federalist*, Madison played a central role in securing the Constitution's ratification. Written by Madison, Alexander Hamilton and John Jay, the eighty-five newspaper essays that comprise *The Federalist* provide an enduring commentary on the nature of government. The second document, taken from *The Federalist*, Number 10, masterfully evaluates republican government and its chances of success in the United States. Less than a decade later, George Washington, nearing the end of his second term as the nation's first president, told the American people that factionalism had taken root in the United States. In the third document, part of his farewell address, Washington warns the nation that the existence of political parties was threatening national unity. Washington's admonitions were ignored, however, and the party system that developed fostered economic sectionalism.

In his essay *Arator*, from which the fourth selection is taken, the Virginia political philosopher and agriculturist John Taylor describes the effect of federal policies on planting and farming in the South. Slavery had not been a sectional issue before the Revolution, but in view of its existence in the South and its absence in the North—and increasing revulsion for the institution among civilized nations—southerners could not take the security of slavery for granted. General Charles Cotesworth Pinckney of South Carolina, was one of many southern leaders who accepted with great reluctance the clause in the Con-

stitution setting a twenty-year time limit on the future importation of slaves into the United States. In a speech to the state's ratifying convention, part of which forms the fifth document, Pinckney stresses that the federal government had no authority to abolish the institution of slavery itself.

The successful overthrow of French rule by black revolutionaries on the Caribbean island of Haiti held great significance for both supporters and detractors of slavery in the United States. Whereas some northerners applauded the revolution as a mirror image of the American struggle for independence, most southerners worried about its effect on the black population in the slave states. In the sixth selection, a speech to the United States Senate, James Jackson of Georgia explains his reasons for supporting a bill to suspend trade between the United States and Haiti. The final document is taken from the writings of Timothy Flint, a New England missionary who traveled extensively in the areas bordering the Ohio and Mississippi rivers. Flint's account suggests that northerners, particularly New Englanders, were resented not only for their antislavery viewpoints but also for their misconceptions of life on the frontier.

Questions for Analysis

1. How did the American Revolution affect society and politics in the South?

2. Did the southern states make too many sacrifices by accepting the United States Constitution?

3. When did the South become conscious of its own regional self-interests?

4. How did the expansion of the cotton economy affect the inland areas of the southern states?

5. How did the formation of parties influence political behavior in the southern states?

6. Apart from slavery, what fostered sectional animosity between the South and the North?

1. *Antifederalist Richard Henry Lee Fears Tyranny, 1787*

New-York, Oct. 16th, 1787

Dear Sir,

I was duly honoured with your favour of September 17th, from Philadelphia, which should have been acknowledged long before now, if the nature of the business it related to had not required time. The establishment of the new plan of government, in its present form, is a question that involves such immense consequences, to the present times and to posterity, that it calls for the deepest attention of the best and wisest friends of their country and mankind. If it be found right, after mature deliberation, adopt it; if wrong, amend it at all events: for to say that a bad government must be established for fear of anarchy, is really saying that we should kill ourselves for fear of dying! Experience, and the actual state of things, show that there is no difficulty in procuring a general convention, the late one having been collected without any obstruction; nor does external war, or internal discord, prevent the most cool, collected, full, and fair discussion of this all-important subject. If, with infinite ease, a convention was obtained to prepare a system, why may not another convention, with equal ease, be obtained to make proper and necessary amendments? Good government is not the work of short time, or of sudden thought. From Moses to Montesquieu the greatest geniuses have been employed on this difficult subject, and yet experience has shown capital defects in the systems produced for the government of mankind. But since it is neither prudent nor easy to make frequent changes in government, and as bad governments have been generally found the most fixed, so it becomes of the last importance to frame the first establishment upon grounds the most unexceptionable, and such as the best theories with experience justify; not trusting, as our new constitution does, and as many approve of doing, to time and future events to correct errors that both reason and experience, in similar cases, now prove to exist in the new system. It has hitherto been supposed a fundamental truth that, in governments rightly balanced, the different branches of legislature should be unconnected, and that the legislative and executive powers should be separate. In the new constitution, the president and senate have all the executive and two-thirds of the legislative; and in some weighty instances (as making all kinds of treaties which are to be the laws of the land) they have the whole legislative and executive powers. They jointly appoint all officers, civil and military, and they (the senate) try all impeachments, either of their own members or of the officers appointed by themselves. Is there not a most formidable combination of power thus created in a few? and can the most critical eye, if a candid one, discover responsibility is this potent corps? or will any sensible man say that great power, without responsibility, can be given to rulers with safety to liberty? It is most clear that the parade of impeachment is nothing to them, or any of them, as little restraint is to be found, I presume, from the fear of offending constituents.

The president is of four years duration, and Virginia (for example) has one vote, out of thirteen, in the choice of him. The senate is a body of six years duration, and as, in the choice of president, the largest state has but a thirteenth part, so is it in the choice of senators; and this thirteenth vote, not of the people, but of electors, two removes from the people. This latter statement is adduced to show that responsibility is as little to be apprehended from amenability to constituents, as from the terror of impeachment. You are, therefore, sir, well warranted in saying that either a monarchy or aristocracy will be generated: perhaps the most grievous system of government may arise! It cannot be denied, with truth, that this new constitution is, in its first principles, most highly and dangerously oligarchic; and it is a point agreed that a government of the few is, of all governments, the worst. The only check to be found in favour of the democratic principle, in this system, is the House of Representatives, which, I believe, may justly be called a mere shred or rag of representation, it being obvious, to the least examination, that smallness of number, and great comparative disparity of power, renders that house of little effect to promote good, or restrain bad government. . . .

In this congressional legislature a bare majority can enact commercial laws, so that the representatives of the seven northern states, as they will have a majority, can, by law, create the most oppressive monopolies upon the five southern states, whose circumstances and productions are essentially different from theirs, although not a single man of their voters are the representatives of, or amenable to, the people of the southern states. Can such a set of men be, with the least colour of truth, called representatives of those they make laws for? It is supposed that the policy of the northern states will prevent such abuses! but how feeble, sir, is *policy* when opposed to interest among trading people, and what is the restraint arising from policy? It is said that we may be forced, by abuse, to become shipbuilders; but how long will it be before a people of agriculture can produce ships sufficient to export such bulky and such extensive commodities as ours; and if we had the ships, from whence

are the seamen to come? four thousand of whom, at least, we shall want in Virginia. In questions so liable to abuses, why was not the necessary vote put to two-thirds of the members of the legislature? Upon the while, sir, my opinion is, that, as this constitution abounds with useful regulations, at the same time that it is liable to strong and fundamental objections, the plan for us to pursue will be to propose the necessary amendments, and express our willingness to adopt it with the amendments; and to suggest the calling of a new convention for the purpose of considering them. To this I see no well-founded objection, but great safety and much good to be the probable result. I am perfectly satisfied that you make such use of this letter as you shall think to be for the public good. And now, after begging your pardon for so great a trespass on your patience, and presenting my best respects to your lady, I will conclude with assuring you that

I am, with the sincerest esteem and regard,
dear sir,
Your most affectionate and obedient servant,

His Excellency,
Gov. Randolph

2. *Federalist James Madison Praises Republican Government, 1787*

. . . [I]t may be concluded that a pure democracy, by which I mean a society, consisting of a small number of citizens, who assemble and administer the government in person, can admit of no cure for the mischiefs of faction. A common passion or interest will, in almost every case, be felt by a majority of the whole; a communication and concert results from the form of government itself; and there is nothing to check the inducements to sacrifice the weaker party, or an obnoxious individual. Hence it is, that such democracies have ever been spectacles of turbulence and contention; have ever been found incompatible with personal security, or the rights of

property; and have in general been as short in their lives, as they have been violent in their deaths. Theoretic politicians, who have patronized this species of government, have erroneously supposed, that by reducing mankind to a perfect equality in their political rights, they would, at the same time, be perfectly equalized, and assimilated in their possessions, their opinions, and their passions.

A republic, by which I mean a government in which the scheme of representation takes place, opens a different prospect, and promises the cure for which we are seeking. Let us examine the points in which it varies from pure democracy, and we shall comprehend both the nature of the cure, and the efficacy which it must derive from the union.

The two great points of difference between a democracy and a republic, are first, the delegation of the government, in the latter, to a small number of citizens elected by the rest; secondly, the greater number of citizens, and greater sphere of country, over which the latter may be extended.

The effect of the first difference is, on the one hand, to refine and enlarge the public views, by passing them through the medium of a chosen body of citizens, whose wisdom may best discern the true interest of their country, and whose patriotism and love of justice, will be least likely to sacrifice it to temporary or partial considerations. Under such a regulation, it may well happen that the public voice pronounced by the representatives of the people, will be more consonant to the public good, than if pronounced by the people themselves convened for the purpose. On the other hand, the effect may be inverted. Men of factious tempers, of local prejudices, or of sinister designs, may by intrigue, by corruption, or by other means, first obtain the suffrages, and then betray the interests of the people. The question resulting is, whether small or extensive republics are most favourable to the election of proper guardians of the public weal; and it is clearly decided in favour of the latter by two obvious considerations.

In the first place it is to be remarked, that however small the republic may be, the representatives must be raised to a certain number, in order to guard against the cabals of a few; and that however large it may be, they must be limited to a certain number, in order to guard against the confusion of a multitude. Hence the number of representatives in the two cases not being in proportion to that of the constituents, and being proportionally greatest in the small republic, it follows, that if the proportion of fit characters be not less in the large than in the small republic, the former will present a greater opinion, and consequently a greater probability of a fit choice.

In the next place, as each representative will be chosen by a greater number of citizens in the large than in the small republic, it will be more difficult for unworthy candidates to practise with success the vicious arts, by which elections are too often carried; and the suffrages of the people being more free, will be more likely to centre on men who possess the most attractive merit, and the most diffusive and established characters.

It must be confessed, that in this, as in most other cases, there is a mean, on both sides of which inconveniences will be found to lie. By enlarging too much the number of electors, you render the representative too little acquainted with all their local circumstances and lesser interests; as by reducing it too much, you render him unduly attached to these, and too little fit to comprehend and pursue great and national objects. The federal constitution forms a happy combination in this respect; the great and aggregate interests being referred to the national, the local and particular to the state legislatures.

The other point of difference is, the greater number of citizens and extent of territory which may be brought within the compass of republican, than of democratic government; and it is this circumstance principally which renders factious combinations less to be dreaded in the former, than in the latter. The smaller the society, the fewer probably will be the distinct parties and interests composing it; the fewer the distinct parties and interests, the more frequently will a majority be found of the same party; and the smaller the number of individuals composing a majority, and the smaller the compass within which they are placed, the more easily will they concert and execute their plans of oppression. Extend the sphere, and you take in a greater variety of parties and interests; you make it less probable that a majority of the whole will have a common motive to invade the rights of other citizens; or if such a common motive exists, it will be more difficult for all who feel it to discover their own strength, and to act in unison with each other. Besides other impediments, it may be remarked, that where there is a consciousness of unjust or dishonourable purposes, communication is always checked by distrust, in proportion to the number whose concurrence is necessary.

Hence it clearly appears, that the same advantage, which a republic has over a democracy, in controlling the effects of faction, is enjoyed by a large over a small republic—is enjoyed by the union over the states composing it. Does this advantage consist in the substitution of representatives, whose enlightened views and virtuous sentiments render them superior to local prejudices, and to schemes of injustice? It will not be denied, that the representation of the union will be most likely to possess these requisite endowments. Does it consist in the greater security afforded by a greater variety of parties, against the event of any one party being able to outnumber and oppress the rest? In an equal degree does the encreased variety of parties, comprised within the union, encrease this security. Does it, in fine, consist in the greater obstacles opposed to the concert and accomplishment of the secret wishes of an unjust and interested majority? Here, again, the extent of the union gives it the most palpable advantage.

The influence of factious leaders may kindle a flame within their particular states, but will be unable to spread a general conflagration through the other states: A religious sect, may degenerate into a political faction in a part of the confederacy; but the variety of sects dispersed over the entire face of it, must secure the national councils against any danger from that source: A rage for paper money, for an abolition of debts, for an equal division of property, or for any other improper or wicked project, will be less apt to pervade the whole body of the union, than a particular member of it; in the sample proportion as such a malady is more likely to taint a particular county or district, than an entire state.

In the extent and proper structure of the union, therefore, we behold a republican remedy for the diseases most incident to republican government. And according to the degree of pleasure and pride, we feel in being republicans, ought to be our zeal in cherishing the spirit, and supporting the character of federalists.

Publius.

3. George Washington Pleads for Unity, 1796

. . . In contemplating the causes which may disturb our Union, it occurs, as a matter of serious concern, that any ground should have been furnished for characterizing parties by geographical discriminations—Northern and Southern—Atlantic and Western: whence designing men may endeavor to excite a belief that there is a real difference of local interests and views. One of the expedients of party to acquire influence within particular districts, is to misrepresent the opinions and aims of other districts. You cannot shield yourselves too much against the jealousies and heartburnings which spring from these misrepresentations; they tend to render alien to each other those who ought to be bound together by fraternal affection. The inhabitants of

our western country have lately had a useful lesson on this head; they have seen in the negotiation by the Executive, and in the unanimous ratification by the Senate, of the treaty with Spain, and in the universal satisfaction at that event throughout the United States, a decisive proof how unfounded were the suspicions propagated among them, of a policy in the General Government, and in the Atlantic States, unfriendly to their interests in regard to the Mississippi: they have been witnesses to the formation of two treaties—that with Great Britain, and that with Spain, which secure to them everything they could desire in respect to our foreign relations, towards confirming their prosperity. Will it not be their wisdom to rely for the preservation of these advantages on the Union by which they were procured? Will they not henceforth be deaf to those advisers, if such there are, who would sever them from their brethren, and connect them with aliens?

To the efficacy and permanency of your Union, a Government for the whole is indispensable. No alliance, however strict between the parts, can be an adequate substitute; they must inevitably experience the infractions and interruptions which all alliances, in all time, have experienced. Sensible of this momentous truth, you have improved upon your first essay, by the adoption of a Constitution of Government better calculated than your former for an intimate Union, and for the efficacious management of your common concerns. This Government, the offspring of our own choice, uninfluenced and unawed, adopted upon full investigation and mature deliberation, completely free in its principles, in the distribution of its powers, uniting security with energy, and containing within itself a provision for its own amendment, has a just claim to your confidence and your support. Respect for its authority, compliance with its laws, acquiescence in its measures, are duties enjoined by the fundamental maxims of true liberty. The basis of our political systems is the right of the people to make and to alter their constitutions of Government: but the Constitution which at any time exists, till changed by an explicit and authentic act of the whole people, is sacredly obligatory upon all. The very idea of the power, and the right of the people to establish Government, presupposes the duty of every individual to obey the established Government.

All obstructions to the execution of the laws, all combinations and associations, under whatever plausible character, with the real design to direct, control, counteract, or awe the regular deliberation and action of the constituted authorities, are destructive to this fundamental principle, and of fatal tendency. They serve to organize faction, to give it an artificial and extraordinary force, to put in the place of the delegated will of the nation, the will of a party, often a small but artful and enterprising minority of the community; and, according to the alternate triumphs of different parties, to make the public administration the mirror of the ill-concerted and incongruous projects of faction, rather than the organ of consistent and wholesome plans, digested by common counsels, and modified by mutual interests.

However combinations or associations of the above description may now and then answer popular ends, they are likely, in the course of time and things, to become potent engines, by which cunning, ambitious, and unprincipled men with be enabled to subvert the power of the people, and to usurp for themselves the reins of Government; destroying, afterwards, the very engines which had lifted them to unjust dominion.

Towards the preservation of your Government, and the permanency of your present happy state, it is requisite, not only that you steadily discountenance irregular oppositions to its acknowledged authority, but also that you resist with care the spirit of innovation upon its principles, however specious the pretexts. . . .

4. *John Taylor Champions the Cause of Agriculture, 1811*

In collecting the causes which have contributed to the miserable agricultural state of the country, as it is a national calamity of the highest magnitude, we should be careful not to be blinded by partiality for our customs or institutions, nor corrupted by a disposition to flatter ourselves or others. I shall begin with those of a political nature. These are a secondary providence, which govern unseen the great interests of society; and if agriculture is bad and languishing in a country and climate, where it may be good and prosperous, no doubt remains with me, that political institutions have chiefly perpetrated the evil; just as they decide the fate of commerce.

The device of subjecting it to the payment of bounties to manufacturing, is an institution of this kind. This device is one item in every system for rendering governments too strong for nations. Such an object never was and never can be effected, except by factions legally created at the public expense. The wealth transferred from the nation to such factions, devotes them to the will of the government, by which it is bestowed. They must render the service for which it was given, or it would be taken away. It is unexceptionably given to support a government against a nation, or one faction against another. Armies, loaning, banking, and an intricate treasury system, endowing a government with the absolute power of applying public money, under the cover of nominal checks, are other devices of this kind. Whatever strength or wealth a government and its legal factions acquire by law, is taken from a nation; and whatever is taken from a nation, weakens and impoverishes that interest, which composes the majority. There, political oppression in every form must finally fall, however it may oscillate during the period of transit from a good to a bad government, so as sometimes to scratch factions. Agriculture being the interest covering a great majority of the people of the United States, every device for getting money or power, hatched by a fellow-feeling or common interest, between a government and its legal creatures, must of course weaken and impoverish it. Desertion, for the sake of reaping without labour, a share in the harvest of wealth and power, bestowed by laws at its expense, thins its ranks; an annual tribute to these legal factions, empties its purse; and poverty debilitates both its soil and understanding.

The device of protecting duties, under the pretext of encouraging manufactures, operates like its kindred, by creating a capitalist interest, which instantly seizes upon the bounty taken by law from agriculture; and instead of doing any good to the actual workers in wood, metals, cotton or other substances, it helps to rear up an aristocratical order, at the expense of the workers in earth, to unite with governments in oppressing every species of useful industry.

The products of agriculture and manufacturing, unshackled by law, would seek each for themselves, the best markets through commercial channels, but these markets would hardly ever be the same; protecting duties tie travellers together, whose business and interest lie in different directions. This ligature upon nature, will, like all unnatural ligatures, weaken or kill. The best markets of our agriculture lie in foreign countries, whilst the best markets of our manufactures are at home. Our agriculture has to cross the ocean, and encounter a competition with foreign agriculture on its own ground. Our manufactures meet at home a competition with foreign manufactures. The disadvantages of the first competition, suffice to excite all the efforts of agriculture to save her life; the advantages of the second suffice gradually to bestow a sound constitution on manufacturing. But the manufacture of an aristocratical interest, under the pretext of encouraging work of a very different nature, may reduce both manufacturers and husbandmen, as Strickland says, is already effected in the case of the latter, "to the lowest state of degradation."

This degradation could never have been seen by a friend to either, who could afterwards approve of protecting duties. Let us take the article of wheat to unfold an idea of the disadvantages which have produced it. If wheat is worth 16s. sterling in England the 70lb. the farmers sell it here at about 6s. sterling. American agriculture then meets English agriculture in a competition, compelling her to sell at little more than one third of the price obtained by her rival. But American manufactures take the field against English on very different terms. These competitors meet in the United States. The American manufactures receive first, a bounty equal to the freight, commission and English taxes, upon their English rivals; and secondly, a bounty equal to our own necessary imposts. Without protecting duties, therefore, the American manufacturer gets for the same article, about 25 per cent more, and the American agriculturist about 180 per cent less, than their English rivals. Protecting duties added to these inequalities, may raise up an order of masters for actual manufacturers, to intercept advantages too enormous to escape the vigilance of capital, impoverish husbandmen, and aid in changing a fair to a fraudulent government; but they will never make either of these intrinsically valuable classes richer, wiser or freer.

5. General Charles Cotesworth Pinckney Defends the Slave Trade, 1788

. . . I am of the same opinion now as I was two years ago, when I used the expressions the gentleman has quoted, that while there remained one acre of swamp-land uncleared of South Carolina I would raise my voice against restricting the importation of negroes. I am as thoroughly convinced as that gentleman is, that the nature of our climate, and the flat, swampy situation of our country, obliges us to cultivate our lands with negroes, and that without them South Carolina would soon be a desert waste.

You have so frequently heard my sentiments on this subject, that I need not now repeat them. It was alleged by some of the members who opposed an unlimited importation, that slaves increased the weakness of any state who admitted them; that they were a dangerous species of property which an invading enemy could easily turn against ourselves and the neighboring states, and that as we were allowed a representation for them in the house of representatives, our influence in government would be increased in proportion as we were less able to defend ourselves. "Shew some period," said the members from the eastern states, "when it may be in our power to put a stop, if we please, to the importation of this weakness, and we will endeavor for your convenience, to restrain the religious and political prejudices of our people on this subject." The middle states and Virginia made us no such proposition; they were for an immediate and total prohibition. We endeavored to obviate the objections that were made in the best manner we could, and assigned reasons for our insisting on the importation, which there is no occasion to repeat, as they must occur to every gentleman in the house: a committee of the states was appointed in order to accommodate this matter, and after a great deal of difficulty, it was settled on the footing recited in the constitution.

By this settlement we have secured an unlimited importation of negroes for twenty years; nor is it declared that the importation shall be then stopped; it may be continued—we have a security that the general government can never emancipate them, for no such authority is granted, and it is admitted on all hands, that the general government has no powers but what are expressly granted by the constitution; and that all rights not expressed were reserved by the several states. We have obtained a right to recover our slaves in whatever part of America they may take refuge, which is a right we had not before. In short, considering all circumstances, we have made the best terms for the security of this species of property it was in our power to make. We would have made better if we could, but on the whole I do not think them bad. . . .

6. The "Bugbear" of a Georgia Senator, 1805

. . . Mr. J. said he wished to begin here, by preventing our own merchants from doing injury to other nations, and then to strike at those who insulted us. He for himself was prepared and willing to attack the first Power who had insulted us with far more superior weapons than arming our ships. He was an agricultural man, and would suffer with the flour makers; but he would call on the honorable gentleman either from Maryland, from New York, from Massachusetts, or Connecticut, to strike at Great Britain or any other nation who had injured us, by a resolution of prohibition of trade or inter-course, and he was the man who would second it and keep it on till the injuring nation should cry *peccavi*—keep it on one twelvemonth, and you would see them all at your feet. Look at the Legislature of Jamaica petitioning their Governor from time to time for American intercourse. Look at Trinidad, the same, in a state of famine. Sir, we have no favors to ask the nations of the earth; they must ask them of us, or their West India colonies must starve.

That however, with respect to documents, he would inform the gentleman from Maryland, that he had seen, though not official, a letter from General Ferrand, Governor of St. Domingo, and which was published in all the principal newspapers of the United States, complaining to the French Government on this subject, and laying all the blame to the American Govern-ment, if not in direct, in the most severe indirect terms. That as to the total separation of the self-created Emperor and nation of Hayti, and its in-dependence of the parent country, and under which gentlemen declared our rights of trade founded on the laws of nations—the late attack on that General by the Emperor proved it did not exist: he was defeated, his army scattered and driven to the mountains; that Ferrand held the island as French Governor for the French na-tion, and the separation was not such as to war-rant the arguments used for a right to trade. It would be a fatal argument used against us as re-spected our Southern States by other Powers. On the same grounds, a parcel of runaways and outcasts from South Carolina and Georgia, to the amount of some hundreds now collected on or near the Okefonokee swamp in Georgia,

might be termed an independent society; or if an insurrection took place in those States, the re-bellious horde, on creating an emperor, be sup-plied with arms and ammunition, as a separate and independent nation. This, as the honorable gentleman from Connecticut had been pleased to term his fears bugbears, might be no bugbear to him, safe and remote from the scene of action, near New Haven; but it was a serious bugbear to him, and would be to the whole southern coun-try, where the horrid scenes of that island would be re-enacted, their property destroyed, and their families massacred. The honorable gentle-man from New York, too, had been pleased to term them bugbears, but had raised up a num-ber of his own to prevent the passing of the bill—he had drawn a most lamentable picture of the state of this country, if this dishonorable trade to this small part of the commercial world was interdicted. Commerce was to languish and agriculture to be annihilated—our fields were to grow up in briers and thorns, and even verdure to disappear. Mr. J. said he did not believe this. The United States, if all the Powers on earth were opposed to us, had within herself enough to eat, to drink, and to clothe her citizens; this was not the case with other Powers. Not a nation existed; which had West India colonies, but was more or less dependent on us, and could not do without us—they must come to our terms or starve. On with your embargo, and in nine months they must lay at your feet. It was certain that we should suffer for that time, but he was willing, and he knew the Southern country willing to submit to it; and at the end of it our fields would resume their usual verdure, and the thorns and briers be rooted out. . . .

7. *Missionary Timothy Flint Encounters Hostility to "Yankees," 1824–1825*

. . . It is well known, that a jealousy, almost a ha-tred of Yankees, prevailed among the mass of this people, during the late war. This feeling, which had been fostered for years, seemed to be now dying away. The popularity of these minis-ters had doubtless contributed to extinguish it. A

respectable traveller from New England, was sure to receive every deserved courtesy. Indeed, the natural progress of literature and philoso-phy, which are diffusing their lights on all sides, is to do away these bitter and baneful jealousies. Fatal will it be to the several members of this great confederation, if the better informed, and those who give tone to public feeling and sentiment, do not feel the necessity of attempting to eradicate every fibre of this root of bitterness from our soil. In times of danger and excitement, which may come even to us, nothing is so terrible as this feeling, exciting distrust and destructive suspicion in the cabinet and in the field. There is but too much of this feeling yet existing, as I shall have occasion to remark elsewhere. A native of the North has no conception of the nature and extent of this feeling, until he finds himself in the South and West. I have felt grieved to see, that too many of our books of travels, and most of the accounts of the West, carried to the East, tend to foster this spirit toward these regions, on our part. The manner in which the slave question is agitated, keeps the embers glowing under the ashes.

In my whole tour through this state, I experienced a frank and cordial hospitality. I entered it with a share of those prejudices, which I had probably fostered unconsciously. I was aware how strongly they existed in the minds of the people, with regard to the inhabitants of the North. The general kindness with which I was every where received, impressed me so much the more forcibly, for being unexpected. The Kentuckians, it must be admitted, are a high minded people, and possess the stamina of a noble character. . . .

References

1. Antifederalist Richard Henry Lee Fears Tyranny, 1787
   Richard Henry Lee to Edmund Randolph, October 16, 1787, in James C. Ballagh, ed., *The Letters of Richard Henry Lee* (New York: The Macmillan Company, 1914), pp. 450–452, 454–455.

2. Federalist James Madison Praises Republican Government, 1787
   James Madison, *The Federalist*, Number 10, November 22, 1787, in Robert Rutland et al., eds., *The Papers of James Madison*, Volume 10, 27 May 1787–3 March 1788 (Chicago: University of Chicago Press, 1977), pp. 267–270.

3. George Washington Pleads for Unity, 1796
   George Washington, "Farewell Address to the People of the United States, September 17, 1796," in John C. Fitzpatrick, ed., *The Writings of George Washington*, Volume 35, March 30, 1796–July 31, 1797 (Washington: United States Government Printing Office, 1940), pp. 223–226.

4. John Taylor Champions the Cause of Agriculture, 1811
   John Taylor, *Arator: Being a Series of Agricultural Essays, Practical and Political: In Sixty One Numbers* (Baltimore: John M. Carter, 1817), pp. 11–13.

5. General Charles Cotesworth Pinckney Defends the Slave Trade, 1788
   Speech of Charles Cotesworth Pinckney, January 17, 1788, in Jonathan Elliot, ed., *The Debates in the Several State Conventions on the Adoption of the Federal Constitution as Recommended by the General Convention at Philadelphia in 1787*, Volume IV (Washington: 1836), pp. 276–277.

6. The "Bugbear" of a Georgia Senator, 1805
   James Jackson, Speech to the United States Senate, *Annals of Congress*, 9th Congress, 1st Session, December 20, 1805, p. 37.

7. Missionary Timothy Flint Encounters Hostility to "Yankees," 1824–1825
   Timothy Flint, *Recollections of the Last Ten Years, Passed in Occasional Residences and Journeyings in the Valley of the Mississippi, from Pittsburg and the Missouri to the Gulf of Mexico, and from Florida to the Spanish Frontier* (Boston: Cummings, Hilliard and Company, 1826), pp. 69–70.

Further Reading

Thomas P. Abernathy, *The South in the New Nation* (1961)

Richard Beeman, *The Old Dominion and the New Nation*, 1788–1801 (1972)

James Broussard, *Southern Federalists*, 1800–1816 (1978)

Noble E. Cunningham, Jr., *The Jeffersonian Republicans: The Formation of Party Organization, 1789–1801* (1957)

David B. Davis, *The Problem of Slavery in the Age of Revolution, 1770–1823* (1975)

David H. Fischer, *The Revolution of American Conservatism: The Federalist Party in the Era of Jeffersonian Democracy* (1965)

David P. Jordan, *Political Leadership in Jefferson's Virginia* (1983)

Robert McColley, *Slavery and Jeffersonian Virginia* (1964)

Duncan J. MacLeod, *Slavery, Race, and the American Revolution* (1974)

Norman K. Risjord, *Chesapeake Politics, 1781–1800* (1978)

Donald L. Robinson, *Slavery in the Structure of American Politics, 1765–1820* (1971)

Robert Shalhope, *John Taylor of Caroline: Pastoral Republican* (1978)

Gordon S. Wood, *The Creation of the American Republic, 1776–1787* (1969)

Document Set 4

Planters and the Proslavery Argument

The debate over slavery took on a new dimension in the 1830s. A resurgence of antislavery sentiment in the North forced the South to reassess its relationship with the "peculiar institution." Americans previously had enjoyed some degree of consensus on the subject. Both northerners and southerners had agreed publicly, for example, that the existence of slavery was tragic. In both sections, people widely viewed the institution as a necessary evil that the British had forced on America. Many northerners and southerners shared the belief that the abolition of slavery—and the emancipation of the nation's large black population, degraded by both slavery and its allegedly barbaric African heritage—would ignite a racial conflict.

Led by William Lloyd Garrison, radical abolitionists increasingly ridiculed this notion and began to level their attacks at the slaveowners as well as slavery itself. Incensed by condemnations of their morals and integrity, southerners responded with an argument designed to prove that slavery was a positive good. Slavery, a benign social system, transformed uncivilized Africans into productive members of society, they declared, with the slaves providing labor in return for the benefits of civilization and conversion to Christianity. The belief that the Bible sanctioned slavery as a divine institution ordained by God underpinned this proslavery argument. Its proponents depicted the plantation as a large familial unit incorporating both masters and slaves. Chattel slavery was an infinitely more humane system of work than wage labor in northern and European cities, the proslavery advocates also argued. Prepared to admit that abuses of the system did occur and that slaves were transferred periodically from one master to another, they nevertheless insisted that such incidents were more the exception than the rule. The interstate

slave trade, forcible separation of families, and indiscriminate acts of cruelty were the fanciful inventions of abolitionists, they claimed. Proslavery Americans maintained that the abolitionist critique of slavery as a brutal, exploitative institution rested largely on hearsay and assumption. Abolitionists' characterization of slavery was closer to the truth, however, than the proslavery depiction. This does not mean that slaveowners ignored the tenets of their own ideology. Rather, the realities of life on southern plantations may have undermined paternalism and patriarchalism among planters, whose actions were heavily influenced by the forces of a market economy and by the behavior of their bondsmen.

The first selection captures the essence of the proslavery argument. It comes from the writings of Virginia's George Fitzhugh, who became the leading apologist for the South's "peculiar institution" in the 1850s. Fitzhugh's defense of slavery, in the abstract and on racial grounds, is accompanied by a fierce assault on the social and economic pattern of development in the North. The second document indicates that some planters sought to establish a clear line between acts of deliberate cruelty and the disciplinary measures that they felt were necessary to run an efficient plantation. The author of the pamphlet, Plowden Weston, whose coastal rice plantations contained more than 300 slaves, relied heavily on his overseers to regulate his slaves' activities. Weston's order to delay the infliction of punishment on slaves is a tacit admission that unrestrained authority affects judgment. The stark reality of the domination of white over black is illustrated to perfection in the third document, an extract from the writings of Frederick Law Olmsted, a northerner who traveled extensively in the South in the 1850s. The fourth selection reveals not just the inhumane treatment inflicted on slaves but also the acquiescence of southern society to incidents of brutality. Social propriety and the intense need to preserve unity among the planter class prevented Thomas Chaplin from voicing his righteous indignation in public. In a system that provided slaves no recourse to justice, the jury's verdict of accidental death was almost inevitable. If errant behavior by slaves occurred under even the most benevolent master, such deviance usually could be attributed to deficiencies in the character of the owner's slaves.

In the fifth document, William Plumer, a minister and strong supporter of temperance, encourages slaveowners to prohibit the use of alcohol among their bondsmen. Abstinence, he naively insists, would prevent slave rebellions of the Nat Turner type (see Document Set 5). An interesting—and perhaps improbable—element of the proslavery argument was the unprofitability of slave labor compared with free labor. Supporters of slavery explained that slaveowners' lower profit margins resulted from masters' spending more in providing for the welfare of their slaves than factory owners paid in wages to their laborers. Olmsted, an astute observer of life and conditions in the slave South, agreed that slavery was not as profitable as the northern wage-labor system but as the next selection shows, he attributes the causes not to the benevolence of masters but to defects in the slave-labor system, and to the escalating price of slaves. One of the most detailed accounts of the events at a slave auction was penned by William Chambers, an English visitor to the United States. His experiences are chronicled in the seventh document. The final selection features one of the many newspaper notices advertising slaves for sale.

Questions for Analysis

1. The new proslavery argument was designed as a defense against abolitionism. To what degree was it also a means of fostering unity in the white population of the South?

2. Were southerners convinced by the "positive good" theory, or did they feel guilty about their ownership of slaves?

3. What constitutes a capitalist society? Was the Old South a feudal, precapitalist society, or was it part of the emerging nineteenth-century capitalist order?

4. How profitable was slavery?

5. How extensive was the interstate slave trade? What was the principal motive for the sale of slaves?

6. Was slavery the most important influence on the development of the antebellum South?

1. George Fitzhugh on the Blessings of Slavery, 1856

Until the lands of America are appropriated by a few, population becomes dense, competition among laborers active, employment uncertain, and wages low, the personal liberty of all the whites will continue to be a blessing. We have vast unsettled territories; population may cease to increase slowly, as in most countries, and many centuries may elapse before the question will be practically suggested, whether slavery to capital be preferable to slavery to human masters. But the negro has neither energy nor enterprise, and, even in our sparser populations, finds, with his improvident habits, that his liberty is a curse to himself, and a greater curse to the society around him. These considerations, and others equally obvious, have induced the South to attempt to defend negro slavery as an exceptional institution, admitting, nay asserting, that slavery, in the general or in the abstract, is morally wrong, and against common right. With singular inconsistency, after making this admission, which admits away the authority of the Bible, of profane history, and of the almost universal practice of mankind—they turn round and attempt to bolster up the cause of negro slavery by these very exploded authorities. If we mean not to repudiate all divine, and almost all human authority in favor of slavery, we must vindicate that institution in the abstract.

To insist that a status of society, which has been almost universal, and which is expressly and continually justified by Holy Writ, is its natural, normal, and necessary status, under the ordinary circumstances, is on its face a plausible and probable proposition. To insist on less, is to yield our cause, and to give up our religion; for if white slavery be morally wrong, be a violation of natural rights, the Bible cannot be true. Human and divine authority do seem in the general to concur, in establishing the expediency of having masters and slaves of different races. The nominal servitude of the Jews to each other, in its temporary character, and no doubt in its mild character, more nearly resembled our wardship and apprenticeship, than ordinary domestic slavery. In very many nations of antiquity, and in some of modern times, the law has permitted the native citizens to become slaves to each other. But few take advantage of such laws; and the infrequency of the practice, establishes the general truth that master and slave should be of different national descent. In some respects, the wider the difference the better, as the slave will feel less mortified by his position. In other respects, it may be that too wide a difference hardens the hearts and brutalizes the feelings of both master and slave. The civilized man hates the savage, and the savage returns the hatred with interest. Hence, West India slavery of newly caught negroes is not a very humane, affectionate, or civilizing institution. Virginia negroes have become moral and intelligent. They love their master and his family, and the attachment is reciprocated. Still, we like the idle, but intelligent house-servants, better than the hard-used, but stupid outhands; and we like the mulatto

better than the negro; yet the negro is generally more affectionate, contented and faithful.

The world at large looks on negro slavery as much the worst form of slavery; because it is only acquainted with West India slavery. Abolition never arose till negro slavery was instituted; and now abolition is only directed against negro slavery. There is no philanthropic crusade attempting to set free the white slaves of Eastern Europe and of Asia. The world, then, is prepared for the defence of slavery in the abstract—it is prejudiced only against negro slavery. These prejudices were in their origin well founded. The Slave Trade, the horrors of the Middle Passage, and West Indian slavery were enough to rouse the most torpid philanthropy.

But our Southern slavery has become a benign and protective institution, and our negroes are confessedly better off than any free laboring population in the world.

How can we contend that white slavery is wrong, whilst all the great body of free laborers are starving; and slaves, white or black, throughout the world, are enjoying comfort?

We write in the cause of Truth and Humanity, and will not play the advocate for master or for slave.

The aversion to negroes, the antipathy of race, is much greater at the North than at the South; and it is very probable that this antipathy to the person of the negro, is confounded with or generates hatred of the institution with which he is usually connected. Hatred to slavery is very generally little more than hatred of negroes.

There is one strong argument in favor of negro slavery over all other slavery: that he, being unfitted for the mechanic arts, for trade, and all skillful pursuits, leaves those pursuits to be carried on by the whites; and does not bring all industry into disrepute, as in Greece and Rome, where the slaves were not only the artists and mechanics, but also the merchants.

Whilst, as a general and abstract question, negro slavery has no other claims over other forms of slavery, except that from inferiority, or rather peculiarity, of race, almost all negroes require masters, whilst only the children, the women, the very weak, poor, and ignorant, &c., among the whites, need some protective and governing relation of this kind; yet as a subject of temporary, but worldwide importance, negro slavery has become the most necessary of all human institutions.

The African slave trade to America commenced three centuries and a half since. By the time of the American Revolution, the supply of slaves had exceeded the demand for slave labor, and the slaveholders, to get rid of a burden, and to prevent the increase of a nuisance, became violent opponents of the slave trade, and many of them abolitionists. New England, Bristol, and Liverpool, who reaped the profits of the trade, without suffering from the nuisance, stood out for a long time against its abolition. Finally, laws and treaties were made, and fleets fitted out to abolish it; and after a while, the slaves of most of South America, of the West Indies, and of Mexico were liberated. In the meantime, cotton, rice, sugar, coffee, tobacco, and other products of slave labor, came into universal use as necessaries of life. The population of Western Europe, sustained and stimulated by those products, was trebled, and that of the North increased tenfold. The products of slave labor became scarce and dear, and famines frequent. Now, it is obvious, that to emancipate all the negroes would be to starve Western Europe and our North. Not to ex-

tend and increase negro slavery, *pari passu*, with the extension and multiplication of free society, will produce much suffering. If all South America, Mexico, the West Indies, and our Union south of Mason and Dixon's line, of the Ohio and Missouri, were slaveholding, slave products would be abundant and cheap in free society; and their market for their merchandise, manufactures, commerce, &c., illimitable. Free white laborers might live in comfort and luxury on light work, but for the exacting and greedy landlords, bosses and other capitalists.

We must confess, that overstock the world as you will with comforts and with luxuries, we do not see how to make capital relax its monopoly— how to do aught but tantalize the hireling. Capital, irresponsible capital, begets, and ever will beget, the *immedicabile vulnus* of so-called Free Society. It invades every recess of domestic life, infects its food, its clothing, its drink, its very atmosphere, and pursues the hireling, from the hovel to the poor-house, the prison and the grave. Do what he will, go where he will, capital pursues and persecutes him. "Hæret lateri lethalis arundo!"

Capital supports and protects the domestic slave; taxes, oppresses and persecutes the free laborer.

2. *A Planter Instructs His Overseers, c. 1858*

The Proprietor, in the first place, wishes the Overseer MOST DISTINCTLY to understand that his first object is to be, under all circumstances, the care and well being of the negroes. The Proprietor is always ready to excuse such errors as may proceed from want of judgment; but he never can or will excuse any cruelty, severity, or want of care towards the negroes. For the well being, however, of the negroes, it is absolutely necessary to maintain obedience, order, and discipline; to see that the tasks are punctually and carefully performed, and to conduct the business steadily and firmly, without weakness on the one hand, or harshness on the other. For

such ends the following regulations have been instituted:

Lists—Tickets.—The names of all the men are to be called over every Sunday morning and evening, from which none are to be absent but those who are sick, or have tickets. When there is evening Church, those who attend are to be excused from answering. At evening list, every negro must be clean and well washed. No one is to be absent from the place without a ticket, which is always to be given to such as ask it, and have behaved well. All persons coming from the Proprietor's other places should shew their tickets to the Overseer, who should sign his name on the back; those going off the plantation should bring back their tickets signed. The Overseer is every now and then to go around at night and call at the houses, so as to ascertain whether their inmates are at home.

Allowance—Food.—Great care should be taken that the negroes should never have less than their regular allowance: in all cases of doubt, it should be given in favor of the largest quantity. The measures should not be *struck*, but rather heaped up over. None but provisions of the best quality should be used. If any is discovered to be damaged, the Proprietor, if at hand, is to be immediately informed; if absent, the damaged article is to be destroyed. The corn should be carefully winnowed before grinding. The small rice is apt to become sour: as soon as this is perceived it should be given out every meal until finished, or until it becomes too sour to use, when it should be destroyed.

Allowances are to be given out according to the following schedule. None of the allowances given out in the big pot are to be taken from the cook until after they are cooked, nor to be taken home by the people. . . .

Work, Holidays, &c.—No work of any sort or kind is to be permitted to be done by negroes on Good Friday, or Christmas day, or on any Sunday, except going for a Doctor, or nursing sick persons; any work of this kind done on any of these days is to be reported to the Proprietor, who will pay for it. The two days following Christmas day; the first Saturdays after finishing threshing, planting, hoeing, and harvest, are also to be holidays, on which the people may work for themselves. Only half task is to be done on every Saturday, except during planting and harvest, and those who have misbehaved or been lying up during the week. A task is as much work as the meanest full hand can do in nine hours, working industriously. The Driver is each morning to point out to each hand their task, and this task is *never* to be increased, and no work is to be done over task except under the *most urgent necessity*; which over-work is to be reported to the Proprietor, who will pay for it. No negro is to be put into a task which they cannot finish with tolerable ease. It is a bad plan to

punish for not finishing tasks; it is subversive of discipline to leave tasks unfinished, and contrary to justice to punish for what cannot be done. *In nothing does a good manager so much excel a bad, as in being able to discern what a hand is capable of doing, and in never attempting to make him do more.*

No negro is to leave his task until the Driver has examined and approved it, he is then to be permitted immediately to go home; and the hands are to be encouraged to finish their tasks as early as possible, so as to have time for working for themselves. Every negro, except the sickly ones and those with suckling children, (who are to be allowed half an hour) are to be on board the flat by sunrise. One Driver is to go down to the flat early, the other to remain behind and bring on all the people with him. He will be responsible for all coming down. The barn-yard bell will be rung by the watchman two hours, and half an hour, before sunrise.

Punishments.—It is desirable to allow 24 hours to elapse between the discovery of the offence, and the punishment. No punishment is to exceed 15 lashes: in cases where the Overseer supposes a severer punishment necessary, he must apply to the Proprietor, or to ——— Esq., in case of the Proprietor's absence from the neighborhood. Confinement (*not* in the stocks) is to be preferred to whipping; but the stoppage of Saturday's allowance, and doing whole task on Saturday, will suffice to prevent ordinary offences. Special care must be taken to prevent any *indecency* in punishing women. No Driver, or other negro, is to be allowed to punish any person in any way, except by order of the Overseer, and in his presence. . . .

Women with six children alive at any *one* time, are allowed all Saturday to themselves.

Fighting, particularly amongst women, and obscene or abusive language, is to be always rigorously punished.

During the summer, fresh spring water must be carried every day on the Island. Any body found drinking ditch or river water must be punished.

Finally.—The Proprietor hopes the Overseer will remember that a system of *strict justice* is necessary to good management. No person should ever be allowed to break a law without being punished, or any person punished who has not broken a well known law. Every person should be made perfectly to understand what they are punished for, and should be made to perceive that they are not punished in anger, or through caprice. All abusive language or violence of demeanor should be avoided: they reduce the man who uses them to a level with the negro, and are hardly ever forgotten by those to whom they are addressed.

Plowden C. J. Weston.

Hagley,   18——.

3. *Frederick Law Olmsted Discovers the Power of a Child, 1854*

. . . Ordinarily there is no show of government any more than at the North: the slaves go about with as much apparent freedom as convicts in a dockyard. There is, however, nearly everywhere, always prepared to act, if not always in service, an armed force, with a military organization, which is invested with more arbitrary and cruel power than any police in Europe. Yet the security of the whites is in a much less degree contingent on the action of the patrols than upon the constant, habitual, and instinctive surveillance and authority of all white people over all black. I have seen a gentleman, with no commission or special authority, oblige negroes to show their passports, simply because he did not recognize them as belonging to any of his neighbors. I have seen a girl, twelve years old, in a district where, in ten miles, the slave population was fifty to one of the free, stop an old man on the public road, demand to know where he was going, and by what authority, order him to face about and return to his plantation, and enforce her command with turbulent anger, when he hesitated, by threatening that she would have him well whipped if he did not instantly obey. The man quailed like a spaniel, and she instantly resumed the manner of a lovely child with me, no more apprehending that she had acted unbecomingly, than that her character had been influenced by the slave's submission to her caprice of supremacy; no more conscious that she had increased the security of her life by strengthening the habit of the slave to the master race, than is the sleeping seaman that he tightens his clutch of the rigging as the ship meets each new billow. . . .

4. *Thomas Chaplin's Jury Service, 1849*

Feb 19th.

Monday I received a summons while at breakfast, to go over to J. H. Sandiford's at 10 o'clock A.M. this day and sit on a jury of inquest on the body of Roger, a Negro man belonging to Sandiford. Accordingly I went. About 12 P.M. there were 12 of us together (the number required to form a jury), viz.—Dr. Scott, foreman, J. J. Pope, J. E. L. Fripp, W. O. P. Fripp, Dr. M. M. Sams, Henry Fripp, Dr. Jenkins, Jn. McTureous, Henry McTureous, P. W. Perry, W. Perry & myself. We were sworn by J. D. Pope, magistrate, and proceeded to examine the body. We found it in an outhouse used as a corn house, and meat house (for there were both in the house). Such a shocking sight never before met my eyes. There was the poor Negro, who all his life had been a complete cripple, being hardly able to walk & used his knees more than his feet, in the most shocking situation, but *stiff dead*. He was placed in this situation by his *master*, to punish him, as he says, *for impertinence*. And what [was] this punishment—this *poor cripple* was sent by his master (as Sandiford's evidence goes) on Saturday the 17th inst., before daylight (cold & bitter weather, as everyone knows, though Sandiford says, "It was *not very* cold"), in a paddling boat down the river to get oysters, and ordering him to return before high water, & cut a bundle of marsh. The poor fellow did not return before ebb tide, but he brought 7 baskets of oysters & a small bundle of marsh (more than the primest of my fellows would have done. Anthony never brought me more than 3 baskets of oyster & took the whole day). His master asked him why he did not return sooner & cut more marsh. He said that the wind was too high. His master said he would whip him for it, & set to work with a cowhide to do the same. The fellow hollered & when told to stop, said he would not, as long as he was being whipped, for which impertinence he received 30 cuts. He went to the kitchen and was talking to another Negro when Sandiford slipped up & overheard this confab, heard Roger, as he says, say, that if he had sound limbs, he would not take a flogging from any white man, but would shoot them down, and turn his back on them (another witness, the Negro that Roger was talking to, says that Roger did not say this, but "that he would turn his back on them if they shot him down," which I think is much the most probable of the two speeches). Sandiford then had him confined, or I should say, murdered, in the manner I will describe. Even if the fellow had made the speech that Sandiford said he did, and even worse, it by no means warranted the punishment he received. The fellow was a cripple, & could not escape from a slight confinement, besides, I don't think he was ever known to use a gun, or even know how to use one, so there was little apprehension of his

putting his threat (if it can be called one) into execution. For these *crimes*, this man, this demon in human shape, this pretended Christian, member of the Baptist Church, had this poor cripple Negro placed in an open outhouse, the wind blowing through a hundred cracks, his clothes wet to the waist, without a single blanket & in freezing weather, with his back against a partition, shackles on his wrists, & chained to a bolt in the floor and a chain around *his neck*, the chain passing through the partition behind him, & fastened on the other side—in this position the poor wretch was left for the night, a position that none but the "most *bloodthirsty* tyrant" could have placed a human being. My heart chills at the idea, and my blood boils at the base tyranny—The wretch returned to his victim about daylight the next morning & found him, as anyone might expect, dead, *choked, strangled,* frozen to death, *murdered*. The verdict of the jury was, that Roger came to his death by choking by a chain put around his neck by his master—*having slipped from the position in which he was placed*. The verdict should have been that Roger came to his death by inhumane treatment to him by his master—by placing him, in very cold weather, in a cold house, with a chain about his neck & fastened to the wall, & otherways chained so that he could in no way assist himself should he slip from the position in which he was placed & must consequently choke to death without immediate assistance. Even should he escape being frozen to death, which we believe would have been the case from the fact of his clothes being wet & the severity of the weather, my *individual* verdict would be *deliberately* but *unpremeditatedly murdered* by his master James H. Sandiford.

5. A Clergyman Denounces Drinking Among Slaves, 1848

. . . It is proper here to state that among the most serious obstacles to the spread of the gospel among this people, the use of ardent spirits has long held and does still hold a prominent place. We once heard a slave-holder say

that if Abolitionists had stirred up as much rebellion and caused as much bloodshed among the negroes as the retailers of ardent spirits had done, there would long ere this have been a civil war.

Nat Turner's insurrection broke out in the region that formerly manufactured vast quantities of apple-brandy. His followers are known to have been highly stimulated with this *liquid fire*. Indeed, we know a clergyman who for many years has resided and travelled extensively in the South, and who testifies that among scores of negroes under sentence of death whom he has visited, he remembers but two, who were not led to commit the crimes that brought them to such sentence by some sort of influence arising from strong drink; and in most cases by drinking just before they committed the crime. It gives us pleasure to state that the sound principles of the Temperance reformation are so few, so plain, and so simple, that they are of easy application to this kind of population. Many recent experiments in the South prove the truth of this assertion, and exhibit most blessed effects arising from the introduction of this reformation among them. Let the friends of morality and religion persevere. Drunkenness is the enemy of the black and the white. It destroys both soul and body, in time and eternity. . . .

6. *Olmsted on the Economy of Slavery, 1854*

. . . It is quite plain, notwithstanding all the drawbacks attending the employment of forced labor, and notwithstanding the high price of slaves, that slave labor is employed profitably by the large planters in Mississippi, and in certain other parts of the South, in the culture of cotton. That the profit, in this case, is not only large compared with the profit of slave labor employed elsewhere, and in other occupations, but that it is moderately good, at least, compared with the profit of other investments of capital and enterprise at the North and in Europe, must also be admitted. There are few enterprises to which capital lends itself more freely than to speculation in slaves, when the seeker for it is already a large cotton planter.

Is slave labor, then, profitable?

To certain individuals, unquestionably.

Nor do I think myself warranted in denying that the production of cotton per acre on many Mississippi plantations may not be as large as it can be economically made with land as low and slaves as high in price as is at present the case.

Is not then this slave agriculture economically conducted?

To the ends had in view by the planter it certainly is.

I answer thus distinctly, because assertions to the same effect have been addressed to me, evidently with the supposition that they invalidated the argument on the economy of Virginia, and of other parts of my first volume. That argument was intended to lead to the conclusions that the cost of such labor as is usually performed by slaves in Virginia, is more than double, in that State, what it is in New York. That in consequence of this excessive cost of labor, the profits of agriculture are much less than they would be if free trade in the commodity of labor could be established. That it is a consequence also of this high cost of labor that enterprise and capital avoid Virginia, especially avoid agriculture in Virginia, and that, as might therefore be supposed, agriculture in Virginia is a wretchedly conducted business, and among the agricultural class, niggardness, surliness, and bigoted ignorance much more prevail than among the farmers of the Free States. In short, that slavery, by unnecessarily adding to the cost of making natural wealth, or the resources of the country, available, and by causing a wasteful use of natural wealth, has the effect of impoverishing and degrading Virginia.

The difference between Virginia and Mississippi is mainly found in the fact that in the latter State cotton grows luxuriantly and matures perfectly. The demand for cotton is such, and the soil on which it can be grown is so limited, that wherever it can be produced with facility a given investment in land, tools, and labor will be much better rewarded than a similar investment can be rewarded in any agricultural enterprise in

Virginia. What is true with regard to Virginia, I believe to be true with regard to Mississippi, with only this difference, that in Mississippi there is one description of natural wealth available with so little labor (having regard to its value in the world) that even with the disadvantages of slavery, capital appears for a time to be well invested in developing it, hence agriculture; that is to say, cotton culture in Mississippi attracts capital, enterprise, and skill, as corn culture would in Virginia if the value of corn bore the same relation to the cost of the labor employed in its production.

The cost of labor merely, is as much increased by slavery in Mississippi as it is in Virginia; the cost of production, the barrier to wealth, is as much more than it needs to be in Mississippi as it is in Virginia. The necessary loss appears to me to be larger in Mississippi, indeed. Substitute a free trade of labor in Mississippi for the present system, and I suppose that you will have, as you would in Virginia, a fourfold value of land, a fourfold economy.

I repeat: Slave labor is to-day undoubtedly profitable to certain owners of slaves in Mississippi.

It was undoubtedly profitable to roll tobacco in casks one hundred miles to market, at one time, in Virginia.

It would probably be profitable in Illinois to reap wheat with sickles, and thrash it with flails, and market it by wagons, if there were no horse reaping machines and horse thrashing machines, and steam locomotive machines, engaged in supplying the demand for wheat, but there is many hundred-fold the wealth in Illinois to-day that there would have been had sickles, flails, and wagon trains been held to there with the bigotry as is slavery in Mississippi; and if it could be made certain that ten years hence the present labor system of Mississippi would be superseded by the free labor system, I have little doubt that twenty years hence the wealth of Mississippi would be at least tenfold what, under the present system, it is likely to be, and the whole country and the whole world be some degrees happier than it is now likely to be. . . .

7. *A British Traveler Visits a Slave Mart, 1853*

. . . Richmond is known as the principal market for the supply of slaves for the south—a circumstance understood to originate in the fact that Virginia, as a matter of husbandry, breeds negro labourers for the express purpose of sale. Having heard that such was the case, I was interested in knowing by what means and at what prices slaves are offered to purchasers. Without introductions of any kind, I was thrown on my own resources in acquiring this information. Fortunately, however, there was no impediment to encounter in the research. The exposure of ordinary goods in a store is not more open to the public than are the sales of slaves in Richmond. By consulting the local newspapers, I learned that the sales take place by auction every morning in the offices of certain brokers, who, as I understood by the terms of their advertisements, purchased or received slaves for sale on commission. . . .

It was already the appointed hour; but as no company had assembled, I entered and took a seat by the fire. The office, provided with a few deal-forms and chairs, a desk at one of the windows, and a block accessible by a few steps, was tenantless, save by a gentleman who was arranging papers at the desk, and to whom I had addressed myself on the previous evening. Minute after minute passed, and still nobody entered. There was clearly no hurry in going to business. I felt almost like an intruder, and had formed the resolution of departing, in order to look into the other offices, when the person referred to left his desk, and came and seated himself opposite to me at the fire.

"You are an Englishman," said he, looking me steadily in the face; "do you want to purchase?"

"Yes," I replied, "I am an Englishman; but I do not intend to purchase. I am travelling about for information, and I shall feel obliged by your letting me know the prices at which negro servants are sold."

"I will do so with much pleasure," was the answer. "Do you mean field-hands or house-servants?"

"All kinds," I replied; "I wish to get all the information I can."

With much politeness, the gentleman stepped to his desk, and began to draw up a note of prices. This, however, seemed to require careful consideration; and while the note was preparing, a lanky person, in a wide-awake hat, and chewing tobacco, entered, and took the chair just vacated. He had scarcely seated himself, when, on looking towards the door, I observed the subjects of sale—the man and boy indicated by the paper on the red flag—enter together, and quietly walk to a form at the back of the shop, whence, as the day was chilly, they edged themselves towards the fire, in the corner where I was seated. I was now between the two parties—the white man on the right, and the old and young negro on the left—and I waited to see what would take place.

The sight of the negroes at once attracted the attention of Wide-awake. Chewing with vigour, he kept keenly eyeing the pair, as if to see what they were good for. Under this searching gaze, the man and boy were a little abashed, but said nothing. Their appearance had little of the repulsiveness we are apt to associate with the idea of slaves. They were dressed in a gray woollen coat, pants, and waistcoat, coloured cotton neckcloths, clean shirts, coarse woollen stockings, and stout shoes. The man wore a black hat; the boy was bareheaded. Moved by a sudden impulse, Wide-awake left his seat, and rounding the back of my chair, began to grasp at the man's arms, as if to feel their muscular capacity. He

then examined his hands and fingers; and, last of all, told him to open his mouth and shew his teeth, which he did in a submissive manner. Having finished these examinations, Wide-awake resumed his seat, and chewed on in silence as before.

I thought it was but fair that I should now have my turn of investigation, and accordingly asked the elder negro what was his age. He said he did not know. I next inquired how old the boy was. He said he was seven years of age. On asking the man if the boy was his son, he said he was not—he was his cousin. I was going into other particulars, when the office-keeper approached, and handed me the note he had been preparing; at the same time making the observation that the market was dull at present, and that there never could be a more favourable opportunity of buying. I thanked him for the trouble which he had taken; and now submit a copy of his price-current:—

Best Men, 18 to 25 years old,	1200 to 1300 dollars.
Fair do. do. do.	950 to 1050 "
Boys, 5 feet,	850 to 950 "
Do.,* 4 feet 8 inches,	700 to 800 "
Do., 4 feet 5 inches,	500 to 600 "
Do., 4 feet,	375 to 450 "
Young Women,	800 to 1000 "
Girls, 5 feet,	750 to 850 "
Do., 4 feet 9 inches,	700 to 750 "
Do., 4 feet,	350 to 452 "

(Signed) —————,

Richmond, Virginia.

[*Do. means ditto.]

8. A Newspaper Advertises Slaves for Sale, 1853

By Thomas N. Gadsden

At private sale, forty prime Negroes, consisting of prime young field men, waitingmen, waiting and house servants, plough boys, well grown families, one tight cask cooper, one blacksmith, two young women, field hands. Apply as above at N. W. Cor. State & Chalmers-Sts., Broker, Auctioneer and General Commission Agent.

References

1. George Fitzhugh on the Blessings of Slavery, 1856
   George Fitzhugh, *Cannibals All! or Slaves Without Masters* (Richmond, Virginia: A. Morris, 1857), pp. 294–299.

2. A Planter Instructs His Overseers, c. 1858
   Plowden C. J. Weston, *Rules for the Government and Management of Plantation to Be Observed by the Overseer* (Charleston, South Carolina: A. J. Burke, n.d.), pp. 5–9, 16.

3. Frederick Law Olmsted Discovers the Power of a Child, 1854
   Frederick L. Olmsted, *A Journey in the Back Country* (New York: Mason Brothers, 1861), pp. 444–445.

4. Thomas Chaplin's Jury Service, 1849
   Entry for February 19, 1849, in Theodore Rosengarten, *Tombee: Portrait of a Cotton Planter with the Plantation Journal of Thomas B. Chaplin (1822–1890)* (New York: McGraw-Hill Book Company, 1987), pp. 456–458.

5. A Clergyman Denounces Drinking Among Slaves, 1848
   W. S. Plumer, D. D., *Thoughts on the Religious Instructions of the Negroes of This Country* (Savannah, Georgia: Edward J. Purse, 1848), p. 16.

6. Olmsted on the Economy of Slavery, 1854
   Olmsted, *In the Back Country*, op. cit., pp. 294–296.

7. A British Traveler Visits a Slave Mart, 1853
   William Chambers, *Things as They Are in America* (London: W. and R. Chambers, 1854), pp. 273, 275–277.

8. A Newspaper Advertises Slaves for Sale, 1853
   Charleston Courier, January 4, 1853.

Further Reading

John B. Boles, ed., *Masters and Slaves in the House of the Lord: Race and Religion in the American South, 1740–1870* (1988)

Marcus Cunliffe, *Chattel Slavery and Wage Slavery: The Anglo-American Context, 1830–1860* (1979)

Clement Eaton, *The Growth of Southern Civilization, 1790–1860* (1961)

Drew G. Faust, *James Henry Hammond and the Old South: A Design for Mastery* (1982)

Robert W. Fogel and Stanley Engerman, *Time on the Cross: The Economics of American Negro Slavery* (1974)

George M. Fredrickson, *The Black Image in the White Mind: The Debate on Afro-American Character and Destiny, 1817–1914* (1971)

Eugene D. Genovese, *The Political Economy of Slavery* (1965)

————, *The World the Slaveholders Made* (1969)

William S. Jenkins, *Pro-Slavery Thought in the Old South* (1935)

Donald G. Mathews, *Religion in the Old South* (1971)

James Oakes, *The Ruling Race: A History of American Slaveholders* (1982)

Laurence Shore, *Southern Capitalists: The Ideological Leadership of an Elite, 1832–1885* (1986)

Julia F. Smith, *Slavery and Plantation Growth in Antebellum Florida* (1973)

Shelton Smith, *In His Image, But . . . : Racism in Southern Religion, 1780–1910* (1972)

Steven M. Stowe, *Intimacy and Power in the Old South: Ritual in the Lives of Planters* (1987)

Michael Tadman, *Speculators and Slaves: Masters, Traders, and Slaves in the Old South* (1989)

Larry E. Tise, *Proslavery: A History of the Defense of Slavery in America, 1701–1840* (1987)

Bertram Wyatt-Brown, *Southern Honor* (1982)

Document Set 5

Slaves and Slavery

In 1956 the historian Kenneth Stampp wrote that "innately Negroes *are*, after all, only white men with black skins, nothing more, nothing less."[1] American liberals heralded Stampp's groundbreaking book *The Peculiar Institution* as the definitive response to the racist defenses of slavery that had dominated the study of the subject for the previous half-century. Yet Stampp's viewpoint implicitly denied the existence of a distinctive slave culture different from the culture of the master class. Only with the rise of black-nationalist movements in the United States in the 1960s did a fresh approach to the study of the African-American experience emerge, bringing about a remarkable reversal in historians' interpretations of slavery. As a result, the traditional notion that slavery can be best understood by examining the evidence left by the white slaveowning class is no longer valid.

Forbidden to learn to read and write by the law and by most slaveowners, slaves nevertheless left considerable written and oral information: narratives by successful runaways, and reminiscences of ex-slaves who related their experiences years later. Historians have questioned the reliability of the oral tradition, but undeniably students of slavery can find a common theme in the slave experience regardless of the source material they use. Most slaves did not share the same worldview as their masters. Psychologists, folklorists, geographers, and experts in the fields of medicine, music, art, and dance have helped to reveal a remarkably complex slave community. Slaves resisted their condition using methods much safer and more subtle than that of open rebellion. Marriage, family relationships, religion, and a vital African heritage were important factors in the creation of a slave community that was not characterized by total submission to the will of the master. The myth of "Sambo" has finally been laid to rest.

Because of the tremendous risks involved, large-scale slave rebellions were extremely uncommon in the Old South. The largest and most famous took place in Southampton County, Virginia, in the summer of 1831, when more than fifty whites were killed in a bloodthirsty insurrection led by Nat Turner, whose confession to his captors is reproduced as the first document. Turner, a preacher and mystic, claimed that divine providence had guided his actions. Although few slaves dared to go as far as Turner, most took solace in religion. The three spirituals reprinted as the second document may have served a dual purpose in the slave community. The slaves' longings for the hereafter is revealed in "Steal Away to Jesus," but all three refrains suggest that escape from bondage and the downfall of slavery were highly desirable in the slaves' present lives.

Permanent escape from slavery was possible in two ways: by running away to the North or to Canada, and by recourse to the law. Bondsmen who lived in the border southern states (Kentucky, Maryland, Missouri) could hope to escape and evade detection long enough to reach freedom in the adjoining northern states. Frederick Douglass, the most renowned of the black abolitionists, made his escape from Baltimore. Intelligent and articulate, Douglass shows in the third document how secretly learning to read and write prepared him for freedom. Fugitive slaves farther south often had no choice but to seek shelter in the most inhospitable terrains if they wanted to retain their freedom. In the fourth selection, one bondsman who was later able to make his way to Canada records his experiences as a fugitive in North Carolina's aptly named Dismal Swamp. The

---

[1] Kenneth M. Stampp, *The Peculiar Institution: Slavery in the Antebellum South* (New York: Alfred A. Knopf, 1956), p. vii.

sense of grief that runaways felt at leaving loved ones behind in captivity indicates that the decision to remain in bondage or to try to escape never came easily.

Some blacks in the South were free, although the opportunities to achieve this status deteriorated after the 1820s as state legislatures increasingly prohibited owners from manumitting (freeing) their slaves. Some free blacks achieved a comfortable life-style. William Johnson, for example, was a prosperous businessman in the Mississippi town of Natchez. Reprinted as the fifth document, the extracts taken from Johnson's diary show that color was a barrier to social equality even when a free black owned land and slaves. The sixth document comprises several accounts by ex-slaves who narrated their memories of slavery to interviewers working for the Federal Writers Project in the 1930s.

Questions for Analysis

1. What were the strengths and weaknesses of the slave community?

2. Did slaves retain a strong sense of their African heritage, or were their cultural values extinguished by their years of servitude in the American South?

3. Were slaves true Christians, or was slave religion a fusion of Christianity and African tribal beliefs? Did slaves accept the version of Christianity delivered to them in the sermons of white preachers?

4. How stable was the slave family?

5. How did slaves cope with their bondage psychologically? How did the actions of slaves influence the attitudes and decisions of their owners?

6. How free were free blacks?

1. Nat Turner Describes His Divine Mission, 1831

. . . To a mind like mine, restless, inquisitive and observant of every thing that was passing, it is easy to suppose that religion was the subject to which it would be directed, and although this subject principally occupied my thoughts—there was nothing that I saw or heard of to which my attention was not directed—The manner in which I learned to read and write, not only had great influence on my own mind, as I acquired it with the most perfect ease, so much so, that I have no recollection whatever of learning the alphabet—but to the astonishment of the family, one day, when a book was shewn to me to keep me from crying, I began spelling the names of different objects—this was a source of wonder to all in the neighborhood, particularly the blacks—and this learning was constantly improved at all opportunities—when I got large enough to go to work, while employed, I was reflecting on many things that would present themselves to my imagination, and whenever an opportunity occurred of looking at a book, when the school children were getting their lessons, I would find many things that the fertility of my own imagination had depicted to me before; all my time, not devoted to my master's service, was spent either in prayer, or in making experiments in casting different things in moulds made of earth, in attempting to make paper, gun-powder, and many other experiments, that although I could not perfect, yet convinced me of its practicability if I had the means.* I was not addicted to stealing in my youth, nor have ever been—Yet such was the confidence of the negroes in the neighborhood, even at this early period of my life, in my superior judgment, that they would often carry me with them when they were going on any roguery, to plan for them. Growing up among

---

*When questioned as to the manner of manufacturing those different articles, he was found well informed on the subject.

them, with this confidence in my superior judgment, and when this, in their opinions, was perfected by Divine inspiration, from the circumstances already alluded to in my infancy, and which belief was ever afterwards zealously inculcated by the austerity of my life and manners, which became the subject of remark by white and black.—Having soon discovered to be great, I must appear so, and therefore studiously avoided mixing in society, and wrapped myself in mystery, devoting my time to fasting and prayer—by this time, having arrived to man's estate, and hearing the scriptures commented on at meetings, I was struck with that particular passage which says: "Seek ye the kingdom of Heaven and all things shall be added unto you." I reflected much on this passage, and prayed daily for light on this subject—As I was praying one day at my plough, the spirit spoke to me, saying "Seek ye the kingdom of Heaven and all things shall be added unto you." *Question*—what do you mean by the Spirit? *Ans*. The Spirit that spoke to the prophets in former days—and I was greatly astonished, and for two years prayed continually, whenever my duty would permit—and then again I had the same revelation, which fully confirmed me in the impression that I was ordained for some great purpose in the hands of the Almighty. Several years rolled round, in which many events occurred to strengthen me in this my belief. At this time I reverted in my mind to the remarks made of me in my childhood, and the things that had been shewn me—and as it had been said of me in my childhood by those by whom I had been taught to pray, both white and black, and in whom I had the greatest confidence, that I had too much sense to be raised, and if I was, I would never be of any use to any one as a slave. Now finding I had arrived to man's estate, and was a slave, and these revelations being made known to me, I began to direct my attention to this great object, to fulfill the purpose for which, by this time, I felt assured I was intended. Knowing the influence I had obtained over the minds of my fellow servants, (not by the means of conjuring and such like tricks—for to them I always spoke of such things with contempt) but by the communion of the Spirit whose revelations I often communicated to them, and they believed and said my wisdom came from God. I now began to prepare them for my purpose, by telling them something was about to happen that would terminate in fulfilling the great promise that had been made to me—. . .

2. *Three Slave Spirituals*

Steal Away to Jesus

Steal away, steal away, steal away to Jesus!
Steal away, steal away home,
I ain't got long to stay here.
Steal away, steal away, steal away to Jesus!
Steal away, steal away home,
I ain't got long to stay here.

My Lord, He calls me,
He calls me by the thunder,
The trumpet sounds within-a my soul,
I ain't got long to stay here.

Steal away, steal away, steal away to Jesus!
Steal away, steal away home,
I ain't got long to stay here.
Steal away, steal away, steal away to Jesus!
Steal away, steal away home,
I ain't got long to stay here.

Green trees a-bending, po' sinner stand a-trembling,
The trumpet sounds within-a my soul,
I ain't got long to stay here,
Oh, Lord I ain't got long to stay here.

Go Down, Moses

Go down, Moses,
  'Way down in Egypt land,
Tell ole Pharaoh,
  To let my people go.
Go down, Moses,
  'Way down in Egypt land,
Tell ole Pharaoh,
  To let my people go.

    When Israel was in Egypts land:
      Let my people go,
    Oppressed so hard they could not stand,
      Let my people go.

    "Thus spoke the Lord," bold Moses said;
      Let my people go,
    If not I'll smite your first born dead,
      Let my people go.

Go down, Moses,
  'Way down in Egypt land,
Tell ole Pharaoh
  To let my people go.
O let my people go.

Joshua Fit de Battle ob Jerico

Joshua fit de battle ob Jerico, Jerico, Jerico,
Joshua fit de battle ob Jerico,
An' de walls come tumblin' down.

You may talk about yo' king ob Gideon,
You may talk about yo' man ob Saul,
Dere's none like good ole Joshua
At de battle ob Jerico.

Up to de walls ob Jerico,
He marched with spear in han'
"Go blow dem ram horns," Joshua cried,
"Kase de battle am in my han'."

Den de lam' ram sheep horns begin to blow,
Trumpets begin to soun',
Joshua commanded de chillen to shout,
An' de walls come tumblin' down.

Dat mornin'
Joshua fit de battle ob Jerico, Jerico, Jerico,
Joshua fit de battle ob Jerico,
An' de walls come tumblin' down.

3. *Frederick Douglass on Learning to Read and Write (1830s), 1845*

I lived in Master Hugh's family about seven years. During this time, I succeeded in learning to read and write. In accomplishing this, I was compelled to resort to various stratagems. I had no regular teacher. My mistress, who had kindly commenced to instruct me, had, in compliance with the advice and direction of her husband, not only ceased to instruct, but had set her face against my being instructed by any one else. It is due, however, to my mistress to say of her, that she did not adopt this course of treatment immediately. She at first lacked the depravity indispensable to shutting me up in mental darkness. It was at least necessary for her to have some training in the exercise of irresponsible power, to make her equal to the task of treating me as though I were a brute.

My mistress was, as I have said, a kind and tender-hearted woman; and in the simplicity of her soul she commenced, when I first went to live with her, to treat me as she supposed one human being ought to treat another. In entering upon the duties of a slaveholder, she did not seem to perceive that I sustained to her the relation of a mere chattel, and that for her to treat me as a human being was not only wrong, but dangerously so. Slavery proved as injurious to her as it did to me. When I went there, she was a pious, warm, and tender-hearted woman. There was no sorrow or suffering for which she had not a tear. She had bread for the hungry, clothes for the naked, and comfort for every mourner that came within her reach. Slavery soon proved its ability to divest her of these heavenly qualities. Under its influence, the tender heart became stone, and the lamblike disposition gave way to one of tiger-like fierceness. The first step in her downward course was in her ceasing to instruct me. She now commenced to practise her husband's precepts. She finally became even more violent in her opposition than her husband himself. She was not satisfied with simply doing as well as he had commanded; she seemed anxious to do better. Nothing seemed to make her more angry than to see me with a newspaper. She seemed to think that here lay the danger. I have had her rush at me with a face made all up of fury, and snatch from me a newspaper, in a manner that fully revealed her apprehension. She was an apt woman; and a little experience soon demonstrated, to her satisfaction, that education and slavery were incompatible with each other.

From this time I was most narrowly watched. If I was in a separate room any considerable length of time, I was sure to be suspected of having a book, and was at once called to give an account of myself. All this, however, was too late. The first step had been taken. Mistress, in teaching me the alphabet, had given me the *inch*, and no precaution could prevent me from taking the *ell*.

The plan which I adopted, and the one by which I was most successful, was that of making friends of all the little white boys whom I met in the street. As many of these as I could, I converted into teachers. With their kindly aid, obtained at different times and in different places, I finally succeeded in learning to read. When I was sent on errands, I always took my book with me, and by going one part of my errand quickly, I found time to get a lesson before my return. I used also to carry bread with me, enough of which was always in the house, and to which I was always welcome; for I was much better off in this regard than many of the poor white children in our neighborhood. This bread I used to bestow upon the hungry little urchins, who, in return, would give me that more valuable bread of knowledge. I am strongly tempted to give the names of two or three of those little boys, as a testimonial of the gratitude and affection I bear them; but prudence forbids;—not that it would injure me, but it might embarrass them; for it is almost an unpardonable offence to teach slaves to read in this Christian country. It is enough to say of the dear little fellows, that they lived on

Philpot Street, very near Durgin and Bailey's ship-yard. I used to talk this matter of slavery over with them. I would sometimes say to them, I wished I could be as free as they would be when they got to be men. "You will be free as soon as you are twenty-one, *but I am a slave for life!* Have not I as good a right to be free as you have?" These words used to trouble them; they would express for me the liveliest sympathy, and console me with the hope that something would occur by which I might be free.

I was now about twelve years old, and the thought of being a *slave for life* began to bear heavily upon my heart. Just about this time, I got hold of a book entitled "The Columbian Orator." Every opportunity I got, I used to read this book. Among much of other interesting matter, I found in it a dialogue between a master and his slave. The slave was represented as having run away from his master three times. The dialogue represented the conversation which took place between them, when the slave was retaken the third time. In this dialogue, the whole argument in behalf of slavery was brought forward by the master, all of which was disposed of by the slave. The slave was made to say some very smart as well as impressive things in reply to his master—things which had the desired though unexpected effect; for the conversation resulted in the voluntary emancipation of the slave on the part of the master.

In the same book, I met with one of Sheridan's mighty speeches on and in behalf of Catholic emancipation. These were choice documents to me. I read them over and over again with unabated interest. They gave tongue to interesting thoughts of my own soul, which had frequently flashed through my mind, and died away for want of utterance. The moral which I gained from the dialogue was the power of truth over the conscience of even a slaveholder. What I got from Sheridan was a bold denunciation of slavery, and a powerful vindication of human rights. The reading of these documents enabled me to utter my thoughts, and to meet the arguments brought forward to sustain slavery; but while they relieved me of one difficulty, they brought on another even more painful than the one of which I was relieved. The more I read, the more I was led to abhor and detest my enslavers. I could regard them in no other light than a band of successful robbers, who had left their homes, and gone to Africa, and stolen us from our homes, and in a strange land reduced us to slavery. I loathed them as being the meanest as well as the most wicked of men. As I read and contemplated the subject, behold! that very discontentment which Master Hugh had predicted would follow my learning to read had already come, to torment and sting my soul to unutterable anguish. As I writhed under it, I would at times feel that learning to read had been a curse rather than a blessing. It had given me a view of my wretched condition, without the remedy. It opened my eyes to the horrible pit, but to no ladder upon which to get out. In moments of agony, I envied my fellow-slaves for their stupidity. I have often wished myself a beast. I preferred the condition of the meanest reptile to my own. Any thing, no matter what, to get rid of thinking! It was this everlasting thinking of my condition that tormented me. There was no getting rid of it. It was pressed upon me by every object within sight or hearing, animate or inanimate. The silver trump of freedom had roused my soul to eternal wakefulness. Freedom now appeared, to disappear no more forever. It was heard in every sound, and seen in every thing. It was ever present to torment me with a sense of my wretched condition. I saw nothing without seeing it, I heard nothing without hearing it, and felt nothing without feeling it. It looked from every star, it smiled in every calm, breathed in every wind, and moved in every storm.

I often found myself regretting my own existence, and wishing myself dead; and but for the hope of being free, I have no doubt but that I should have killed myself, or done something for which I should have been killed. While in this state of mind, I was eager to hear any one speak of slavery. I was a ready listener. Every little while, I could hear something about the abolitionists. It was some time before I found what the word meant. It was always used in such connections as to make it an interesting word to me. If a slave ran away and succeeded in getting

clear, or if a slave killed his master, set fire to a barn, or did any thing very wrong in the mind of a slaveholder, it was spoken of as the fruit of *abolition*. Hearing the word in this connection very often, I set about learning what it meant. The dictionary afforded me little or no help. I found it was "the act of abolishing"; but then I did not know what was to be abolished. Here I was perplexed. I did not dare to ask any one about its meaning, for I was satisfied that it was something they wanted me to know very little about. After a patient waiting, I got one of our city papers, containing an account of the number of petitions from the north, praying for the abolition of slavery in the District of Columbia, and of the slave trade between the States. From this time I understood the words *abolition* and *abolitionist*, and always drew near when that word was spoken, expecting to hear something of importance to myself and fellow-slaves. The light broke in upon me by degrees. I went one day down on the wharf of Mr. Waters; and seeing two Irishmen unloading a scow of stone, I went, unasked, and helped them. When we had finished, one of them came to me and asked me if I were a slave. I told him I was. He asked, "Are ye a slave for life?" I told him that I was. The good Irishman seemed to be deeply affected by the statement. He said to the other that it was a pity so fine a little fellow as myself should be a slave for life. He said it was a shame to hold me. They both advised me to run away to the north; that I should find friends there, and that I should be free. I pretended not to be interested in what they said, and treated them as if I did not understand them; for I feared they might be treacherous. White men have been known to encourage slaves to escape, and then, to get the reward, catch them and return them to their masters. I was afraid that these seemingly good men might use me so; but I nevertheless remembered their advice, and from that time I resolved to run away. I looked forward to a time at which it would be safe for me to escape. I was too young to think of doing so immediately; besides, I wished to learn how to write, as I might have occasion to write my own pass. I consoled myself with the hope that I should one day find a good chance. Meanwhile, I would learn to write.

The idea as to how I might learn to write was suggested to me by being in Durgin and Bailey's ship-yard, and frequently seeing the ship carpenters, after hewing, and getting a piece of timber ready for use, write on the timber the name of that part of the ship for which it was intended. When a piece of timber was intended for the larboard side, it would be marked thus—"L." When a piece was for the starboard side, it would be marked thus—"S." A piece for the larboard side forward, would be marked thus—"L.F." When a piece was for starboard side forward, it would be marked thus—"S.F." For larboard aft, it would be marked thus—"L.A." For starboard aft, it would be marked thus—"S.A." I soon learned the names of these letters, and for what they were intended when placed upon a piece of timber in the ship-yard. I immediately commenced copying them, and in a short time was able to make the four letters named. After that, when I met with any boy who I know could write, I would tell him I could write as well as he. The next word would be, "I don't believe you. Let me see you try it." I would then make the letters which I had been so fortunate as to learn, and ask him to beat that. In this way I got a good many lessons in writing, which it is quite possible I should never have gotten in any other way. During this time, my copy-book was the board fence, brick wall, and pavement; my pen and ink was a lump of chalk. With these, I learned mainly how to write. I then commenced and continued copying the Italics in Webster's Spelling Book, until I could make them all without looking on the book. By this time, my little Master Thomas had gone to school, and learned how to write, and had written over a number of copy-books. These had been brought home, and shown to some of our near neighbors, and then laid aside. My mistress used to go to class meeting at the Wilk Street meeting-house every Monday afternoon, and leave me to take care of the house. When left thus, I used to spend the time in writing in the spaces left in Master Thomas's copy-book, copying what he had written. I continued to do this until I could write a hand very similar to that of Master Thomas. Thus, after a long, tedious effort for years, I finally succeeded in learning how to write.

4. *A Runaway Seeks Refuge in Dismal Swamp, 1859*

. . . Best water in Juniper Swamp ever tasted by man. Dreadful healthy place to live, up in de high land in de cane-brake. 'Speck ye've heern tell on it? There is reefs ob land—folks call de high lands. In dar de cane-brake grow t'irty feet high. In dem ar cane-brakes de ground is kivered wit leaves, kinder makin' a nat'ral bed. Dar be whar de wild hogs, cows, wolves, and bars (bears) be found. De swamp is lower land, whar dar's de biggest trees most ever was. De sypress is de handsomest, an' anudder kind called de gum tree.

Dismal Swamp is divided into tree or four parts. Whar I worked da called it Company Swamp. When we wanted fresh pork we goed to Gum Swamp, 'bout sun-down, run a wild hog down from de cane-brakes into Juniper Swamp, whar dar feet can't touch hard ground, knock dem over, and dat's de way we kill dem. De same way we ketch wild cows. We troed dar bones, arter we eated all de meat off on 'em up, to one side de fire. Many's de time we waked up and seed de bars skulking round our feet for de bones. Da neber interrupted us; da knowed better; coz we would gin dem cold shot. Hope I shall live long enough to see de *slaveholders* feared to interrupt us!

. . . I tort a sight 'bout my wife, and used allers be planin' how I get to see her agin. Den I heern dat old mass'r made her live wid anudder man, coz I left her. Dis 'formation nearly killed me. I mout 'spected it; for I knowed de mass'rs neber ingard de marriage 'stution 'spectin' dar slaves. Dey hab de right to make me be selled from my wife, and dey had de right of makin' her live wid anudder man if she hated him like pisin. I do n't blame Lizzie; but I hoped she would b'lieve dat I was dead; den she would n't fret herself to def, as I knowed she would if she reckoned I was livin'. She loved me, I knowed, but dat warn't no 'count at all. De slaves are ingarded as dey must marry jist for dar mass'r's int'rest. Good many on dem jist marry widout any more respect for each oder den if dey was hogs. . . . I and my wife warn't so. I married Lizzy, and had a ceremony over it, coz I loved her an' she loved me. Well, arter I heern dat she was livin' wid 'nudder man, dat ar made me to come to Canada.

Ole man Fisher was us boys' preacher. He runned away and used to pray, like he's 'n earnest. I camped wid him. Many's been de 'zortation I have 'sperienced, dat desounded t'rough de trees, an' we would almos' 'spect de judgment day was comin', dar would be such loud nibrations, as de preacher called dem; 'specially down by de lake. I b'lieve God is no inspector of persons; an' he knows his childer, and kin hear dem jest as quick in de Juniper Swamp as in de great churches what I seed in New York, whar dey don't 'low a man, as I'm told, to go in thar, if he hasn't been allers customed to sit on spring bottomed cheers, and sofas and pianners and all dem sort of tings. Tank de Lord, he don't tink so much 'bout spring-bottom cheers as his poor critters do—dat's a fac'. I was fered to peep inside dem ar rich churches, and I 'spects de blessed Lord hisself dunno much more 'bout dar insides dan I does. . . . Oh, dey were nice prayers we used to have sometimes, an' I dunno but de old preacher is dar now.

Dar is families growed up in dat ar Dismal Swamp dat never seed a white man, an' would be skeered most to def to see one. Some runaways went dere wid dar wives, an' dar childers are raised dar. We never had any trouble 'mong us boys; but I tell you pretty hard tings sometimes 'cuz dat makes ye shiver all over, as if ye was frozed. De master will offer a reward to some one in de swamp to ketch his runaway. So

de colored folks got jist as much devil in dem as white folks; I sometimes tink de are jist as voracious arter money. Da 'tray de fugitives to dar masters. Sometimes de masters comes and shoots dem down dead on de spot. . . . I saw wid my own eyes when dey shot Jacob. Dat is too bad to 'member. God will not forget it; never, I bet ye. Six white men comed upon him afore he knowed nothin' at all 'bout it most. Jist de first ting Jacob seed was his old master, Simon Simms, of Suffolk, Virginny, standing right afore him. Dem ar men—all on em—had a gun apiece, an' dey every one of dem pointed right straight to de head of poor Jacob. He felt scared most to def. Old Simms hollored out to him—"Jake! You run a step, you nigger, and I'll blow yer brains out." Jacob did n't know for de life on him what to do. He feared to gin up: he too scared to run; he dunno what to do. Six guns wid number two shot, aimed at your head isn't nothin', I tell ye. Takes brave man to stand dat, 'cordin' to my reck'nin'.

Jacob lifts up his feet to run. Marcy on him! De master and one ob de men levelled dar guns, and dar guns levelled poor Jacob. His whole right side from his hip to his heel was cut up like hashmeat. He bleeded orfull. Dey took some willow bark—made a hoop orn't—run a board trough it—put Jacob on it like as if he war dead; run a pole t'rough de willow hoop, and put de poles on dar shoulders.

Dreadful scenes, I tell ye, 'sperienced in de Dismal Swamp, sometimes, when de masters comes dar. Dey shoot down runaways, and tink no more sendin' a ball t'rough dar hearts and sendin' dar hearts into 'Ternity dan jist nothin' at all. But de balls will be seen in 'Ternity, when de master gets dar 'spectin' to stay; 'spect dey'll get dispinted a heap!

I feared to stay dar arter I seed such tings; so I made up my mind to leave. . . . 'Spect I better not tell de way I comed: for dar's lots more boys comin' same way I did. . . .

5. *A Free Black in Natchez, 1837, 1838, 1842*

September 18, 1837

Mr. W. H. Perkins Sent for me to day Stating that he wanted to see me in the afternoon, and if I would be Kind Enough to Come up, Saying that he was unwell or he would come down, I promised him to come up. I went up to day to Mr Pitcher to get my House Insured. I Left a Discription of the Property and came away. He promised me to act on it & Let me Know the rates, After Dinner I walked up to See Mr Perkins, I Knocked at the door, it was opened by his Miss, She showed me in to his bed Room where he Lay asleep She Commenced Calling him by saying, Willy, Willy. He at Length awoke and she told him that a Gentleman had came to see him He saw me, shook hands together, he then got up, invited me to take a seate, I did so, wanted me to drink, I refused. We then talked about One thing or other In the mean time the Miss walked up Stairs He after awhile came to the Point—he wanted to Borrow a hundred and fifty Dollars from me, I told him that I had not the Surplus about me and that I could not

March 22, 1838

I wrote the following Lines and gave them to Mr Umphrys Ranaway from the subscriber in Natchez on the 21st July 1837, a negro man by the name of Walker. He is about forty years of age—very Black Complection, smiles when spoken to and shows his teeth which are very sound and white tho he chews tobacco to Excess—Walker is about six feet High, raw Boned and muscular. He was brought to this Country by Mr Merret Williams and Granville Smith and was sold by them to Dr Duncan & Preston and was by them returned to Williams and Smith and was sold at Sorias Auction Room where I purchased him as an unsound Slave—Mr. John Clay of Bourbon County Ky. now owns a wife of Walkers and I presume he is now in that neighbourhood He has a full head of hair and a heavy Beard, tho no grey hairs in his head that I Know of I think that he is inclined to stoop or Lean to one side when walking. His feet is pretty Large—He I am told professes to belong to the Babtiste Church I know of no marks on his person—If he is taken up in Ky I will Give a reward of two hundred Dollars when [he] is Delivered to me in Natchez or if he is in Ohio I will Give three hundred Dollars for his safe Delivery to me in Natchez or I will Take three Hundred Dollars for the Chance of Him William Johnson

July 9, 1842

I Spoke to A. L. Willson the other day to procure me a passage on the Steam Boat, Maid of Arkensaw, which he promised to do and to day when the Boat Came I went down to see about it and I saw him and He told me that he had spoke to the Capt. and that he had Refused to Let a State Room, But that my wife Could have the whole of the Ladies Cabbin to Herself but it was a Rule on his Boat not to Let any Col persons have State Rooms on Her—I asked him to go with me on Bourd—He went on Board and showd me the Capt. and I asked him if he could not spare a State Room and he told me that He Could not spare one that it was against the Rules of His Boat and that he had said it once and that was Enough and that he was a man of his word and Spoke of Prejudice of the Southern people, it was damd Foolish &c, and that he was a doing a Business for other people and was Compelld to adopt those Rules—I did not prevail by no means—He then said that I Could Have a State Room on Conditions which I told him would answer.

6. Ex-Slaves Recall Their Bondage, 1930s

My mammy larned me a lot of doctorin' what she larnt from old folkses from Africy, and some de Indians larnt her.

If you has rheumatism, jes' take white sassafras root and bile it and drink de tea.

Eat black-eyed peas on New Year, and have luck all dat year.

When anybody git cut, I allus burns woolen rags and smokes de wound, or burns a piece of fat pine and drops tar from it on scorched wool and binds it on de wound.

For headache, put a horseradish poultice on de head, or wear a nutmeg on a string, round you neck.

If you kills de first snake you sees in spring, you enemies ain't gwine git de best of you dat year.

All dese doctorin' things come clear from Africy, and dey allus worked for Mammy and for me, too.

—Harriet Collins

When I growed up, I married Exter Durham. He belonged to Marse Snipes Durham, who had de plantation 'cross de county line, in Orange County. We had a big weddin'. We was married on de front po'ch of de big house. Marse George killed a shoat, an' Mis' Betsy had Georgianna, de cook, to bake a big weddin' cake, all iced up white as snow wid a bride an' groom standin' in de middle holdin' han's. De table was set out in de yard under de trees, an' you ain't never seed de like of eats. All de niggers come to de feas', an' Marse George had a dram for everybody. Dat was some weddin'. I had on a white dress, white shoes, an' long white gloves dat come to my elbows, an' Mis' Betsy done made me a weddin' veil out of a white net window curtain. When she played de weddin' ma'ch on de piano, me an' Exter ma'ched down de walk an' up on de po'ch to de alter Mis' Betsy done fixed.

Uncle Edmond Kirby married us. He was de nigger preacher dat preached at de plantation church. After Uncle Edmond said de las' words over me an' Exter, Marse George got to have his little fun. He say, "Come on, Exter, you an' Tempie got to jump over de broomstick backwards. You got to do dat to see which one gwine be boss of your househol'." Everybody come stan' roun' to watch. Marse George hold de broom 'bout a foot high off de floor. De one dat jump over it backwards an' never touch de handle gwine boss de house, an' if bofe of dem jump over widout touchin' it, dey ain't gwine be no bossin'; dey jus' gwine be 'genial.

I jumped fus', an' you ought to seed me. I sailed right over dat broomstick, same as a cricket. But when Exter jump, he done had a big dram an' his feets was so big an' clumsy dat dey got all tangled up in dat broom, an' he fell headlong. Marse George, he laugh an' laugh, an' tole Exter he gwine be bossed till he skeered to speak less'n I tole him to speak.

After de weddin', we went down to de cabin Mis' Betsy done all dressed up, but Exter couldn' stay no longer den dat night, 'cause he belonged to Marse Snipes Durham an' he had to go back home. He lef' de nex' day for his plantation, but he come back every Saturday night an' stay till Sunday night. We had eleven chillun. Nine was bawn befo' Surrender an' two after we was set free. I was worth a heap to Marse George, 'kaze I had so many chillun.

—Tempie Durham

It took a smart nigger to know who his father was, in slavery time. I just can remember my mother.

—Elias Thomas

My mammy am owned by Massa Fred Tate and so am my pappy and all my brudders and sisters. How many brudders and sisters? Lawd A'mighty! I'll tell you, 'cause you asks, and dis nigger gives de facts as 'tis. Let's see; I can't 'lect de number. My pappy have twelve chillun by my mammy and twelve by anudder nigger, name' Mary. You keep de count. Den, dere am Lisa. Him have ten by her. And dere am Mandy. Him have eight by her. And dere am Betty. Him have six by her. Now, let me 'lect some more. I can't bring de names to mind, but dere am two or three others what have jus' one or two chillun by my pappy. Dat am right—close to fifty chillun, 'cause my mammy done told me. It's disaway: my pappy am de breedin' nigger.

—Lewis Jones

It come to de time Old Marster have so many slaves he don't know what to do wid them all. He give some of them off to his chillun. He give them mostly to his daughters, Mis' Marion, Mis' Nancy, and Mis' Lucretia. I was give to his grandson, Marse John Mobley McCrory, just to wait on him and play wid him. Little Marse John treat me

good sometime, and kick me round sometime'. I see now dat I was just a little dog or monkey, in his heart and mind, dat it 'mused him to pet or kick, as it pleased him.

—Henry Gladney

Whenever white folks had a baby born, den all de old niggers had to come th'ough the room, and the master would be over 'hind the bed, and he'd say, "Here's a new little mistress or master you got to work for." You had to say, "Yessuh, Master," and bow real low, or the overseer would crack you. Them were slavery days, dog days.

—Harriett Robinson

References

1. Nat Turner Describes His Divine Mission, 1831
   "The Confession of Nat Turner," in John B. Duff and Peter M. Mitchell, eds., *The Nat Turner Rebellion: The Historical Event and the Modern Controversy* (New York: Harper & Row, 1971), pp. 16–18.

2. Three Slave Spirituals
   "Steal Away to Jesus," "Go Down, Moses," and "Joshua Fit de Battle ob Jerico," in Willard Thorp, ed., *A Southern Reader* (New York: Alfred A. Knopf, 1955), pp. 630–632.

3. Frederick Douglass on Learning to Read and Write (1830s), 1845
   Michael Meyer, ed., *Frederick Douglass: The Narrative and Selected Writings* (New York: The Modern Library, 1984), pp. 50–56.

4. A Runaway Seeks Refuge in Dismal Swamp, 1859
   James Redpath, *The Roving Editor: Or Talks with Slaves in the Southern States* (New York: A. B. Burdick, 1859), pp. 291–295.

5. A Free Black in Natchez, 1837, 1838, 1842
   Entries for September 18, 1837; March 22, 1838; July 9, 1842; in William R. Hogan and Edwin A. Davis, eds., *William Johnson's Natchez: The Antebellum Diary of a Free Negro* (Baton Rouge: Louisiana University Press, 1951), pp. 192–193, 224–225, 391.

6. Ex-Slaves Recall Their Bondage, 1930s
   James Mellon, ed., *Bullwhip Days: The Slaves Remember* (New York: Weidenfeld & Nicolson, 1988), pp. 94, 146–147, 149.

Further Reading

Ira Berlin, *Slaves Without Masters: The Free Negro in the Antebellum South* (1974)

John W. Blassingame, *The Slave Community* (1972)

Margaret Creel, *"A Peculiar People": Slave Religion and Community Culture Among the Gullahs* (1988)

Stanley Elkins, *Slavery: A Problem in American Institutional and Intellectual Life* (1959)

Dena J. Epstein, *Sinful Tunes and Spirituals: Black Folk Music to the Civil War* (1977)

Eugene D. Genovese, *Roll, Jordan, Roll: The World the Slaves Made* (1974)

Herbert G. Gutman, *The Black Family in Slavery and Freedom, 1750–1925* (1976)

Charles W. Joyner, *Down by the Riverside: A South Carolina Slave Community* (1984)

Lawrence W. Levine, *Black Culture and Black Consciousness: Afro-American Thought from Slavery to Freedom* (1977)

Stephen B. Oates, *The Fires of Jubilee: Nat Turner's Fierce Rebellion* (1975)

Leslie H. Owens, *This Species of Property: Slave Life and Slave Culture in the Old South* (1976)

Ulrich B. Phillips, *American Negro Slavery* (1918)

Albert S. Raboteau, *Slave Religion* (1978)

George P. Rawick, *From Sundown to Sunup: The Making of a Black Community* (1972)

Todd L. Savitt, *Medicine and Slavery: The Diseases and Health Care of Blacks in Antebellum Virginia* (1978)

Kenneth M. Stampp, *The Peculiar Institution: Slavery in the Ante-Bellum South* (1956)

Sterling Stuckey, *Slave Culture: Nationalist Theory and the Foundations of Black America* (1987)

Thomas L. Webber, *Deep Like the Rivers: Education in the Slave Community, 1831–1865* (1978)

Document Set 6

Women's Culture in the Old South

In recent decades historical scholarship has broadened its horizons considerably. Nowhere has this trend been more evident than in the field of women's studies. The American South provides an invaluable focus for investigations into women's experiences because of the unique juxtaposition of gender and race in the region. The idea that southern women represented the essence of virtue in civilized society was principally a creation of self-serving Old South propagandists and became a central feature of the proslavery argument.

This "cult of womanhood" served a dual purpose: it reinforced racial unity among the white population as a whole, and it attempted to convince women that their functions as genteel wives and loving mothers of numerous offspring were both obligatory and desirable. There is little to suggest, however, that southern women blindly accepted their designated roles. In the closed society that the South had become by the mid-nineteenth century, opportunities for collective action were much more limited than for women who lived in the North, where social reform, especially abolitionism, provided a forum for the transmission of ideas. Women everywhere could and did voice opinions, however—privately to their husbands and closest friends and confidentially to their diaries.

The cult of pure womanhood reserved a place for slave women. Unlike white women, whose qualities were instrumental in molding all that was good about slavery, slave women were perceived as passive recipients of the civilizing influences of the "peculiar institution." In actuality, the stability of the slave community depended on the roles that bondswomen could forge for themselves. The harsh reality of life on the plantation also condemned slave women to suffer the worst abuses of the slave system. Victimized both racially and sexually, slave women needed an inner strength of character to survive physically and psychologically. In the annals of human endurance against overwhelming odds, the story of slave women in the American South, so much of it still untold, is one of the most remarkable.

The first document comprises selections from the writings of Professor Thomas Dew, the president of the College of William and Mary, and Dr. Samuel Cartwright of Louisiana. These excerpts reflect the views of two of the leading proslavery advocates. Cartwright's treatise on the maternal instincts of southern women is accompanied by opinions not generally found in proslavery tracts, notably affirmation that absentee ownership of plantations was prevalent and that the interstate slave trade was flourishing. Many women were less concerned with social niceties than with the struggle to survive. Mary Chaplin's married life was a continuous round of pregnancies and debilitating illnesses that resulted in her premature death at the age of twenty-nine. Consequently, she played very little part in the day-to-day running of the plantation. As the second document reveals, she disliked her husband Thomas's principal character flaw, which was excessive drinking, while he found her habit of ingesting snuff equally objectionable.

Dissent within the family was more common than might be supposed, as the third, fourth, and fifth documents indicate. Women were prepared to question the mores and values of the southern male in general and of their own spouses in particular. Elizabeth Perry, the wife of a prominent South Carolina state legislator, repeatedly admonished her husband for his lack of ambition. Her letters to him show that she had strong opinions not only on the course of his political career but also on the disunionist sentiment that plagued South Carolina in the early 1850s. The letters of Ann Elizabeth Middleton to her slave-owning husband are remarkable because of their favorable comments on *Uncle Tom's Cabin*, an antislavery book universally condemned in the South. Mary Chesnut confines her reservations about the evils of slavery to her diary. Her rage at the presence of mulatto children on the plantation is directed firmly at what she considers the deplorable moral conduct of her own father-in-law. Chesnut, the wife of a former United States sen-ator, displays little sympathy for the black female victims of her kinsman's sexual aggression.

A vastly different impression of the relationship between slave and master appears in the next selection. Susan Smedes contributes to the "moonlight and magnolias" tradition of the plantation with her nostalgic reminiscences of life in the Old South. The final document is an extract from the autobiography of Harriet Jacobs, a slave girl whose experiences confirm Chesnut's observations on lustful masters and self-pitying mistresses.

Questions for Analysis

1. What measures, if any, could women in the Old South take to free themselves from the cult of pure womanhood reserved for them by a male-dominated society?

2. How did women influence the development of antebellum southern society?

3. How did the existence of slavery affect women's perceptions of male behavior in the Old South?

4. What was the relationship between plantation mistresses and white women of other social groups?

5. How did plantation mistresses interact with slave women? Was racism an insurmountable barrier to unity based on gender?

6. What was the role of black women in the slave community?

1. Professor Thomas Dew and Dr. Samuel Cartwright Exalt Southern Womanhood, 1832, 1858

The "Weaker Sex"

Influence of slavery on the condition of the female sex.—The bare name of this interesting half of the human family, is well calculated to awaken in the breast of the generous the feeling of tenderness and kindness. The wrongs and sufferings of meek, quiet, forbearing woman, awaken the generous sympathy of every noble heart. Man never suffers without murmuring, and never relinquishes his rights without a struggle. It is not always so with woman; her physical weakness incapacitates her for the combat; her sexual organization, and the part which she takes in bringing forth and nurturing the rising generation, render her necessarily domestic in her habits, and timid and patient in her sufferings. If man chooses to exercise his power against woman, she is sure to fall an easy prey to his oppression. Hence, we may always consider her progressing elevation in society as a mark of advancing civilization, and, more particularly, of the augmentation of disinterested and generous *virtue*. . . .

. . . [L]et us proceed at once to inquire if the institution of slavery is not calculated to relieve the sufferings and wrongs of injured woman, and elevate her in the scale of existence? Slavery, we have just seen, changes the hunting to the shepherd and agricultural states,—gives rise to augmented productions, and consequently, furnishes more abundant supplies for man. The labor of the slaves thus becomes a substitute for that of the woman; man no longer wanders through the forest, in quest of game; and woman, consequently, is relieved from following on his track, under the enervating and harassing burthen of her children. She is now surrounded by her domestics, and the abundance of their labor lightens by the toil and hardships of the whole family. She ceases to be a mere *"beast of burthen"*; becomes the cheering and animating centre of the family circle—time is afforded for reflection and the cultivation of all those mild and fascinating virtues, which throw a charm and delight around our homes and firesides, and calm and tranquillize the harsher tempers and more restless propensities of the male: Man, too, relieved from that endless disquietude about subsistence for the morrow—relieved of the toil of wandering over the forest—more amply provided for by the productions of the soil—finds his habits changed, his temper moderated, his kindness and benevolence increased; he loses that savage and brutal feeling which he had before indulged towards all his unfortunate dependants; and, consequently, even the slave, in the agricultural, is happier than the free man in the hunting state.

In the very first remove from the most savage state, we behold the marked effects of slavery on the condition of woman—we find her at once elevated, clothed with all her charms, mingling with and directing the society to which she belongs, no longer the slave, but the equal and the idol of man. The Greeks and Trojans, at the siege of Troy, were in this state, and some of the most interesting and beautiful passages in the Iliad relate to scenes of social intercourse and conjugal affection, where woman, unawed and in all the pride of conscious equality, bears a most conspicuous part. Thus, Helen and Andromanche are frequently represented as appearing in company with the Trojan chiefs, and mingling freely in conversation with them. Attended only by one or two maid servants, they walk through the streets of Troy, as business or fancy directs: even the prudent Penelope, persecuted as she is by her suitors, does not scruple

occasionally to appear among them; and scarcely more reserve seems to be imposed on virgins than married women. Mitford has well observed, that "Homer's elegant eulogiums and Hesiod's severe sarcasm, equally prove woman to have been in their days important members of society. The character of Penelope in the Odyssee, is the completest panegyric on the sex that ever was composed; and no language even give a more elegant or more highly colored picture of conjugal affection, than is displayed in the conversation of Hector and Andromanche, in the 6th book of the Iliad."

The Teutonic races who inhabited the mountains and fastnesses of Germany, were similarly situated to the Greeks; and even before they left their homes to move down upon the Roman Empire, they were no more distinguished by their deeds in arms, than for devotion and attention to the weaker sex. So much were they characterized by this elevation of the female sex, that Gilbert Stuart does not hesitate to trace the institution of chivalry, whose origin has never yet been satisfactorily illustrated, to the German manners.

Again: if we descend to modern times, we see much the largest portion of Africa existing in this second stage of civilization, and, consequently, we find woman in an infinitely better condition than we any where find her among the aborigines on the American continent. And thus is it a most singular and curious fact, that woman, whose sympathies are ever alive to the distress of others; whose heart is filled with benevolence and philanthropy, and whose fine feelings, unchecked by considerations of interest or calculations of remote consequences, have ever prompted to embrace with eagerness even the wildest and most destructive schemes of emancipation, has been in a most peculiar and eminent degree indebted to slavery, for that very elevation in society which first raised her to an equality with man. We will not stop here to investigate the advantages resulting from the ameliorated condition of woman: her immense influence on the destiny of our race is acknowledged by all: upon her must ever devolve, in a peculiar degree, the duty of rearing into manhood a creature, in its infancy the frailest and feeblest which Heaven has made—of forming the plastic mind—of training the ignorance and imbecility of infancy into virtue and efficiency. There is, perhaps, no moral power, the magnitude of which swells so far beyond the grasp of calculation, as the influence of the female character on the virtues and happiness of mankind: it is so searching, so versatile, so multifarious, and so universal: it turns on us like the eye of a beautiful portrait, wherever we take our position; it bears upon us in such an infinite variety of points, on our instincts, our passions, our vanity, our tastes, and our necessities; above all, on the first impressions of education and the associations of infancy. The *rule* which woman should act in the great drama of life, is truly an important and an indispensable one; it must and will be acted, and that too, either for our weal or woe: all must wish then, that she should be guided by virtue, intelligence, and the purest affection; which can only be secured by elevating, honoring, and loving *her*, in whose career we feel so deep an interest. . . .

"Nursemaids" to the Slaves

. . . [T]he black man requires government even in his meat and drink, his clothing, and hours of repose. Unless under the government of one man to prescribe the rules of conduct to him, he will eat too much meat and not enough of bread and vegetables; he will not dress to suit the season, or kind of labor he is engaged in, nor retire to rest in due time to get sufficient sleep, but sit up and doze by the fire nearly all night. Nor will the women undress the children and put them regularly to bed. Nature is no law unto them. They let their children suffer and die, or unmercifully abuse them, unless the white man or woman prescribes rules for them to go by. Whenever the white woman superintends the nursery, whether the climate be cold or hot, they increase faster than any other people on the globe; but on large plantations, remote from her influence, the negro population invariably diminishes, unless the overseer takes upon himself those duties in the lying-in and nursery department, which on small estates are attended to by the mistress. She often sits up at night with sick children and administers to their wants, when their own mothers are nodding by them, and would be sound asleep if it were not for her presence. The care that white women bestow on the nursery is one of the principal causes why three hundred thousand Africans, originally imported into the territory of the United States, have increased to four millions, while in the British West Indies the number imported exceeded, by several millions, the actual population. It is also the cause why the small proprietors of negro property in Maryland, Virginia, Kentucky, and Missouri are able to supply the loss in the large Southern plantations, which are cut off from the happy influence of the presiding genius over civilization, morality, and population—the white woman.

2. *Bad Habits in the Chaplin Family, 1850–1851*

Oct. 24th

Must confess that I wish wife back at the village, for more reasons than one. She is dissatisfied with everything & everybody, myself *in particular*, and so intolerably cross—but poor soul, she is *ailing*, & I must only hold my peace, & so *prevent* her finding fault with what *I say*, if she does with what *I do*. I must bear with what I have brought on myself, by doing that which has given her power over me, to *upbraid* me *justly*, and she knows how to take advantage of this power. But "those who live [in] glass houses should not throw stones."

Nov. 5th

. . . Query. Can there be anything more unpleasant to a man of family than that his wife should be a victim to the following demoralizing and injurious habit? Habits which entirely destroy all social and domestic enjoyments & comforts and prevent all chances of prosperity. The wife says it rather makes her appearance (this is, when she makes it atall for the day).

Sometime between 11 A.M. & 1 P.M. remains out of her chamber one or two hours more or less, *sometimes* takes her place at the dinner table, but always takes her breakfast in bed. After dinner, retires for an hour or two to *indulge* either in [   ] or what is worse, to half fill her mouth with snuff, and lie in bed, when, if per chance a little of the saliva escapes down her throat, a fit of vomiting is invariably the consequence, then farewell to the small quantity of nourishment her sedentary habit allowed her to take at dinner. She leaves her chamber *generally* just about dusk, when she walks out, to take a [   ] walking about the yard—frequently remaining out of [   ] after dark. Sometimes remains down to tea, but should she retire before, & her tea is sent to her, [   ] the servant not unfrequently finds her unable to speak, and why? Her mouth is *full of snuff*; should she remain to tea, she retires immediately after, not to bed, to sleep, oh! no, but to put *snuff in her mouth*, take a *novel* & lie on her back till twelve or one o'clock at night, unless, per chance, she

enacts the vomiting scene over again, & thereby loses her *tea*. At a late hour she goes to bed finally in a very ill humor with her "good man," & everybody else for she is perhaps sleepy by this time, there to remain till the late hours previously mentioned, the next day, to live the same routine of life over & over again, each succeeding day, not to mention one or two *other* items. I envy not that man's conjugal blessings. . . .

March 17th

Dear husband, I opened your book to put a little extract in it and read your last items, one when you comment about Turner not giving credit on *my account*. Don't give yourself uneasiness for *me*. I have always endeavored to spare you any trouble I could, in this case I only reap the punishment due to my own weakness, believe me *you* are one of the best husbands. I can only hope you will not long be troubled with a wife so frail, weak and suffering. God help you my husband. You have but one fault that may work your ruin—for the sake of *our* children check it. Think not of the poor frail wife. I will pray for you here and if it be possible, hereafter——

3. *Elizabeth Perry Advises Her Husband, 1850–1851*

Elizabeth Perry to Benjamin Perry

March 30, 1850

. . . [Y]ou have no ambition, that is your failing & in that lies your bad success; when a man wishes, & is determined to gain what he wishes, he is certain to succeed but you are too lazy sometimes.

November 30, 1850

. . . You always decline too soon, you ought to let your friends find out, before you decline, what your prospects are; & if they find out they are not good, then it is time to decline. . . .

December 5, 1851

. . . [Y]ou know *nothing* is to be expected from the *present Legislature*, they were elected before the people were *enlightened* & go against *all reform*, the *next Legislature* will be *different*. You can then introduce all the reforms you wish, & be *supported*. You are now voting *against* the *current*, next session the current will *go along with you*. . . . The *Cooperationists* & *Secessionists* I have no sympathy for; they are *both equally bad*, but the latter more dangerous, they both act from *selfish motives*, for their own *aggrandisement*; where they do not, they are ignorant or under a delusion that amounts to derangement.

. . . Do your duty as a *legislator* & a *patriot* & a *member* from the *Upper Country*. The Secessionists had better do all they wish *now* before another session. I hope their power will have departed, & all their acts repealed, *then* I hope *you* will be the leader, and for *once* in a *majority*; & I hope you will be rewarded. So do not be discouraged; if you fail in your endeavors to free the *Upper Country* from the bondage of the *Lower*, all reformers you know have to *persevere*, meet with *opposition* at *first*, but in the *end* are *appreciated*. . . .

4. A Southern Woman Defends Uncle Tom's Cabin, *1852*

*Ann Elizabeth Middleton
to Nathaniel Middleton*

July 25, 1852

. . . I have been reading at odd moments in ''Uncle Tom's Cabin.'' I suppose I have read enough in the first hundred pages to judge the spirit of the work—a year ago I should have said it was overdrawn and false, but the experience and information which I have had within the last few months—particularly regarding the method of *hunting* fugitives render all the other pictures as *possibilities*—which though they have never come within my experience, certainly might occur under the protection of our *laws*. . . . I do not feel as if *any thing* could tempt me to sell Lydia and her family. . . .

August 6, 1852

. . . Do you think there is *any* place like that of the monster Legree? It seems to [*sic*] horrible to think of, but I do not see but our laws make it *possible*. I cannot express what a new view of the whole subject, the consideration of these *possibilities* has opened to me. I do not know what you will think of me, but I feel that, if those things are *possible* I am willing to give up all claim that I may have to *any property* for the sake of reducing even those yet unborn from so fearful a doom. . . .

August 9, 1852

. . . The evil of slavery seems to me to be the most *palpable* now before the gross sensual eyes of the world. When that is cleared away others (evils) of a more spiritual nature (and perhaps on that very account of a deeper die) will rise up for correction. But what I feel most strongly at present is our own *personal* responsibility. *We at least are striving* to have *our marriage union in God*. *We*, at least, *desire* to govern our children according to the will of God, and to render to *all* their dues. What have *we* then to do with an institution whose results are only paralleled to the reverse of all we aim at? . . .

. . . Oh the N. has as much if not more to answer for than the S.—but it is nothing to *us*. We have our own work to do. I can only say that I firmly believe that our blessed God will support us in any circumstances we may come to in doing His will. . . .

5. Mary Chesnut Denounces Miscegenation, *1861*

. . . This [life?] is full of strange vicissitudes, and in nothing more remarkable than the way people are reconciled, ignore the past, and start afresh in life, here to incur more disagreements and set to bickering again. . . .

I wonder if it be a sin to think slavery a

curse to any land. Sumner said not one word of this hated institution which is not true. Men and women are punished when their masters and mistresses are brutes and not when they do wrong—and then we live surrounded by prostitutes. An abandoned woman is sent out of any decent house elsewhere. Who thinks any worse of a negro or mulatto woman for being a thing we can't name? God forgive us, but ours is a *monstrous* system and wrong and iniquity. Perhaps the rest of the world is as bad—this *only* I see. Like the patriarchs of old our men live all in one house with their wives and their concubines, and the mulattoes one sees in every family exactly resemble the white children—and every lady tells you who is the father of all the mulatto children in everybody's household, but those in her own she seems to think drop from the clouds, or pretends so to think. Good women we have, *but* they talk of all *nastiness*—tho' they never do wrong, they talk day and night of [*erasures illegible save for the words* "all unconsciousness"] my disgust sometimes is boiling over—but they are, I believe, in conduct the purest women God ever made. Thank God for my countrywomen—alas for the men! No

worse than men everywhere, but the lower their mistresses, the more degraded they must be.

My mother-in-law told me when I was first married not to send my female servants in the street on errands. They were then tempted, led astray—and then she said placidly, so they told *me* when I came here, and I was very particular, *but you see with what result*.

Mr. Harris said it was so patriarchal. So it is—flocks and herds and slaves—and wife Leah does not suffice. Rachel must be *added*, if not *married*. And all the time they seem to think themselves patterns—models of husbands and fathers.

Mrs. Davis told me everybody described my husband's father as an odd character—"a millionaire who did nothing for his son whatever, left him to struggle with poverty, &c." I replied—"Mr. Chesnut Senior thinks himself the best of fathers—and his son thinks likewise. I have nothing to say—but it is true. He has no money but what he makes as a lawyer." And again I say, my countrywomen are as pure as angels, tho' surrounded by another race who are the social evil! . . .

6. Susan Smedes Recalls the "Black Mammy," 1886

. . . Managing a plantation was something like managing a kingdom. The ruler had need of a great store, not only of wisdom, but of tact and patience as well.

When there was trouble in the house the real kindness and sympathy of the servants came out. They seemed to anticipate every wish. In a thousand touching little ways they showed their desire to give all the comfort and help that lay in their power. They seemed to claim a right to share in the sorrow that was their master's, and to make it their own. It was small wonder that the master and mistress were forbearing and patient when the same servants who sorrowed with them in their affliction should, at times, be perverse in their days of prosperity. Many persons said that the Burleigh servants were treated with overindulgence. It is true that at times some of them acted like spoiled children, seeming not

to know what they would have. Nothing went quite to their taste at these times. The white family would say among themselves, "What is the matter now? Why these martyr-like looks?" Mammy Maria usually threw light on these occasions. She was disgusted with her race for posing as martyrs when there was no grievance. A striking illustration of this difficulty in making things run smoothly occurred one summer, when the family was preparing to go to the Pass. The mistress made out her list of the servants whom she wished to accompany her. She let them know that they were to be allowed extra time to get their houses and clothes in order for the three months' absence from home. Some of them answered with tears. It would be cruel to be torn from home and friends, perhaps husband and children, and not to see them for all that time. Sophia regretfully made out a new list, leaving out the most clamorous ones. There were no tears shed nor mournful looks given by the newly elected, for dear to the colored heart was the thought of change and travel. It was a secret imparted by Mammy Maria to her mistress that great was the disappointment of those who had overacted their part, thereby cutting themselves off from a much-coveted pleasure. . . .

7. *Harriet Jacobs Faces Her Jealous Mistress (c. 1829), 1861*

I would ten thousand times rather that my children should be the half-starved paupers of Ireland than to be the most pampered among the slaves of America. I would rather drudge out my life on a cotton plantation, till the grave opened to give me rest, than to live with an unprincipled master and a jealous mistress. The felon's home in a penitentiary is preferable. He may repent, and turn from the error of his ways, and so find peace; but it is not so with a favorite slave. She is not allowed to have any pride of character. It is deemed a crime in her to wish to be virtuous.

Mrs. Flint possessed the key to her husband's character before I was born. She might have used this knowledge to counsel and to screen the young and the innocent among her slaves; but for them she had no sympathy. They were the objects of her constant suspicion and malevolence. She watched her husband with unceasing vigilance; but he was well practised in means to evade it. What he could not find opportunity to say in words he manifested in signs. He invented more than were ever thought of in a deaf and dumb asylum. I let them pass, as if I did not understand what he meant; and many were the curses and threats bestowed on me for my stupidity. One day he caught me teaching myself to write. He frowned, as if he was not pleased; but I suppose he came to the conclusion that such an accomplishment might help to advance his favorite scheme. Before long, notes were often slipped into my hand. I would return them, saying, "I can't read them, sir." "Can't you?" he replied; "then I must read them to you." He always finished the reading by asking, "Do you understand?" Sometimes he would complain of the heat of the tea room, and order his supper to be placed on a small table in the piazza. He would seat himself there with a well-satisfied smile, and tell me to stand by and brush away the flies. He would eat very slowly, pausing between the mouthfuls. These intervals were employed in describing the happiness I was so foolishly throwing away, and in threatening me with the penalty that finally awaited my stubborn disobedience. He boasted much of the forbearance he had exercised towards me, and reminded me that there was a limit to his patience. When I succeeded in avoiding opportunities for him to talk to me at home, I was ordered to come to his office, to do some errand. When there, I was obliged to stand and listen to such language as he saw fit to address to me. Sometimes I so openly expressed my contempt for him that he would become violently enraged, and I wondered why he did not strike me. Circumstanced as he was, he probably thought it was better policy to be forbearing. But the state of things grew worse and worse daily. In desperation I told him that I must and would apply to my grandmother for protection. He threatened me with death, and worse than death, if I made any complaint to her. Strange to say, I did not despair. I was naturally of a buoyant disposition, and always I had a hope of somehow getting out of his clutches. Like many a poor, simple slave before me, I trusted that some threads of joy would yet be woven into my dark destiny.

I had entered my sixteenth year, and every day it became more apparent that my presence was intolerable to Mrs. Flint. Angry words frequently passed between her and her husband. He had never punished me himself, and he would not allow any body else to punish me. In that respect, she was never satisfied; but, in her angry moods, no terms were too vile for her to bestow upon me. Yet I, whom she detested so bitterly, had far more pity for her than he had, whose duty it was to make her life happy. I never wronged her, or wished to wrong her; and one word of kindness from her would have brought me to her feet.

After repeated quarrels between the doctor and his wife, he announced his intention to take his youngest daughter, then four years old, to sleep in his apartment. It was necessary that a servant should sleep in the same room, to be on hand if the child stirred. I was selected for that office, and informed for what purpose that arrangement had been made. By managing to keep within sight of people, as much as possible, during the day time, I had hitherto succeeded in eluding my master, though a razor was often held to my throat to force me to change this line of policy. At night I slept by the side of my great aunt, where I felt safe. He was too prudent to come into her room. She was an old woman, and had been in the family many years. More-over, as a married man, and a professional man, he deemed it necessary to save appearances in some degree. But he resolved to remove the obstacle in the way of his scheme; and he thought he had planned it so that he should evade suspicion. He was well aware how much I prized my refuge by the side of my old aunt, and he determined to dispossess me of it. The first night the doctor had the little child in his room alone. The next morning, I was ordered to take my station as nurse the following night. A kind Providence interposed in my favor. During the day Mrs. Flint heard of this new arrangement, and a storm followed. I rejoiced to hear it rage.

After a while my mistress sent for me to come to her room. Her first question was, "Did you know you were to sleep in the doctor's room?"

"Yes, ma'am."

"Who told you?"

"My master."

"Will you answer truly all the questions I ask?"

"Yes, ma'am."

"Tell me, then, as you hope to be forgiven, are you innocent of what I have accused you?"

"I am."

She handed me a Bible, and said, "Lay your hand on your heart, kiss this holy book, and swear before God that you tell me the truth."

I took the oath she required, and I did it with a clear conscience.

"You have taken God's holy word to testify your innocence," said she. "If you have deceived me, beware! Now take this stool, sit down, look me directly in the face, and tell me all that has passed between your master and you."

I did as she ordered. As I went on with my account her color changed frequently, she wept, and sometimes groaned. She spoke in tones so sad, that I was touched by her grief. The tears came to my eyes; but I was soon convinced that her emotions arose from anger and wounded pride. She felt that her marriage vows were des-ecrated, her dignity insulted; but she had no compassion for the poor victim of her husband's perfidy. She pitied herself as a martyr; but she was incapable of feeling for the condition of shame and misery in which her unfortunate, helpless slave was placed.

Yet perhaps she had some touch of feeling for me; for when the conference was ended, she spoke kindly, and promised to protect me. I should have been much comforted by this assur-ance if I could have had confidence in it; but my experiences in slavery had filled me with dis-trust. She was not a very refined woman, and had not much control over her passions. I was an object of her jealousy, and, consequently, of her hatred; and I knew I could not expect kind-ness or confidence from her under the circum-stances in which I was placed. I could not blame her. Slaveholders' wives feel as other women would under similar circumstances. The fire of her temper kindled from small sparks, and now the flame became so intense that the doctor was obliged to give up his intended arrangement.

I knew I had ignited the torch, and I expected to suffer for it afterwards; but I felt too thankful to my mistress for the timely aid she rendered me to care much about that. She now took me to sleep in a room adjoining her own. There I was an object of her especial care, though not of her especial comfort, for she spent many a sleep-less night to watch over me. Sometimes I woke up, and found her bending over me. At other times she whispered in my ear, as though it was her husband who was speaking to me, and lis-tened to hear what I would answer. If she startled me, on such occasions, she would glide stealthily away; and the next morning she would tell me I had been talking in my sleep, and ask who I was talking to. At last, I began to be fearful for my life. It had been often threatened; and you can imagine, better than I can describe, what an unpleasant sensation it must produce to wake in the dead of night and find a jealous woman bending over you. Terrible as this experience was, I had fears that it would give place to one more terrible.

My mistress grew weary of her vigils; they did not prove satisfactory. She changed her tactics. She now tried the trick of accusing my master of crime, in my presence, and gave my name as the author of the accusation. To my utter astonishment, he replied, "I don't believe it: but if she did acknowledge it, you tortured her into exposing me." Tortured into exposing him! Truly, Satan had no difficulty in distinguishing the color of his soul! I understood his object in making this false representation. It was to show me that I gained nothing by seeking the protection of my mistress; that the power was still all in his own hands. I pitied Mrs. Flint. She was a second wife, many years the junior of her husband; and the hoary-headed miscreant was enough to try the patience of a wiser and better woman. She was completely foiled, and knew not how to proceed. She would gladly have had me flogged for my supposed false oath; but, as I have already stated, the doctor never allowed any one to whip me. The old sinner was politic. The application of the lash might have led to remarks that would have exposed him in the eyes of his children and grandchildren. How often did I rejoice that I lived in a town where all the inhabitants knew each other! If I had been on a remote plantation, or lost among the multitude of a crowded city, I should not be a living woman at this day.

The secrets of slavery are concealed like those of the Inquisition. My master was, to my knowledge, the father of eleven slaves. But did the mothers dare to tell who was the father of their children? Did the other slaves dare to allude to it, except in whispers among themselves? No, indeed! They knew too well the terrible consequences.

My grandmother could not avoid seeing things which excited her suspicions. She was uneasy about me, and tried various ways to buy me; but the neverchanging answer was always repeated: "Linda does not belong to *me*. She is my daughter's property, and I have no legal right to sell her." The conscientious man! He was too scrupulous to *sell* me; but he had no scruples whatever about committing a much greater wrong against the helpless young girl placed under his guardianship, as his daughter's property. Sometimes my persecutor would ask me whether I would like to be sold. I told him I would rather be sold to any body than to lead such a life as I did. On such occasions he would assume the air of a very injured individual, and reproach me for my ingratitude. "Did I not take you into the house, and make you the companion of my own children?" he would say. "Have I ever treated you like a negro? I have never allowed you to be punished, not even to please your mistress. And this is the recompense I get, you ungrateful girl!" I answered that he had reasons of his own for screening me from punishment, and that the course he pursued made my mistress hate me and persecute me. If I wept, he would say, "Poor child! Don't cry! don't cry! I will make peace for you with your mistress. Only let me arrange matters in my own way. Poor, foolish girl! you don't know what is for your own good. I would cherish you. I would make a lady of you. Now go, and think of all I have promised you."

I did think of it.

Reader, I draw no imaginary pictures of southern homes. I am telling you the plain truth. Yet when victims make their escape from this wild beast of Slavery, northerners consent to act the part of bloodhounds, and hunt the poor fugitive back into his den, "full of dead men's bones, and all uncleanness." Nay, more, they are not only willing, but proud, to give their daughters in marriage to slaveholders. The poor girls have romantic notions of a sunny clime, and of the flowering vines that all the year round shade a happy home. To what disappointments are they destined! The young wife soon learns that the husband in whose hands she has placed her happiness pays no regard to his marriage vows.

Children of every shade of complexion play with her own fair babies, and too well she knows that they are born unto him of his own household. Jealousy and hatred enter the flowery home, and it is ravaged of its loveliness.

Southern women often marry a man knowing that he is the father of many little slaves. They do not trouble themselves about it. They regard such children as property, as marketable as the pigs on the plantation; and it is seldom that they do not make them aware of this by passing them into the slavetrader's hands as soon as possible, and thus getting them out of their sight. I am glad to say there are some honorable exceptions.

I have myself known two southern wives who exhorted their husbands to free those slaves towards whom they stood in a "parental relation";

and their request was granted. These husbands blushed before the superior nobleness of their wives' natures. Though they had only counselled them to do that which it was their duty to do, it commanded their respect, and rendered their conduct more exemplary. Concealment was at an end, and confidence took the place of distrust.

Though this bad institution deadens the moral sense, even in white women, to a fearful extent, it is not altogether extinct. I have heard southern ladies say of Mr. Such a one, "He not only thinks it no disgrace to be the father of those little niggers, but he is not ashamed to call himself their master. I declare, such things ought not to be tolerated in any decent society!"

References

1. Professor Thomas Dew and Dr. Samuel Cartwright Exalt Southern Womanhood, 1832, 1858
   The "Weaker Sex": Thomas R. Dew, "Review of the Debate in the Virginia Legislature of 1831 and 1832," in *The Pro-Slavery Argument* (Charleston: Walker, Richards & Co., 1852), pp. 336–341.
   "Nursemaids" to the Slaves: Samuel Cartwright, "Dr. Cartwright on the Caucasians and the Africans," *De Bow's Review* (July 1858), pp. 54–55.

2. Bad Habits in the Chaplin Family, 1850–1851
   Entries for October 24 and November 5, 1850, and March 17, 1851, in Theodore Rosengarten, *Tombee: Portrait of a Cotton Planter* (New York: William Morrow and Company, Inc., 1986), pp. 506–508, 526.

3. Elizabeth Perry Advises Her Husband, 1850–1851
   Elizabeth Perry to Benjamin Perry, March 30 and November 30, 1850, and December 5, 1851, Benjamin Franklin Perry Papers, South Caroliniana Library, University of South Carolina.

4. A Southern Woman Defends *Uncle Tom's Cabin*, 1852
   Ann Elizabeth Middleton to Nathaniel Middleton, July 25, August 6, and August 9, 1852, Nathaniel Russell Middleton Papers, Southern Historical Collection, Library of the University of North Carolina at Chapel Hill.

5. Mary Chesnut Denounces Miscegenation, 1861
   Entry for March 18, 1861, in C. Vann Woodward, ed., *Mary Chesnut's Civil War* (New Haven: Yale University Press, 1981), pp. 29, 31.

6. Susan Smedes Recalls the "Black Mammy," 1886
   Susan Dabney Smedes, *A Southern Planter* (New York: James Pott & Co., 1892), pp. 116–117.

7. Harriet Jacobs Faces Her Jealous Mistress (c. 1829), 1861
   Harriet Jacobs, *Incidents in the Life of a Slave Girl* (Boston, 1861), pp. 49–57.

Further Reading

Catherine G. Clinton, *The Plantation Mistress: Women's World in the Old South* (1982)

Elizabeth Fox-Genovese, *Within the Plantation Household: Black and White Women of the Old South* (1988)

Walter J. Fraser, Jr., Frank Saunders, Jr., and Jon Wakelyn, eds., *The Web of Southern Social Relations: Women, Family, and Education* (1985)

Jean E. Friedman, *The Enclosed Garden: Women and Community in the Evangelical South, 1830–1900* (1985)

Joanne V. Hawks and Sheila L. Skemp, eds., *Sex, Race, and the Role of Women in the South* (1983)

Jacqueline Jones, *Labor of Love, Labor of Sorrow: Black Women, Work, and the Family from Slavery to the Present* (1985)

Suzanne Lebsock, *The Free Women of Petersburg: Status Culture in a Southern Town, 1784–1860* (1984)

Gerda Lerner, *The Grimké Sisters from South Carolina: Rebels Against Slavery* (1967)

Sally G. McMillen, *Motherhood in the Old South: Pregnancy, Childbirth, and Infant Rearing* (1990)

Elizabeth Muhlenfeld, *Mary Boykin Chesnut* (1981)

Jeanne L. Noble, *Beautiful, Also, Are the Souls of My Black Sisters: A History of the Black Woman in America* (1978)

Anne F. Scott, *The Southern Lady: From Pedestal to Politics, 1830–1930* (1970)

Deborah Gray White, *Ar'n't I a Woman? Female Slaves in the Plantation South* (1985)

Document Set 7

The Southern Nonslaveholder

Scholars recently have come to understand—since the majority of white southerners did not own slaves—that it is impossible to determine the social and cultural values of the Old South solely by analyzing the actions and beliefs of the small but highly visible planter class. In a pioneering work published in 1949, Frank Owsley studied southern nonslaveholders, characterizing them as plain folk who earned a profitable living from the land and who clearly benefited from the Jacksonian promise of economic mobility for all Americans. Historians have widely acknowledged Owsley's valuable contribution to a little explored facet of antebellum southern life. Subsequently, however, some scholars have detected serious flaws in the methodology and interpretation of the "Owsley school."

Undoubtedly, as several recent studies have shown, some nonslaveholders were indeed—as Owsley believed—hardworking, fiercely independent yeoman farmers, although their ability to retain possession of their property may have diminished as cotton culture expanded inland and as wealthy planters sought new lands in place of the much used and worn-out soil nearer the coast. Still other nonslaveholders were townspeople; skilled artisans and semiskilled or unskilled industrial workers. Our knowledge of other groups of nonslaveholders is extremely vague. For example, the sand hills and piney woods of the piedmont contained nonslaveholding vagrants and squatters who left little or no record of their way of life. Most nonslaveholders could not afford to buy slaves, especially during the cotton boom of the 1850s, when prices for slaves soared to unprecedented heights. Given the prevalence of debtors, the use of slaves as collateral to pay debts, and the fact that most slaveowners possessed only a handful of slaves, it appears likely that a considerable number of southerners—depending on their economic circumstances—were intermittently slaveholders and nonslaveholders.

The idea that nonslaveholders were proud and industrious farmers first found critical expression in an analysis of southern society written in 1860. The author was Daniel Hundley, a defender of the plantation-slavery system. In addition to describing these hardworking farmers, Hundley identified a less respected social group, composed of poverty-stricken rural dwellers, and the first document contrasts these two nonslaveowning elements of the southern population. In the second document, William Gregg, a prosperous mill owner, outlines the advantages to less privileged people of life and work in a factory town. The role of the "sand hiller" in local elections is the theme of the third document, written by an anonymous visitor to Columbia, South Carolina, a city with a national reputation for corrupt politics.

The fourth, fifth, and sixth selections illustrate the aversion of some southerners to the institution of slavery. Cassius Marcellus Clay, a slaveowner who freed his slaves, argues in the fourth document that the white population of Kentucky had nothing to fear from the emancipation of the slaves. A meeting between the Swedish traveler Fredrika Bremer and a former plantation overseer affords in the fifth document a fascinating glimpse of one man's attitude toward slavery. The letter and petition that compose the sixth document demonstrate the existence of great hostility to the slaveowners' practice of hiring out their own slaves to trades that brought the bondsmen into competition with white mechanics and craftsmen. In the letter, J. J. Flournoy's concern for the white laboring class was rooted in an intense dislike of blacks.

The final selections reveal a growing concern among southerners that white unity based on an awareness of white racial superiority might be sorely tested if the sectional struggle erupted into open conflict. Hinton Helper, a former resident of North Carolina, was branded a traitor by south-erners for his inflammatory appeals to nonslave-holders to take action against a domineering planter class. James De Bow, the premier propa-gandist for southern culture in the late 1850s, insisted that the interests of slaveholders and nonslaveholders so nearly matched that class conflict could not exist in the South. Daniel Hamilton, a secessionist from South Carolina, was less certain, as the closing excerpt shows.

Questions for Analysis

1. What was the relationship between slaveholders and nonslaveholders?

2. Did nonslaveholders value the institution of slavery? Was entry into the slaveowning ranks their ultimate goal?

3. Did the nonslaveholding majority compose a distinct class of people with clearly defined class interests, or did the existence of racial slavery inhibit the formation of class consciousness?

4. Slaveowning interests were grossly overrepresented in southern state legislatures. Did this imbalance result in the political and eco-nomic domination of nonslaveholders by the planter elite?

5. What was the relationship between the yeoman farmers and the land they cultivated? Was land ownership more important to them than the possession of slaves?

6. Were urban artisans, mechanics, and craftsmen a potential threat to southern unity on the eve of the Civil War? Did discord between social groups precipitate the movement toward secession?

1. Daniel Hundley Identifies Southern Nonslaveholders, 1860

. . . For while princes, presidents, and governors may boast of their castles and lands, their silken gowns and robes of ceremony—all which can be made the sport of fortune, and do often vanish away in a moment, leaving their sometime own-ers poor indeed—the Common People, as the masses are called, possess in and of themselves a far richer inheritance, which is the ability and the will to earn an honest livelihood (not by the tricks of trade and the lying spirit of barter, nor yet by trampling on any man's rights, but) by the toilsome sweat of their own brows, delving patiently and trustingly in old mother earth, who, under the blessings of God, never deceives or disappoints those who put their trust in her generous bosom. And of all the hardy sons of toil, in all free lands the Yeomen are most deserving of our esteem. With hearts of oak and thews of steel, crouching to no man and fearing no danger, these are equally bold to handle a musket on the field of battle or to swing their reapers in times of peace among the waving stalks of yellow grain. For, in the language of the poet:

"———Each boasts his hearth
And field as free as the best lord his barony,
Owing subjection to no human vassalage
Save to their king and law. Hence are they
     resolute,
Leading the van on every day of battle,
As men who know the blessings they defend.
Hence are they frank and generous in peace,
As men who have their portion in its plenty."

*But you have no Yeomen in the South, my
dear Sir?* Beg your pardon, our dear Sir, but we
have—hosts of them. *I thought you had only
poor White Trash?* Yes, we dare say as much—
and that the moon is made of green cheese! You
have fully as much right or reason to think the
one thing as the other. *Do tell, now; want to
know?* Is that so, our good friend? do you really
desire to learn the truth about this matter? If so,
to the extent of our poor ability, we shall
endeavor to enlighten you upon a subject,
which not one Yankee in ten thousand in the
least understands.

Know, then, that the Poor Whites of the
South constitute a separate class to themselves;
the Southern Yeomen are as distinct from them
as the Southern Gentleman is from the Cotton
Snob. Certainly the Southern Yeomen are nearly
always poor, at least so far as this world's goods
are to be taken into the account. As a general
thing they own no slaves; and even in case they
do, the wealthiest of them rarely possess more
than from ten to fifteen. . . .

. . . Now, the Poor White Trash are about the
only paupers in our Southern States, and they
are very rarely supported by either the State or
parish in which they reside; nor have we ever
known or heard of a single instance in the
South, in which a pauper was farmed out by the
year to the lowest or highest bidder, (whichever
it be,) as is the custom in the enlightened States
of New-England. Moreover, the Poor White
Trash are wholly rural; hence, the South will
ever remain secure against any species of agrarianism, since such mob violence always originates
in towns and cities, wherein are herded together
an unthinking rabble, whom Dryden fitly
describes as,

"The scum
That rises up most, when the nation boils."

The Poor Whites of the South live altogether
in the country, in hilly and mountainous regions
generally, in communities by themselves, and far
removed from the wealthy and refined settle-
ments. Why it is they always select the hilly, and
consequently unproductive districts for their
homes, we know not. It can not be, however, as
urged by the abolitionists, because the slaveholders have seized on all the fertile lands; for it
is well known, that some of the most inex-
haustible soils in the South have never yet felt
the touch of the ploughshare in their virgin
bosoms, and are still to be had at government
prices. Neither can it be pleaded in behalf of the
Poor White Trash, that they object to labor by
the side of slaves; for, as we have already shown,
the Southern Yeomanry, who, as a class, are
poor, work habitually in company with negroes,
and usually prefer to own a homestead in the
neighborhood of wealthy planters. We appre-
hend, therefore, that it is a natural feeling with
Messrs. Rag Tag and Bobtail—an idiosyncrasy for
which they themselves can assign no good
reason—why they delight to build their pine-pole
cabins among the sterile sand hills, or in the very
heart of the dismal solitude of the burr-oak or
pine barrens. We remember to have heard an
overseer who had spent some time among the
Sandhillers, relate something like the following
anecdote of a youthful Bobtail whom he per-
suaded to accompany him out of the hill-country
into the nearest alluvial bottoms, where there
was any number of extensive plantations in a
high state of cultivation, which will aptly illustrate this peculiarity of the class. So soon as the
juvenile Bobtail reached the open country, his
eyes began to dilate, and his whole manner and
expression indicated bewilderment and uneasiness. "Bedadseized!" exclaimed he at last, "ef
this yere ked'ntry haint got nary sign ov er tree!
How in thunder duz folks live down yere? By G-
o-r-j! this beats all that Uncle Snipes tells about
Carlina. Tell yer what, I'm goin' ter make tracks
fur dad's—yer heer my horn toot?" And he did
make tracks for dad's, sure enough.

But, whatever may be said of the poverty of Rag Tag and Bobtail, of their ignorance and general spiritual degradation, it is yet a rare thing that any of them suffer from hunger or cold. As a class, indeed, they are much better off than the peasantry of Europe, and many a poor mechanic in New York City even—to say nothing of the thousands of day-laborers annually thrown out of employment on the approach of winter— would be most happy at any time from December to March, to share the cheerful warmth of the blazing pine fagots which glow upon every poor man's hearth in the South; as well as to help devour the fat haunches of the noble old buck, whose carcass hangs in one corner suspended from one of the beams of the loft overhead, ready at all times to have a slice cut from its sinewy hams and broiled to delicious juiciness upon the glowing coals. . . .

2. A Factory Owner's Solution to Southern Poverty, 1855

. . . When Graniteville was established, there had been no systematic effort made for the moral and religious culture of factory operatives in any of the southern States. The prevailing opinion was, that the calling was a degrading one, and there was much truth in it. To this cause may be traced the difficulty that previously existed in procuring steady and efficient white operatives to work cotton factories. People, however poor, are not easily induced to place their children in the way of temptation and vice, or in situations that will degrade them. Of the two evils, immoral and vicious associations, or idleness coupled with extreme poverty and ignorance, I do not know but the latter was the choice of wisdom. Our system has more than realized our expectations. We have always had a pressure upon us for situations, and could in a month stock another factory with hands, while the Augusta and Columbus companies are always short of help, not withstanding they pay much higher wages than we do.

I believe that our population at Graniteville, in general, is as pure and virtuous a community as can be found anywhere in the State. The ministers of the Gospel that have been located here all concur with me on that point. We are now beginning to feel the effects of our school, in the good order and discipline that prevails among the hands in the mill. All agree that we have as efficient a working force as can be found in any country.

Mr. Montgomery, who has had much experience in Scotland, and had charge of large mills in New England and New York, thinks that for stability, controllability and productive power, they are not surpassed anywhere. A majority of our skilful manufacturing overseers are South Carolinians, who learned the business here. We may really regard ourselves as the pioneers in developing the real character of the poor people of South Carolina. Graniteville is truly the home of the poor widow and helpless children, or for a family brought to ruin by a drunken, worthless father. Here they meet with protection, are educated free of charge, and brought up to habits of industry under the care of intelligent men. The population of Graniteville is made up mainly from the poor of Edgefield, Barnwell, and Lexington districts. From extreme poverty and want, they have become a thrifty, happy, and contented people. When they were first brought together, the *seventy-nine* out of a hundred grown girls who could neither read nor write were a by-word around the country; that reproach has long since been removed. We have night, Sunday and week-day schools. Singing-masters, music-teachers, writing-masters, and itinerant lecturers all find patronage in Graniteville, where the people can easily earn all the necessaries of life, and are in the enjoyment of the usual luxuries of country life. The finest silk dresses abound, and, in some instances, pianos may be seen that have been purchased with the surplus earnings of the girls. Our Savings Bank has 8 or $9,000 on deposit from the operatives, and when our new stock is issued you will find our operatives among the subscribers. Were our shares $100, instead of $500, very many of them would be found among the owners of Graniteville.

It is by this occupation, and this alone, (at the present day,) that the poor people can be made profitable to themselves, and to the country at large. When a taste for manufacturing prevails, and our intelligent capitalists are placed in situations which will require them to look after such people, they will all be brought out from their cabins of poverty, to mingle with enlightened men in accelerating the spirit of progress of the present age. There will then be no difficulty in the disbursement of the free school fund of South Carolina—when these people are brought together in villages, the difficulty that has puzzled our wisest politicians will cease to exist. As manufacturers, they will in a few years become a regenerated people, and do more for our State than all the cotton planters have yet done; for the prevailing policy of the planter seems to have been to exhaust the soil as rapidly as possible, with a view of abandoning the country.

The laborers of a cotton factory must of necessity be drawn from the poorest class of a country—hardy, economical and simple in all their habits. With a little attention to the education and moral training of their children, and opportunities afforded for the religious culture of such a people, they may be collected together in villages isolated and away from the corrupting influence of city vices, as they are at Graniteville, and be made industrious, intelligent and happy, and withal quite as available in the production of wealth to the State, and in advancing general prosperity, as any people on earth. Remove the same class of people into cities to work factories, and what becomes of them? The pay is insufficient for the artificial wants of a city life; they will be regarded by the community around them as little better than paupers and outcasts, will soon enter into the most corrupting dissipation and vice, and will not remain such steady and efficient operatives as are necessary to the profitable prosecution of manufacturing. Aside from the all absorbing profits which should be the pole star with those who expect to thrive in any branch of business, there is a charity in the matter, which will attract many good men who have been fortunate enough to become retired capitalists. . . .

3. A Visitor to Columbia Witnesses a Corrupt Election, 1854

. . . We have just passed through an exciting election in which Mr. Preston having the most money has come out victorious. About 500 of the sovereigns in this district are always up for sale, which is a sufficient number to turn the scale. The most amusing thing occurred at the polls that I have seen for a long time. Adams, the opposition candidate to Preston, saw a venerable "sand-hiller" somewhat the worse for liquor in charge of a Preston man. Adams gave chase & seizing the antiquity by the coat, dragged him up to the polls to vote for him, the Preston man holding on tight to the other side of his collar. When he got to the window the confusion became very great and before Adams could pre-

vent it Wade Hampton slipped a Preston ticket in the voter's hand and Adams had the satisfaction of knowing that he had dragged up a man to vote against him. The laugh and shout that went up brought a little additional redness to Adams' cheek, seeing the tide was setting in irresistibly against him. . . .

In speaking of the election I forgot to mention the scenes I witnessed on the night succeeding the announcement of the result. Some two or three thousand visited the houses of the different candidates who had been successful and were treated to champagne, etc. At Preston's they drank three wagon loads of champagne & from there went to Boyce's house where beside drinking an unlimited amount, they broke about $200 worth of glass and have destroyed the shrubbery, etc. Such an irruption of these vandals, I have never seen before. . . .

4. Cassius Clay on the Benefits of Emancipation, 1845

. . . "What," says the slaveholder, "shall the blacks be turned loose among us?" Permit me to ask, in the most childlike simplicity, if they are not loose already? Men talk as if all the slaves were chained to a block, and some mad hand was about to sever the links, and let them go, like wild bears to ravage the land! Now, all this bugaboo is founded upon the false idea that the aggregate power of the community is less than that of an individual slaveholder, which is absurd. By liberation we do not withdraw the force of *legal restraint, but enlarge it*; because we bring a high moral power to sustain the civil arm in the execution of justice. The whole population of Kentucky, we take to be now, 840,000: blacks, 180,000; for since the last census of '40, the whites must have increased, whilst the blacks, perhaps, have remained about stationary, owing to the Southern trade: that is 660,000 whites, to 180,000 blacks; an excess of whites over blacks, which would insure the whites absolute power of control, for ever, over the blacks, in case of liberation: more especially, as statistics of the North and South show that, upon the same basis, the black increases faster in slavery than in a state of freedom, *among whites, when all the stimulants of acquiring position in society, and rising to eminence, are withdrawn*. To say then, that turning them loose, would endanger the peace of society, is absolutely contrary to all experience, as proven in the West Indies, and in the Northern states; and contrary to every law of the human mind; for it involves the gross absurdity, that a man would revenge a favor, or love his enemies, not as well as, but better than his friends! We are not for turning any man *loose, black* or *white*; but in case of liberation, we repeat, we would not only have the same civil power over the blacks, which we now have, but the *superadded power* of the combined moral power of the master and the slave! The master strengthened in his position by a sense of being based upon justice, and the freedman constrained to quiet subjection to the laws, by every grateful affection of the heart. But if we do not turn them "*loose*," they will go on increasing, till they get in a majority: when, at last, they will turn themselves loose, for *every law of nature*, in time, vindicates itself. Man never has, and never will hold his fellow man in perpetual slavery. South Carolina has gone on with the "let alone" system, and [with the] "right itself" policy, till she is on the very eve of utter ruin. A single citizen, from the state of Massachusetts, where Bunker Hill lifts its eternal granite brow to the eyes of equal freedom, throws the whole state into a consternation, greater than if an hundred thousand mail-clad men, with fire and sword, had landed on the shores of a *just* people. In spite of all the silly vaporing of this unhappy state, we are full of pity when we look upon such a "sorry sight." They are now set about giving the slaves "moral and religious culture," most tame and impotent conclusion: the only remedy is to slay them—remove them—or make them *free*. Kentuckians, you know the right, you feel the wrong: in South Carolina you see *the end*.

5. *Fredrika Bremer Encounters a Man with a Conscience, 1850*

One day I went to see, in the forest, some of the poor people called "clay-eaters"; these are a kind of wretched white people, found in considerable numbers both in Carolina and Georgia, who live in the woods, without churches, without schools, without hearths, and sometimes, also, without homes, but yet independent and proud in their own way, and who are induced by a diseased appetite to eat a sort of unctuous earth which is found here, until this taste becomes a passion with them, equally strong with the love of intoxicating liquors; although, by slow degrees, if consumes its victim, causes the complexion to become gray, and the body soon to mingle with the earth on which it has nourished itself. Clay-eaters is the name given to these miserable people. No one knows whence they come, and scarcely how they exist; but they and the people called "Sand-hill people"—poor whites who live in the barren, sandy tracts of the Southern States—are found in great numbers here. The Sand-hill people are commonly as immoral as they are ignorant; for as by the law of the States it is forbidden to teach the negro slaves to read and write, and in consequence there would be no support for schools, where half the population consists of slaves, and the country in consequence is thinly inhabited; therefore the indigent white people in the country villages are without schools, and very nearly without any instruction at all. Besides which, these people have no feeling for the honor of labor and the power of activity. The first thing which a white man does when he has acquired a little money is to buy a slave, either male or female, and the slave must work for the whole family. The poor slaveholder prides himself on doing nothing, and letting the whole work be done by the slave. Slave labor is generally careless labor, and all the more so under a lazy master. The family is not benefited by it. If the master and mistress are famished, the slaves are famished also, and all become miserable together. But again to the clay-eaters.

Mr. G. and his family were a good specimen of this class of people. They lived in the depths of a wood quite away from any road. It was a hot and sultry day, and it was sultry in the wood. The poison-oak (a kind of dwarf oak, said to be extremely poisonous) grew thickly on all sides of the sand. Deep in the wood we found a newly-built shed, which had been roofed in for the poor family by some benevolent persons. Here lived the husband and wife, with five or six children. They had a roof over their heads, but that was all; I saw no kind of furniture whatever, not even a fire-place, and door there was none. But Mr. G., an affable little man of about fifty, seemed delighted with his world, with himself, his children, and in particular with his wife, whom he described as the best wife in the world, and with whom he seemed to be enchanted. The wife, although gray as the earth, both in complexion and dress, and pitifully thin, was evidently still quite young, and possessed real beauty of feature. She looked good but not gay, was silent, and kept her eyes very much fixed on her children, the handsomest, the most magnificent, unbaptized young creatures that any one can imagine, tumbling about with one another in perfect freedom, with natural grace, liveliness, and agility—very excellent human material, thought I, and better than many a baptized, over-indulged drawing-room urchin. Mr. G. was talkative, and volunteered us various passages out of his life's history.

He had at one time been the overseer of a slaveholder and churchman; but the office was one of so much cruelty that he gave it up. He could not endure having to flog the slaves himself, nor yet to have them flogged. But his master would not permit him to abstain from it. And others were no better. He had tried them. This one, it seemed to him, ought to have been better, as he was a religious man. "And in the beginning he was not bad," said he; "but after a while he married a rich planter's daughter, which changed him greatly, and he grew worse and worse very year. But that was the fault of his marriage, for he was unhappy with his wife."

The clay-eater in the forest looked down with compassion upon the rich planter—religious professor though he was—unhappy with his wife and cruel to his people. He, the freeman in the wild forest, with his pretty, gentle wife, and his handsome children, was richer and happier than he! Mr. G. seemed proud as a king in his free, innocent poverty. . . .

6. Two Appeals for the Protection of White Labor, 1838, 1858

To the Contractors for Mason's and Carpenter's Work, Athens, Georgia

Gentlemen: I desire your candid consideration of the views I shall here express. I ask no reply to them except at your own volition. I am aware that most of you have too strong antipathy to encourage the masonry and carpentry trades of your poor white brothers, that your predilections for giving employment in your line of business to ebony workers have either so cheapened the white man's labor, or expatriated hence with but a few solitary exceptions, all the white masons and carpenters of this town.

The white man is the only real, legal, moral and civil proprietor of this country and state. The right of his proprietorship reaches from the date of the studies of those white men, Copernicus and Gallileo, who indicated from the seclusion of their closets the sphericity of the earth: which sphericity hinted to another white man, Columbus, the possibility by a westerly course of sailing, of finding land. Hence by white man alone was this continent discovered; by the prowess of white men alone (though not always properly or humanely exercised), were the fierce and active Indians driven occidentally: and if swarms and hordes of infuriated red men pour down now from the Northwest, like the wintry blast thereof, the white men alone, aye, those to whom you decline to give money for bread and clothes, for their famishing families, in the logic matter of withholding work from them, or employing negroes, in the sequel, to cheapen their wages to a rate that amounts to a moral and physical impossibility for them either to live here and support their families—would bare their breasts to the keen and whizzing shafts of the savage crusaders—defending negroes too in the bargain, for if left to themselves without our aid, the Indians would or can sweep the negroes hence, "as dew drops are shaken from the lion's mane."

The right, then, gentlemen, you will no doubt candidly admit, of the white man to employment in preference to negroes, who *must* defer to us since they live well enough on plantations, cannot be considered impeachable by contractors. It is a right more virtual and indisputable than that of agrarianism. As masters of the polls in a majority, carrying all before them, I am surprised the poor do not elect faithful members to the Legislature, who will make it penal to prefer negro mechanic labor to white men's. But of the premises as I have now laid them down, you will candidly judge for yourselves, and draw a conclusion with me, that white bricklayers and house joiners must henceforward have ample work and remuneration; and yourselves and other contractors will set the example, and pursue it for the future without deviation. Your respectfully

J. J. Flournoy

Petition from Mechanics and Laborers of Atlanta, Georgia, to the City Council, 1858

We, the undersigned, would respectfully represent to your honorable body that there exists in the city of Atlanta a number of men who, in the opinion of your memorialists are of no benefit to the city. We refer to negro mechanics whose masters reside in other places, and who pay nothing toward the support of the city government, and whose negro mechanics can afford to underbid the regular resident citizen mechanics of your city to their great injury, and without benefit to the city in any way. We most respectfully request your honorable body to take the matter in hand, and by your action in the premises afford such protection to the resident mechanics of your city as your honorable body may deem meet in the premises, and in duty bound your petitioners will ever pray.

7. *Hinton Helper Reveals Nonslaveholders' Plight, 1857*

. . . Black slave labor, though far less valuable, is almost invariably better paid than free white labor. The reason is this: The fiat of the oligarchy has made it *fashionable* to "have negroes around," and there are, we are grieved to say, many non-slaveholding whites, (lickspittles), who, in order to retain on their premises a hired slave whom they falsely imagine secures to them not only the appearance of wealth, but also a position of high social standing in the community, keep themselves in a perpetual strait.

Last Spring we made it our special business to ascertain the ruling rates of wages paid for labor, free and slave, in North Carolina. We found sober, energetic white men, between twenty and forty years of age, engaged in agricultural pursuits at a salary of $84 per annum—including board only; negro men, slaves, who performed little more than half the amount of labor, and who were exceedingly sluggish, awkward, and careless in all their movements were hired out on adjoining farms at an average of about $115 per annum, including board, clothing, and medical attendance. Free white men and slaves were in the employ of the North Carolina Railroad Company; the former, whose services, in our opinion, were at least twice as valuable as the services of the latter, received only $12 per month each; the masters of the latter received $16 per month for every slave so employed. Industrious, tidy white girls, from sixteen to twenty years of age, had much difficulty in hiring themselves out as domestics in private families for $40 per annum—board only included; negro wenches, slaves, of corresponding ages, so ungraceful, stupid and filthy that no decent man would ever permit one of them to cross the threshold of his dwelling, were in brisk demand at from $65 to $70 per annum, including victuals, clothes, and medical attendance. These are facts, and in considering them, the students of political and social economy will not fail to arrive at conclusions of their own.

Notwithstanding the greater density of population in the free States, labor of every kind is, on an average, about one hundred per cent higher there than it is in the slave States. This is another important fact, and one that every non-slaveholding white should keep registered in his mind.

Poverty, ignorance, and superstition, are the three leading characteristics of the non-slaveholding whites of the South. Many of them grow up to the age of maturity, and pass through life without ever owning as much as five dollars at any one time. Thousands of them die at an advanced age, as ignorant of the common alphabet as if it had never been invented. All are more or less impressed with a belief in witches, ghosts, and supernatural signs. Few are exempt from habits of sensuality and intemperance. None have anything like adequate ideas of the duties which they owe either to their God, to themselves, or to their fellow-men. Pitiable, indeed, in the fullest sense of the term, is their condition.

It is the almost utter lack of an education that has reduced them to their present unenviable situation. In the whole South there is scarcely a publication of any kind devoted to their interests. They are now completely under the domination of the oligarchy, and it is madness to suppose that they will ever be able to rise to a position of true manhood, until after the slave power shall have been utterly overthrown. . . .

8. *James De Bow Praises Nonslaveholders, 1860*

The non-slaveholders of the South may be classed as either such as desire and are incapable of purchasing slaves, or such as have the means to purchase and do not because of the absence of the motive, preferring to hire or employ cheaper white labor. A class conscientiously objecting to the ownership of slave-property, does not exist at the South, for all such scruples have long since been silenced by the profound and unanswerable arguments to which Yankee controversy has driven our statesmen, popular orators and clergy. . .

The non-slaveholders are either urban or rural, including among the former the merchants, traders, mechanics, laborers and other classes in the towns and cities; and among the latter, the tillers of the soil in sections where slave property could, or could not be profitably employed.

As the competition of free labor with slave labor is the gist of the argument used by the opponents of slavery, and as it is upon this that they rely in support of a future conflict in our midst, it is clear that in cases where the competition cannot possibly exist, the argument, whatever weight it might otherwise have, must fall to the ground. . . . .

I will proceed to several general considerations which must be found powerful enough to influence the non-slaveholders, if the claims of patriotism were inadequate, to resist any attempt to overthrow the institutions and industry of the section at which they belong.

1. The non-slaveholder of the South is assured that the remuneration afforded by his labor, over and above the expense of living, is larger than that which is afforded by the same labor in the free States.

2. The non-slaveholders, as a class, are not reduced by the necessity of our condition, as is the case in the free States, to find employment in crowded cities and come into competition in close and sickly workshops and factories, with remorseless and untiring machinery.

3. The non-slaveholder is not subjected to that competition with foreign pauper labor, which has degraded the free labor of the North and demoralized it to an extent which perhaps can never be estimated.

4. The non-slaveholder of the South preserves the status of the white man, and is not regarded as an inferior or a dependant.

5. The non-slaveholder knows that as soon as his savings will admit, he can become a slaveholder, and thus relieve his wife from the necessities of the kitchen and the laundry, and his children from the labors of the field.

6. The large slaveholders and proprietors of the South begin life in great part as non-slaveholders.

7. But should such fortune not be in reserve for the non-slaveholder, he will understand that by honesty and industry it may be realized to his children.

8. The sons of the non-slaveholder are and always have been among the leading and ruling spirits of the South; in industry as well as in politics.

9. Without the institution of slavery, the great staple products of the South would cease to be grown, and the immense annual results, which are distributed among every class of the community, and which give life to every branch of industry, would cease.

10. If emancipation be brought about as will undoubtedly be the case, the encroachments of the fanatical majorities of the North are resisted now the slaveholders, in the main, will escape the degrading equality which must result, by emigration, for which they would have the means, by disposing of their personal chattels: whilst the non-slaveholders, without these resources, would be compelled to remain and endure the degradation.

9. A Secessionist Questions
Nonslaveholders' Loyalty, 1860

D. H. Hamilton to W. P. Miles

January 23, 1860

February 2, 1860

. . . When the South becomes fairly embarked in a contest which will shake the world, you will find an element of great weakness in our non-slaveholding population. . . . [W]e have chosen to bring the issue upon the question of Slavery, & we must take the consequences. . . .

. . . [T]hink you that 360,000 slaveholders will dictate terms for 3,000,000 of non-slaveholders at the South. I fear not, I mistrust our own people more than I fear all the efforts of the Abolitionists. . . .

References

1. Daniel Hundley Identifies Southern Nonslaveholders, 1860
    Daniel R. Hundley, *Social Relations in Our Southern States* (New York: H. B. Price, 1860), pp. 192–193, 258–261.

2. A Factory Owner's Solution to Southern Poverty, 1855
    William Gregg, "Practical Results of Southern Manufactures," *De Bow's Review* XVIII (June 1855), pp. 788–790.

3. A Visitor to Columbia Witnesses a Corrupt Election, 1854
    Anonymous, Columbia, October 17, 1854, Daniel Augustus Tomkins Papers, Duke University Library.

4. Cassius Clay on the Benefits of Emancipation, 1845
    Horace Greeley, ed., *The Writing of Cassius Marcellus Clay* (New York: Arno Press, 1969), pp. 248–249.

5. Fredrika Bremer Encounters a Man with a Conscience, 1850
    Fredrika Bremer, *The Homes of the New World: Impressions of America*, Volume 1 (New York: Harper and Brothers, 1853), pp. 365–367.

6. Two Appeals for the Protection of White Labor, 1838, 1858
    J. J. Flournoy, "To the Contractors for Mason's and Carpenter's Work, Athens, Georgia," and "Petition from Mechanics and Laborers of Atlanta, Georgia, to the City Council, 1858," in John Commons et al., *A Documentary History of American Industrial Society*, Volume II, *Plantation and Frontier* (New York: Russell & Russell, 1958), pp. 360–361, 367–368.

7. Hinton Helper Reveals Nonslaveholders' Plight, 1857
    Hinton R. Helper, *The Impending Crisis of the South: How to Meet It* (New York: Burdick Brothers, 1857), pp. 380–382.

8. James De Bow Praises Nonslaveholders, 1860
    J. D. B. De Bow, *The Interest in Slavery of the Southern Nonslaveholder*, 1860 Association, Tract No. 5 (Charleston, South Carolina: Evans and Cogswell, 1860).

9. A Secessionist Questions Nonslaveholders' Loyalty, 1860
   D. H. Hamilton to W. P. Miles, January 23 and February 2, 1860,
   William Porcher Miles Papers, University of North Carolina at
   Chapel Hill.

Further Reading

Orville V. Burton and Robert C. McMath, Jr., *Class, Conflict, and Consensus: Antebellum Southern Community Studies* (1982)

Blanche H. Clark, *The Tennessee Yeomen, 1840–1860* (1942)

Bruce Collins, *White Society in the Antebellum South* (1985)

Lacy K. Ford, Jr., *The Origins of Southern Radicalism: The South Carolina Upcountry* (1988)

Alison G. Freehling, *Drift Toward Dissolution: The Virginia Slavery Debate of 1831–1832* (1982)

Steven Hahn, *The Roots of Southern Populism: Yeomen Farmers and the Transformation of the Georgia Upcountry, 1850–1890* (1983)

J. William Harris, *Plain Folk and Gentry in a Slave Society: White Liberty and Black Slavery in Augusta's Hinterlands* (1985)

Edward Magdol and Jon Wakelyn, eds., *The Southern Common People: Studies in Nineteenth Century Social History* (1980)

Frank L. Owsley, *Plain Folk of the Old South* (1949)

Herbert Weaver, *Mississippi Farmers, 1850–1860* (1945)

Document Set 8

Sectionalism and Secession

The election in 1860 of Abraham Lincoln of the antislavery Republican party convinced the southern states that they were no longer safe in the Union. Lincoln's election precipitated secession and ultimately led to civil war. Sectionalism, defined as an exaggerated devotion to the interests of a geographical region, had become a largely southern phenomenon from the 1820s, when popular attacks on slavery took political form. Southerners were convinced that the U.S. Constitution protected slavery and that abolitionism threatened the rights of the states to regulate the "peculiar institution." Sectionalism had also assumed an economic aspect, as high protective tariffs benefited northern manufacturing interests and contributed to the tumbling market price of cotton.

Before midcentury, compromise between North and South had always been possible, because neither the Democrats nor the Whigs dared to risk internal division over slavery, which the leaders of both parties recognized as the most explosive political issue of the day. But the end of the second-party system in the early 1850s paved the way for the birth and rapid progress of the Republican party, whose strength lay entirely in the North and whose members were united by a determination to prevent the spread of slavery into the new territories opening up in the West. Lincoln did not profess to be an abolitionist, but many leading Republicans certainly were. Widespread support in the North for John Brown's raid on Harpers Ferry strongly suggested to southerners that future assaults on slavery would be more substantial than mere political rhetoric.

A united Democratic party, with strong electoral support throughout the nation, might have withstood the Republican challenge in 1860, but the party convention at Charleston was torn by dissension over safeguards for slavery. The hopelessly divided Democrats ran two presidential candidates, effectively handing the election to the Republican party, which captured the presidency without securing a single electoral vote in the southern states. For southern "fire eaters" like William Yancey, Edmund Ruffin, and Robert Barnwell Rhett, who had advocated separation from the Union throughout the 1850s, only secession would solve the South's problems. But most southerners were not radical fire eaters, and the level of support for the secessionist cause is uncertain and still hotly debated among historians. Thus we should not interpret the decision for secession as a decision for war. In the unsettled atmosphere of late 1860 and early 1861, the key figure was Lincoln, whose political experience was limited but whose responses to the secession of the South clearly dictated the subsequent course of events.

Until his death in 1850, John C. Calhoun led in defense of southern interests in national politics. The selections composing the first document illustrate Calhoun's transition from nationalist to sectionalist. As a novice congressman in the House of Representatives, Calhoun became a "war hawk," one of a group of young politicians whose patriotic speeches helped to persuade a reluctant President James Madison to propose war against Great Britain. Calhoun's 1811 speech is a response to the antiwar sentiment of Virginia's John Randolph. High protective tariffs that hurt the South's cotton economy convinced Calhoun, who had become vice president of the United States in 1825, that the federal government had become the master, not the servant, of the states. Nullification—a state's declaring null and void any federal legislation that it judged to be unconstitutional—was a constitutional remedy that Calhoun believed would protect state sovereignty. The "Fort Hill Address," featured in the second excerpt, defines Calhoun's position and at the same time elevated him to the leadership of the nullification movement in South Carolina. Calhoun claimed that the doctrine of nullification would restore state sovereignty and federal authority to their proper relationship. Unchecked abolitionism in the North further disillusioned Calhoun. His final speech in the United States Senate in 1850 demonstrates his sense of resignation that a separation of the southern from the northern states was imminent.

The admission of California as a free state in 1850 generated impassioned debate over the future of the South in the Union. South Carolina favored secession, but most southern states advocated a moderate approach of the type adopted by the Georgia state convention in the second document. The possibility of compromise as a solution to sectional problems diminished in the wake of the rapid rise of the Republican party. Few Republicans were as vitriolic in their denunciation of slavery as the Massachusetts senator Charles Sumner, whose "Crime Against Kansas" speech, excerpted in the third document, led to violence in the halls of the United States Congress itself. After the speech, which cast aspersions on the moral character of Senator Andrew Butler of South Carolina, Sumner was beaten unconscious by Representative Preston Brooks, Butler's nephew. The fourth document, a speech by James Henry Hammond, Butler's suc-cessor in the Senate, expresses the view that the value of cotton exports underpinned the American economy. That there was some substance to this claim was confirmed in the Panic of 1857, which hurt the North but barely affected southern cotton. Indeed, cotton prices in the late 1850s had reached an all-time high.

John Brown's 1859 raid on the federal armory at Harpers Ferry mobilized the South to organize in defense of its institutions. The fifth document typifies the resolutions passed in the aftermath of Harpers Ferry by southern rights associations, which formed or re-formed all over the South in the winter of 1859–1860. Southern fears that the Republican party would win the 1860 election hardened into conviction when the Democrats failed to unite around a single candidate. The final three selections show one state's response to the impending crisis. Always the most radical of southerners, South Carolinians created the 1860 Association as a propaganda agency to ensure that secessionist fervor did not abate as it had done a decade earlier. In December 1860, South Carolina became the first state to secede from the Union. The last document reveals the division of opinion among Carolinians about the repercussions of their actions. James McCarter was a merchant and a unionist; Henry Ravenel, a slaveowner and a scientist; and William Henry Trescot, assistant secretary of state in the closing months of the lame-duck James Buchanan administration.

Questions for Analysis

1. How did the South differ from the North in the mid-nineteenth century? Were those differences irreconcilable?

2. Did northern threats to the security of slavery constitute the principal motive of southerners in their decision to secede?

3. How important to southerners was the extension of slavery into the territories? Did the Republican party's determination to prevent the spread of slavery cause secession?

4. How harmonious was southern society on the eve of secession? Was secession a device to alleviate tensions and to reinforce unity in the white South?

5. Was the act of secession a conspiracy or an inevitable consequence of Abraham Lincoln's election?

6. Was secession constitutional?

1. *John C. Calhoun: From Nationalist to Sectionalist*

The Young "War Hawk," 1811

. . . The first argument of the gentleman [John Randolph] which I shall notice, is the unprepared state of the country. Whatever weight this argument might have, in a question of immediate war, it surely has little in that of preparation for it. If our country is unprepared, let us remedy the evil as soon as possible. Let the gentleman submit his plan; and if a reasonable one, I doubt not it will be supported by the House. But, sir, let us admit the fact and the whole force of the argument; I ask whose is the fault? Who has been a member for many years past, and has seen the defenceless state of his country even near home, under his own eyes, without a single endeavor to remedy so serious an evil? Let him not say "I have acted in a minority." It is no less the duty of the minority than a majority to endeavor to serve our country. For that purpose we are sent here; and not for that of opposition. We are next told of the expences of the war; and that the people will not pay taxes. Why not? Is it a want of capacity? What, with 1,000,000 tons of shipping; a trade of near 100,000,000 dollars; manufactures of 150,000,000 dollars, and agriculture of thrice that amount, shall we be told the country wants capacity to raise and support 10,000 or 15,000 additional regulars? No; it has the ability, that is admitted; but will it not have the disposition? Is not the course a just and necessary one? Shall we then utter this libel on the nation? Where will proof be found of a fact so disgraceful? It is said, in the history of the country 12 or 15 years ago. The case is not parallel. The ability of the country is greatly increased since. The object of that tax was unpopular. But on this, as well as my memory and almost infant observation at that time serve me, the objection was not to the tax, or its amount, but the mode of collection. The eye of the nation was frightened by the number of officers; its love of liberty shocked with the multiplicity of regulations. We, in the vile spirit of imitation, copied from the most oppressive part of European laws on that subject, and imposed on a young and virtuous nation all the severe provisions made necessary by corruption and long growing chicane. If taxes should become necessary, I do not hesitate to say the people will pay cheerfully. It is for their government and their cause, and would be their interest and duty to pay. But it may be, and I believe was said, that the nation will not pay taxes, because the rights violated are not worth defending; or that the defence will cost more than the profit. Sir, I here enter my solemn protest against this low and "calculating avarice" entering this hall of legislation. It is only fit for shops and counting houses, and ought not to disgrace the seat of sovereignty by its squalid and vile appearance. Whenever it touches sovereign power the nation is ruined. It is too short sighted to defend itself. It is an unpromising spirit, always ready to yield a part to save the balance. It is too timid to have in itself the laws of self preservation. It is never safe but under the shield of honor. Sir, I only know of one principle to make a nation great, to produce in this country not the form but real spirit of union, and that is, to protect every citizen in the lawful pursuit of his business. He will then feel that he is backed by the government, that its arm is his arms, and will rejoice in its increased strength and prosperity. Protection and patriotism are reciprocal. This is the road that all great nations have trod. Sir, I am not versed in this calculating policy; and will not therefore pretend to estimate in dollars and cents the value of national independence, or national affection. I cannot dare to measure in shillings and pence the misery, the stripes and the slavery of our impressed seamen; nor even to value our shipping, commercial and agricultural losses, under the Orders in Council and the British system of blockade. I hope I have not condemned any prudent estimate of the means of a country, before it enters on a war. This is wisdom, the other folly.

Sir, the gentleman from Virginia has not failed to touch on the calamity of war; that fruitful source of declamation by which pity becomes the advocate of cowardice; but I know not what we have to do with that subject. If the gentleman desires to repress the gallant ardor of our countrymen by such topics; let me inform him, that true courage regards only the cause, that it is just and necessary; and that it despises the pain and danger of war. If he really wishes to promote the cause of humanity, let his eloquence be addressed to Lord Wellesley or Mr. Perceval, and not the American Congress. Tell them if they persist in such daring insult and injury to a neutral nation, that, however inclined to peace, it will be bound in honor and interest to resist; that their patience and benevolence, however great, will be exhausted; that the calamity of war will ensue, and that they, in the opinion of wounded humanity will be answerable for all its devastation and misery. Let melting pity, a regard to the interest of humanity, stay the hand of injustice, and my life on it, the gentleman will not find it difficult to call off his country from the bloody scenes of war.

We are next told of the danger of war! I believe we are all ready to acknowledge its hazard and accidents; but I cannot think we have any extraordinary danger to contend with, at least so much as to warrant an acquiescence in the injuries we have received. On the contrary, I believe no war can be less dangerous to internal peace, or national existence. But we are told of the black population of the Southern States. As far as the gentleman from Virginia speaks of his own personal knowledge, I will not pretend to contradict him—I only regret that such is the dreadful state of his particular part of the country. Of the Southern section, I too have some personal knowledge, and can say, that in South Carolina no such fears in any part are felt. But, sir, admit the gentleman's statement; will a war with Great Britain increase the danger? Will the country be less able to repress insurrection? Had we any thing to fear from that quarter, which I sincerely disbelieve; in my opinion, the precise time of the greatest safety is during a war in which we have no fear of invasion—then the country is most on its guard; our militia the best prepared; and standing force the greatest. Even in our Revolution no attempts were made by that portion of our population; and, however the gentleman may frighten himself with the disorganising effects of French principles, I cannot think our ignorant blacks have felt much of their baneful influence. I dare say more than one half of them never heard of the French Revolution. . . .

In Defense of Nullification, 1831 (The "Fort Hill Address")

. . . The great and leading principle is, that the General Government emanated from the people of the several States, forming distinct political communities, and acting in their separate and sovereign capacity, and not from all of the people forming one aggregate political community; that the Constitution of the United States is, in fact, a compact, to which each State is a party, in the character already described; and that the several States, or parties, have a right to judge of its infractions; and in case of a deliberate, palpable, and dangerous exercise of power not delegated, they have the right, in the last resort, to use the language of the Virginia Resolutions, "*to interpose for arresting the progress of the evil, and for maintaining, within their respective limits, the authorities, rights, and liberties appertaining to them.*" This right of interposition, thus solemnly asserted by the State of Virginia, be it called what it may,—State-right, veto, nullification, or by any other name,—I conceive to be the fundamental principle of our system, resting on facts historically as certain as our revolution itself, and deductions as simple and demonstrative as that of any political or moral truth whatever; and I firmly believe that on its recognition depend the stability and safety of our political institutions.

I am not ignorant that those opposed to the doctrine have always, now and formerly, regarded it in a very different light, as anarchical and revolutionary. Could I believe such, in fact, to be its tendency, to me it would be no recommendation. I yield to none, I trust, in a deep and sincere attachment to our political institutions and the union of these States. I never breathed an opposite sentiment; but, on the contrary, I have ever considered them the great instruments of preserving our liberty, and promoting the happiness of our selves and our posterity; and next to these I have ever held them most dear.

Nearly half my life has been passed in the service of the Union, and whatever public reputation I have acquired is indissolubly identified with it. To be too national has, indeed, been considered by many, even of my friends, my greatest political fault.

With these strong feelings of attachment, I have examined, with the utmost care, the bearing of the doctrine in question; and, so far from anarchical or revolutionary, I solemnly believe it to be the only solid foundation of our system, and of the Union itself; and that the opposite doctrine, which denies to the States the right of protecting their reserved powers, and which would vest in the General Government (it matters not through what department) the right of determining, exclusively and finally, the powers delegated to it, is incompatible with the sovereignty of the States, and of the Constitution itself, considered as the basis of a Federal Union. As strong as this language is, it is not stronger than that used by the illustrious Jefferson, who said, to give to the General Government the final and exclusive right to judge of its powers, is to make "*its discretion*, and *not the Constitution, the measure of its powers*", and that, "*in all cases of compact between parties having no common judge, each party has an equal right to judge for itself, as well of the infraction as of the mode and measure of redress.*" Language cannot be more explicit, nor can higher authority be adduced.

That different opinions are entertained on this subject, I consider but as an additional evidence of the great diversity of the human intellect. Had not able, experienced, and patriotic individuals, for whom I have the highest respect, taken different views, I would have thought the right too clear to admit of doubt; but I am taught by this, as well as by many similar instances, to treat with deference opinions differing from my own. The error may, possibly, be with me; but if so, I can only say that, after the most mature and conscientious examination, I have not been able to detect it. But, with all proper deference, I must think that theirs is the error who deny what seems to be an essential attribute of the conceded sovereignty of the States, and who attribute to the General Government a right

utterly incompatible with what all acknowledge to be its limited and restricted character: an error originating principally, as I must think, in not duly reflecting on the nature of our institutions, and on what constitutes the only rational object of all political constitutions.

It has been well said by one of the most sagacious men of antiquity, that the object of a constitution is, to *restrain the government, as that of laws* is to restrain *individuals*. The remark is correct; nor is it less true where the government is vested in a majority, than where it is in a single or a few individuals—in a republic, than a monarchy or aristocracy. No one can have a higher respect for the maxim that the majority ought to govern than I have, taken in its proper sense, subject to the restrictions imposed by the Constitution, and confined to objects in which every portion of the community have similar interests; but it is a great error to suppose, as many do, that the right of a majority to govern is a natural and not a conventional right, and therefore absolute and unlimited. By nature, every individual has the right to govern himself; and governments, whether founded on majorities or minorities, must derive their right from the assent, expressed or implied, of the governed, and be subject to such limitations as they may impose. Where the interests are the same, that is, where the laws that may benefit one will benefit all, or the reverse, it is just and proper to place them under the control of the majority; but where they are dissimilar, so that the law that may benefit one portion may be ruinous to another, it would be, on the contrary, unjust and absurd to subject them to its will; and such I conceive to be the theory on which our Constitution rests.

That such dissimilarity of interests may exist, it is impossible to doubt. They are to be found in every community, in a greater or less degree, however small or homogeneous; and they constitute every where the great difficulty of forming and preserving free institutions. To guard against the unequal action of the laws, when applied to dissimilar and opposing interests, is, in fact, what mainly renders a constitution indispensable; to overlook which, in reasoning on our Constitution, would be to omit the principal element by which to determine its character. Were there no contrariety of interests, nothing would be more simple and easy than to form and preserve free institutions. The right of suffrage alone would be a sufficient guarantee. It is the conflict of opposing interests which renders it the most difficult work of man. . . .

A Final Plea to the North, 1850

. . . [W]hat is the cause of this discontent? It will be found in the belief of the people of the southern states, as prevalent as the discontent itself, that they cannot remain, as things now are, consistently with honor and safety, in the Union. The next question to be considered is: what has caused this belief?

One of the causes is, undoubtedly, to be traced to the long-continued agitation of the slavery question on the part of the North, and the many aggressions which they have made on the rights of the South during the time. . . .

There is another lying back of it—with which this is intimately connected—that may be regarded as the great and primary cause. This is to be found in the fact, that the equilibrium between the two sections, in the government as it stood when the Constitution was ratified and the government put in action, has been destroyed. At that time there was nearly a perfect equilibrium between the two, which afforded ample means to each to protect itself against the aggression of the other; but, as it now stands, one section has the exclusive power of controlling the government, which leaves the other without any adequate means of protecting itself against its encroachment and oppression. . . .

. . . The census is to be taken this year, which must add greatly to the decided preponderance of the North in the House of Representatives and in the Electoral College. The prospect is, also, that a great increase will be added to its present preponderance in the Senate, during the period of the decade, by the addition of new states. Two territories, Oregon and Minnesota, are already in progress, and strenuous efforts are making to bring in three additional states from the territory recently conquered from Mexico; which, if suc-

cessful, will add three other states in a short time to the northern section, making five states; and increasing the present number of its states from fifteen to twenty, and of its Senators from thirty to forty. On the contrary, there is not a single territory in progress in the southern section, and no certainty that any additional state will be added to it during the decade. The prospect then is, that the two sections in the Senate, should the effort now made to exclude the South from the newly acquired territories succeed, will stand before the end of the decade, twenty northern states to fourteen southern (considering Delaware as neutral), and forty northern Senators to twenty-eight southern. This great increase of Senators, added to the great increase of members of the House of Representatives and the Electoral College on the part of the North, which must take place under the next decade, will effectually and irretrievably destroy the equilibrium which existed when the government commenced.

Had this destruction been the operation of time, without the interference of government, the South would have had no reason to complain; but such was not the fact. It was caused by the legislation of this government, which was appointed as the common agent of all, and charged with the protection of the interests and security of all. The legislation by which it has been effected may be classed under three heads. The first is, that series of acts by which the South has been excluded from the common territory belonging to all the states as members of the Federal Union—which have had the effect of extending vastly the portion allotted to the northern section, and restricting within narrow limits the portion left the South. The next consists in adopting a system of revenue and disbursements, by which an undue proportion of the burden of taxation has been imposed upon the South, and an undue proportion of its proceeds appropriated to the North; and the last is a system of political measures, by which the original character of the government has been radically changed. . . .

The result of the whole of those causes combined is, that the North has acquired a decided ascendency over every department of this government, and through it a control over all the powers of the system. A single section governed by the will of the numerical majority, has now, in fact, the control of the government and the entire powers of the system. What was once a constitutional federal republic is now converted, in reality, into one as absolute as that of the Autocrat of Russia, and as despotic in its tendency as any absolute government that ever existed.

As, then, the North has the absolute control over the government, it is manifest that on all questions between it and the South, where there is a diversity of interests, the interest of the latter will be sacrificed to the former, however oppressive the effects may be; as the South possesses no means by which it can resist, through the action of the government. But if there was no question of vital importance to the South, in reference to which there was a diversity of views between the two sections, this state of things might be endured without the hazard of destruction to the South. But such is not the fact. There is a question of vital importance to the southern section, in reference to which the views and feelings of the two sections are as opposite and hostile as they can possibly be.

I refer to the relation between the two races in the southern section, which constitutes a vital portion of her social organization. Every portion of the North entertains views and feelings more or less hostile to it. Those most opposed and hostile, regard it as a sin, and consider themselves under the most sacred obligation to use every effort to destroy it. Indeed, to the extent that they conceive that they have power, they regard themselves as implicated in the sin, and responsible for not suppressing it by the use of all and every means. Those less opposed and hostile, regarded it as a crime—an offense against humanity, as they call it; and, although not so fanatical, feel themselves bound to use all efforts to effect the same object; while those who are least opposed and hostile, regard it as a blot and a stain on the character of what they call the Nation, and feel themselves accordingly bound to give it no countenance or support. On the contrary, the southern section regards the relation as one which cannot be destroyed without

subjecting the two races to the greatest calamity, and the section to poverty, desolation, and wretchedness; and accordingly they feel bound, by every consideration of interest and safety, to defend it.

This hostile feeling on the part of the North toward the social organization of the South long lay dormant, and it only required some cause to act on those who felt most intensely that they were responsible for its continuance, to call it into action. The increasing power of this government, and of the control of the northern section over all its departments, furnished the cause. It was this which made the impression on the minds of many, that there was little or no restraint to prevent the government from doing whatever it might choose to do. This was sufficient of itself to put the most fanatical portion of the North in action, for the purpose of destroying the existing relation between the two races in the South.

Having now shown what cannot save the Union, I return to the question with which I commenced, how can the Union be saved? There is but one way by which it can with any certainty; and that is, by a full and final settlement, on the principle of justice, of all the questions at issue between the two sections. The South asks for justice, simple justice, and less she ought not to take. She has no compromise to offer, but the Constitution; and no concession or surrender to make. She has already surrendered so much that she has little left to surrender. . . .

But can this be done? Yes, easily; not by the weaker party, for it can, of itself do nothing,—not even protect itself—but by the stronger. The North has only to will it to accomplish it—to do justice by conceding to the South an equal right in the acquired territory, and to do her duty by causing the stipulations relative to fugitive slaves to be faithfully fulfilled, to cease the agitation of the slave question, and to provide for the insertion of a provision in the Constitution, by an amendment, which will restore to the South, in substance, the power she possessed of protecting herself, before the equilibrium between the sections was destroyed by the action of this government. There will be no difficulty in devising such a provision—one that will protect the South, and which, at the same time, will improve and strengthen the government, instead of impairing and weakening it. . . .

It is time, Senators, that there should be an open and manly avowal on all sides, as to what is intended to be done. If the question is not now settled, it is uncertain whether it ever can hereafter be; and we, as the representatives of the states of this Union, regarded as governments, should come to a distinct understanding as to our respective views, in order to ascertain whether the great questions at issue can be settled or not. If you, who represent the stronger portion, cannot agree to settle on the broad principle of justice and duty, say so; and let the states we both represent agree to separate and part in peace. If you are unwilling we should part in peace, tell us so, and we shall know what to do, when you reduce the question to submission or resistance. If you remain silent, you will compel us to infer by your acts what you intend. In that case, California will become the test question. If you admit her, under all the difficulties that oppose her admission, you compel us to infer that you intend to exclude us from the whole of the acquired territories, with the intention of destroying, irretrievably, the equilibrium between the two sections. We would be blind not to perceive in that case, that your real objects are power and aggrandizement; and infatuated, not to act accordingly.

2. *Georgia Accepts the Compromise of 1850*

To the end that the position of this State may be clearly apprehended by her Confederates of the South and of the North, and that she may be blameless of all future consequences —

Be it resolved by the people of Georgia in Convention assembled, First. That we hold the American Union secondary in importance only to the rights and principles it was designed to perpetuate. That past associations, present fruition, and future prospects, will bind us to it so long as it continues to be the safeguard of those rights and principles.

Second. That if the thirteen original Parties to the Compact, bordering the Atlantic in a narrow belt, while their separate interests were in embryo, their peculiar tendencies scarcely developed, their revolutionary trials and triumphs still green in memory, found Union impossible without compromise, the thirty-one of this day may well yield somewhat in the conflict of opinion and policy, to preserve that Union which has extended the sway of Republican Government over a vast wilderness to another ocean, and proportionately advanced their civilization and national greatness.

Third. That in this spirit the State of Georgia has maturely considered the action of Congress, embracing a series of measures for the admission of California into the Union, the organization of Territorial Governments for Utah and New Mexico, the establishment of a boundary between the latter and the State of Texas, the suppression of the slave-trade in the District of Columbia, and the extradition of fugitive slaves, and (connected with them) the rejection of propositions to exclude slavery from the Mexican Territories, and to abolish it in the District of Columbia; and, whilst she does not wholly approve, will abide by it as a permanent adjustment of this sectional controversy.

Fourth. That the State of Georgia, in the judgment of this Convention, will and ought to resist, even (as a last resort) to a disruption of every tie which binds her to the Union, any future Act of Congress abolishing Slavery in the District of Columbia, without the consent and petition of the slaveholders thereof, or any Act abolishing Slavery in places within the slaveholding States, purchased by the United States for the erection of forts, magazines, arsenals, dock-yards, navy-yards, and other like purposes; or in any Act suppressing the slave-trade between slave-holding States; or in any refusal to admit as a State any Territory applying because of the existence of Slavery therein; or in any Act prohibiting the introduction of slaves into the

Territories of Utah and New Mexico; or in any Act repealing or materially modifying the laws now in force for the recovery of fugitive slaves.

Fifth. That it is the deliberate opinion of this Convention, that upon the faithful execution of the Fugitive Slave Bill by the proper authorities, depends the preservation of our much loved Union.

3. Senator Charles Sumner Insults Southern Honor, 1856

. . . I must say something of a general character, particularly in response to what has fallen from Senators who have raised themselves to eminence on this floor in championship of human wrong: I mean the Senator from South Carolina [Mr. Butler] and the Senator from Illinois [Mr. Douglas], who, though unlike as Don Quixote and Sancho Panza, yet, like this couple, sally forth together in the same adventure. I regret much to miss the elder Senator from his seat; but the cause against which he has run a tilt, with such ebullition of animosity, demands that the opportunity of exposing him should not be lost; and it is for the cause that I speak. The Senator from South Carolina has read many books of chivalry, and believes himself a chivalrous knight, with sentiments of honor and courage. Of course he has chosen a mistress to whom he has made his vows, and who, though ugly to others, is always lovely to him,—though polluted in the sight of the world, is chaste in his sight: I mean the harlot Slavery. For her his tongue is always profuse in words. Let her be impeached in character, or any proposition be made to shut her out from the extension of her wantonness, and no extravagance of manner or hardihood of assertion is then too great for this Senator. The frenzy of Don Quixote in behalf of his wench Dulcinea del Toboso is all surpassed. The asserted rights of Slavery, which shock equality of all kinds, are cloaked by a fantastic claim of equality. If the Slave States cannot enjoy what, in mockery of the great fathers of the Republic, he misnames Equality under the Constitution,—in other words, the full power in the National Territories to compel fellow-men to unpaid toil, to separate husband and wife, and to sell little children at the auction-block,—then, Sir, the chivalric Senator will conduct the State of South Carolina out of the Union! Heroic knight! Exalted Senator! A second Moses come for a second exodus!

Not content with this poor menace, which we have been twice told was "measured," the Senator, in the unrestrained chivalry of his nature, has undertaken to apply opprobrious words to those who differ from him on this floor. He calls them "sectional and fanatical"; and resistance to the Usurpation of Kansas he denounces as "an uncalculating fanaticism." To be sure, these charges lack all grace of originality and all sentiment of truth; but the adventurous Senator does not hesitate. He is the uncompromising, unblushing representative on this floor of a flagrant *sectionalism*, now domineering over the Republic,—and yet, with a ludicrous ignorance of his own position, unable to see himself as others see him, or with an effrontery which even his white head ought not to protect from rebuke, he applies to those here who resist his *sectionalism* the very epithet which designates himself. The men who strive to bring back the Government to its original policy, when Freedom and not Slavery was national, while Slavery and not Freedom was sectional, he arraigns as *sectional*. This will not do. It involves too great a perversion of terms. I tell that Senator that it is to himself, and to the "organization" of which he is the "committed advocate," that this epithet belongs. I now fasten it upon them. For myself, I care little for names; but, since the question is raised here, I affirm that the Republican party of the Union is in no just sense *sectional*, but, more than any other party, *national*,—and that it now goes forth to dislodge from the high places that tyrannical sectionalism of which the Senator from South Carolina is one the maddest zealots. . . .

4. Senator James Henry Hammond on the Power of "King Cotton," 1858

. . . With an export of $220,000,000 under the present tariff, the South organized separately would have $40,000,000 of revenue. With one-fourth the present tariff, she would have a revenue with the present tariff adequate to all her wants, for the South would never go to war; she would never need an army or a navy, beyond a few garrisons on the frontiers and a few revenue cutters. It is commerce that breeds war. It is manufactures that require to be hawked about the world, and that give rise to navies and commerce. But we have nothing to do but to take off restrictions on foreign merchandise and open our ports, and the whole world will come to us to trade. They will be too glad to bring and carry us, and we never shall dream of a war. Why the South has never yet had a just cause of war except with the North. Every time she has drawn her sword it has been on the point of honor, and that point of honor has been mainly loyalty to her sister colonies and sister States, who have ever since plundered and calumniated her.

But if there were no other reason why we should never have war, would any sane nation make war on cotton? Without firing a gun, without drawing a sword, should they make war on us we could bring the whole world to our feet. The South is perfectly competent to go on, one, two, or three years without planting a seed of cotton. I believe that if she was to plant but half her cotton, for three years to come, it would be an immense advantage to her. I am not so sure but that after three years' entire abstinence she would come out stronger than ever she was before, and better prepared to enter afresh upon her great career of enterprise. What would happen if no cotton was furnished for three years? I will not stop to depict what every one can imagine, but this is certain: England would topple headlong and carry the whole civilized world with her, save the South. No, you dare not make war on cotton. No power on earth dares to make war upon it. Cotton *is* king. Until lately the Bank of England was king; but she tried to put

her screws as usual, the fall before the last, upon the cotton crop, and was utterly vanquished. The last power has been conquered. Who can doubt, that has looked at recent events, that cotton is supreme? When the abuse of credit had destroyed credit and annihilated confidence; when thousands of the strongest commercial houses in the world were coming down, and hundreds of millions of dollars of supposed property evaporating in thin air; when you came to a dead lock, and revolutions were threatened, what brought you up? Fortunately for you it was the commencement of the cotton season, and we have poured in upon you one million six hundred thousand bales of cotton just at the crisis to save you from destruction. That cotton, but for the bursting of your speculative bubbles in the North, which produced the whole of this convulsion, would have brought us $100,000,000. We have sold it for $65,000,000, and saved you. Thirty-five million dollars we, the slaveholders of the South, have put into the charity box for your magnificent financiers, your "cotton lords," your "merchant princes."

But, sir, the greatest strength of the South arises from the harmony of her political and social institutions. This harmony gives her a frame of society, the best in the world, and an extent of political freedom, combined with entire security, such as no other people ever enjoyed upon the face of the earth. Society precedes government; creates it, and ought to control it; but as far as we can look back in historic times we find the case different; for government is no sooner created than it becomes too strong for society, and shapes and moulds, as well as controls it. In later centuries the progress of civilization and of intelligence has made the divergence so great as to produce civil wars and revolutions; and it is nothing now but the want of harmony between governments and societies which occasions all the uneasiness and trouble and terror that we see abroad. It was this that brought on the American Revolution. We threw off a Government not adapted to our social system, and made one for ourselves. The question is, how far have we succeeded? The South, so far as that is concerned, is satisfied, harmonious, and prosperous, but demands to be let alone. . . .

5. Virginia Reacts to John Brown's Raid, 1859

Resolved, That the late outbreak at Harpers Ferry, of a long-concocted and wide-spread Northern conspiracy, for the destruction by armed violence and bloodshed of all that is valuable for the welfare, safety, and even existence of Virginia and the other Southern States, was, in the prompt and complete suppression of the attempt, and in all its direct results, a failure no less abortive and contemptible than the design and means employed, and objects aimed at, were malignant, atrocious, and devilish.

Resolved, That, nevertheless, the indirect results of this Northern conspiracy, and attempted deadly assault and warfare on Virginia, are all-important for the consideration and instruction of the Southern people, and especially in these respects, to wit: 1st, As proving to the world the actual condition of entire submission, obedience, and general loyalty of our negro slaves, in the fact that all the previous and scarcely impeded efforts of Northern abolitionists and their emissaries, aided by all that falsehood and deception could effect, did not operate to seduce a single negro in Virginia to rebel, or even to evince the least spirit of insubordination. 2d, As showing, in the general expression of opinion in the Northern States, through the press and from the pulpit, from prominent or leading public men, and also in the only public meetings yet held, and generally by the great popular voice of the North, that the majority, or at least the far greater number of all whose opinions have yet been expressed, either excuse, or desire to have pardoned, or sympathise with, or openly and heartily applaud the actors in this conspiracy and attack, which could have been made successful only by the means of laying waste the South and extinguishing its institutions and their defenders by fire and sword, and with outrages more horrible then merely general massacre—while the Northern friends of the South, and of the cause of right and law, are too few, or too timid to speak openly in our support, or even to make their dissent heard, and too weak to contend with the more numerous and violent assaults of the South.

Resolved, That the time has come when every State and every man of the South should determine to act promptly and effectively for the defence of our institutions and dearest rights, as well as for other important, though less vital interests; and we earnestly appeal, especially to the legislature of Virginia, and also to the legislatures of all others of the slaveholding States, that they will hasten to consult and to deliberate, and will maturely consider and discuss the condition of the Southern States, under all past aggressions and wrongs, especially this last and crowning aggression of Northern usurpation and hatred, and devise suitable and efficient measures for the defense of the Southern people and their institutions, from the unceasing hostility and unscrupulous assaults of Northern enemies, fanatics and conspirators.

6. *The 1860 Association Agitates the Sectional Crisis, 1860*

Executive Chamber, The 1860 Association
Charleston, 19 November, 1860

In September last, several gentlemen of Charleston, met to confer in reference to the position of the South in the event of the accession of Mr. Lincoln and the Republican party to power. This informal meeting was the origin of the organization known in the community as The 1860 Association.

Aims:

1st. To conduct a correspondence with leading men in the South, and, by an interchange of information and views, prepare the Slave States to meet the impending crisis.

2nd. To prepare, print and distribute in the Slave States, tracts, pamphlets, &c., designed to awaken them to a conviction of their danger and to urge the necessity of resisting Northern and Federal aggression.

3rd. To enquire into the defenses of the State and to collect and arrange information which may aid the Legislature to establish promptly, an effective military organization.

—136,000 pamphlets published—and several pamphlets passing through 2nd. and 3rd. editions.

The Conventions in several of the Southern States, will soon be elected. The North is preparing to soothe and conciliate the South, by disclaimers and overtures. The success of this policy would be disastrous to the cause of Southern Union and Independence, and it is necessary to resist and defeat it. The Association is preparing pamphlets with this special object. Funds are necessary to enable it to act promptly. The 1860 Association is laboring for the State and for the South, and asks your aid.

Robert N. Gourdin
Chairman of Executive Committee

7. *South Carolina Secedes, 1860*

At a Convention of the people of the State of South Carolina, begun and holden at Columbia on the seventeenth day of December, in the year of our Lord 1860, and thence continued by adjournment to Charleston and there, by divers adjournments, to the 20th day of December in the same year:

An ordinance to dissolve the union between the State of South Carolina and other states united with her under the compact entitled "The Constitution of the United States of America":

We, the people of the State of South Carolina in Convention assembled, do declare and ordain, and it is hereby declared and ordained, that the ordinance adopted by us in Convention on the twenty-third day of May, in the year of our Lord 1788, whereby the Constitution of the United States of America was ratified, and also all acts and parts of acts of the General Assembly of this State ratifying amendments of the said Constitution, are hereby repealed; and that the union now subsisting between South Carolina and the other States, under the name of the "United States of America" is hereby dissolved.

Done at Charleston the twentieth day of December, in the year of our Lord, 1860.

8. *Carolinians Debate the Possibility of War, 1860–1861*

A "Fire Eater's" Contempt for "Cowardly" Yankees, 1860

November 1860

On Monday a large concourse of people assembled in front of the Congress House Columbia and several gentlemen addressed the crowd. I well remember the language of Mr. R. B. Rhett—who assured his audience that secession was a great and easy remedy for an intolerable tyranny. That there was not the slightest danger of exciting the Yankees into a fight—that they were a poor, pusillanimous, cowardly race who loved the Almighty Dollar too well to risk the wealth they had already filched from the South by going to war, for the preservation of the Union: That they could not fight, and were only by nature and education to manufacture wooden nutmeg and patent cucumber seeds and that the only weapons we would need in a war with them would be a raw hide and cow skins. . . .

. . . Other speakers continued to pour out similar sentiments, all concurring with Mr. R that secession was a peaceable and quiet remedy and we could not adopt it too soon.

Henry Ravenel Anticipates a Bloody Conflict, 1861

February 15, 1861

We are now rapidly approaching a critical period in the complicated relations which the last two months have brought into existence between the states of the old Confederacy. Six states (Texas the seventh has spoken also by her convention, but has not yet consummated the act of secession) have passed formal acts of Secession and have met together and have formed for themselves an independent government. They have no intention of returning to the old Union. They will enter into war before abandoning their position of independence under a separate Confederacy. They will in a few days send commissioners to Washington and also to European powers, to demand a recognition of their government. It is generally believed from indications in the papers of England and France that our government will be immediately recognized by these nations. But at Washington, there is much doubt if we shall be recognized at once. The larger and stronger portion of the Republican party, as yet has shown no willingness to do so. They do not admit by any of their acts, either the right or the fact of Secession. Lincoln says the laws must be enforced in all the States and the Federal property retaken. Of course this leads to war at once if persisted in. On the other hand the eight border states, North Carolina, Virginia, Maryland, Delaware, Tennessee, Kentucky, Arkansas and Missouri have taken the strongest ground against any attempt at coercion, and have pledged themselves to resist it, and join their fortunes with the Cotton States if the attempt is made. The "Peace Conference" (as it is termed) or informal Convention now in session at Washington are endeavoring to agree upon some form of compromise or guarantee which will be acceptable to the South. So far they have been able to effect nothing. In the mean time, the day of inauguration of Lincoln is approaching, and Fort Sumter in Charleston harbor, and Fort Pickens in Pensacola Bay are held by Federal troops. As soon as our demand for recognition is refused there is but one course left, and that is to dislodge these foreign troops and take possession. They cannot be suffered to remain there a standing menace and insult on our soil. This will be the opening of a civil war, which if carried out will be one of the bloodiest the world has ever seen. . . . Every day is hurrying us onwards to the crisis which must be shortly reached, and upon which will depend the great issues at stake. In a little over two weeks, the Black Republican party come into power, and Lincoln assumes command. . . .

William Henry Trescot Predicts Peace, 1861

Trescot to Miles, March 3, 1861

What is going on in Charleston I do not know. As I have said to you from the first I do not expect war or an attack upon the Fort. You will have negotiation if not recognition and if not a surrender of the Fort some mutual arrangement pending the termination of the negotiation. I would not be surprised to see both surrender and absolute recognition. . . .

References

1. John C. Calhoun: From Nationalist to Sectionalist
   The Young "War Hawk,": 1811: "Speech on the Report of the Foreign Relations Committee," December 12, 1811, in Robert L. Meriwether, ed., *The Papers of John C. Calhoun*, Volume I, 1801–1817 (Columbia, South Carolina: University of South Carolina Press, 1959), pp. 78–81. In Defense of Nullification, 1831 (The "Fort Hill Address"): "Address on the Relation Which the States and General Government Bear to Each Other," July 26, 1831, in Richard K. Crallé, ed., *Reports and Public Letters of John C. Calhoun*, Volume VI (New York: D. Appleton & Co., 1857), pp. 278–281. A Final Plea to the North, 1850: "Speech on Henry Clay's Compromise Resolution on the Bill to Admit California," March 4, 1850, in David B. Davis, ed., *Antebellum American Culture: An Interpretive Anthology* (Lexington, Massachusetts: D. C. Heath and Company, 1979), pp. 203–207.

2. Georgia Accepts the Compromise of 1850
   "Georgia Platform of 1850," in Alexander H. Stephens, *A Constitutional View of the Late War Between the States*, Volume II, Appendix B (Philadelphia: National Publishing Company, 1870), pp. 676–677.

3. Senator Charles Sumner Insults Southern Honor, 1856
   "Speech of the Hon. C. Sumner, of Massachusetts, in the Senate, May 19, 1856," *Appendix to the Congressional Globe*, 34th Congress, 1st Session, p. 530.

4. Senator James Henry Hammond on the Power of "King Cotton," 1858
   "Speech of Hon. J. H. Hammond, of South Carolina, in the Senate, March 4, 1858," *Appendix to the Congressional Globe*, 35th Congress, 1st Session, pp. 70–71.

5. Virginia Reacts to John Brown's Raid, 1859
   "Resolution of the Central Southern Rights Association" in *De Bow's Review* XXVIII (March 1860), p. 356.

6. The 1860 Association Agitates the Sectional Crisis, 1860
   "Circular of the 1860 Association," in Archibald Rutledge Papers, Southern Historical Collection, Library of the University of North Carolina at Chapel Hill.

7. South Carolina Secedes, 1860

   "South Carolina Ordinance of Secession" in *The War of the Rebellion: A Compilation of the Records of the Union and Confederate Armies*, Series I, Volume I (Washington: Government Printing Office, 1880), p. 110.

8. Carolinians Debate the Possibility of War, 1860−1861

   A "Fire Eater's" Contempt for "Cowardly" Yankees, 1860: McCarter's Journal, November 1860, Manuscripts Division, Library of Congress, pp. 10−11. Henry Ravenel Anticipates a Bloody Conflict, 1861: Entry for February 15, 1861, in Arney R. Childs, ed., *The Private Journal of Henry William Ravenel* (Columbia: University of South Carolina Press, 1947), pp. 53−54. William Henry Trescot Predicts Peace, 1861: Trescot to W. P. Miles, March 3, 1861, William Porcher Miles Papers, Southern Historical Collection, University of North Carolina at Chapel Hill.

Further Reading

Steven A. Channing, *Crisis of Fear: Secession in South Carolina* (1970)

William J. Cooper, Jr., *The South and the Politics of Slavery, 1852−1856* (1978)

Avery O. Craven, *The Growth of Southern Nationalism, 1848−1861* (1953)

Daniel W. Crofts, *Reluctant Confederates: Upper South Unionists in the Secession Crisis* (1989)

David Donald, *Charles Sumner and the Coming of the Civil War* (1970)

William W. Freehling, *Prelude to Civil War: The Nullification Controversy in South Carolina, 1816−1836* (1965)

Holman Hamilton, *Prologue to Conflict: The Crisis and Compromise of 1850* (1966)

Michael F. Holt, *The Political Crisis of the 1850s* (1978)

Thelma Jennings, *The Nashville Convention* (1980)

Michael P. Johnson, *Toward a Patriarchal Republic: The Secession of Georgia* (1977)

John McCardell, *The Idea of a Southern Nation: Southern Nationalists and Southern Nationalism* (1979)

John Niven, *John C. Calhoun and the Price of Union* (1988)

Stephen B. Oates, *To Purge This Land with Blood: A Biography of John Brown* (1970)

David M. Potter, *The South and the Sectional Conflict* (1968)

Ronald L. Takaki, *A Proslavery Crusade: The Agitation to Reopen the African Slave Trade* (1971)

J. Mills Thornton III, *Alabama: Politics and Power in a Slave Society* (1978)

Laura A. White, *Robert Barnwell Rhett: Father of Secession* (1931)

Ralph A. Wooster, *The Secession Conventions of the South* (1962)

Document Set 9

The Civil War

No experience traumatized the South more than the Civil War. At its outset, southerners anticipated an early victory that would vindicate their decision to secede and justify their belief that the southern way of life was superior to that of the North. Optimism ran high after the resounding defeat of a Union army at Manassas (Bull Run), the first of a string of military triumphs that appeared to confirm the brilliance of Confederate battle tactics and strategies. The Confederacy's chances of achieving its war goals deteriorated, however, as the Union utilized its full industrial and technological power in the war effort. The appointment of Ulysses S. Grant as commander-in-chief of the Union armies brought forward a man who followed to the letter Lincoln's objective of bringing the Confederate forces to battle and defeating them in the field.

The South and its sympathizers have always claimed that the war's outcome was determined by the infinitely greater resources of the enemy. Comforting as this explanation may be to contemporary southerners who cherish tales of valor and heroic exploits, other, less satisfying factors have to be taken into consideration. For example, not only was the southern desertion rate high but some state governors refused to implement conscription to replenish the undermanned Confederate armies. Moreover, the southern commitment to states' rights retarded the development of nationalism and unity in the Confederacy. Cabinet members in the Confederate government resigned, or were replaced, with monotonous regularity. Finally, Jefferson Davis's overestimation of his own military worth, and his personal intervention in the military conduct of the war, undermined the undoubted skills of his leading generals.

Still, history abounds with instances of wars won in the face of adverse circumstances. Abraham Lincoln encountered equally daunting obstacles as members of his own cabinet—and the majority of the northern people—opposed his war policies. The success of the U. S. president in overcoming divisiveness in his party and in the country was crucial to the northern war effort. Driven by a belated sense of unity and urgency, which was largely absent in the South, the North used every means at its disposal to achieve victory.

Morale in war depends as much upon the material welfare of the soldiers as it does on repeated successes in the battlefield. The first document, a letter from Lieutenant Colonel Samuel Walkup to North Carolina's governor, Zebulon Vance, reveals that Confederate soldiers were ill equipped, disgruntled, and ripe for desertion as early as the autumn of 1862. The price of desertion was high. Despite the anguished concern that Mary Cooper expresses for her children in the second document, a letter read at the court-martial hearing of her deserter husband, Edward Cooper, he was sentenced to death (Cooper was later pardoned by Robert E. Lee). A much discussed proposal to reinforce the dwindling Confederate armies with slaves met with great hostility from southern troops. In the third selection, Confederate general Patton Anderson claims that the implementation of such a policy would not be worth the price of victory.

For those who believe that wars are won on the battlefield, the campaign at Gettysburg marked the turning point of the conflict. In the aftermath of the war, some southerners laid the blame for this adversity squarely on the shoulders of James Longstreet, one of Lee's commanders in the Army of Northern Virginia, and indeed, the unfortunate Longstreet was the perfect scapegoat. His cooperation with the Republican party, which controlled southern state governments during the Reconstruction era, alienated Longstreet from southerners who already held the noble Lee blameless for the defeat of the Confederacy. The fourth document, taken from the memoirs of General Edward Porter Alexander, an artillery officer on Longstreet's staff and an eyewitness to the Battle of Gettysburg, exposes flaws in the tactical planning of both Longstreet and Lee.

Southerners had always prided themselves on their honor and chivalry, but as John M. Daniel, the wartime editor of the *Richmond Examiner* explains in the fifth document, such qualities were disadvantages in the kind of total conflict that the Civil War gradually became. The South realized too late that Lincoln's win-at-all-costs policy, carried out to perfection by Union generals Grant and William Tecumseh Sherman, doomed the Confederate war effort to failure. General Wade Hampton's letter to Sherman, the sixth selection, is a lecture on codes of conduct in wartime. The message clearly indicates Hampton's reluctance to contravene time-honored but increasingly obsolete methods of waging war.

Some, perhaps many, southerners were not committed to the goal of independence. Jonathan Worth of North Carolina gives his opinion in the seventh document that a restoration of the Union offered the best hope for the perpetuation of slavery. In 1864, such a prospect was wildly unrealistic; however, Worth's denunciation of administrative ineptitude was not misplaced. Factionalism and rivalry were rife in the Confederate government, especially in the relationship between Jefferson Davis, president of the Confederate States of America, and Alexander Stephens, his vice president. In the final selection, Stephens outlines some of his objections to what he claims is Davis's assumption of dictatorial powers.

Questions for Analysis

1. Could the South have won the Civil War by using different battle strategies and tactics?
2. Was the Battle of Gettysburg the turning point of the war?
3. If conditions in Confederate armies were so bad, why did southern soldiers continue to fight?
4. Did the existence of slavery in the South have any perceptible influence on the course of the war?
5. To what extent did adherence to a philosophy of states' rights hinder the Confederate war effort? Did the belief in states' rights prevent the emergence of a genuine southern nationalism?
6. As president of the Confederate States of America, Jefferson Davis is inevitably compared as a political leader to Abraham Lincoln. Are such comparisons fair? Was Davis a liability to the Confederacy?

1. A Confederate Officer on Discontent in a North Carolina Regiment, 1862

Camp Near Winchester Va.   Oct 11th 1862.

I lay before you for your consideration the destitute condition of our Regt with the hope that you, who have experienced some of the severe trials of a soldiers life, may hasten up the requisite relief—

We have present Six hundred & nineteen men rank file in the 48th Regt. N. C. Troops—There are of that number Fifty one who are completely

& absolutely Barefooted—& one hundred & ninety four who are nearly as bad off, as Barefooted, & who will be altogether so, in less than one month. There are but Two hundred & ninety seven Blankets in the Regt among the 619 men present which is less than one Blanket to every two men. In truth there is one Compy (I) having 66 men & only Eleven Blankets in the whole company—The pants are generally ragged & out at the seats—& there are less than three cooking utensils to each Company—This sir is the condition of our Regt. upon the eve of winter here among the mountains of Va. Cut off from all supplies from home, & worn down & thinned with incessant marchings, fighting & diseases—can any one wonder that our Regt. numbering over 1250 rank & file has more than half its no. absent from camp, & not much over one third 449 of them fit for duty? The country is filled with strangers, deserters, & sick men & the hospitals are crowded from the exposures. A spirit of disaffection is rapidly engendering among the soldiers which threatens to show itself in general straggling & desertions if it does not lead to open mutiny.

Add to this that our surgeons have no medicines & dont even pretend to prescribe for the sick in camp, having no medicines & you have an outline of the sufferings & prospective trials & difficulties under which we labor.

What is said of the 48th N. C. is equally true of other Regts in the service from N. C. & from other States too.—But you are aware how the matter stands with N. C. The State agreed to & did receive from the Confed. Govmt. The commutation money & assumed to furnish the Clothing, Shoes Blankets &c to the soldier. This she has utterly failed to do, or to give the commutation money in lieu thereof. She has received the money & has failed to furnish the clothing for which she has been paid by the Confed. Govmt.—Our Regt. entered the service 1st of April last They recd *generally* one suit each except socks, & nearly all recd, one pair of shoes—Only about one third of them received any Blankets & very few of those who furnished their own blankets have been paid any money by way of commutation—We have passed six Months in the service & you well know we have

seen hard service during that time. Our scanty clothing, which we had independent of the government of either N. C. or the C. S. has been lost for the want of the means of transportation; & finally all that we had, except what we had on our persons, was lost when we crossed the Potomac after the late battle of Sharpsburg, Septr. 17th. This of course was no fault of N. C. but one of the misfortunes of war. I mention these things to show that our destitution is no fault of the Regt. It was in fact mainly the fault of the misfortune of the C. S. government in not furnishing us with sufficient means of transportation & the casualties incident to War. But what I do insist upon now is that North Carolina who always has maintained a character for the prompt & faithful performance of all her contracts, Should now exert herself to her utmost capacity with her most patriotic energy & zeal to supply these just & pinching wants of her own citizens & save them from the extreme sufferings now rapidly approaching & already felt in the coming winter—Just think of our *ragged & barefooted* men with *one* blanket only & scarcely one to any *two* men & having *no tents*, or even *flies* to shield them from the cold rains & winter blasts in this Northern clime, Having so few cooking utensils that their constant use cannot supply the demands of the Regt. & having no medical supplies. And having *no other* rations except of flour & *eternal* Beef—And think of the sick, who constitute nearly two thirds of our army, in such a condition. And surely, surely with these facts before them, the generous & patriotic State of N. C. will be just & faithful in fulfilling the engagements which she has made to & been paid for by the Confederate States. She will thus alleviate the miseries likely to befall her *own sons*, and save them & herself from the disgrace that may otherwise obscure their fair fame, & darken her history now proudly standing forth among the brightest of the Southern States or of the nations of the earth.

What we most pressingly need just now is our full supply of *Blankets*, of *Shoes* & of *pants* & *socks*. We need very much all our other clothing too. But we are in the greatest need of these indispensable articles & *Must* have them, & have them *Now*. Otherwise how can the government blame the soldier for failing to render service, when it fails to fulfil its stipulated & *paid for* contracts? A contract broken on *one* side is broken on all sides & void.—If N. C. cannot fulfil her contract for clothing, blankets & shoes. She ought to rescind it & refund the money & let the C. S. Govmt. do it. Or measures should be immediately taken to give *free transportation*, with *security* from *loss by the way*, to such articles as the parents, wives & friends of the suffering soldiers would immediately & joyfully send from home to their relief; And the State should pay over the commutation money to those furnishing the supplies, which indeed they would generously furnish at any sacrifice, without pay, if they were assured the gift would reach the beloved objects of their bounty & not be lost on the way. The State should however promptly pay for it & thus relieve the destitute family of the soldiers for the sacrifice made to him in his necessities & thus doubly bless in both giving & receiving favours.

The soldiers of the 48th N. C. & from all the State will patriotically suffer & bear their hardships & privations as long as those from any other State, or as far as human endurance can tolerate such privations, But it would not be wise to experiment to far in such circumstances as now surround us upon the extent of their endurance. With Lincolns proclamation promising freedom to the slaves, what might be the suffering, exhausted, ragged, barefooted & dying *Non* slaveholders of the South, who are neglected by their government & whose suffering families at home are exposed to so many evils, begin to conclude? Would it not be dangerous to tempt them with too great trials?—

Dear Sir, you will please not to consider me obtrusive in this communication to your excellency. I feel the very earnest & solemn responsibility of my position as commander of this Regt. at this critical period & under these trying circumstances & wish to do all I can to remove from my Skirts the heavy responsibility by doing all that I can to remove the evils by seeking a speedy supply of Blankets Shoes & clothing. & therefore beg your earnest attention to the premises & your zealous & I hope efficient aid to supply our necessity—I send with this paper Lt. R. H. Stitt of Co. A 48th Regt. N. C. in whose care any clothing &c. will be attended to in the promptest manner, & who also can give any further information required of the condition of this Regt. The Quarter Master, Capt. Hayne, is too sick to leave his post—. . .

2. *A Soldier's Wife Fears for Her Children, c. 1863*

My dear Edward:—I have always been proud of you, and since your connection with the Confederate army, I have been prouder of you than ever before. I would not have you do anything wrong for the world, but before God, Edward, unless you come home, we must die. Last night, I was aroused by little Eddie's crying. I called and said 'What is the matter, Eddie?' and he said, "O mamma! I am so hungry." And Lucy, Edward, your darling Lucy; she never complains, but she is growing thinner and thinner every day. And before God, Edward, unless you come home, we must die.

Your Mary.

3. A Confederate General Opposes Slave Enlistments, 1864

(Confidential)

Dalton, Ga., Jan. 14, 1864

To Lieutenant General L. Polk,
Enterprise, Miss.

General: After you have read what I am about to disclose to you I hope you will not think I have assumed any unwarrantable intimacy in marking this communication as "confidential." My thoughts for ten days past have been so oppressed with the weight of the subject as to arouse in my mind the most painful apprehensions of future results, and have caused me to cast about for a friend of clear head, ripe judgment and pure patriotism with whom to confer and take counsel. My choice has fallen upon you, sir, and I proceed at once to lay the matter before you.

On January 2d I received a circular order from the headquarters of Hindman's corps informing me that the commanding general of the army desired division commanders to meet him at his quarters at seven o'clock that evening. . . .

General Cleburn proceeded to read an elaborate article on the subject of our past disasters, present condition and inevitable future ruin unless an entire change of policy might avert it.

That change he boldly and proudly proposed to effect by emancipating our slaves and putting muskets in the hands of all of them capable of bearing arms, thus securing them to us as allies and equals, and insuring a superiority of numbers over our enemies, &c.

Yes, sir, this plain, but in my view monstrous, proposition was calmly submitted to the generals of this army for their sanction and adoption, with the avowed purpose of carrying it to the rank and file.

I will not attempt to describe my feelings on being confronted by a project so startling in its character—may I say, so revolting to Southern sentiment, Southern pride and Southern honor?

And not the least painful of the emotions awakened by it was the consciousness which forced itself upon me that it met with favor from others besides the author in high station then present. You have a place, General, in the Southern heart perhaps not less exalted than that you occupy in her army. No one knows better than yourself all the hidden powers and secret springs which move the great moral machinery of the South. You know whence she derived that force which three years ago impelled her to the separation and has since that time to this present hour enabled her to lay all she has, even the blood of her best sons, upon the altar of independence, and do you believe that that South will now listen to the voices of those who would ask her to stultify herself by entertaining a proposition which heretofore our insolent foes themselves have not even dared to make in terms so bold and undisguised?

What are we to do? If this thing is once openly proposed to the army the total disintegration of that army will follow in a fortnight, and yet to speak and work in opposition to it is an agitation of the question scarcely less to be dreaded at this time and brings down the universal indignation of the Southern people and the Southern soldiers upon the head of at least one of our bravest and most accomplished officers. Then, I repeat, what is to be done?

What relief it would afford me to talk to you about this matter, but as that may not be, do I go too far in asking you to write me?

I start in a few days to go to my home in Monticello, Fla., where I expect to spend twenty days with my family, and I assure you, General, it would add much to the enjoyment of my visit if you would favor me by mail with some of the many thoughts which this subject will arouse in your mind.

Believe me, General, very truly your friend,

Patton Anderson.

4. A Confederate Officer Remembers
Gettysburg (1863), 1898–1899

. . . 1. The question of all, at the inception of the campaign, was whether to play what I've already called the Pennsylvania, or, the Tennessee gambit. By the rules of the game, the Tennessee, with its interior lines was the safest game. But, perhaps, one consideration which may have influenced Gen. Lee was that Pa. was nearest the enemy's vitals. There was reason to believe that, if we could take Washington, the moral effect on the enemy would be much more potent than to capture Cincinnati. And the narrative of the battle I think has put it beyond all question that it was not the *choice of the gambit* which lost the game. We took into Pa. an amount of fight, so to express it, which would have defeated Meade's army, if it had been judiciously concentrated & applied, & not expended upon physical obstacles, and at non-vital times & places.

2. Hooker seems to me to have lost a great chance when he found, at Fredericksburg, only A. P. Hill between himself & Richmond; Longstreet at Culpeper, & Ewell in the Valley. By all means, he should have marched to Richmond, overwhelming Hill as he went; which would have been sure & easy with his immense force. A somewhat similar situation was presented to Sherman in 1864, when, at Atlanta, he found Hood threatening Nashville in his rear. He knew that Hood could do nothing serious, even if he took Nashville, so he let him alone, & marched for Savannah. But, as I have before written, the Federals were ridiculously & insanely afraid of our capturing Washn. City; in spite of their superb triple circle of fortifications. Gen. Lee appreciated their weaknesses, and boldly played upon it—indeed I think he must sometimes have enjoyed very hearty laughs over his successful but marvellous audacity in practising on the enemy's fears.

3rd. The next point in the game was Stuart's cavalry move, around Hooker's army. I've already said that I am sure that was bad play, on general principles. We should have *always* had our *whole* army in *easy reach, & supporting distance* of each other. Such a raid could cut no

real figure on the grand result, & was taking chances for no good.

4. When Heth's division was authorized to go to Gettysburg to get shoes, I think it should surely have had a similar caution to that given Gen. Ewell, on the afternoon of the first day's battle, when he was directed to occupy Cemetery Hill but cautioned "*not to bring on a general engagement*." The principle involved in such cautions, which are very often given, is not to waste the fighting spirit & power of the army on side issues. It is simply that of saving & concentrating every energy for the vital point at the critical time. This fighting spirit in the troops, after a period of rest, is something as real, though not as tangible, as ammunition, & should be economised in the same way. Even the best divisions, after one really severe & bloody action, cannot be expected to exhibit the highest development of spirit, particularly on the offensive, until after a little rest; during which new offers & fresh leaders among them acquire influence, & replace those who have been lost. Note the better spirit of Pickett's fresh division in his charge than that of the troops badly cut up two days before.

5. On the first day we had taken the aggressive. Although a casual reading of Gen. Lee's report suggests that the aggressive on [the] second day seemed forced upon him, yet the statement is very much qualified by the expression "in a measure," & also by the reference to the hopes inspired by our partial success. I think it must be frankly admitted that there was no real difficulty, whatever, in our taking the defensive the next day; & in our so manouvring afterward as to have finally forced Meade to attack us.

I think it a reasonable estimate to say that 60 per cent of our chances for a great victory were lost by our continuing the aggressive. And we may easily imagine the boon it was to Gen. Meade (who was neither a man of any high degree of decision, or of aggression; & who was now entirely new to his great responsibility, & evidently oppressed by it) to be relieved from the burden of making any difficult decision, such as he would have had to do if Lee had been satisfied with his victory of the first day; & then taken a strong position & stood on the defensive. Now the gods had flung to Meade more than impudence itself could have dared to pray for—a position unique among all the battlefields of the war, certainly adding fifty per cent to his already superior force, and an adversary stimulated by success to an utter disregard of all physical disadvantages & ready to face for nearly three quarters of a mile the very worst that all his artillery & infantry could do. For I am impressed by the fact that the strength of the enemy's position seems to have cut no figure in the consideration [of] the question of the aggressive; nor does it seem to have been systematically examined or inquired into—nor does the night seem to have been utilized in any preparation for the morning. Verily that night *it was pie for Meade*!

6. There seems no doubt that had Longstreet's attack on the 2nd been made materially sooner, we would have gained a decided victory. Nor is there any doubt that it could have been—or that Gen. Lee much desired it to be made very much earlier. But he yielded to Longstreet's request to wait for Law's brigade; and the delay caused by Longstreet's infantry being taken in sight of Round Top seems to have entirely escaped his attention, & that of all his staff. He was present on the field all the time, & was apparently consenting to the situation from hour to hour. Longstreet is bitterly blamed for asking for delay, & subsequent events showed that it lost us a great opportunity. But it seems to me that while he might blame himself for it general criticism must be modified by the fact that Gen. Lee's granting the request justified it as apparently prudent, at the time.

7. I have sufficiently discussed, in my narrative, the very great mistake made, in my judgment, in the selection of the point of attack. Here again, as when the question of the aggressive or the defensive was up, on the night of the first day, there seems a lack of appreciation of the immense figure which the character of the ground may cut in the results of an aggressive fight. Not only was the selection about as bad as possible, but there does not seem to have been any special thought given to the matter. It seems to have been allowed almost to select itself as if it was a matter of no consequence....

5. A Southern Editor Criticizes Southern Chivalry, 1863

May 12, 1863

We have had recently some remarkable returns for the pretty civilities showered by Stuart and Hampton on the Dutch farmers of Pennsylvania during their raid to Chambersburg. That souvenir of chivalry is forcibly brought to mind by the sharp contrast of recent occurrences. It has long been a laughing-stock for the North; and the narrative which was published by Colonel McClure, the Yankee commander at Chambersburg, of the polite phrases and punctilios of the "soft-mannered rebels" who invaded his military dominions, still survives among the Yankee humors of the war. We still have the picture before us of the sleek Yankee watching from the cover of his porch the wet, weary, and hungry "rebels" exposing themselves to a drenching rain, rather than invade the sanctity of the homes of the citizens of Chambersburg; "begging" a few coals to light their fires, and humbly asking permission to buy food from the negro wenches in the kitchens; while the officers made their salaams to Colonel McClure, and "thanked him for his candor" when he informed them that he was a red-hot abolitionist. It never seemed to have occurred to these damp knights that it was their duty to their men to take from an enemy what they wanted of food and shelter; they were too intent on pruning their manners, practising the knighthood of the middle ages in Pennsylvania, and establishing a chivalric fraternity with the Dutch civilization they had invaded.

We have had enough, in the recent Yankee raids, to put to the blush these recollections of "chivalry," and to teach us that the gentle knight-errantry of rose-water is but a poor way of opposing an enemy whose mission is that of savage warfare.

From our Southern exchanges we gather some accounts of the conduct of the Yankees on their recent raid in Mississippi. We might prolong the frightful tissue of these barbarities; but it is not necessary to exhibit the brutal and despicable character of the enemy whom we are so courteously fighting.

During the excursion of Stoneman's bandits in this State, no opportunity was lost by them to insult females, to search the chambers of ladies, and to steal jewelry, chickens, and whatever articles of merchandising they could conveniently pocket.

In Kentucky, the conduct of the Yankee marauders, who are constantly spying out the land, is licensed and uninterrupted outrage.

The contrast which these recent Yankee raids have afforded between the savage conduct of the enemy and the false tenderness of such knights as those who made the cavalcade to Chambersburg, not only disgusts and offends the true patriotism of the South, but it presents a case of rank injustice to our own people, who are debarred from retaliation, and whose interests are subordinated to the ambition of some officer to make a reputation for "chivalry" in the North,

and earn a compliment in the *New York Tribune*. Again and again have Southern people had occasion to know the ridiculous figure they make, the contempt they bring upon themselves, and the positive injury they invite, by their sentimental tenderness for Yankees and their monkey chivalry to their enemy. But court to Yankees is a fashion that seems to be ingrained in the Southern mind. An opportunity never seems to be lost, whether they invade districts occupied by the enemy, or come in contact with him, or take prisoners, for some vain Confederate commander to make a display of stilted wanderer, and dance some ridiculous jig of politeness, to the edification of the varlets who surround him.

Chivalry is a very noble quality. But we do not get our idea of it from the mincings of dandy preachers and parlor geldings. We do not deprive our interpretation of the codes of war from sprigs dressed up in Confederate uniform of uncertain moral gender. We know that we are in a dreadful war; that we are fighting a base and deadly enemy. While it is not for the South to fight with any mean advantage, it is time for her to abandon those polite notions of war which she has got from the Waverley novels, and to fight with fire and sword. If any retaliation is to be made for the recent Yankee raids (and present opportunities invite it), its history should be written in broad tracks of blood and destruction. There should be no re-enactment of the scenes at Chambersburg. We must pay the enemy back in the savage coin of vengeance, and settle our accounts in blood.

6. *Confederate General Wade Hampton Denounces Union General William T. Sherman as a Murderer, 1865*

Headquarters,
In the Field, February 27, 1865

Maj. Gen. W. T. Sherman, U.S. Army:

General: Your communication of the 24th instant reached me to-day. In it you state that it

has been officially reported that your foraging parties are "murdered" after capture. You go on to say that you have "ordered a similar number of prisoners in our hands to be disposed of in like manner"; that is to say, you have ordered a number of Confederate soldiers to be "murdered." You characterize your order in proper terms, for the public voice, even in your own country, where it seldom dares to express itself in vindication of truth, honor, or justice, will surely agree with you in pronouncing you guilty of murder if your order is carried out. Before dismissing this portion of your letter, I beg to assure you that for every soldier of mine "murdered" by you, I shall have executed at once two of yours, giving in all cases preferences to any officers who may be in my hands.

In reference to the statement you make regarding the death of your foragers, I have only to say that I know nothing of it; that no orders given by me authorize the killing of prisoners after capture, and that I do not believe my men killed any of yours, except under circumstances in which it was perfectly legitimate and proper that they should kill them. It is a part of the system of the thieves whom you designate as your foragers to fire the dwellings of those citizens whom they have robbed. To check this inhuman system, which is justly execrated by every civilized nation, I have directed my men to shoot down all of your men who are caught burning houses. This order shall remain in force so long as you disgrace the profession of arms by allowing your men to destroy private dwellings. . . .

You are particular in defining and claiming "war rights." May I ask if you enumerate among these the right to fire upon a defenseless city without notice: to burn that city to the ground after it had been surrendered by the inhabitants who claimed, though in vain, that protection which is always accorded in civilized warfare to non-combatants; to fire the dwelling houses of citizens after robbing them; and to perpetrate even darker crimes than these crimes too black to be mentioned?

You have permitted, if you have not ordered, the commission of these offenses against humanity and the rules of war; you fired into the city of Columbia without a word of warning; after its surrender by the mayor, who demanded protection to private property, you laid the whole city in ashes, leaving amidst its ruins thousands of old men and helpless women and children, who are likely to perish of starvation and exposure. Your line of march can be traced by the lurid light of burning houses, and in more than one household there is now an agony far more bitter than that of death. The Indian scalped his victim regardless of age or sex, but with all his barbarity he always respected the persons of his female captives. Your soldiers, more savage than the Indian, insult those whose natural protectors are absent.

In conclusion, I have only to request that whenever you have any of my men "murdered" or "disposed of," for the terms appear to be synonymous with you, you will let me hear of it, that I may know what action to take in the matter. In the meantime I shall hold fifty-six of your men as hostages for those whom you have ordered to be executed.

I am yours, &c.,

Wade Hampton
Lieutenant-General

7. *A Unionist's Plan to End the War, 1864*

Raleigh   Feb. 6th 1864

. . . If you abhor the war in which we are involved as much as I do, it is, perhaps, fortunate for your personal comfort that you have nothing to do with public affairs; but however terrible and chaotic appearances may be they may be made worse by misrule and made better by wise and good rulers. For myself I retain my early convictions that the government established by our forefathers was admirably adapted to promote the happiness and prosperity of its people, and that none is likely to be constructed on its ruins so well calculated to effect these ends: I have uniformly believed that no sufficient cause existed to justify the rupture, and so strong were these convictions that I would not be a member of the Convention when the demand seemed to be universal for a despoliation of the Union, and I now think, bitter as the animosity has grown to be, that a Union on the old basis will be better for both sections, than separate independence—and I am not sure this is not the opinion of a majority of the people of both sections. I am sure it is the opinion of a majority of the people of North Carolina. It is an opinion, however, which the dominant powers of the Southern Confederacy denounce as traitorous—and which subjects the man who utters it to the monstrous imputation, of deserving to die by the gallows. The free expression of opinion is thus restrained. I believe, if a Convention were now called in this State, the people would elect delegates who would propose a general pacification on this basis. If it succeeded, it would be a blessing to the whole land and would prevent that universal emancipation and the curse of an enormous free negro population making the country unfit to live in:—If the North would not make peace on this basis, it would produce a unity among us which would render us invincible.

You must regard the whole of this letter as confidential. I an conscious of being as patriotic as any man who lives. Every thing dearest to me is in North Carolina: and I would be as far as any man from doing any thing which would, in my judgment, derogate from her dignity and honor. I would do nothing to weaken our military arm until it could be ascertained that peace could be made on this basis.

Windsor

8. Confederate Vice President Alexander Stephens Fears a Dictatorship, 1864

Crawfordville, Ga., April 8, 1864

Hon. H. V. Johnson,
Sandy Grove, Ga.:

. . . As for Mr. Davis, I repeat again I have no feelings of antipathy, much less hostility. What opinions you may think I entertain of him as you intimate I know not, but I have no hesitancy in stating to you freely and frankly, and most confidentially, what my opinions of him are. They are much more akin to suspicion and jealousy than of animosity or hate. While I do not and never have regarded him as a great man or statesman on a large scale, or a man of any marked genius, yet I have regarded him as a man of good intentions, weak and vascillating, timid, petulant, peevish, obstinate, but not firm. Am now beginning to doubt his good intentions. I say doubt, for after watching him closely I am not satisfied in my own mind, or arrived at any conclusion, whether some of his shortcomings are to be attributed to weakness or bad purposes. These are my real sentiments, and my reasons for them are these: Since his first elevation to power he has changed many of his former State's rights principles, as in case of conscription. His whole policy on the organization and discipline of the Army is perfectly consistent with the hypothesis that he is aiming at absolute power. Not a word has come from him of military usurpation in the orders for martial law by Bragg and Van Dorn on the whole system of passports and provost-marshals, which is utterly wrong and without authority of law. After all that may be said or written by myself and others against these usurpations, not one word has escaped Mr. Davis showing his disapproval of them. Again, it is well known that the subject of a dictatorship has been mooted, talked of, and discussed in private and in the public journals, and that the most earnest advocates of such a course, the virtual doing away with Congress and the Constitution, have been editors near him—right under his nose; editors of journals recognized at the time to be the organs of the Administration. Now, it seems to me strange that this should be so, and men holding and advocating such sentiments for months should hold such near relations to him if such sentiments were distasteful to him. These are bad signs to me, yet they are not conclusive evidences of bad objects or intentions on his part. They leave me in doubt, but certainly awaken my suspicion and watchful jealousy. They teach me to be on my guard, and they should, in my opinion, put the whole country on their guard. The price of liberty is eternal vigilance. But again I assure you I feel no more hostility to him than I do to you and great numbers I meet with who see no danger in these things. My hostility and wrath (and I have enough of it to burst ten thousand bottles) is not against him, or any man or men, but against the thing—the measures and the policy which I see is leading us to despotism. If you can understand and appreciate this position and these feelings, then you can understand me; and if you cannot, then you do not understand me, and cannot. But I trust you do. How you could have got the impression, or entertained the thought, that I had an antipathy to Mr. Davis, or was hostile to him, is strange and unaccountable to me. You surely have heard me in conversation speak of his weakness and imbecility, but certainly with no bitterness of feeling, and what I have said on this subject has always been more in sorrow than anger. I had no more feeling of resentment toward him for these than I had toward the defects and infirmities of my poor old blind and deaf dog that you saw when you were here. Poor old Ris; he is dead now and gone to his long rest. Peace to his ashes and honor to his memory. While I deplore his infirmities I certainly have no feeling of unkindness to him. As to what you say about the

Administration, one word: I hardly know what idea you attach to this term as used by you. If you mean the Cabinet, then they are sustained by neither the Congress nor country, and when their recommendations were rejected by Congress, if they had had any self-respect they would have resigned their places. If you mean the acts and messages of Congress, then I am confident not one-tenth of the people of this country approve them. I would stake my head upon the issue that not ten districts in the Confederacy could be carried in a Congressional election for a candidate running on the advocacy of the four leading measures of the last Congress and pledged to sustain them as the settled policy of the country. This cry of sustaining the Administration, you will allow me to say, with all due respect to you, is nothing but a stupid, senseless cachination. Nobody approves it. I heard that General Cobb, in his speech at Milledgeville, said all these acts of Congress were proper, wise, and just; and yet I do know that General Cobb spoke very differently to me of some of them before they were passed. Why will men thus degrade themselves by attempting to bamboozle the people; and how are we to get better laws if bad ones, that all feel and know to be bad, are not denounced and true principles proclaimed?

I said but little about the tax and currency question in Milledgeville, because money at best, in my estimation, is but trash. Greater and more vital interests were in jeopardy. . . .

References

1. A Confederate Officer on Discontent in a North Carolina Regiment, 1862
   Colonel Samuel H. Walkup to Governor Vance, October 11, 1862, in Frontis W. Johnson, ed., *The Papers of Zebulon Vance*, Volume I, 1843–1862 (Raleigh: State Department of Archives and History), pp. 258–261.
2. A Soldier's Wife Fears for Her Children, c. 1863
   Ella Lonn, *Desertion During the Civil War* (New York: The Century Company, 1928), p. 13.

3. A Confederate General Opposes Slaves Enlistments, 1864
   General Patton Anderson to Leonidas Polk, January 14, 1864, in "History of Walthall's Brigade, C.S.A.," *Publications of the Mississippi Historical Society* (1916), pp. 552–554.

4. A Confederate Officer Remembers Gettysburg (1863), 1898–1899
   Gary W. Gallagher, ed., *Fighting for the Confederacy: The Personal Recollections of General Edward Porter Alexander* (Chapel Hill: University of North Carolina Press, 1989), pp. 276–278.

5. A Southern Editor Criticizes Southern Chivalry, 1863
   Frederick Daniel, ed., *The* Richmond Examiner *During the War: or, The Writings of John M. Daniel* (New York, 1868), pp. 84–85.

6. Confederate General Wade Hampton Denounces Union General William T. Sherman as a Murderer, 1865
   Wade Hampton to W. T. Sherman, February 27, 1865, in *The War of the Rebellion: A Compilation of the Union and Confederate Armies*, Series I, Volume XLVII (Washington: Government Printing Office, 1900), pp. 596–597.

7. A Unionist's Plan to End the War, 1864
   Jonathan Worth to John Pool, February 6, 1864, in J. G. de Roulhac Hamilton, ed., *The Correspondence of Jonathan Worth* (Raleigh: Edwards & Broughton Printing Company, 1909), pp. 288–289.

8. Confederate Vice President Alexander Stephens Fears a Dictatorship, 1864
   Alexander Stephens to Herschel Johnson, April 8, 1864, in *The War of the Rebellion: A Compilation of the Official Records of the Union and Confederate Armies*, Series IV, Volume III (Washington: Government Printing Office, 1900), pp. 279–280.

Further Reading

Thomas B. Alexander and Richard E. Beringer, *The Anatomy of the Confederate Congress* (1972)

Richard E. Beringer et al., *Why the South Lost the Civil War* (1986)

James H. Brewer, *The Confederate Negro* (1969)

Edward B. Coddington, *The Gettysburg Campaign: A Study in Command* (1968)

Thomas L. Connelly and Archer Jones, *The Politics of Command: Factions and Ideas in Confederate Strategy* (1973)

David Donald, ed., *Why the North Won the Civil War* (1960)

Clement Eaton, *A History of the Southern Confederacy* (1954)

Paul D. Escott, *After Secession: Jefferson Davis and the Failure of Southern Nationalism* (1978)

Shelby Foote, *The Civil War: A Narrative*, 3 vols. (1958–1974)

Douglas S. Freeman, *R. E. Lee: A Biography*, 4 vols. (1941–1943)

Ella Lonn, *Desertion During the Civil War* (1928)

James M. McPherson, *Battle Cry of Freedom* (1988)

Grady McWhiney and Perry D. Jamieson, *Attack and Die: Civil War Military Tactics and the Southern Heritage* (1981)

Albert B. Moore, *Conscription and Conflict in the Confederacy* (1963)

Frank L. Owsley, *King Cotton Diplomacy: Foreign Relations of the Confederate States of America* (1931)

Georgia L. Tatum, *Disloyalty in the Confederacy* (1934)

Emory Thomas, *The Confederate Nation, 1861–1865* (1979)

Bell I. Wiley, *The Plain People of the Confederacy* (1943)

Steven E. Woodworth, *Jefferson Davis and His Generals: The Failure of Confederate Command in the West* (1990)

W. Buck Yearns, ed., *The Confederate Governors* (1985)

Document Set 10

Emancipation and Reconstruction

For nearly a century, Reconstruction was widely regarded as an unmitigated disaster for the South. Critics of the federal government's Reconstruction policies claimed that a more lenient solution would have facilitated reconciliation between the sections and smoothed the tortured path of race relations between whites and African-Americans in the South. These commentators observed that the violent methods used to attempt to return the South to the political control of the Democratic party might then have been averted. In the case of the Republican party, the traditional interpretation of its role in the South was completely negative. The Radical Republican coalition of plundering northern carpetbaggers, degraded southern scalawags, and vengeful blacks used its political power to ruin the economies of the southern states, the traditional argument ran. Critics claimed that Reconstruction was an era of unprecedented graft and fraud.

As in many other areas of American history, the 1960s produced a strongly revisionist argument, which has gradually gained acceptance by all but the most "unreconstructed" southerners. Revisionist scholars assert that the majority of white southerners, unrepentant and defiant, were not prepared to alter their political and racial beliefs. The Republican party therefore remained the deadly enemy of the South, and emancipation brought to the fore all the fears among whites of the presence in their midst of a large, uncontrollable, uncivilized black population. Even before the Republican plan for Reconstruction went into operation, southern states implemented "black codes" to replace slavery as a mechanism for controlling ex-slaves' activities.

The revisionists further observe that conservative white southerners exaggerated the deficiencies of the Republican state governments. Compared to the corruption associated with Ulysses S. Grant's presidential administration, and the schemings of ambitious politicians in big northern cities, fraud in the southern states was not extensive. Rather, inexperience in government often underlay inefficient Republican administration, and the immense task of physically reconstructing the prostrate South necessitated heavy drains on state treasuries. Many carpetbaggers, the revisionists point out, displayed a genuine concern for the future of the South, and some scalawags worked diligently to improve conditions in their states. Southern blacks rarely used their political power vindictively. Fully comprehending that social equality between the races was an anathema to southern whites, black leaders instead pressed for land reform, greater educational opportunities, and full participation in the political process. By the end of Reconstruction, some southern states had better schools and judicial systems, enjoyed more effective local and state governments, and had a greater degree of democracy in their institutions than at any time previously. Thus Reconstruction was far from a dismal failure. Neither was it an unqualified success, however, for few southern blacks received their much anticipated "forty acres and a mule," and African-Americans' resulting economic dependency on southern whites made emancipation something less than full freedom.

To the Radical Republicans who dominated the United States Congress in the 1860s, the federal government had little choice but to treat the South as a conquered province. The first document in this section is the Fourteenth Amendment, which guarantees citizenship to all persons born or naturalized in the United States. Fully aware that the South would not accede voluntarily to any legislation designed to benefit the newly freed blacks,

Congress demanded that the former Confederate states ratify the amendment before being allowed back into the Union. It became law in July 1868.

The future welfare of the black population centered on its ability to achieve a measure of economic independence from whites, who controlled the resources of the South. As the second document, a plea to the federal government by the freedmen of Hampton, Virginia, makes clear, however, the chances of African-Americans' becoming landowners were deteriorating as early as the autumn of 1865. As President Andrew Johnson and the Radical Republicans quarreled over Reconstruction policy in Washington, southern state governments sought to find an effective substitute for slavery. Black codes regulated the conduct and restricted the movements of freedmen. Labor contracts, like the one reprinted as the third document, indicate that the plantation system continued to function chiefly as an instrument for supervision and control of the black race. Not all employers honored their part of the contract, as is shown by the fourth selection, a complaint by a black hotel worker to the superintendent of the Freedmen's Bureau in Louisville, Kentucky.

Unable to influence economic change in the South, blacks leapt to their own defense when their newly won political privileges were threatened. The fifth document is a petition by black citizens of Savannah, Georgia, to their congressional representative, protesting the abuses of the political process in Georgia. The amount of political power enjoyed by blacks varied from state to state. The South Carolina Constitution of 1868, written by a predominantly black convention, was by far the most democratic in the history of that troubled state. Unwilling to accept that blacks could make responsible decisions, white opponents launched fierce condemnations of both the constitutional convention and the legislature that governed South Carolina until its redemption by the Democrats in 1877. James Pike, a northern newspaper correspondent who visited the state in 1873, published his revelations of administrative ineptitude the following year, part of which is reprinted as the sixth document.

In their attempts to end the Radical Republican regimes and restore the Democratic party to power, white southerners resorted to intimidation and violence to influence elections in the South. The Ku Klux Klan, formed in 1866 by a group of Tennessee war veterans, was the most notorious of the many white supremacist groups that sprang up in the South during Reconstruction. The first part of the seventh document identifies the Klan as an extralegal organization dedicated to the preservation of law and order. Testimony submitted in the trials of its members four years later reveals a much more sinister side to Klan activities. By the mid-1870s, the beleaguered Radical Republican coalition of carpetbaggers, scalawags, and blacks was in retreat. Although the Klan had been forced out of existence by the military power of the federal government, organized violence continued, especially in Mississippi, where the Democratic party resolved at all costs to win the next election and capture the state government. The eighth selection, a letter from Governor Adelbert Ames, a carpetbagger from New England, to his wife, graphically illustrates the conflict.

The presidential election of 1876 signaled Reconstruction's end. In one of the closest electoral contests in American history, and after much conniving between the parties, the Republican party retained the presidency, while the Democratic party secured control of the three southern states still under Republican rule. Despite all the evidence to the contrary, President Rutherford B. Hayes, in his inaugural address, the final document, predicts a harmonious future for race relations in the South. Southern Republicans and the few remaining Radicals in the United States Congress knew differently. These Republicans were fully aware that Democratic party control of the South would mean a return to subservient status for African-Americans. They urged Hayes to use the federal government's power to monitor the South and condemned what they correctly regarded as a "hands off" southern policy.

Questions for Analysis

1. Should the federal government have been more lenient with the conquered South? Would southerners have cooperated with a milder Reconstruction policy?

2. What did emancipation mean to the freedmen? How did they view their role in postbellum southern society?

3. Did the federal government err in failing to redistribute land in the South? In a country that holds the preservation of private property sacred, would such a policy have been feasible?

4. How did the Radical Republican coalition change the political and social institutions of the South?

5. How important was organized violence in the overthrow of Republican state governments? Did the use of violence to influence elections set a precedent for future political behavior in the South?

6. Why did the federal government abandon its Reconstruction policies?

1. *The Fourteenth Amendment, 1868*

Sec. 1. All persons born or naturalized in the United States, and subject to the jurisdiction thereof, are citizens of the United States and of the State wherein they reside. No State shall make or enforce any law which shall abridge the privileges or immunities of citizens of the United States; nor shall any State deprive any person of life, liberty, or property, without due process of law; nor deny to any person within its jurisdiction the equal protection of the laws.

Sec. 2. Representatives shall be apportioned among the several States according to their respective numbers, counting the whole number of persons in each State, excluding Indians not taxed. But when the right to vote at any election for the choice of electors for President and Vice President of the United States, Representatives in Congress, the Executive and Judicial officers of a State, or the members of the Legislature thereof, is denied to any of the male inhabitants of such State, being twenty-one years of age, and citizens of the United States, or in any way abridged, except for participation in rebellion, or other crime, the basis of representation therein shall be reduced in the proportion which the number of such male citizens shall bear to the whole number of male citizens twenty-one years of age in such State.

Sec. 3. No person shall be a Senator or Representative in Congress, or elector of President and Vice President, or hold any office, civil or military, under the United States, or under any State, who, having previously taken an oath, as a member of Congress, or as an officer of the United States, or as a member of any State legislature, or as an executive or judicial officer of any State, to support the Constitution of the United States, shall have engaged in insurrection or rebellion against the same, or given aid or comfort to the enemies thereof. But Congress may by a vote of two-thirds of each House, remove such disability.

Sec. 4. The validity of the public debt of the United States, authorized by law, including debts incurred for payment of pensions and bounties for services in suppressing insurrection or rebellion, shall not be questioned. But neither the United States nor any State shall assume or pay any debt or obligation incurred in aid of insurrection or rebellion against the United States, or any claim for the loss or emancipation of any slave; but all such debts, obligations and claims shall be held illegal and void.

Sec. 5. The Congress shall have power to enforce, by appropriate legislation, the provisions of this article.

2. *The Freedmen's Plea for Land, 1865*

After the burning of Hampton by the rebel inhabitants, the abandoned and confiscated lots within the town and the [Sinclair] farm, containing 600 acres of land, and the farm of Shields, containing about 400 acres, was set apart by the United States Government for the use of the colored refugees. There are now 800 families upon said lands, each with a humble tenement erected by themselves. The value of the property owned by them amounts to $51,006. We have five churches built by ourselves since the Rebellion and pay our pastors $1,050 per annum. We have a store of our own in Hampton, filled with groceries and goods of all sorts, kept and managed by an Association of our own selection, for the benefit of the colored people.

Our settlement on Sinclair's farm is laid out in streets, with order and regularity. The farms of Sinclair and Shields will this year yield better, richer and heavier crops than was ever known under the system of Slavery. More than thirty-seven of us were raised upon these farms and we know whereof we speak, that *free black labor* is altogether more remunerative than slave labor.

We are anxious and willing, and believe we are able, to build up a city upon our lands, as orderly, as prosperous, as religious, as patriotic, and as intelligent as could be done by any other people, provided we can secure the fee to the lands.

In the midst of our happiness and prosperity, the former owners of the lands we occupy have just returned and are seeking to take from us our happy homes. Our attorney and counsel have offered to pay these men liberal sums of money to obtain the land without controversy; but we are told by Sinclair and Shields that they will have all that they before possessed. Therefore

Resolved, That we will not leave our happy homes unless compelled to do so by legal authority; that we will purchase or lease, at fair prices, of the United States Government its interests in these lots; that we will oppose, in all legal ways, the opening of the decrees of confiscation.

Resolved, That we have confidence and faith that the United States Government will be just and generous with us in the disposition of these lands and that we hail *the Freedmen's Bureau* as a wise and beneficent institution for the protection of our rights and interests and that we invoke its aid and cooperation in the social and political demonstration we are making; and we promise that nothing shall be wanting on our part to make us worthy of the great boon of *freedom*.

Resolved, That we respectfully request all papers in the United States friendly to our interest to publish these proceedings.

3. *South Carolina Freedmen Sign a Labor Contract, 1865*

**State of South Carolina
Darlington District**

Articles of Agreement

This Agreement entered into between Mrs. Adele Allston Exect of the one part, and the Freedmen and Women of The Upper Quarters plantation of the other part *Witnesseth*:

That the latter agree, for the remainder of the present year, to reside upon and devote their labor to the cultivation of the Plantation of the former. And they further agree, that they will in all respects, conform to such reasonable and necessary plantation rules and regulations as Mrs. Allston's Agent may prescribe; that they will not keep any gun, pistol, or other offensive weapon, or leave the plantation without permission from their employer; that in all things connected with their duties as laborers on said plantation, they will yield prompt obedience to all orders from Mrs. Allston or his [*sic*] agent; that they will be orderly and quiet in their conduct, avoiding drunkenness and other gross vices; that they will not misuse any of the Plantation Tools, or Agricultural Implements, or any Animals entrusted to their care, or any Boats, Flats, Carts or Wagons; that they give up at the expiration of this Contract, all Tools &c., belonging to the Plantation, and in case any property, of any description belonging to the Plantation shall be willfully or through negligence destroyed or injured, the value of the Articles so destroyed, shall be deducted from the portion of the Crops which the person or persons, so offending, shall be entitled to receive under this Contract.

Any deviations from the condition of the foregoing Contract may, upon sufficient proof, be punished with dismissal from the Plantation, or in such other manner as may be determined by the Provost Court; and the person or persons so dismissed, shall forfeit the whole, or a part of his, her or their portion of the crop, as the Court may decide.

In consideration of the foregoing Services duly performed, Mrs. Allston agrees, after deducting Seventy five bushels of Corn for each work Animal, exclusively used in cultivating the Crops for the present year; to turn over to the said Freedmen and Women, one half of the remaining Corn, Peas, Potatoes, made this season. He [sic] further agrees to furnish the usual rations until the Contract is performed.

All Cotton Seed Produced on the Plantation is to be reserved for the use of the Plantation. The Freedmen, Women and Children are to be treated in a manner consistent with their freedom. Necessary medical attention will be furnished as heretofore.

Any deviation from the conditions of this Contract upon the part of the said Mrs. Allston or her Agent or Agents shall be punished in such manner as may be determined by a Provost Court, or a Military Commission. This agreement to continue till the first day of January 1866.

Witness our hand at The Upper Quarters this 28th day of July 1865.

Signed and delivered in the presence of
W. H. Evans
A. Vander Horst

Adele Allston *Executrix*
by her Agent
Ben Allston

His
1. George X Gunn
mark

His
2. Billy X Grice
mark

his
3. William X [illegible]
mark

her
4. Sybanna X Keith
mark

her
5. Sally X Brown
mark

his
6. Murphy X Keith
mark

4. An Ex-Slave Is Refused His Wages, 1865

Louisville Ky   Aug 10th 1865

Colonel I have the honor to make the following statement. I was formerly the slave of Mr Morris of Louisville Ky. On the 5th day of July 1865 I contracted with the Steward of the National Hotel, to work for Mr Kean the proprietor of said hotel for the sum of Twenty Dollars per month— that I commenced working for said Mr Kean in accordance with said contract, On the 5th day of July 1865 and continued so to work without loss of time until the 5th day of August 1865—that on the 5th day of August 1865 I demanded of said Mr Kean the amount of my wages under the aforesaid contract—that the said Mr Kean refused to pay me and still refuses to pay me the amount of my wages giving as a reason that I cannot show my Freedom Papers, nor the written consent of my former master to entitle me to draw my wages. My former master Mr Morris told me repeatedly that he wanted me to leave his place—that if I did not he would drive me off and he has never attempted to take me back home since I left him. I have the honor to be Very Respectfully Your Most Obt Servt

his
Willis X Stillman
mark

5. Savannah Blacks Defend Their Political Rights, 1868

Savannah, December 28, 1868

Dear Sir: At a mass meeting, of this date, of the republican party, when the entire colored vote of said party in the city of Savannah was represented, called to give expression of opinion in regard to the present status of political affairs in the State of Georgia, and at the same time urge upon the Congress of the United States the absolute necessity of further legislation, in order to secure to every citizen of this State the rights of citizens of the United States, as contemplated under the reconstruction acts of Congress, it was unanimously

Resolved, 1st. That the action of the Georgia legislature, in expelling the duly elected colored representatives from that body, was an unjust deprivation of our most sacred rights as citizens, a high-handed outrage on a large political element in this community, in direct contravention of the voice of a majority of the legal voters of the State as expressed at the ballot-box, and contrary to the plain letter and spirit of the reconstruction acts, under which the constitution of Georgia was framed, adopted, and presented for congressional acceptance.

2d. That we cannot hope to have justice done us, to enjoy in security the rights of person or property, freedom of political opinion or thought, or the free exercise of the franchise extended us, as citizens of this State or of the United States, while such fraudulent and unrepublican proceedings of the legislature are permitted to remain valid and of binding force. Further, that the persecutions we have suffered, the barbarities committed in the name of the law, and in defiance of all law, by those in power by virtue of the action of said legislature, satisfies us that unless the power of the federal government is brought to bear in our favor our last estate must prove worse than our first, our freedom only another and worse form of slavery.

[The original document does not show a third resolution.]

4th. That we are opposed to the admission of the so-called senators elect of this State, Messrs. Hill and Miller, on the ground that they were elected by the vote of those who were in fact ineligible as members in the legislature choosing said senators, and that the legislature itself did afterwards declare a large number of its members, who were allowed to participate in said election, ineligible, and expel them therefrom, thereby with strange inconsistency and utter disregard of all principle vitiate and nullify its own action in the premises.

5th. That we uphold Governor R. B. Bullock in his efforts to correct the abuses hereinbefore mentioned, endorse his plans and suggestions to Congress for the accomplishment of this most desirable end, and make this our humble prayer to Congress to speedily adopt such measures for our relief as in its wise judgment the necessities of the case may require.

6th. That these resolutions be forwarded to our representative in Congress, Hon. J. W. Clift, and through him presented to that body.

> Moses H. Bentley,
> *Chairman of the Committee*
>
> Richard W. White
> Frederick Allen
> Per R. W. White

Hon. J. W. Clift,
Washington, D.C.

6. *A Northern Journalist Condemns South Carolina's "Black Parliament," 1873*

In the Legislature there is a tendency to retrenchment and reform in such points as the expenditures in the departments, and on appropriations generally; the members had to promise this in the late canvass. But the economies are rather nominal than real, as the gross appropriations this year exceed those of the previous year.

It has been made a question whether the property-holders of the State would not save money by giving every sable representative a house and lands, that he might personally taste the sweets of taxation. This would seem to be the only way of bringing it home to him. If it were not that the term of service were so short, the proposition would be worth considering.

It is not harsh to criticise members of this black Parliament in the way we do, for we only say of them what they say of themselves. They are in the habit of charging one another with ignorance and venality and corruption without stint, and it is not deemed any offense. The thieves were obliged, as we have said, to make a sort of compact with their supporters at the last election that they would stop robbing the State.

But like the drunkard who promised to quit drinking, and still drank to intoxication by spells, and defended himself by saying he "always excepted his sprees," so these legislative robbers claim the right to extort pay from everybody who is to profit by their legislation, taking the ground that it is no violation of their pledges, when a senatorial election comes round, to sell their votes to the highest bidder. This is not corruption in their sense of the term. It is only to turn an honest penny.

In regard to all such shameless acts as this, and the refusing of charters to responsible persons to make needed improvements in the State because the members are not bribed, the respectable white men of the Legislature say they should blush with shame if they felt that the real character of the State was represented in the body. But as it is, they can only plead that scoundrelism is dominant, and that all legislation is in the hands of unscrupulous knaves who belong in the penitentiary. The facts fill every decent citizen with mortification, but, outside the gang who hold control, every one claims exemption from all responsibility for the degradation into which the State has fallen.

The only drawback to the country, the only hinderance to an immediate accession of population from the best agricultural classes abroad, is this scoundrel government, which has so long rioted, and is yet rioting, in its robberies. There seems to be no way of even checking their intolerable practices but to flash the flambeaux of an outside execration in their faces. They defy the indignation of the people they have ruined, but they are not proof against the indignation of the country at large. It becomes a public duty

"To lash the rascals naked through the land,"

and aid this prostrate State to recover possession of itself, retrieve its standing before the world, and drag to condign punishment the culprits who have so long rioted in its spoils, and who so persistently prey upon its remains.

7. *The Life and Trials of the Ku Klux Klan, 1868, 1872*

A Chivalrous Order, 1868

Appellation

This Organization shall be styled and denominated, the Order of the ———.

Creed

We, the Order of the ———, reverentially acknowledge the majesty and supremacy of the Divine Being, and recognize the goodness and providence of the same. And we recognize our relation to the United States Government, the supremacy of the Constitution, the Constitutional Laws thereof, and the Union of States thereunder.

Character and Objects of the Order

This is an institution of Chivalry, Humanity, Mercy, and Patriotism; embodying in its genius and its principles all that is chivalric in conduct, noble in sentiment, generous in manhood, and patriotic in purpose; its peculiar objects being

First: To protect the weak, the innocent, and the defenseless, from the indignities, wrongs, and outrages of the lawless, the violent, and the brutal; to relieve the injured and oppressed; to succor the suffering and unfortunate, and especially the widows and orphans of Confederate soldiers.

Second: To protect and defend the Constitution of the United States, and all laws passed in conformity thereto, and to protect the States and the people thereof from all invasion from any source whatever.

Third: To aid and assist in the execution of all constitutional laws, and to protect the people from unlawful seizure, and from trial except by their peers in conformity to the laws of the land.

Titles

Section 1. The officers of this Order shall consist of a Grand Wizard of the Empire, and his ten Genii; a Grand Dragon of the Realm, and his eight Hydras; a Grand Titan of the Dominion, and his six Furies; a Grand Giant of the Province, and his four Goblins; a Grand Cyclops of the Den, and his two Night-hawks; a Grand Magi, a Grand Monk, a Grand Scribe, a Grand Exchequer, a Grand Turk, and a Grand Sentinel.

Sec. 2. The body politic of this Order shall be known and designated as "Ghouls."

Territory and its Divisions

Section 1. The territory embraced within the jurisdiction of this Order shall be coterminous with the States of Maryland, Virginia, North Carolina, South Carolina, Georgia, Florida, Alabama, Mississippi, Louisiana, Texas, Arkansas, Missouri, Kentucky, and Tennessee; all combined constituting the Empire.

Sec. 2. The Empire shall be divided into four departments, the first to be styled the Realm, and coterminous with the boundaries of the several States; the second to be styled the Dominion and to be coterminous with such counties as the Grand Dragons of the several Realms may assign to the charge of the Grand Titan. The third to be styled the Province, and to be coterminous with the several counties; *provided*, the

Grand Titan may, when he deems it necessary, assign two Grand Giants to one Province, prescribing, at the same time, the jurisdiction of each. The fourth department to be styled the Den, and shall embrace such part of a Province as the Grand Giant shall assign to the charge of a Grand Cyclops.

[Questions to Be Asked Candidates]

1st. Have you ever been rejected, upon application for membership in the ——, or have you ever been expelled from the same?

2d. Are you now, or have you ever been, a member of the Radical Republican party, or either of the organizations known as the "Loyal League" and the "Grand Army of the Republic?"

3d. Are you opposed to the principles and policy of the Radical party, and to the Loyal League, and the Grand Army of the Republic, so far as you are informed of the character and purposes of those organizations?

4th. Did you belong to the Federal army during the late war and fight against the South during the existence of the same?

5th. Are you opposed to negro equality, both social and political?

6th. Are you in favor of a white man's government in this country?

7th. Are you in favor of Constitutional liberty, and a Government of equitable laws instead of a Government of violence and oppression?

8th. Are you in favor of maintaining the Constitutional rights of the South?

9th. Are you in favor of the re-enfranchisement and emancipation of the white men of the South, and the restitution of the Southern people to all their rights, alike proprietary, civil, and political?

10th. Do you believe in the inalienable right of self-preservation of the people against the exercise of arbitrary and unlicensed power?

The Klan Exposed, 1872

King Edwards

I was twenty-one years old last April; I joined the Horse Creek Klan last March; I joined it through ignorance, I reckon; I can't read or write much; Alfred Harris initiated me; I was on six or seven raids, I guess; we first went on Dick Roberts; Alfred Harris, Jervey Gidney, Thomas Tait, Christenburg Tait, and Jonas Vassey were on the raid; Dick Roberts was a white man; he had been stealing things from another man, and we talked to him; the next raid was on John Harris; he was a black man, and we whipped him; it was 9 or 10 o'clock at night, I reckon; we pulled him out of bed and whipped him a little with hickories; some of them said they gave him about sixty licks altogether; we whipped another black boy whose name was Mage Cash, and we whipped another named Humphries; he was whipped for whipping his young master; we didn't talk to him about politics; we next went on Martha Jolly, but we didn't do anything with her; we next hunted for Jack Bark, but we didn't find him; Alfred Harris led the first raid, and Jonas Vassey led the other; we made a raid on John Harris, and Billy Scruggs led us that night.

Six months' imprisonment.

Christenberry Tait

I belong to the Horse Creek Klan; I am going on for eighteen years, old, I guess; I cannot read or write; I joined the Klan last January; I joined it because they shouldn't raid on me; they told me I had better join for fear of being killed; I have been on three or four raids; the first was on Richard Roberts; we raided on him because there had been talk about his selling whisky on Sabbath day; he lived near the church, and had a bar room, and we ordered him to stop selling whisky on meeting day; then we went to old Ride's; he was a boy that wouldn't mind his mother, and we told him he had better mind her, and some of them struck him about ten licks with a peach tree switch; we went into another black man's house, but we didn't do anything to him; I do not know but that I have heard that Banks Lyle was Chief of the Klan; there were some respectable people in our neighborhood; there is Mr. Watkins and Mr. Collins, William McKinney and Miller McKinney; they are respectable men, and well off; I joined the organization because they told me I would not be safe if I did not; William McKinney was taken out just before this thing was broken up; and he would have been whipped if he had not joined.

Three months' imprisonment.

8. A Carpetbagger Describes a Riot, 1875

Jackson, Miss., September 5, 1875

Dear Blanche: I had finished my letter to you yesterday and was looking for George to mail it when Capt. Fisher came to me out of breath and out of heart to tell me of a riot which had just taken place at Clinton (a village ten miles west of here) and from which he had just escaped, with his wife. He was speaking when the riot began. It was a premeditated riot on the part of the Democracy which resulted in the death of some four white men and about the same number of Negroes and quite a large number of Negroes wounded. There were present at a Republican barbecue about fifteen hundred colored people, men, women and children. Seeking the opportunity white men, fully prepared, fired into this crowd. Two women were reported killed, also two children. As the firing continued, the women ran away with the men in many instances, leaving their children on the ground. Today there are some forty carriages, wagons and carts which were abandoned by the colored people in their flight. Last night, this morning and today squads of white men are scouring the county killing Negroes. Three were killed at Clinton this morning—one of whom was an old man, nearly one hundred years old—defenseless and helpless. Yesterday the Negroes, though unarmed and unprepared, fought bravely and killed four of the ringleaders, but had to flee before the muskets which were at once brought onto the field of battle. This is but in keeping with the programme of the Democracy at this time. They know we have a majority of some thirty thousand and to overcome it they are resorting to intimidation and murder. It is cold-blooded murder on the part of the "white liners"—but there are other cases exactly like this in other parts of the state. You ask what are we to do. That is a question I find it difficult to answer. I told you a day or two ago that the whole party has been opposed to organizing the militia and furthermore I have been unable to find anyone who was willing to take militia appointments.

The Mansion has been crowded all day long with Republican friends and Negroes from the field of battle. I have run off to the northwest chamber for my daily chat with you, leaving a crowd in the other rooms. There has also been a crowd at the front gate all day long. The town is full of Negroes from the country who come to escape harm. The whites here are afraid of the Negroes who have come in. A committee of white men have just waited on me and offer to keep the peace so far as may be in their power. The Sheriff has selected a number of them to act as a posse to go out into the country and arrest those who are murdering Negroes. This last step has caused a subsidence of the excitement felt by the whites as well as blacks.

I anticipate no further trouble here at this time. The "white liners" have gained their point—they have, by killing and wounding, so intimidated the poor Negroes that they can in all human probability prevail over them at the election. I shall at once try to get troops from the general government. Of course it will be a difficult thing to do.

I send a world of love.

Adelbert

9. President Rutherford B. Hayes Abandons the South, 1877

The permanent pacification of the country upon such principles and by such measures as will secure the complete protection of all its citizens in the free enjoyment of all their constitutional rights is now the one subject in our public affairs which all thoughtful and patriotic citizens regard as of supreme importance.

Many of the calamitous effects of the tremendous revolution which has passed over the Southern States still remain. The immeasurable benefits which will surely follow, sooner or later, the hearty and generous acceptance of the legitimate results of that revolution have not yet been realized. Difficult and embarrassing questions meet us at the threshold of this subject. The people of those States are still impoverished, and the inestimable blessing of wise, honest, and peaceful local self-government is not fully enjoyed. Whatever difference of opinion may exist as to the cause of this condition of things, the fact is clear that in the progress of events the time has come when such government is the imperative necessity required by all the varied interests, public and private, of those States. But it must not be forgotten that only a local government which recognizes and maintains inviolate the rights of all is a true self-government.

With respect to the two distinct races whose peculiar relations to each other have brought upon us the deplorable complications and perplexities which exist in those States, it must be a government which guards the interests of both races carefully and equally. It must be a government which submits loyally and heartily to the Constitution and the laws—the laws of the nation and the laws of the States themselves—accepting and obeying faithfully the whole Constitution as it is.

Resting upon this sure and substantial foundation, the superstructure of beneficent local governments can be built up, and not otherwise. In furtherance of such obedience to the letter and the spirit of the Constitution, and in behalf of all that its attainment implies, all so-called

party interests lose their apparent importance, and party lines may well be permitted to fade into insignificance. The question we have to consider for the immediate welfare of those States of the Union is the question of government or no government; of social order and all the peaceful industries and the happiness that belong to it, or a return to barbarism. It is a question in which every citizen of the nation is deeply interested, and with respect to which we ought not to be, in a partisan sense, either Republicans or Democrats, but fellow-citizens and fellow-men, to whom the interests of a common country and a common humanity are dear.

The sweeping revolution of the entire labor system of a large portion of our country and the advance of 4,000,000 people from a condition of servitude to that of citizenship, upon an equal footing with their former masters, could not occur without presenting problems of the gravest moment, to be dealt with by the emancipated race, by their former masters, and by the General Government, the author of the act of emancipation. That it was a wise, just, and providential act, fraught with good for all concerned, is now generally conceded throughout the country. That a moral obligation rests upon the National Government to employ its constitutional power and influence to establish the rights of the people it has emancipated, and to protect them in the enjoyment of those rights when they are infringed or assailed, is also generally admitted.

The evils which afflict the Southern States can only be removed or remedied by the united and harmonious efforts of both races, actuated by motives of mutual sympathy and regard; and while in duty bound and fully determined to protect the rights of all by every constitutional means at the disposal of my Administration, I am sincerely anxious to use every legitimate influence in favor of honest and efficient local *self*-government as the true resource of those States for the promotion of the contentment and prosperity of their citizens. In the effort I shall make to accomplish this purpose I ask the cordial cooperation of all who cherish an interest in the welfare of the country, trusting that party ties and the prejudice of race will be freely surrendered in behalf of the great purpose to be accomplished. In the important work of restoring the South it is not the political situation alone that merits attention. The material development of that section of the country has been arrested by the social and political revolution through which it has passed, and now needs and deserves the considerate care of the National Government within the just limits prescribed by the Constitution and wise public economy.

But at the basis of all prosperity, for that as well as for every other part of the country, lies the improvement of the intellectual and moral condition of the people. Universal suffrage should rest upon universal education. To this end, liberal and permanent provision should be made for the support of free schools by the State governments, and, if need be, supplemented by legitimate aid from national authority.

Let me assure my countrymen of the Southern States that it is my earnest desire to regard and promote their truest interests—the interests of the white and of the colored people both and equally—and to put forth my best efforts in behalf of a civil policy which will forever wipe out in our political affairs the color line and the distinction between North and South, to the end that we may have not merely a united North or a united South, but a united country.

References

1. The Fourteenth Amendment, 1868
   "The Fourteenth Amendment," in Albert P. Blaustein and Robert L. Zangrando, *Civil Rights and the American Negro: A Documentary History* (New York: Trident Press, 1968), pp. 226–227.

2. The Freedmen's Plea for Land, 1865
   The National Freedman, September 15, 1865.

3. South Carolina Freedmen Sign a Labor Contract, 1865
   "A Freedmen's Contract, 1865," in J. H. Easterby, ed., *The South Carolina Rice Plantation as Revealed in the Papers of Robert F. W. Allston* (Chicago: University of Chicago Press, 1945), pp. 354–355.

4. An Ex-Slave Is Refused His Wages, 1865
   "Kentucky Former Slave to the Freedmen's Bureau Superintendent of the Subdistrict of Louisville, Kentucky," in Ira Berlin et al., eds., *Freedom: A Documentary History of Emancipation 1861–1867*, Volume I, *The Destruction of Slavery* (Cambridge: Cambridge University Press, 1985), pp. 636–637.

5. Savannah Blacks Defend Their Political Rights, 1868
   "Resolutions Passed by a Mass Meeting of Colored Citizens of Savannah, Georgia," in *The Condition of Affairs in Georgia: Statement of Hon. Nelson Tift to the Reconstruction Committee of the House of Representatives, February 18, 1869* (Freeport, New York: Books for Libraries Press, 1971), pp. 89–90.

6. A Northern Journalist Condemns South Carolina's "Black Parliament," 1873
   James S. Pike, *The Prostrate State: South Carolina Under Negro Government* (New York: D. Appleton & Co., 1874), pp. 110–113.

7. The Life and Trials of the Ku Klux Klan, 1868, 1872
   A Chivalrous Order, 1868: "Organization and Principles of the Ku Klux Klan," in Walter Fleming, *Documentary History of Reconstruction*, Volume 2 (Cleveland, Ohio: Arthur H. Clark Company, 1906), pp. 347–348. The Klan Exposed, 1872: "Testimony of King Edwards and Christenberry Tait," in *U.S. Circuit Court Ku Klux Trials at Columbia, S.C.*, 1872, pp. 772–773.

8. A Carpetbagger Describes a Riot, 1875
   Adelbert Ames to Blanche Ames, September 5, 1875, in Blanche Ames Ames, *Adelbert Ames 1835–1933: General, Senator, Governor* (New York: Argosy-Antiquarian Ltd., 1964), pp. 419–420.

9. President Rutherford B. Hayes Abandons the South, 1877
   "Inaugural Address of Rutherford B. Hayes, March 5, 1877," in James D. Richardson, *A Compilation of the Messages and Papers of the Presidents, 1789–1897*, Volume VII (Washington: Government Printing Office, 1898), pp. 442–444.

Further Reading

Richard H. Abbott, *The Republican Party and the South, 1855–1877* (1986)

Dan T. Carter, *When the War Was Over: Self-Reconstruction in the South, 1865–1877* (1985)

Richard N. Current, *Those Terrible Carpetbaggers* (1988)

Eric Foner, *Reconstruction: America's Unfinished Revolution, 1863–1877* (1988)

William C. Harris, *The Day of the Carpetbagger: Republican Reconstruction in Mississippi* (1979)

Jacqueline Jones, *Soldiers of Light and Love: Northern Teachers and Georgia Blacks, 1865–1873* (1980)

Peter Kolchin, *First Freedom: The Responses of Alabama's Blacks to Emancipation and Reconstruction* (1972)

Leon Litwack, *Been in the Storm So Long: The Aftermath of Slavery* (1979)

Edward Magdol, *A Right to the Land: Essays on the Freedmen's Community* (1977)

Otto Olsen, ed., *Reconstruction and Redemption in the South* (1980)

Claude F. Oubre, *Forty Acres and a Mule: The Freedmen's Bureau and Black Land Ownership* (1978)

James Roark, *Masters Without Slaves: Southern Planters in the Civil War and Reconstruction* (1978)

Willie Lee Rose, *Rehearsal for Reconstruction: The Port Royal Experiment* (1964)

Kenneth M. Stampp, *The Era of Reconstruction, 1865–1877* (1965)

Allen W. Trelease, *White Terror: The Ku Klux Klan Conspiracy and Southern Reconstruction* (1971)

Ted Tunnell, *Crucible of Reconstruction: War, Radicalism, and Race in Louisiana, 1862–1877* (1984)

William P. Vaughan, *Schools for All: The Blacks and Public Education in the South, 1865–1877* (1974)

Jonathan M. Wiener, *Social Origins of the New South: Alabama, 1860–1885* (1978)

Joel Williamson, *The Negro in South Carolina During Reconstruction, 1861–1877* (1965)

Document Set 11

The New South

The individuals who promoted the cause of economic progress through industrialization challenged southerners to question their commitment to a cherished agrarian heritage. As the defeat of the Confederacy clearly affirmed, a rural, agricultural society was also a vulnerable society. Beginning in the 1870s, advocates of the New South creed argued that the region would remain economically backward unless it unleashed its full potential for growth. The resultant postwar transformation in the South's economic life was considerable. Drawing on the region's abundant natural resources and from its deep pool of cheap labor, towns and cities quickly sprang up to accommodate iron- and steel-producing factories. The southern countryside underwent a physical transformation, with cotton mill villages dotting the piedmont landscape. Railroad construction spurred further industrialization and urbanization. In James Buchanan Duke, the founder of the American Tobacco Company, the South could boast a rags-to-riches story to rival any of the achievements of the great captains of industry in the North.

External and internal factors, however, limited the extent to which the South could change. Bereft of banking and credit facilities, southern industry relied heavily on massive infusions of northern capital, creating an economic dependency that reduced the South to a neocolonial status, enriching northern investors yet failing to pull southerners out of poverty. By the end of the nineteenth century, per capita income in the South was less than half that of the North. Not only were wages and conditions in the factories deplorable, but agriculture offered no relief from poverty as a declining world demand for cotton exposed the fallacy of the belief that cotton would provide the South's salvation. The development of a crop-lien system had promoted a reliance on the single crop of cotton rather than on the diversification of agricultural production so necessary to help the embattled farmers, many of whom became debt-ridden sharecroppers and tenant farmers. Psychologically, southerners were not prepared for life in an industrialized, mechanized society. Their hearts and their minds were rooted firmly in an idyllic past. Although largely fictitious, this past heritage nevertheless inured them against the depressing reality of the present and the uncertainty of the future.

The champion of the New South creed was Henry Grady, the editor of the *Atlanta Constitution*. Even as he promoted his vision of progress through speeches and newspaper articles, Grady took pains to avoid alienating southerners when it came to their revered past. In the first document, selections from his book *The New South*, Grady stresses the great continuity of the southern tradition and minimizes northerners' role in southern economic development. Urbanization, slow by contemporary northern standards, but rapid compared to the South's own past, provided visible evidence of southern progress. Grady described the emerging urban centers as "magic cities," symbols of the South's unlimited potential for economic growth. James Kitson, a member of the British Iron and Steel Institute, was part of an international team of entrepreneurs and industrialists who visited the South in 1890. The second document, an excerpt from a magazine article, notes the transition of Birmingham, Alabama, from a small town to a thriving and populous center of the iron industry. Walter Hines Page, a native of North Carolina and a publisher in the North, tempered his support of industrialization with some harshly realistic observations on southern society. As the third selection indicates, Page believed that the attitudes of the southern people retarded the section's development. The result was a society in limbo, trapped in its own mythic past and unable to commit itself to a new and uncertain future. Fears that the New South would diminish the imagined glories of the Old prompted the poet Paul Hamilton Hayne to write a sonnet on the subject, reprinted as the fourth document.

Fond reminiscences of a tranquil age played little part in the lives of the working classes, who labored for long hours and low wages in southern mills and factories. A spirit of progressivism, a reform movement associated largely with northern cities, found some fertile soil in an otherwise ultraconservative South. Edgar Gardner Murphy, an Episcopalian minister, from whose writings the

fifth selection is taken, provides valuable information on working conditions in the South. The disastrously low price of cotton in the 1890s forced hundreds of thousands of farmers from the land and into southern factory towns and northern cities. The exodus continued in the twentieth century with the arrival of the boll weevil, an insect that devastated the cotton plant. In the final document, Nate Shaw, a black Alabama sharecropper, shows both a hatred and a healthy respect for the tiny creature that could inflict so much damage. Ironically, the boll weevil was something of a boon to southern farmers because it finally forced them to diversify their crop production.

Questions for Analysis

1. What was new about the New South? Was the southern experience in the late nineteenth century marked by continuity or change?

2. To what degree did northern control of southern business contribute to the South's economic backwardness?

3. How did race relations between blacks and whites affect the course of the New South?

4. How did sharecropping and farm tenancy differ from slavery? Were black agricultural laborers better or worse off in the New South than in the Old?

5. How much did the southern desire to return to a simple agrarian past inhibit the desire for economic development?

6. Did the Progressive movement enjoy any success in the New South?

1. Henry Grady Articulates His New South Vision, 1890

. . . The new South is simply the old South under new conditions. It rejoices that slavery has been swept forever from American soil. It rejoices that the American Union was saved from the storm of war. Not one in a thousand of its sons would reverse if they could the results of the war into which they threw without stint their lives and their property. They are thankful that the issues at stake in the great civil war were adjudged by higher wisdom than their own. And the Republic has no better citizens in peace and would have no braver soldiers in war than the

men who twenty-five years ago wore the gray and followed the Confederate flag.

The courage in which the new South makes these declarations, and the sincerity in which it maintains them, are a heritage of the old South. If it involved the surrender to perfect love and reverence for that civilization that produced Washington and Jefferson, and Clay and Calhoun—or for the memory of those who fought with Lee and Jackson and Johnston—the New South would be dumb and motionless. It is from the foot of the monuments, illumined with the names of her dead, that she makes her fullest renunciation of the past and her best pledge for the future. Always she will honor above all men the men who sleep beneath those towering shafts. The sign of nobility in her families for generations to come will be the gray cap or the stained coat, on which, in the ebb of losing battle, God laid the sword of His imperishable knighthood. Those, who ask her to turn away from the memory of her heroes who died hopeless but unfearing in defeat, ask her to sacrifice that without which no people can be steadfast or great.

. . . The South has been re-built by the Southern people. I shall often use Atlanta as an example, for it is a typical Southern city. None is more generally thought to be so largely the result of Northern capital and enterprise. And yet the census of 1880 shows that of 47,588 people in Fulton county (of which Atlanta is the capital), less than 1,000 were of Northern birth. This will astound those Northern men who, amazed at Atlanta's simple and comprehensive growth, have declared the South never had built and never could build such a city, but that it was a "Yankee city" in the South. Let me particularize. The census shows that of the 47,588 people in Fulton county, 38,648 were born in Georgia. Of the rest, 2,102 were born in South Carolina, 752 in North Carolina, 1,464 in Alabama, 1,200 in Virginia, 795 in Tennessee, and 472 in other Southern States. This gives us 44,951 Southern born. To this add 1,391 foreigners, and we have 46,814. Deduct this from the total, 47,588, and we have 774 as the total of Northern-born citizens of Atlanta. This is the city that is oftenest cited as a "Northern city in the South." Since 1860 the South has lost nearly one-fourth of its foreign born population in spite of the tremendous tide of foreign immigration that flows in at Northern ports. Further—the South had less Northern-born citizens in 1880 than in 1860. In the eight South Atlantic States there were even fewer Northerners in 1880 than in 1870. In Georgia in 1870 there were 6,613 citizens of foreign birth; in 1880 only 5,848—this in a total population of 1,542,180. In 1880 there were 139,971 more Southern people living North than Northern people living South.

The South has been rebuilt by Southern brains and energy. . . .

. . . Atlanta now sends plows into Mexico, and ships agricultural implements to Central America. She is even competing with the North in nearer markets, and we have our eyes on the Pan-American delegates now traveling over the continent. They shall not escape to their homes without being told in indifferent Spanish that the South is their nearest and their best market.

The growth of the iron industries provoked other ventures. In Atlanta the best gold watches are now made, the finest pianos, double concave razors and sewing-machines. In Birmingham pins, in Gainesville matches. It is curious to note how the industries of the South have been built up, step by step, and how the system has grown of its own growth. A few years ago a firm in Atlanta began making paper bags. It sold these all over America, having a branch depot in Chicago. It then added cloth bags. It then built a cotton factory to supply the cloth for its bags. Later it doubled the factory. And now it has just added a bleachery at a cost of $100,000 to prepare the cloth. A number of men established successful proprietary medicines in Atlanta. Two box factories followed—and now a glass and bottle factory, with $90,000 capital, supplies them with bottles. Each item grows out of another. And so vast and varied are our resources that the system is a miracle of success and expansion. The last census shows that Atlanta stands third in the list of American cities in the proportion of actual workers to entire population. Lawrence, Mass., is first; Lowell, Mass., second; and Fall River, Mass., and Atlanta, Ga., tie at third place! . . .

2. An English Visitor Describes a New South City, 1890

. . . Our party, which, with American friends, numbered over a thousand, divided at Chicago, one section going North to visit the iron ore districts of Michigan, Wisconsin and Minnesota, the copper mines of Lake Superior and the iron, copper and nickel mines of Canada, the other proceeding southwards to visit Alabama and other Southern States which are fast being opened up to new industries and becoming industrial rivals of the Northern States. I accompanied the southern contingent. We left Chicago deeply regretting that we had seen only a small part of its wonderful industrial capabilities, and that we were unable to utilise a tithe of the opportunities which the manufacturers and citizens afforded us. We travelled by night to Louisville, thence all day to Nashville, Tennessee, and arrived at Birmingham, Alabama, on the following evening, February 16. Birmingham is a conspicuous example of rapid development. In the course of a few years it has grown into a town of 50,000 inhabitants, with eight trunk lines of railway converging on it, seventy miles of street railways, excellent hotels, parks, many beautiful buildings, and an opera house. The social surroundings give evidence of the spread of education and material advancement. The progress of the town of Birmingham has been contemporaneous with the general development of the State of Alabama. The rapid growth of the iron trade in this State is attributable to the close proximity and abundance of coal and iron ore rather than to any excellence in methods of mining or manufacture. Owing to these geological conditions, it is claimed, and apparently with reason, that the cheapest pig iron in the United States is produced here. The furnaces of Birmingham are mainly supplied from a red hematite band of iron ore, which extends with the Alleghany Mountains from Canada, through Pennsylvania and Virginia, to the Cahaba river in Alabama. The district of Birmingham produces 20,000 tons of coal and 2200 tons of iron per day. There is also a large production of malleable iron, and a healthy expansion of manufactures dependent on the iron trade, such as pipe works, engine works, nail factories, and iron foundries. As illustrating the vast and rapid expansion of the Southern States—a phenomenon which will have an important bearing on the commercial policy and future of the Republic—it may be interesting to note that Alabama produced 62,000 tons of iron in 1880, and 1,780,000 tons in 1890. The coloured population are largely employed as miners and as labourers about blast-furnaces and ironworks. They are cheap and slow. They are not as energetic or as regular as white men. To cope with their irregularities it is necessary to keep twice the staff for the same work. They are sluggish, and are quite content to earn a livelihood by working continually half-time. Their social wants are few. They live cheaply, often herding together in insanitary conditions. They do not act as foremen, nor are they often placed in responsible positions. White men must superintend and direct them. It is very noticeable how the white and coloured population of the South keep absolutely distinct. There is no intermingling or social intercourse between them. The groups of women and children seen in the streets and at the railway stand entirely apart. The white people apparently hold no communication with the blacks.

We were not long in finding out that the manufacturers of the South hold different opinions on fiscal questions from the people of Pennsylvania. In the Birmingham district the views of the people in favour of free trade are very pronounced. They expressed themselves as convinced that it was fortunate that the struggle for supremacy between the North and the South ended as it did in a victory for the North, but the Southerners are now as resolute in commerce as they were in arms, and strive against their Northern competitors for supremacy in trade and industry. They are confident that, with their abundant resources and the cheapness of production, they can hold their own with all competitors without the aid of protective duties.

There is strong evidence that the Free Trade party in the South has extensive support, as this opinion was repeated in other places in Alabama, and also in Tennessee, Kentucky, and West Virginia. In going to the iron ore mines we passed by railway along the range of hills above Birmingham, and had a magnificent view of the brown amphitheatre of hill and valley below. The scene before us, and the tone and hues of the landscape, reminded us very much of the panorama around Florence. Extensive iron-pipe works were being erected for casting pipes, so as to consume the pig iron on the spot. It is anticipated that the development of Southern towns, and the necessity for pipes for new water-works, will utilise all the pipes and manufactured products which can be produced in this district for many years to come. . . .

3. Walter Hines Page Identifies Southern Problems, 1902

. . . [I]n the country, only a few miles from almost any of these towns, men and women live and think as men and women did fifty years ago, or eighty years, or even a hundred. The farmers have more money than their grandfathers had, but the general structure of their life is the same,—a dull succession of the seasons where agriculture is practiced in old-fashioned ways, where weary housewives show resignation rather than contentment, and where ignorance has become satisfied with itself. The country is somewhat more densely populated than it was twenty years ago, but the growth of population suggests only a denser stagnation.

These men and women are not poor, that is, they do not feel poor. They have a civilization of their own of which they are proud. They have for a hundred years been told to be proud of it. The politicians have told them that they are the best people on earth, that the state they live in is the most important in the Union, that the ideas they stand for are the bulwarks of our liberties. Do they not own land? Are they not independent? What more could men ask? One in five is illiterate. But what matter? Some of the illiterate are more successful than some others that can read. What does it profit a man, then, to read? They have a self-satisfied personal dignity that prevents near approach. If you propose to change a law or a custom, or are suspected of such a wish, or if you come with a new idea, the burden of proving its value rests on you. What they are they regard as the normal state of human society. If you would change it or them, you are under suspicion as a disorganizer of social life. There was talk in one household, I recall, about the possibility that the son of one of the more prosperous men in the neighborhood might go away to study medicine. "I don't see the use," said the father. "We've got two doctors nigh enough, and there ain't no room for a third." The preacher, too, has hardened their self-contentment, especially the self-contentment of the women. A profession of faith after "conversion" prepares them for the life to come, and breeds an indifference to the transitory inconveniences of the life that is.

A country schoolmaster in this region told me last year (truly enough) that the ability to read was not a good test even of a man's intelligence, to say nothing of his character. "Why, do you know," said he, "how many of the Confederate soldiers were illiterate? Yet they were the best soldiers that ever went to war."

"Suppose they had all been trained,—trained to some useful occupation,—some as geologists, some as miners, some as machinists, some as shipwrights, some as gun-makers. The iron in Alabama, the wood and coal near by, would these not have been utilized in war?"

"Utilized? We'd 'ave whipped the Yankees—shore!"

"What would you think of schools where men should now be trained to occupations, schools here in this neighborhood, to make ploughs, wagons, furniture, everything useful?"

"That'd be a mighty good thing; but it ain't education."

There is a considerable variety of social conditions in these rural communities, as everywhere else. Near one home, where both children and grandchildren are illegitimate, is the residence of a man who holds his land by direct descent in his family from a colonial grant, and whose sons are successful lawyers and preachers and physicians in four states. A good many youth go to the towns and find wider opportunities. From this same neighborhood a youth went to New York, and he is now a rich merchant; another went to college by his own exertions, and he is an electrical engineer in a great manufacturing city; another is a partner in a factory in New England; another is a judge in Oregon. The most ambitious are those who go away; and the general level of life seems as low as it was generations ago. The emigration from the older Southern states has been enormous.

Three influences have held the social structure stationary: first slavery, which pickled all Southern life and left it just as it found it; then the politician, and the preacher. One has for a hundred years proclaimed the present social state as the ideal condition; and, if any has doubted this declaration, the other has told him that this life counts for little at best. Thus gagged and bound, Southern rural society has remained stationary longer than English-speaking people have remained stationary anywhere else in the world. It is a state of life that keeps permanently the qualities of the frontier civilization long after the frontier has receded and been forgotten. The feeling that you bring away with you is a feeling that something has intervened to hold these people back from their natural development. They have a capacity that far outruns their achievement. They are citizens of an earlier time and of a narrower world, who have not had the development that a democracy implies. The cue to a proper understanding of them is the historic fact that they are a capable people whose growth, when democracy began to develop men, was interrupted.

The familiar classification of the Southern people as "gentlemen" and "poor whites" is misleading. The number of the large landed proprietors and of large slaveholders has been greatly exaggerated by tradition. Smaller, too, than is thought is the class that may properly be called "white trash" or "buckra." The great mass of these country people came of sturdy English and Scotch-Irish stock, and they are very like the country population that settled the other states eighty years ago. They are not poorer nor "trashier" than the rural population of New Jersey, or Pennsylvania, or New York, or New England were several generations ago, or than they now are in certain remote regions.

If the rural parts of New York, or of New Jersey, or of Pennsylvania were to-day depopulated, and all the machinery of the present civilization were removed, and if to-morrow the population of eighty years ago were to reappear just as it was, this would be a community very like these Southern communities. What an interesting field for sociological experiment such a reappearance of a part of the past would present! Peddlers and missionaries and reorganizers of social life would overwhelm their "contemporary ancestors." It would be a pleasure to help them forward in a decade or two as far as their descendants traveled in eighty years, but it would not be an easy task. After many impatient efforts we should learn the wisdom of trying to find out their point of view, and of contenting ourselves with gently helping them to advance in their own way, even if they came slowly and seemed stupid. Teaching one's ancestors is at best a difficult undertaking; for it is not the same task as teaching one's descendants. What a lot of disappointing effort this generation might have saved if it had known this simple truth somewhat sooner! . . .

4. *Paul Hamilton Hayne's Sonnet on the New South, 1885*

To the New South

"New South! "new South!" we hail your
    radiant rise
The morning sunshine flasht across your
    crest—.
  Your Eagle-wings, & proudly swelling breast—,
  The soul that burns & brightens in your eyes—
—But while you dare to storm the loftiest skies,
—Foul not the fairness of your natal nest,

—Nor, in high Orient soaring scorn the West,
  Wherein your Fathers' sunset-glory lies!—

How oft is sunset beautiful & grand!
  Its very *clouds* are steeped in light & grace,—
—The glow and pathos of a farewell-time;—
—'Tis thence the Past uplifts her dying face,
—And if that Past hath been like ours, sublime,—
—Ah, show her reverence in the sunset-land!

5. *A Southern Progressive on the Evils of Child Labor, 1904*

. . . Upon a personal investigation of a large number of mills, one will find, among managers, superintendents, and foremen, the representatives of almost every social class. Although the mill can hardly be called the instrument of an industrial democracy, there will sometimes be found men in the ranks of factory administration who have worked themselves forward from the vague multitude of the unlettered and unskilled. It is from this multitude, however,—from the great army of the non-participants,—that the population of the factory is chiefly drawn. From their little homes in the "hill-country" of the Piedmont, where for years they have maintained a precarious existence upon a difficult and forbidding soil, thousands of them have been drawn within the precincts of the new industrial life. Some of them have come from the heavier lands in the malarial sections of the "Black Belt." Whether from the hills or from the valleys,—and most of them are a "hill-people,"—they have sometimes found in the factory an instrument of industrial rescue. In many instances, however, the change from agriculture—however hard the old life—has represented a loss of freedom without a compensating gain of ease. I have known cases where the bright promises of the factory's labor agent have lured families from their little holdings of poor land to a fate even more dreary and more pitiless. In other cases the change has represented more of gain than of loss. The family has found in the opportunity presented by the mill a new chance for a real foothold in the struggle for existence. Having failed under the conditions of agriculture, it has found under the conditions of manufacture at least the possibility of another world.

On the farm the whole family has usually worked together, and so the family still remains, under the changed conditions, the working unit. Often at the week's end they will find themselves in possession of more real money than they have seen in months before, and, not clearly perceiving that more of money does not always mean more of life,—an error not unusual among more favored classes,—and feeling the magic spell of fellowship, of closer social contact with other human souls and other human forces, they soon forget whatever of advantage the old life may have contained.

Nor is the promise of the new world always vain. With some the possibilities of promotion are perceived, and steadily and sometimes successfully pursued. The more important factories are now seldom found without the factory school, where—in spite of the many calls to the mill, to meet the exigencies of "rush orders"— the children, or a fraction of them, are given an elementary training in "the three R's." When the more ambitious boy or the more capable girl is advanced to "piece-work," the result of an active day is often a gratifying wage. But the period of satisfactory earning power reaches its maximum at about the eighteenth or nineteenth year, and the operative is held by the rewards of the industry at the only time when another career might seem possible and practicable. When it is clearly perceived that the strain of the long factory hours does not bring a really satisfactory adult wage, it is too late to change; and the few who pass upward in the mill are but a small proportion of the mass. These, under the pressure of the economic situation just suggested, yield to that class tendency which is just as active among the poor as among the rich. The forces of a common origin, of neighborhood life, of a social experience shut in by the factory enclosure,—with no opportunity for the home, that best basis of social differentiation,—all conspire to emphasize the distinctions and the barriers of caste, and we find in process of creation a "factory people." They are marked by certain characteristic excellences and by certain characteristic evils. I would not forget the first in dwelling here upon the latter. There will be found among them, in frequent and appalling evidence, two symbols of a low industrial life,—the idle father and the working child.

Neither could exist without the partial complicity of the mills. The adult men among the new recruits have untrained hands and awkward fingers. The younger children are taken at first as the "pupils of the industry," but the mills have clung to them with a tenacity which indicates that while their immediate labor may be profitless, the net rewards of their "instruction" do not fall exclusively to the children. Upon the little farm among the hills the family worked and lived close to the very limit of existence. The father, there, had often done the hunting and the fishing while the women and the children labored. The family earnings in the new environment at the mill present a small but appreciable margin. As there has rarely been a thought or a plan beyond a little fuller measure of subsistence,—subsistence of the same kind and according to the same standards,—it is now obviously possible when this measure is attained

for some one in the number of the workers to "fall out." The father does not seem to be seriously in demand, the children are. The member of the family who ceases work is thus not the youngest, but the oldest. If the father has never entered the mill,—as is sometimes the case,—and if there still appears a little margin in the family wage beyond the limit of subsistence, the one who falls out is the mother. The children work on. . . .

The system of child labor, especially at the South, is at war, not only with the welfare of the child, the parent, the industry, but with democracy itself. It stands, not only for arrested development in the individual, for ignorance and industrial helplessness, but for arrested development in the social class to which the child belongs. These have been the white non-participants of the older civilization. The greater number of them, . . . are now being incorporated within the general body of democratic life. They are becoming conscious participants in the fulness and freedom of their century. Those who have become involved in the industrial movement represented by the mill might well find through the mill,—as a few have done,—not only more to eat and more to wear, but more to live for. The mill might well be to all, as it has been to some, the instrument of their transplanting,—out of a life of barren and isolated non-participation into a life of fruitful and generous relationship with men, with work, with the rewarding world. But it has too often seemed to be the policy of the factory to save only in order that it might consume.

The isolated family is called in from the barren lands about its rural cabin, but too often it is redeemed from isolation only that its helplessness may bring profit to the instrument of its redemption. It is put to dwell within the factory enclosure; its instinctive desire to live somewhat to itself, to own a little land, to have a home, is denied; it must be "the company's" tenant, it must—usually—trade at "the company's store," its children are to go upon "the company's roll." The child is trained almost from infancy into a certain human and economic dependence upon one particular industry. If it have a few months, now and then, for schooling, it must go to "the company's school." If the family go to worship, there is at the larger mills "the company's church," a chapel in which the salary of the minister and his helpers is defrayed by the same resourceful and generous "company"—the company, by the way, which has charged that the enactment of a child-labor law would be paternalism!

Here and there the exceptional child, through an exceptional virility, rises out of the enfolding powers of the system; here and there a life escapes. But as a rule the system is effective; and the familiar saying, "once an operative, always an operative," rings all too seriously true. The operatives remain a fixed and semi-dependent class. One manufacturer bluntly informed me that he wished them to remain so, upon the double ground that they would then "never organize and would never want or get high wages." "My business," said he, "is a low-wages business." I will not charge that his temper is representative. Many of the manufacturers honestly and earnestly desire the progress of their people. But the fact remains that the factory system, as a system, betrays a tendency to hold its humbler industrial forces in a state of arrested development; which, from the broader social standpoint and in relation to the larger life of democracy, means an arrested participation. Here is an eddy in the fuller and freer current of democratic life; here, in the industrial imprisonment of the child, is a contradiction—however temporary—of those juster and deeper forces which are claiming the human possibilities of the individual—however lowly—as elements in the power and happiness of the State.

6. Sharecropper Nate Shaw Encounters the Boll Weevil, 1923

1923, I got what the boll weevil let me have—six bales. Boll weevil et up the best part of my crop. Didn't use no poison at that time, just pickin up squares. All you could do was keep them boll weevils from hatchin out and goin back up on that cotton. Couldn't kill em.

The boll weevil come into this country in the teens, between 1910 and 1920. Didn't know about a boll weevil when I was a boy comin up. They blowed in here from the western countries. People was bothered with the boll weevil way out there in the state of Texas and other states out there before we was here. And when the boll weevil hit this country, people was fully ignorant of their ways and what to do for em. Many white employers, when they discovered them boll weevils here, they'd tell their hands out on their plantations—some of em didn't have plantations, had land rented in their possession and put a farmin man out there; he was goin to gain that way by rentin land and puttin a man out there to work it; he goin to beat the nigger out of enough to more than pay the rent on it. And the white man didn't mind rentin land for a good farmer. That rent weren't enough to hurt him; he'd sub-rent it to the fellow that goin to work it or put him out there on halves. Didn't matter how a nigger workin a crop, if he worked it it's called his until it was picked out and ginned and then it was the white man's crop. Nigger delivered that cotton baled up to the white man—so they'd tell you, come out to the field to tell you or ask you when you'd go to the store, "How's your crop gettin along?" knowin the boll weevil's eatin away as he's talkin. Somebody totin news to him every day bout which of his farmers is pickin up the squares and which ones aint.

"You seen any squares fallin on the ground?"

Sometimes you'd say, "Yes sir, my crop's losin squares."

He'd tell you what it was. Well, maybe you done found out. He'd tell you, "Pick them squares up off the ground, keep em picked up;

boll weevil's in them squares. If you don't, I can't furnish you, if you aint goin to keep them squares up off the ground."

Boss man worryin bout his farmers heavy in debt, if he ever goin to see that money. Mr. Lemuel Tucker, when I was livin down there on Sitimaches Creek, he come to me, "You better pick them squares up, Nate, or you won't be able to pay me this year."

Don't he know that I'm goin to fight the boll weevil? But fight him for my benefit. He goin to reap the reward of my labor too, but it aint for him that I'm laborin. All the time it's for myself. Any man under God's sun that's got anything industrious about him, you don't have to make him work—he goin to work. But Tucker didn't trust me to that. If a white man had anything booked against you, well, you could just expect him to ride up and hang around you to see that you worked, especially when the boll weevil come into this country. To a great extent, I was given about as little trouble about such as that as any man. I didn't sit down and wait till the boss man seed my sorry acts in his field. I worked. I worked.

Me and my children picked up squares sometimes by the bucketsful. They'd go out to the field with little sacks or just anything to hold them squares and when they'd come in they'd have enough squares to fill up two baskets. I was industrious enough to do somethin about the boll weevil without bein driven to it. Picked up them squares and destroyed em, destroyed the weevil eggs. Sometimes, fool around there and see a old weevil himself.

I've gived my children many pennies and nickels for pickin up squares. But fact of the business, pickin up squares and burnin em—it weren't worth nothin. Boll weevil eat as much as he pleased. Consequently, they come to find out pickin up them squares weren't worth a dime. It was impossible to get all them squares and the ones you couldn't get was enough to ruin your crop. Say like today your cotton is illuminated with squares; come up a big rain maybe tonight, washin them squares out of the fields. Them boll weevils hatches in the woods, gets up and come right back in the field. You couldn't keep your fields clean—boll weevil schemin to eat your crop faster than you workin to get him out.

My daddy didn't know what a boll weevil was in his day. The boll weevil come in this country after I was grown and married and had three or four children. I was scared of him to an extent. I soon learnt he'd destroy a cotton crop. Yes, all God's dangers aint a white man. . . .

References

1. Henry Grady Articulates His New South Vision, 1890
   Henry W. Grady, *The New South* (New York: Robert Bonner's Sons, 1890), pp. 146–148, 182–184, 200–202.

2. An English Visitor Describes a New South City, 1890
   James Kitson, "Iron and Steel Industries of America," in *The Contemporary Review*, Volume 59 (May 1891), pp. 635–637.

3. Walter Hines Page Identifies Southern Problems, 1902
   Walter Hines Page, "The Rebuilding of Old Commonwealths," in *Atlantic Monthly*, Volume 89 (May 1902), pp. 653–654.

4. Paul Hamilton Hayne's Sonnet on the New South, 1885
   John Archer Carter, "Paul Hayne's 'Sonnet to the New South,' " in *Georgia Historical Quarterly*, Volume 48 (June 1964), p. 194.

5. A Southern Progressive on the Evils of Child Labor, 1904
   Edgar Gardner Murphy, *Problems of the Present South* (New York: The Macmillan Company, 1904), pp. 104–107, 123–125.

6. Sharecropper Nate Shaw Encounters the Boll Weevil, 1923
Theodore Rosengarten, ed., *All God's Dangers: The Life of Nate Shaw* (New York: Vintage Books, 1984), pp. 221–223.

Further Reading

Orville V. Burton and Robert C. McMath, Jr., eds., *Towards a New South? Studies in Post–Civil War Southern Communities* (1982)

David L. Carlton, *Mill and Town in South Carolina, 1880–1920* (1982)

Pete Daniel, *The Shadow of Slavery: Peonage in the South, 1901–1969* (1973)

Steven J. DeCanio, *Agriculture in the Postbellum South* (1975)

Gaines M. Foster, *Ghosts of the Confederacy: Defeat, the Lost Cause, and the Emergence of the New South, 1865 to 1913* (1987)

Paul M. Gaston, *The New South Creed: A Study in Southern Mythmaking* (1970)

Thavolia Glymph and John J. Kushma, eds., *Essays on the Postbellum Southern Economy* (1985)

Jacqueline D. Hall et al., *Like a Family: The Making of a Southern Cotton Mill World* (1987)

Joy J. Jackson, *New Orleans in the Gilded Age: Politics and Urban Progress, 1880–1896* (1969)

Melton A. McLaurin, *Paternalism and Protest: Southern Cotton Mill Workers and Organized Labor* (1971)

Jay R. Mandle, *The Roots of Black Poverty: The Southern Plantation Economy After the Civil War* (1978)

Broadus Mitchell, *The Rise of the Cotton Mills in the South* (1921)

Idus A. Newby, *Plain Folk in the New South* (1986)

John F. Stover, *The Railroads of the South, 1865–1900* (1955)

Peter Wallenstein, *From Slave South to New South: Public Policy in Nineteenth Century Georgia* (1987)

C. Vann Woodward, *Origins of the New South, 1877–1913* (1951)

Gavin Wright, *Old South, New South: Revolutions in the Southern Economy Since the Civil War* (1986)

Document Set 12

White Supremacy in the Segregated South, 1896–1954

The relationship between whites and blacks, always the most volatile feature of the southern experience, reached a low point in the late nineteenth and early twentieth centuries. By the time the United States entered World War I in 1917 to help preserve democracy in the world, the American South had disfranchised almost all its black population. Whites and blacks lived in separate worlds as local governments passed Jim Crow laws to circumvent the rights and privileges that black southerners had gained through Reconstruction legislation. The demise of Reconstruction and the "redemption" of the South from Republican rule in the late 1870s had not heralded an immediate decline in the political status of blacks because white economic power had at first coerced African-Americans into voting Democratic.

The security of white Democrats was temporarily shattered, however, by the challenge of a new political party, the Populist party, which had emerged in response to the economic crisis confronting the nation in the 1880s and 1890s. Populism had found strong support among the impoverished farmers of the South. For Democrats, the prospects of an interracial coalition, coupled with an unprecedented, radical program for reform, had galvanized their party to action.

Racist demagoguery consequently took root as a standard feature of Democratic party rhetoric. The effectiveness of racist appeals ensured their continuation as an electioneering strategy long after the Populist party ceased to exist. In the one-party political system that the South had become, Democratic candidates sought to outdo each other in lurid tales about, and drastic remedies for, alleged black depravity. Lawmakers, to avert what they considered an imminent threat to the purity of the white race, worked to ensure the segregation of African-Americans from southern white society, and gradually Jim Crow replaced slavery as a mechanism for controlling blacks. An almost total acceptance of the white-supremacy doctrine, and of a rationale for maintaining it, dictated the course of the South until the second half of the twentieth century. Workers in the South went as far as to shy away from class conflict and even put aside the promotion of their own economic well-being in the greater interest of "racial purity." Racial bigotry bred an atmosphere of intellectual mediocrity and a shocking neglect of education at all levels. Southerners who flocked by the hundreds to witness the lynching of blacks became impervious to the brutal nature of the society that they were creating—a system that endured until the civil-rights movement began to breach the barriers of segregation in the middle of the twentieth century.

Amid the political and economic crises of the late nineteenth century, African-Americans became the obvious scapegoats for the misfortunes that had befallen the South. One repercussion of the Populist upheaval of the 1890s was a systematic attempt to deprive blacks of the right to vote. Early disfranchisement techniques affected both blacks and the poorer class of white voters until the state of Louisiana passed its "grandfather" plan, reproduced here as the first document, which protected poor whites from disqualification.

The admission by some southern whites that the abolition of slavery benefited the South was nevertheless a far cry from an acceptance of racial equality. When Homer Plessy a light-skinned African-American, violated a Louisiana law by sitting in the white-only section of a railroad car, the case went all the way to the U.S. Supreme Court. The second document excerpts the Court's opinion, which all but one of the nine justices supported. The *Plessy* v. *Ferguson* decision approved the constitutionality of the establishment of separate facilities for whites and blacks as long as those facilities were equal.

Disfranchisement was necessary because the right to vote constituted a privilege that southern blacks had not earned, argued Benjamin Ryan Tillman before the U.S. Senate in 1900. In this speech, reprinted as the third document, Tillman's defense of the brutal practice of lynching reveals the extent to which southerners had convinced themselves that black males possessed an abnormal sexual craving for white women. Tillman's fiery racial demagoguery was particularly successful in his native state of South Carolina, which had had a black majority for more than a century. The fourth document demonstrates the sense of relief felt by Carolinians that the state's population was in the process of acquiring a white majority.

The fifth selection exposes the brutality of a lynching in the town of Ocilla, Georgia, one of many documented instances collected by Arthur Raper, field secretary of the Commission on Interracial Co-operation. (This organization was formed by a group of southern liberals in 1920 to promote harmony between the races by eliminating the more distasteful aspects of discrimination.) The victim, James Irwin, had allegedly raped a sixteen-year-old white girl. The white-

supremacist notion of "the black male as rapist" served a dual purpose. It not only intimidated black males but also perpetuated the image of white female chastity and innocence. The cult of pure womanhood demanded constant protection because of the perception by southern white males that it was becoming increasingly vulnerable. Their greatest fear was racial intermixture, which, they believed, would create a hybrid, or mongrel, race. A leading proponent of this argument was Theodore Bilbo, a governor of and member of congress for Mississippi. The sixth selection is taken from his 1947 book, which was written as a warning to white America. Not all southern women accepted the notion that they needed guardians of their virtue. In 1930 the Association of Southern Women for the Prevention of Lynching was formed to protest the extralegal and violent methods used to enforce white supremacy. The seventh document is an opinion on lynching written by Jesse Daniel Ames, the association's first executive director.

Although more and more white southerners were beginning to question the validity of segregation by the 1950s, racial prejudice remained deeply rooted in the southern psyche. The final document is a remarkable account of an initially trivial incident during a basketball game, elevated to enormous importance by the fears passed down by generations of white southerners. The author is Melton McLaurin, then a youth in the small North Carolina town of Wade and today a professor of history.

Questions for Analysis

1. Did southerners institutionalize segregation to replace slavery as a method of controlling the black population? How similar were slavery and segregation?

2. How much did the political and economic disturbances of the late nineteenth century contribute to the decision by white southerners to disfranchise and segregate blacks?

3. Were Democratic party politicians responsible for fomenting racial intolerance and violence in the South?

4. Was white supremacy a means for controlling the actions and beliefs of women and working-class whites in the South?

5. Why did so few white southerners express disapproval of segregationist practices?

6. Was segregation in the American South similar to the present-day system of apartheid in South Africa?

1. Louisiana Adopts the "Grandfather" Plan, 1898

[Article 197] Sec. 3. He [the elector] shall be able to read and write, and shall demonstrate his ability to do so when he applies for registration, by making, under oath administered by the registration officer or his deputy, written application therefor, in the English language, or his mother tongue, which application shall contain the essential facts necessary to show that he is entitled to register and vote, and shall be entirely written, dated and signed by him, in the presence of the registration officer or his deputy, without assistance or suggestion from any person or any memorandum whatever, except the form of application. . . .

Sec. 4. If he be not able to read and write, as provided by Section three . . . then he shall be entitled to register and vote if he shall, at the time he offers to register, be the bona fide owner of property assessed to him in this State at a valuation of not less than three hundred dollars . . . and on which, if such property be personal only, all taxes due shall have been paid. . . .

Sec. 5. No male person who was on January 1st, 1867, or at any date prior thereto, entitled to vote under the Constitution or statutes of any State of the United States, wherein he then resided, and no son or grandson of any such person not less than twenty-one years of age at the date of the adoption of this Constitution, and no male person of foreign birth, who was naturalized prior to the first day of January, 1898, shall be denied the right to register and vote in this State by reason of his failure to possess the educational or property qualifications

prescribed by this Constitution; provided, he shall have resided in this State for five years next preceding the date at which he shall apply for registration, and shall have registered in accordance with the terms of this article prior to September 1, 1898, and no person shall be entitled to register under this section after said data. . . .

A separate registration of voters applying under this section, shall be made by the registration officer of every parish. . . .

The registration of voters under this section [5] shall close on the 31st day of August, 1898, and immediately thereafter the registration officer of every parish shall make a sworn copy, in duplicate, of the list of persons registered under this section, showing in detail whether the applicant registered as a voter of 1867, or prior thereto, or as the son of such voter, or as the grandson of such voter, and deposit one of said duplicates in the office of the Secretary of State . . . and the other of said duplicates shall be by him filed in the office of the Clerk of the District Court of the parish. . . .

All persons whose names appear on said registration lists shall be admitted to register for all elections in this State without possessing the educational or property qualification prescribed by this Constitution, unless otherwise disqualified, and all persons who do not by personal application claim exemption from the provisions of sections 3 and 4 of this article before September 1st, 1898, shall be forever denied the right to do so. . . .

2. The Supreme Court Upholds "Separate-but-Equal," 1896

. . . The object of the [Fourteenth] Amendment was undoubtedly to enforce the absolute equality of the two races before the law, but in the nature of things it could not have been intended to abolish distinctions based upon color, or to enforce social, as distinguished from political, equality, or a commingling of the two races upon terms unsatisfactory to either. Laws permitting, and even requiring, their separation in places where they are liable to be brought into contact do not necessarily imply the inferiority of either race to the other, and have been generally, if not universally, recognized as within the competency of the state legislatures in the exercise of their police power. The most common instance of this is connected with the establishment of separate schools for white and colored children, which has been held to be a valid exercise of the legislative power even by courts of States where the political rights of the colored race have been longest and most earnestly enforced. . . .

Laws forbidding the intermarriage of the two races may be said in a technical sense to interfere with the freedom of contract, and yet have been universally recognized as within the police power of the State. . . .

The distinction between laws interfering with the political equality of the negro and those requiring the separation of the two races in schools, theatres, and railway carriages has been frequently drawn by this court. . . .

. . . Every exercise of the police power must be reasonable, and extend only to such laws as are enacted in good faith for the promotion of the public good, and not for the annoyance or oppression of a particular class. . . .

So far, then, as a conflict with the Fourteenth Amendment is concerned, the case reduces itself to the question of whether the statute of Louisiana is a reasonable regulation, and with respect to this there must necessarily be a large discretion on the part of the legislature. In determining the question of reasonableness it is at liberty to act with reference to the established usages, customs and traditions of the people, and with a view to the promotion of their comfort, and the preservation of the public peace and good order. Gauged by this standard, we cannot say that a law which authorizes or even requires the separation of the two races in public conveyances is unreasonable, or more obnoxious to the Fourteenth Amendment than the acts of Congress requiring separate schools for colored children in the District of Columbia, the constitutionality of which does not seem to have been questioned, or the corresponding acts of State legislatures.

We consider the underlying fallacy of the plaintiff's argument to consist in the assumption that the enforced separation of the two races stamps the colored race with a badge of inferiority. If this be so, it is not by reason of anything found in the act, but solely because the colored race chooses to put that construction upon it. . . . The argument also assumes that social prejudices may be overcome by legislation, and that equal rights cannot be secured to the negro except by an enforced commingling of the two races. We cannot accept this proposition. If the two races are to meet on terms of social equality, it must be the result of natural affinities, a mutual appreciation of each other's merits and a voluntary consent of individuals. . . . Legislation is powerless to eradicate racial instincts or to abolish distinctions based upon physical differences, and the attempt to do so can only result in accentuating the difficulties of the present situation. If the civil and political rights of both races be equal, one cannot be inferior to the other civilly or politically. If one race be inferior to the other socially, the Constitution of the United States cannot put them upon the same plane. . . .

3. Senator Benjamin R. Tillman
Defends Lynching, 1900

. . . And he [Senator John C. Spooner, of Wisconsin] said we had taken their rights away from them. He asked me was it right to murder them in order to carry the elections. I never saw one murdered. I never saw one shot at an election. It was the riots before the election, precipitated by their own hot-headedness in attempting to hold the government, that brought on conflicts between the races and caused the shotgun to be used. That is what I meant by saying we used the shotgun.

I want to call the Senator's attention to one fact. He said that the Republican party gave the negroes the ballot in order to protect themselves against the indignities and wrongs that were attempted to be heaped upon them by the enactment of the black code. I say it was because the Republicans of that day, led by Thad Stevens, wanted to put white necks under black heels and to get revenge. There is a difference of opinion. You have your opinion about it, and I have mine, and we can never agree.

I want to ask the Senator this proposition in arithmetic: In my State there were 135,000 negro voters, or negroes of voting age, and some 90,000 or 95,000 white voters. General Canby set up a carpetbag government there and turned our State over to this majority. Now, I want to ask you, with a free vote and a fair count, how are you going to beat 135,000 by 95,000? How are you going to do it? You had set us an impossible task. You had handcuffed us and thrown away the key, and you propped your carpetbag negro government with bayonets. Whenever it was necessary to sustain the government you held it up by the Army.

Mr. President, I have not the facts and figures here, but I want the country to get the full view of the Southern side of this question and the justification for anything we did. We were sorry we had the necessity forced upon us, but we could not help it, and as white men we are not sorry for it, and we do not propose to apologize for anything we have done in connection with it. We took the government away from them in 1876.

We did take it. If no other Senator has come here previous to this time who would acknowledge it, more is the pity. We have had no fraud in our elections in South Carolina since 1884. There has been no organized Republican party in the State.

We did not disfranchise the negroes until 1895. Then we had a constitutional convention convened which took the matter up calmly, deliberately, and avowedly with the purpose of disfranchising as many of them as we could under the fourteenth and fifteenth amendments. We adopted the educational qualification as the only means left to us, and the negro is as contented and as prosperous and as well protected in South Carolina to-day as in any State of the Union south of the Potomac. He is not meddling with politics, for he found that the more he meddled with them the worse off he got. As to his "rights"—I will not discuss them now. We of the South have never recognized the right of the negro to govern white men, and we never will. We have never believed him to be equal to the white man, and we will not submit to his gratifying his lust on our wives and daughters without lynching him. I would to God the last one of them was in Africa and that none of them had ever been brought to our shores. But I will not pursue the subject further.

I want to ask permission in this connection to print a speech which I made in the constitutional convention of South Carolina when it convened in 1895, in which the whole carpetbag régime and the indignities and wrongs heaped upon our people, the robberies which we suffered, and all the facts and figures there brought out are incorporated, and let the whole of the facts go to the country. I am not ashamed to have those facts go to the country. They are our justification for the present situation in our State. If I can get it, I should like that permission; otherwise I shall be forced to bring that speech here and read it when I can put my hand on it. I will then leave this matter and let the dead past bury its dead. . . .

4. South Carolina Becomes a "White" State, 1927

Change from Negro to white majority in the population of South Carolina has been the most important if not the most interesting event in the state's history in the last twenty-five years. The bureau of the census estimated the population of the state July 1, 1925, at 1,804,000—893,900 colored and 910,100 white. As will be seen from the table appended, the colored outnumbered the whites by the census of 1820 and in every census succeeding.

The Negro majority in proportion to the whites has been rapidly diminishing since 1900. In that year the Negroes were 782,321 and the whites 557,807, the Negro majority being 224,514. In 1910, it was 156,682, but by 1920, when the whites were 818,538 and the Negroes 864,719, it had dropped to 46,181. The census bureau's estimate for July, 1925, was that the number of whites exceeded that of the Negroes by 16,200.

In these five years of the current census decade, the estimate of gain for the state, both races, was 120,000, the difference between 1,683,000, disregarding hundreds, and 1,803,000.

In the first ten years of the present century the percentage of increase, as shown by the thirteenth census, was 21.8 per cent for whites and 6.8 per cent for Negroes. In the second, as shown by the census for 1920, it was 20.5 per cent for whites and 3.5 for Negroes. In these sharply contrasting percentages for the twenty years, migration of Negroes was not the commanding factor—indeed, it was scarcely important. Considerable Negro migration from South Carolina did not begin until after the census of 1920, general infestation of South Carolina cotton fields by boll weevils not having taken place until 1922. That, and coincident in time with it, strong demand for unskilled labor in the North caused Negroes to leave South Carolina farms in numbers for two or three years, though for the last two years the number has been smaller.

The departure of Negroes upon the arrival of the weevils was not in an economic sense calamitous. For the most part they left lands which they had rented and which had not had skillful tillage. These lands were worn and usually had been yielding meager support to the colored labor that occupied them as renters or sharecroppers.

The lands vacated by Negro migrants are an open opportunity to ambitious newcomers. They are, of course, purchasable at low prices. They are not, as a rule, naturally unfertile. Hundreds of thousands of acres require no drainage. They can in a very few years be brought to high productivity. Almost no districts of South Carolina are now remote from improved highways or from railroads. Scarcely is a point to be found not quickly and easily accessible to a market town.

In South Carolina are broad acreages of $10 an acre land, rolling, or level land, much of it on improved highways, and they offer assurances of a competence and independence to the newcomer of small capital, able-bodied and resolved to get along.

A farmer who could hardly hope in the Corn Belt to possess 50 acres of $300 an acre land short of a lifetime of toil may, in many parts of South Carolina, acquire 100 acres for $1,000 which in a few years may be brought to the profit-making level of Corn Belt harvests.

The existence of a Negro majority for more than a full century in South Carolina, fifty-five years of it after slave emancipation, has had political, social and economic results, depressing in character, which can hardly be measured. Only one other state has had a Negro majority. Hardly does one risk exaggeration in saying that a great, if not the greater, part of the troubles that the commonwealth has endured is explained by it. Despite the census bureau's estimate of 1925, placing the white majority at 16,200, made with no consideration of the unusual migration since 1920, one hazards the opinion that this majority will appear close to 75,000 or 100,000 in 1930.

This means a new freedom for South Carolina. It is the removal of a vague but always present shadow. South Carolina at last has become a white state. . . .

The following table gives the population of the state for the 14 censuses, with the division and percentages of white and colored:

Census Year	Population	White	Colored	Percentage of Negroes
1790	249,073	140,178	108,805	43.7
1810	415,115	214,196	200,919	48.4
1820	502,741	237,440	265,301	52.8
1830	581,185	257,863	323,322	55.6
1840	594,398	259,084	335,314	56.4
1850	668,507	274,563	393,944	58.9
1860	703,708	291,300	412,320	58.6
1870	705,706	289,667	415,814	58.9
1880	995,577	391,105	604,332	60.7
1890	1,150,942	462,008	688,934	59.9
1900	1,340,316	557,807	782,321	58.4
1910	1,515,400	679,161	835,843	55.2
1920	1,683,724	818,538	864,719	51.4
1925 (est.)	1,804,000	910,100	893,900	49.5

5. An Investigator Describes a Lynching in Georgia, 1930

Protracted Tortures, Followed by Fire and Bullets

Upon reaching the place where the body of the girl was found, Irwin was tied to a tree with chains. The tortures began. Approximately a thousand people were present, including some women and children on the edge of the crowd. Members of the mob cut off his fingers and toes, joint by joint, Mob leaders carried them off as souvenirs. Next, his teeth were pulled out with wire pliers. When ever he expressed pain or tried to evade the approaches of his sadistic avengers, he was jabbed in the mouth with a pointed pole. Because of their nature, the remaining mutilations and tortures will not be described. Suffice it to say that they were indecent and brutal beyond belief.

After these mutilations, which lasted more than an hour, Irwin's mangled but living body was hung upon a tree by the arms. Logs and underbrush were piled beneath. Gasoline was poured on. A match was struck. As the flames engulfed the body, it was pierced by bullets.

James Irwin was dead. All day his body, burned past recognition, hung in the tree by the public road. Thousands of white people, including women and children, rode out to see the spectacle. At nightfall the county authorities took the body down and buried it.

6. *Theodore Bilbo Warns Against Mongrelization, 1947*

THE TITLE of this book is TAKE YOUR CHOICE—SEPARATION OR MONGRELIZATION. Maybe the title should have been "You Must Take or You Have Already Taken Your Choice—Separation or Mongrelization," but regardless of the name of this book it is really and in fact a S.O.S. call to every white man and white woman within the United States of America for immediate action, and it is also a warning of equal importance to every right-thinking and straight-thinking American Negro who has any regard or respect for the integrity of his Negro blood and his Negro race.

For nine years I have read, studied and analyzed practically all the records and everything written throughout the entire world on the subject of race relations, covering a period of close on to thirty thousand years. For more than three years I have been writing the message of warning to the white men and women, regardless of nationality, of the United States that you will find recorded on the pages of this book.

This book is not a condemnation or denunciation of any race, white, black or yellow because I entertain no hatred or prejudice against any human being on account of his race or color—God made them so. I have endeavored to bring to the attention of the white, the yellow, and the black races the incontrovertible truths of history over a span of thirty thousand years, all in an honest attempt to conserve and protect and perpetuate my own white race and white civilization, and at the same time impress especially the black and yellow races with the fact that they must join in an effort to protect the integrity of their own race, blood, and civilization.

Be it said to the credit of the black or Negro race in the United States that no right-thinking and straight-thinking Negro desires that the blood of his black race shall be contaminated or destroyed by the commingling of his blood with either the white or yellow races. The desire to mix, commingle, interbreed or marry into the white race by the Negro race is advocated largely by the mulattoes or mongrels who are now to an alarming degree found within the Negro race in this country.

Surely every decent white man and woman in America should have cause to be alarmed over the mongrelization of their white race and the loss of their white civilization when Dr. Ralph S. Linton, a leading Professor of Anthropology of Columbia University, New York City, said just recently that at the present rate of intermarrying, interbreeding, and intermixing within nine generations, which is only 300 years, that there would be no white race nor black race in America—that all would be yellow. And in a recent article entitled "Who Is a Negro," Herbert Asbury makes the alarming and sickening statement that "more than two million United States Negroes have crossed the color line, contributing, among other things, an ever-widening stream of black blood to the native white stock."

In the face of these two startling statements, the truth of which is established beyond every reasonable doubt by the contents of this book, the time has arrived—the clock has struck, when something must be done immediately by every white man and woman in this great and glorious country to stay or to escape the certain and tragic fate that awaits the future of our children's children of generations yet to be born.

It is indeed a sorry white man and white woman who when put on notice of the inevitable result of mongrelization of their race and their civilization are yet unwilling to put forth any effort or make any sacrifice to save themselves and their off-spring from this great and certain calamity. YOU MUST TAKE YOUR CHOICE!

Personally, the writer of this book would rather see his race and his civilization blotted out with the atomic bomb than to see it slowly but surely destroyed in the maelstrom of miscegenation, interbreeding, intermarriage, and mongrelization. The destruction in either case would be inevitable—one in a flash and the other by the slow but certain process of sin, degradation, and mongrelization.

It is not too late—we can yet save the integrity and civilization of both the white and the black races. Many great men of the past have suggested the only solution—the only salvation. A physical separation as advocated from the days of Thomas Jefferson to the present is the only solution. To do this may be a Herculean task, but it is not impossible. . . .

There is no middle ground on the question of interracial marriage. A person either favors or condemns such unions. The Negroes and negrophiles in the United States today who are waging the campaign for complete racial equality must be assumed to favor the amalgamation of the races unless they have openly stated their opposition.

The danger of amalgamation may be stated very simply—it means the destruction of the white race. When the blood of the white and Negro races mix, the fair-skinned Caucasian is lost beneath the black flood. This result can not be denied. And because miscegenation means the death of the white race, every white person not only has the right but the duty to do all in his power to prevent such destruction.

Just as every white man has the right to marry a white woman in preference to a Negress so he has the right to join with the majority of his fellow citizens to prohibit any other member of his race from forming such a union. When the majority believes that society is endangered by the marriage of whites with Negroes or Mongolians, they may prohibit such unions by statute. This right is a fundamental principle of our Republican form of government.

The fact that a white man believes that white-Negro marriages should be prohibited is no indication that he thinks the Negro should be treated with cruelty or injustice. It is often true that those who criticize the Southern policy of racial segregation recognize no neutral ground between love and hatred. They seem to think that the races must be either at daggers' points or in physical embrace. There is, of course, no excuse for such ignorance. A man may use all the power at his command to see that Negroes are treated with fairness, justice, and consideration and still refuse to marry a Negress or to recognize socially any white person who crosses the color line.

Southern white people have been greatly alarmed by the intensity of the current campaign for racial equality in this Nation. They have lived with the race problem for generations and have gained knowledge which many of their Northern friends had had no opportunity to gain. Southern white people know and realize the dangers of amalgamation, and they have been quick to condemn the agitators and troublemakers who have been attempting to spread the doctrine of social equality of the races in the Southland. The following quotation from a resolution passed by the House of Representatives of South Carolina's General Assembly in 1944 is typical:

We indignantly and vehemently denounce the intentions of all organizations seeking the amalgamation of the white and Negro races by a commingling of the races upon any basis of equality as being destructive to the identity and characteristics and integrity of both races, and as being un-American and hostile to the existence and preservation of the American Union of States.

We reaffirm our belief in and our allegiance to established white supremacy as now prevailing in the South, and we solemnly pledge our lives and our sacred honor to maintain it, whatever the cost, in war and in peace.

At the close of the War Between the States, a Confederate soldier inscribed a poem on the back of a Confederate note. These are the words which he wrote on the worthless piece of paper:

Representing nothing on God's Earth now
And naught in the waters below it
As the pledge of a nation that passed away
Keep it, dear friend, and show it.

Show it to those who will lend an ear
To the tale this trifle will tell
Of Liberty born of a patriot's dream
Of a storm cradled nation that fell.

Amalgamation can write the same obituary for the United States of America by insuring that the future generations of Americans will sink into hopeless depths of mongrelization from which there can be no return. On the other hand, a white America can guard and protect the white blood in her veins, guarantee the right of Caucasian racial integrity to generations yet unborn, maintain her civilization and continue to rise in strength and power.

7. *Southern Women Condemn Lynching, 1942*

. . . Fundamentally the white South is not yet fixed in any new ideals expressive of a genuine regeneration of mind and spirit. The white South still believes in the inherent right of the white race to rule supreme over Negroes. It still believes that the rights and privileges of democracy can be limited by force; that certain jobs are the exclusive prerogative of white people; that equal pay for equal work, equal protection and administration of the law for all, and the free exercise of the ballot imperil white racial supremacy. The need to hang together in the present days in order to keep from hanging separately later on will hold in abeyance any widespread outbreak of racial violence, but this need, or at least the recognition of it, will pass with the passing of war.

Decrees and edicts by the President protecting the status of Negroes will be honored in the breach unless the white people of the South come to realize that the future of the South and of the Nation depends upon the extending of certain inalienable rights to the Negro race. If the South is saved from a post-war era of violence, bloodshed, lynching, and torture, it will be because sane white Southerners begin now to work for, as well as talk for, the principles of Democracy. But the task is not alone that of the white South. As there are arrogant and unruly white people, so are there arrogant, unruly, and embittered Negroes. The responsibility of Southern Negroes for the kind of South they will live in is as great as is that of the white people, in the same direction and toward the same end. . . .

In general, the program of the Southern women has been directed to exposing the falsity of the claim that lynching is necessary to their protection and to emphasizing the real danger of lynching to all the values of the home and religion. Its methods have been in part those followed by the Commission on Interracial Cooperation and in part those devised to meet the situations as women saw them. State Associations have been set up; methods to prevent lynchings developed and followed; investigations made of lynchings allegedly involving crimes against white women; public forums held in small towns and county seats; flyers, pamphlets, posters, one-act plays written, published, and distributed.

By 1940, having tried out and established its most effective methods of education, the Association, through its Central Council extended its program of education of public opinion against lynching to include a presentation of the effect of the white primary on white people. This decision was reached as the result of a growing realization that Negroes as a voteless people in a Democracy were a helpless people, and that this condition of helplessness contributed to a belief in inherent racial superiority on the part of white people and encouraged disregard for the rights of minorities.

One danger that the Association of Southern Women for the Prevention of Lynching foresaw, as lynching decreased, was that some lynchings, with little reader interest outside the localities where they were committed, would not come to the attention of the general public. To meet this situation, the Association has organized its machinery to check on rumored lynchings and to give adequate publicity to the facts obtained. . . .

8. A Southern Youth Confronts His Worst Fear, c. 1954

. . . We were using Howard Lee's ball, which presented a challenge because it leaked air and had to be reinflated every thirty minutes or so. Since there was an air compressor at the store, I was charged with keeping the ball inflated. Although we played on a black playground, the white kids controlled the situation because we controlled the ball. None of the black players had a ball, so without us there was no game. Under the circumstances it made little difference which team won. However, had the black players challenged what Howard and I perceived as our rights on the court, we probably would have taken the ball and left the game.

We played into the afternoon, our play interrupted by frequent trips to the air compressor. When enough air leaked from the ball to cause it to lose its bounce and begin to interfere with the game, I would take it to the air compressor to pump it up. Some of the other boys, their game halted and lacking even a flat ball to shoot at the basket in the meantime, would accompany me from the playground to the store. On what turned out to be our last trip, Bobo and Howard strolled over with me as I went to inflate the ball. As we walked the three of us created brilliant passes and incredible moves with the flabby sphere, all of which we dreamed we would someday employ in the perfect game. When we reached the air compressor I pulled from my pocket the needle required to inflate the ball and without thinking handed it to Bobo.

The procedure followed for inserting a needle into a basketball had long been sanctioned by the rituals of kids playing on dirt and asphalt courts. First, someone wet the needle by sticking it into his mouth or spitting on it. Thus lubricated, the instrument was popped neatly into the small rubber valve through which the ball was inflated. This time chance dictated that playground procedure would fail; we couldn't insert the needle into the valve. Bobo stuck the needle in his mouth, applied the usual lavish amount of saliva, and handed it to Howard Lee, who held the ball. Howard struggled to push the

needle into the valve, with no luck. Irritated by what struck me as their incompetence and anxious to return to the game I decided to inflate the ball myself. I took the ball from Howard, pulled the needle from the valve, and placed it in my mouth, convinced that my spit would somehow get the needle into the ball and us back onto the court. A split second after placing the needle in my mouth, I was jolted by one of the most shattering emotional experiences of my young life. Instantaneously an awareness of the shared racial prejudices of generations of white society coursed through every nerve in my body. Bolts of prejudice, waves of prejudice that I could literally feel sent my head reeling and buckled my knees.

The realization that the needle I still held in my mouth had come directly from Bobo's mouth, that it carried on it Bobo's saliva, transformed my prejudices into a physically painful experience. I often had drunk from the same cup as black children, dined on food prepared by blacks. It never occurred to me that such actions would violate my racial purity. The needle in my mouth, however, had been purposely drenched with Negro spit, and that substance threatened to defile my entire being. It threatened me with germs which, everyone said, were common among blacks. These blacks germs would ravage my body with unspeakable diseases, diseases from the tropics, Congo illnesses that would rot my limbs, contort my body with pain. Visions pulled from foreign missions films occasionally shown at the Presbyterian church flashed through my mind. I saw the white jungle doctor, Schweitzer at Lamborini, dressed in a white linen suit, walking among row on row of rickety cots, each occupied by some wretched, rotting black. Those awful African diseases, I now imagined, would claim me as a victim.

The tainted substance on the needle also threatened, in a less specific but equally disturbing manner, my white consciousness, my concept of what being white meant. Bobo's spit threatened to plunge me into a world of voodoo chants and tribal drums. Suddenly the *Saturday Evening Post* cartoon world of black savages dancing about boiling cauldrons filled with white hunters and missionaries seemed strangely real. I felt deprived of the ability to reason, to control the situation. All threats to mind and body, however, failed to compare to the ultimate danger posed by the saliva on the needle. It placed in jeopardy my racial purity, my existence as a superior being, the true soul of all southern whites. The needle was the ultimate unclean object, carrier of the human degeneracy that black skin represented. It transmitted to me Bobo's black essence, an essence that degraded me and made me, like him, less than human.

I felt compelled to jerk the needle from my mouth, to spit it to the ground and rid myself of the unclean thing. I wanted desperately to wipe my mouth with the back of my hand, to remove with my pure white skin any trace of this defiling substance. The urge to gag, to lean over and vomit out any of the black saliva that might remain to spread its contamination throughout my body, was almost unbearable. Yet I could neither gag nor vomit, nor could I wipe my mouth with the back of my hand. Ironically, the same prejudices that filled me with loathing and disgust also demanded that I conceal my feelings. The emotional turmoil exploding inside me had to be contained, choked off. Not for a second could I allow Bobo to suspect that I was in the least upset, or to comprehend the anguish his simple act of moistening the needle with his saliva had caused me. The rules of segregation which I had absorbed every waking moment of my life, and which were now an essential part of my consciousness, demanded that I retain my position as the superior, that I remain in control of the situation. More than the poison of Bobo's saliva I feared the slightest indication of loss of self-control, the merest hint that this black child I knew so well had the power to cut me to the emotional quick, to reach the innermost regions of my being and challenge the sureties of my white world. He could never be allowed to cause me to deviate in the least from the prescribed pattern of white behavior.

Thirteen years of conditioning in a segregationist society squelched my confusion. The unswerving assurance of racial dogma suppressed any instinct to flinch, any inclination to hesitate. Infuriated with myself because I had momentarily allowed a black—even worse, a black my age—to intimidate me, I grabbed the needle from my mouth and slammed it through the valve into the basketball. I jerked the air hose from its rack and inflated the ball to its normal hardness. Still angry, I flung the ball at Bobo, striking him in the stomach. Startled, he clutched the ball with both hands, holding it tightly against his midriff. He and Howard Lee glanced at me, Bobo's eyes filled with anger, Howard's with surprise, as each probed to find a reason for my outburst. No one spoke, and I met their gaze. Bobo turned, bounced the ball once, hard, caught it, and moved toward the basketball court. He paused and glanced at me again, this time his eyes expressing puzzlement rather than anger. Howard followed him. My white heritage defended, I stood and watched them walk toward the three black boys who nonchalantly awaited our return and the resumption of the game.

I had triumphed. I had preserved my status as the superior. I had prevented Bobo from guessing that his actions had destroyed my emotional composure. I had challenged him in front of another white and forced him to confront my claim to superiority. By refusing to question my actions and returning to the game, he had acquiesced in that claim, though he never acknowledged it. I had upheld the doctrine of white supremacy and observed the rules of segregated society. And I suspect that Bobo realized, as I did, that those same rules governed his response to me. He must have understood that he could not respond to my challenge because of who he was within the village social structure, and because we stood in the shadow of Granddaddy's store, in a white world.

Yet my vindication of white supremacy was incomplete. While I had asserted my superiority and my right to that status because of my skin color, I still felt defiled. The thought that some residual contamination, some lingering trace of the essence of Bobo's blackness remained with me became an obsession. I could feel his germs crawling through my body, spreading their black pestilence from head to toe. I had to cleanse myself—to purify my body of Bobo's contaminants and to rid my person of any remaining trace of his negritude. Only then could I fully reclaim my racial purity and restore my shaken sense of superiority. And I had to do so quickly, without the knowledge of others, before I could return to the game.

I walked to the other side of the store, out of sight of the five boys on the basketball court who had begun to shoot goals at random while waiting for my return. From the side of the building protruded a faucet, used by thirsty ball players who had no money for Cokes. Bending over, I turned the tap and watched the clear, clean water burst from the spigot and spatter into the sand. I cupped my hands beneath the flow, watched them fill with the crystal liquid, then splashed it to my face, felt it begin to cleanse me of Bobo's black stain. Bending farther, I placed my mouth against the grooved lip of the faucet. I filled my mouth with water, swished the water from cheek to cheek, then forced it through my teeth and onto the ground. Tilting my head, mouth still against the faucet, I let the cleansing stream trickle through my mouth, removing any remaining Negro contaminant. I splashed more water over my face and head, then washed my hands and forearms. Finally, I swallowed a large gulp of water, felt it slide down my throat, and in my mind's eye saw it wash away the last traces of Bobo's blackness. My rite of purification was completed. With this baptism of plain tap water I was reborn, my white selfhood restored. I stood straight, shook the water from my face and hands, and walked back to rejoin the game.

I don't remember if the game resumed at midpoint, if new sides were chosen, or who won or lost. What I remember is an awareness that things had changed. I knew that Bobo was black, that he would always be black, and that his blackness set him apart from me in ways that I had never understood. I realized, too, that his blackness threatened me, that in a way I did not comprehend it challenged my most securely held concepts about who I was and what I might become. For the first time I understood that Bobo and I belonged to two fundamentally different worlds, and that society demanded that we each stay in the world designated for us. And for the first time I understood that segregation was not a happenstance, an everyday reality of no import. I realized now that segregation was serious, as serious as life and death, perhaps as serious as heaven or hell. I knew, too, that Bobo was unchanged, that I was still me, that none of the blacks with whom I played or worked were any different than they had been. I also knew that there was something very wrong, even sinister, about this power Bobo held over me, this ability to confound my world simply because he was black. None of it made much sense at the time. But the knowledge, the understanding that segregation was so powerful a force, that it could provoke such violent emotional responses within me, for the first time raised questions in my mind about the institution, serious questions that adults didn't want asked and, as I would later discover, that they never answered.

References

1. Louisiana Adopts the "Grandfather" Plan, 1898
"Constitution of the State of Louisiana, Adopted May 12, 1898," in Walter L. Fleming, ed., *Documentary History of Reconstruction*, Volume II (Cleveland, Ohio: The Arthur H. Clark Company, 1906), pp. 451—453.

2. The Supreme Court Upholds "Separate-but-Equal," 1896
"*Plessy* v. *Ferguson*, 1896," in Richard Bardolph, ed., *The Civil Rights Record: Black Americans and the Law, 1849—1970* (New York: Thomas Y. Crowell Company, 1970), pp. 149—150.

3. Senator Benjamin R. Tillman Defends Lynching, 1900
"Speech of Senator Benjamin R. Tillman, March 23, 1900," in *Congressional Record*, 56th Congress, 1st Session, pp. 3223–3224.

4. South Carolina Becomes a "White" State, 1927
"Whites Come to Be a Majority," in *South Carolina: A Handbook* (Columbia, South Carolina: The State Co., 1927), pp. 20–24.

5. An Investigator Describes a Lynching in Georgia, 1930
Arthur Raper, *The Tragedy of Lynching* (Chapel Hill, North Carolina: University of North Carolina Press, 1933), pp. 133–134.

6. Theodore Bilbo Warns Against Mongrelization, 1947
Theodore G. Bilbo, *Take Your Choice: Separation or Mongrelization* (Poplarville, Mississippi: Dream House Publishing Company, 1947), preface and pp. 219–221.

7. Southern Women Condemn Lynching, 1942
Jesse Daniel Ames, *The Changing Character of Lynching* (Atlanta, Georgia: Commission on Interracial Co-operation, Inc., 1942), pp. ix–x, 19, 21.

8. A Southern Youth Confronts His Worst Fear, c. 1954
Melton McLaurin, *Separate Pasts: Growing up White in the Segregated South* (Athens, Georgia: University of Georgia Press, 1987), pp. 36–41.

Further Reading

Dan T. Carter, *Scottsboro: A Tragedy of the American South* (1964)

Bertram Doyle, *The Etiquette of Race Relations in the South: A Study in Social Control* (1937)

George M. Fredrickson, *The Black Image in the White Mind* (1971)

——, *White Supremacy: A Comparative Study in American and South African History* (1981)

Lawrence J. Friedman, *The White Savage: Racial Fantasies in the Postbellum South* (1970)

Dewey Grantham, *Hoke Smith and the Politics of the New South* (1958)

A. Wigfall Green, *The Man Bilbo* (1963)

Robert Haws, ed., *The Age of Segregation: Race Relations in the South, 1890–1945* (1978)

V. O. Key, Jr., *Southern Politics in State and Nation* (1949)

J. Morgan Kousser, *The Shaping of Southern Politics: Suffrage Restriction and the Establishment of the One-Party South, 1880–1910* (1974)

Claude Nolen, *The Negro's Image in the South: The Anatomy of White Supremacy* (1968)

H. Leon Prather, *We Have Taken a City: Wilmington Racial Massacre and the Coup of 1898* (1984)

Howard N. Rabinowitz, *Race Relations in the Urban South* (1978)

James Silver, *Mississippi: The Closed Society* (1964)

Morton Sosna, *In Search of the Silent South: Southern Liberals and the Race Issue* (1977)

Joel Williamson, *The Crucible of Race: Black/White Relations in the American South Since Emancipation* (1984)

C. Vann Woodward, *The Strange Career of Jim Crow* (1966)

Document Set 13

Blacks in the Jim Crow South

The ease with which segregation became a southern way of life reveals the black population's impotence to influence the course of events in the South. In fact, blacks' resistance to white supremacy invited both economic and physical reprisal. Overworked and underpaid, even by southern standards, African-Americans could not risk losing their slender means of livelihood. Even more intimidating were the threats of physical violence, against which the law offered little or no protection. Once again, the survival of southern blacks depended on their outward acquiescence to a society that exploited and oppressed them.

Perhaps worse than the grinding poverty and the appalling conditions under which African-Americans lived and worked was the psychological effect of segregation. Blacks in the Jim Crow South experienced nothing less than internal colonialism by which white southerners belittled African-American culture and sought to convince black people that their values and standards were worthless. Blacks should strive to emulate the achievements of the superior white race, white southerners argued. The white strategy of systematically withholding from African-Americans the economic means to achieve upward mobility was a deliberate attempt to nurture a sense of inferiority and hopelessness.

Convinced that the South held no future other than misery for the race, and spurred on by a desire to escape from the ravaged cotton fields, many blacks migrated to the North in the hope of finding less discrimination and greater economic opportunity there. Blacks who chose or were forced to remain in the South, however, continued to live as second-class citizens. At the mercy of employers who manipulated ethnic divisions in the work force, and politicians who used blatant race baiting to secure office, blacks were kept firmly on the bottom rung of society's ladder: as debt-ridden sharecroppers and tenant farmers or as factory laborers performing only the most menial and undesirable jobs. Family separations were common as husbands despaired of providing adequately for wives and children. Just as they had in the days of slavery, however, black people found the determination to survive segregation. The majority of African-American families remained intact; churches provided much needed bulwarks of support for the black community; and education, separate but certainly not equal, held the promise of a better life.

Nothing illustrates the contradictions of the African-American experience in the Jim Crow South more than the careers of Booker T. Washington and Richard Wright. The founder of Tuskegee Institute in Alabama, Washington had been born into slavery on a Virginia plantation in 1856. One of the foremost educators of the age, Washington nevertheless found it expedient to advocate a gradualist and accommodationist approach to segregation. His speech at the Atlanta Cotton States and International Exposition in 1895, reproduced as the first document, generally received the approval of white southerners but was denounced by some black leaders who felt that Washington's solution to race problems was a tacit acceptance of segregation.

Inquisitive and intelligent, Richard Wright, the son of a sharecropper, was forced to stifle his natural talents in the interests of self-preservation. The tale of his tortured childhood is the subject of the second selection, taken from his autobiographical novel *Black Boy*, first published in 1937. Wright's youthful fantasies that the North was a haven from racial prejudice were dashed, and he spent the last fourteen years of his life in France until his death in 1960.

Posing less of a threat than black men to the doctrine of white supremacy, African-American women could frequently voice dissent without the consequent risk of violent reprisal. In the third document, schoolteacher and newspaper editor Ida B. Wells explains why she proposed a black boycott of white-owned businesses in Memphis, Tennessee, in 1892 in retaliation for the violent deaths of African-Americans there.

The legal process in the South discriminated strongly against black defendants. In the most notorious court case of the Jim Crow era, eight black youths were sentenced to death by a court in Scottsboro, Alabama, in 1931 for raping two white women. The case, which attracted national attention, exposed the true nature of southern justice, especially after one of the women admitted that the Scottsboro Boys, as they became known, had not committed the crime of which they had been convicted. All the defendants were later released, some after serving long prison sentences. The fourth document is an account of the trial by Haywood Patterson, one of the defendants.

The appalling conditions under which poverty-stricken blacks lived are revealed fully in the fifth selection, taken from the autobiography of Jane Edna Hunter, a black nurse in South Carolina. Job discrimination was a vital weapon in the white-supremacist armory. As North Carolinian Sam Mayhew explains in the final document, college-trained blacks were deprived of positions of responsibility in southern business and industry.

Questions for Analysis

1. To what degree did white supremacy fulfill its goal of instilling a sense of inferiority in black southerners?

2. Was the psychological impact of racism on southern blacks worse than the physical effects?

3. What strategies and tactics were open to black southerners in their efforts to fight racism in the segregated South?

4. How stable was the African-American family in the Jim Crow era?

5. How important were black churches and church leaders in helping to maintain a sense of worth among the black population of the South?

6. Were living and working conditions for African-Americans in the South better in the cities than in the countryside?

1. Booker T. Washington's Atlanta Address, 1895

Mr. President and Gentlemen of the Board of Directors and Citizens:

One-third of the population of the South is of the Negro race. No enterprise seeking the material, civil, or moral welfare of this section can disregard this element of our population and reach the highest success. I but convey to you, Mr. President and Directors, the sentiment of the masses of my race when I say that in no way have the value and manhood of the American Negro been more fittingly and generously recog-

nized than by the managers of this magnificent Exposition at every stage of its progress. It is a recognition that will do more to cement the friendship of the two races than any occurrence since the dawn of our freedom.

Not only this, but the opportunity here afforded will awaken among us a new era of industrial progress. Ignorant and inexperienced, it is not strange that in the first years of our new life we began at the top instead of at the bottom; that a seat in Congress or the state legislature was more sought than real estate or industrial skill; that the political convention or stump speaking had more attractions than starting a dairy farm or truck garden.

A ship lost at sea for many days suddenly sighted a friendly vessel. From the mast of the unfortunate vessel was seen a signal, "Water, water; we die of thirst!" The answer from the friendly vessel at once came back, "Cast down your bucket where you are." A second time the signal, "Water, water; send us water!" ran up from the distressed vessel, and was answered, "Cast down your bucket where you are." And a third and fourth signal for water was answered, "Cast down your bucket where you are." The captain of the distressed vessel, at last heeding the injunction, cast down his bucket, and it came up full of fresh, sparkling water from the mouth of the Amazon River. To those of my race who depend on bettering their condition in a foreign land or who underestimate the importance of cultivating friendly relations with the Southern white man, who is their next-door neighbour, I would say: "Cast down your bucket where you are"—cast it down in making friends in every manly way of the people of all races by whom we are surrounded.

Cast it down in agriculture, mechanics, in commerce, in domestic service, and in the professions. And in this connection it is well to bear in mind that whatever other sins the South may be called to bear, when it comes to business, pure and simple, it is in the South that the Negro is given a man's chance in the commercial world, and in nothing is this Exposition more eloquent than in emphasizing this chance. Our greatest danger is that in the great leap from slavery to freedom we may overlook the fact that the masses of us are to live by the productions of our hands, and fail to keep in mind that we shall prosper in proportion as we learn to dignify and glorify common labour and put brains and skill into the common occupations of life; shall prosper in proportion as we learn to draw the line between the superficial and the substantial, the ornamental gewgaws of life and the useful. No race can prosper till it learns that there is as much dignity in tilling a field as in writing a poem. It is at the bottom of life we must begin,

and not at the top. Nor should we permit our grievances to overshadow our opportunities.

To those of the white race who look to the incoming of those of foreign birth and strange tongue and habits for the prosperity of the South, were I permitted I would repeat what I say to my own race, "Cast down your bucket where you are." Cast it down among the eight millions of Negroes whose habits you know, whose fidelity and love you have tested in days when to have proved treacherous meant the ruin of your firesides. Cast down your bucket among these people who have, without strikes and labour wars, tilled your fields, cleared your forests, built your railroads and cities, and brought forth treasures from the bowels of the earth, and helped make possible this magnificent representation of the progress of the South. Casting down your bucket among my people, helping and encouraging them as you are doing on these grounds, and to education of head, hand, and heart, you will find that they will buy your surplus land, make blossom the waste places in your fields, and run your factories. While doing this, you can be sure in the future, as in the past, that you and your families will be surrounded by the most patient, faithful, law-abiding, and unresentful people that the world has seen. As we have proved our loyalty to you in the past, in nursing your children, watching by the sick-bed of your mothers and fathers, and often following them with tear-dimmed eyes to their graves, so in the future, in our humble way, we shall stand by you with a devotion that no foreigner can approach, ready to lay down our lives, if need be, in defence of yours, interlacing our industrial, commercial, civil, and religious life with yours in a way that shall make the interests of both races one. In all things that are purely social we can be as separate as the fingers, yet one as the hand in all things essential to mutual progress.

There is no defence or security for any of us except in the highest intelligence and development of all. If anywhere there are efforts tending to curtail the fullest growth of the Negro, let these efforts be turned into stimulating, encouraging, and making him the most useful and intelligent citizen. Effort or means so invested will pay a thousand per cent interest. These efforts will be twice blessed—"blessing him that gives and him that takes."

There is no escape through law of man or God from the inevitable:—

The laws of changeless justice bind
    Oppressor with oppressed;
And close as sin and suffering joined
    We march to fate abreast.

Nearly sixteen millions of hands will aid you in pulling the load upward, or they will pull against you the load downward. We shall constitute one-third and more of the ignorance and crime of the South, or one-third its intelligence and progress; we shall contribute one-third to the business and industrial prosperity of the South, or we shall prove a veritable body of death, stagnating, depressing, retarding every effort to advance the body politic.

Gentlemen of the Exposition, as we present to you our humble effort at an exhibition of our progress, you must not expect overmuch. Starting thirty years ago with ownership here and there in a few quilts and pumpkins and chickens (gathered from miscellaneous sources), remember the path that has led from these to the inventions and production of agricultural implements, buggies, steam-engines, newspapers, books, statuary, carving, paintings, the management of drug-stores and banks, has not been trodden without contact with thorns and thistles. While we take pride in what we exhibit as a result of our independent efforts, we do not for a moment forget that our part in this exhibition would fall far short of your expectations but for the constant help that has come to our educational life, not only from the Southern states, but especially from Northern philanthropists, who have made their gifts a constant stream of blessing and encouragement.

The wisest among my race understand that the agitation of questions of social equality is the extremest folly, and that progress in the enjoyment of all the privileges that will come to us must be the result of severe and constant struggle rather than of artificial forcing. No race that has anything to contribute to the markets of the world is long in any degree ostracized. It is important and right that all privileges of the law be ours, but it is vastly more important that we be prepared for the exercises of these privileges. The opportunity to earn a dollar in a factory just now is worth infinitely more than the opportunity to spend a dollar in an opera-house.

In conclusion, may I repeat that nothing in thirty years has given us more hope and encouragement, and drawn us so near to you of the white race, as this opportunity offered by the Exposition; and here bending, as it were, over the altar that represents the results of the struggles of your race and mine, both starting practically empty-handed three decades ago, I pledge that in your effort to work out the great and intricate problem which God has laid at the doors of the South, you shall have at all times the patient, sympathetic help of my race; only let this be constantly in mind, that, while from representations in these buildings of the product of field, of forest, of mine, of factory, letters, and art, much good will come, yet far above and beyond material benefits will be that higher good, that, let us pray God, will come, in a blotting out of sectional differences and racial animosities and suspicions, in a determination to administer absolute justice, in a willing obedience among all classes to the mandates of law. This, this, coupled with our material prosperity, will bring into our beloved South a new heaven and a new earth.

2. Richard Wright Recalls His Troubled Childhood, 1918

. . . I soon made myself a nuisance by asking far too many questions of everybody. Every happening in the neighborhood, no matter how trivial, became my business. It was in this manner that I first stumbled upon the relations between whites and blacks, and what I learned frightened me. Though I had long known that there were people called "white" people, it had never meant anything to me emotionally. I had seen white men and women upon the streets a thousand times, but they had never looked particularly "white." To me they were merely people like other people, yet somehow strangely different because I had never come in close touch with any of them. For the most part I never thought of them; they simply existed somewhere in the background of the city as a whole. It might have been that my tardiness in learning to sense white people as "white" people came from the fact that many of my relatives were "white"-looking people. My grandmother, who was white as any "white" person, had never looked "white" to me. And when word circulated among the black people of the neighborhood that a "black" boy had been severely beaten by a "white" man, I felt that the "white" man had had a right to beat the "black" boy, for I naïvely assumed that the "white" man must have been the "black" boy's father. And did not all fathers, like my father, have the right to beat their children? A paternal right was the only right, to my understanding, that a man had to beat a child. But when my mother told me that the "white" man was not the father of the "black" boy, was no kin to him at all, I was puzzled.

"Then why did the 'white' man whip the 'black' boy?" I asked my mother.

"The 'white' man did not *whip* the 'black' boy," my mother told me. "He *beat* the 'black' boy."

"But why?"

"You're too young to understand."

"I'm not going to let anybody beat me," I said stoutly.

"Then stop running wild in the streets," my mother said.

I brooded for a long time about the seemingly causeless beating of the "black" boy by the "white" man and the more questions I asked the more bewildering it all became. Whenever I saw "white" people now I stared at them, wondering what they were really like. . . .

A dread of white people now came to live permanently in my feelings and imagination. As the war drew to a close, racial conflict flared over the entire South, and though I did not witness any of it, I could not have been more thoroughly affected by it if I had participated directly in every clash. The war itself had been unreal to me, but I had grown able to respond emotionally to every hint, whisper, word, inflection, news, gossip, and rumor regarding conflicts between the races. Nothing challenged the totality of my personality so much as this pressure of hate and threat that stemmed from the invisible whites. I would stand for hours on the doorsteps of neighbors' houses listening to their talk, learning how a white woman had slapped a black woman, how a white man had killed a black man. It filled me with awe, wonder, and fear, and I asked ceaseless questions.

One evening I heard a tale that rendered me sleepless for nights. It was of a Negro women whose husband had been seized and killed by a mob. It was claimed that the woman vowed she would avenge her husband's death and she took a shotgun, wrapped it in a sheet, and went humbly to the whites, pleading that she be allowed to take her husband's body for burial. It seemed that she was granted permission to come to the side of her dead husband while the whites, silent and armed, looked on. The woman, so went the story, knelt and prayed, then proceeded to unwrap the sheet; and, before the white men realized what was happening, she had taken the gun from the sheet and had slain four of them, shooting at them from her knees.

I did not know if the story was factually true or not, but it was emotionally true because I had already grown to feel that there existed men against whom I was powerless, men who could violate my life at will. I resolved that I would emulate the black woman if I were ever faced with a white mob; I would conceal a weapon, pretend that I had been crushed by the wrong done to one of my loved ones; then, just when they thought I had accepted their cruelty as the law of my life, I would let go with my gun and kill as many of them as possible before they killed me. The story of the woman's deception gave form and meaning to confused defensive feelings that had long been sleeping in me.

My imaginings, of course, had no objective value whatever. My spontaneous fantasies lived in my mind because I felt completely helpless in the face of this threat that might come upon me at any time, and because there did not exist to my knowledge any possible course of action which could have saved me if I had ever been confronted with a white mob. My fantasies were a moral bulwark that enabled me to feel I was keeping my emotional integrity whole, a support that enabled my personality to limp through days lived under the threat of violence.

These fantasies were no longer a reflection of my reaction to the white people, they were a part of my living, of my emotional life; they were a culture, a creed, a religion. The hostility of the whites had become so deeply implanted in my mind and feelings that it had lost direct connection with the daily environment in which I lived; and my reactions to this hostility fed upon itself, grew or diminished according to the news that reached me about the whites, according to what I aspired or hoped for. Tension would set in at the mere mention of whites and a vast complex of emotions, involving the whole of my personality, would be aroused. It was as though I was continuously reacting to the threat of some natural force whose hostile behavior could not be predicted. I had never in my life been abused by whites, but I had already become as conditioned to their existence as though I had been the victim of a thousand lynchings.

I lived in West Helena an undeterminedly long time before I returned to school and took up regular study. My mother luckily secured a job in a white doctor's office at the unheard-of wages of five dollars per week and at once she announced that her "sons were going to school again." I was happy. But I was still shy and half paralyzed when in the presence of a crowd, and my first day at the new school made me the laughingstock of the classroom. I was sent to the blackboard to write my name and address; I knew my name and address, knew how to write it, knew how to spell it; but standing at the blackboard with the eyes of the many girls and boys looking at my back made me freeze inside and I was unable to write a single letter.

"Write your name," the teacher called to me.

I lifted the white chalk to the blackboard and, as I was about to write, my mind went blank, empty; I could not remember my name, not even the first letter. Somebody giggled and I stiffened.

"Just forget us and write your name and address," the teacher coaxed.

An impulse to write would flash through me, but my hand would refuse to move. The children began to twitter and I flushed hotly.

"Don't you know your name?" the teacher asked.

I looked at her and could not answer. The teacher rose and walked to my side, smiling at me to give me confidence. She placed her hand tenderly upon my shoulder.

"What's your name?" she asked.

"Richard," I whispered.

"Richard what?"

"Richard Wright."

"Spell it."

I spelled my name in a wild rush of letters, trying desperately to redeem my paralyzing shyness.

"Spell it slowly so I can hear it," she directed me.

I did.

"Now, can you write?"

"Yes, ma'am."

"Then write it."

Again I turned to the blackboard and lifted my hand to write, then I was blank and void within. I tried frantically to collect my senses, but I could remember nothing. A sense of the girls and boys behind me filled me to the exclusion of everything. I realized how utterly I was failing and I grew weak and leaned my hot forehead against the cold blackboard. The room burst into a loud and prolonged laugh and my muscles froze.

"You may go to your seat," the teacher said.

I sat and cursed myself. Why did I always appear so dumb when I was called upon to perform something in a crowd? I knew how to write as well as any pupil in the classroom, and no doubt I could read better than any of them, and I could talk fluently and expressively when I was sure of myself. Then why did strange faces make me freeze? I sat with my ears and neck burning, hearing the pupils whisper about me, hating myself, hating them; I sat still as stone and a storm of emotion surged through me. . . .

3. *Ida B. Wells Crusades Against Lynching, 1892*

. . . Although I had been warned repeatedly by my own people that something would happen if I did not cease harping on the lynching of three months before, I had expected that happening to come when I was at home. I had bought a pistol the first thing after Tom Moss was lynched, because I expected some cowardly retaliation from the lynchers. I felt that one had better die fighting against injustice than to die like a dog or a rat in a trap. I had already determined to sell my life as dearly as possible if attacked. I felt if I could take one lyncher with me, this would even up the score a little bit. But fate decided that the blow should fall when I was away, thus settling for me the question whether I should go West or East. My first thought after recovering from the shock of the information given me by Mr. Fortune was to find out if Mr. Fleming got away safely. I went at once to the telegraph office and sent a telegram to B. F. Booth, my lawyer, asking that details be sent me at the home address of Mr. Fortune.

In due time telegrams and letters came assuring me of Mr. Fleming's safety and begging me not to return. My friends declared that the trains and my home were being watched by white men who promised to kill me on sight. They also told me that colored men were organized to protect me if I should return. They said it would mean more bloodshed, more widows and orphans if I came back, and now that I was out of it all, to stay away where I would be safe from harm.

Because I saw the chance to be of more service to the cause by staying in New York than by returning to Memphis, I accepted their advice, took a position on the *New York Age*, and continued my fight against lynching and lynchers. They had destroyed my paper, in which every dollar I had in the world was invested. They had made me an exile and threatened my life for hinting at the truth. I felt that I owed it to myself and my race to tell the whole truth.

So with the splendid help of T. Thomas Fortune and Jerome B. Peterson, owners and editors of the *New York Age*, I was given an opportunity to tell the world for the first time the true story of Negro lynchings, which were becoming more numerous and horrible. Had it not been for the courage and vision of these two men, I could never have made such headway in emblazoning the story to the world. These men gave me a one-fourth interest in the paper in return for my subscription lists, which were afterward furnished me, and I became a weekly contributor on salary.

The readers will doubtless wonder what caused the destruction of my paper after three months of constant agitation following the lynching of my friends. They were killed on the ninth of March. The *Free Speech* was destroyed 27 May 1892, nearly three months later. I thought then it was the white southerner's chivalrous defense of his womanhood which caused the mob to destroy my paper, even though it was known that the truth had been spoken. I know now that it was an excuse to do what they had wanted to do before but had not dared because they had no good reason until the appearance of that famous editorial.

For the first time in their lives the white people of Memphis had seen earnest, united action by Negroes which upset economic and business conditions. They had thought the excitement would die down; that Negroes would forget and become again, as before, the wealth producers of the South—the hewers of wood and drawers of water, the servants of white men. But the excitement kept up, the colored people continued to leave, business remained at a standstill, and there was still a dearth of servants to cook their meals and wash their clothes and keep their homes in order, to nurse their babies and wait on their tables, to build their houses and do all classes of laborious work.

Besides, no class of people like Negroes spent their money like water, riding on streetcars and railroad trains, especially on Sundays and excursions. No other class bought clothes and food with such little haggling as they or were so easily satisfied. The whites had killed the goose that laid the golden egg of Memphis prosperity and Negro contentment; yet they were amazed that colored people continued to leave the city by scores and hundreds. . . .

4. A Scottsboro Boy Stands Trial, 1931

I was tried on April 7, the second day of the trials. Solicitor H. G. Bailey, the prosecutor, he talked excited to the jurymen. They were backwoods farmers. Some didn't even have the education I had. I had only two short little periods of reading lessons. But these men passed a decision on my life. . . .

The girls I and the others were accused of raping I saw for the third time in court. The first I saw them was at Paint Rock when we were all picked up. The second was in Scottsboro jail when they were brought to our cell. And now in court. This time they were not wearing men's overalls, but dresses. Victoria Price, the older girl, she was to me a plain-looking woman. Ruby Bates was more presentable.

Solicitor Bailey, he asked me questions. The way he handled me was the same way he handled all of us. Like this:

"You ravished that girl sitting there."

"I ravished nobody. I saw no girl."

"You held a knife to her head while the others ravished her."

"I had no knife. I saw no knife. I saw no girl."

"You saw this defendant here ravish that girl there."

"I saw nobody ravish nobody. I was in a fight. That's all. Just a fight with white boys."

"You raped that girl. You did rape that girl, didn't you?"

"I saw no girl. I raped nobody."

Bailey, he kept firing that story at me just like that. He kept pounding the rape charge against me, against all of us. We all kept saying no, we saw no girls, we raped nobody, all we knew of was a fight.

The girls got up and kept on lying. There was only one thing the people in the courtroom wanted to hear. Bailey would ask, "Did the niggers rape you?"

"Yes," the girls would answer.

That's all the people in that court wanted to hear, wanted to hear "yes" from the girls' mouths.

When Bailey finished with me he said to the jury:

"Gentlemen of the jury, I don't say give that nigger the chair. I'm not going to tell you to give him the electric chair.

"*You know your duty.*

"I'm not going to tell you to give the nigger a life sentence. All I can say is, *hide him. Get him out of our sight.*

"Hide them. Get them out of our sight.

"They're not our niggers. Look at their eyes, look at their hair, gentlemen. They look like something just broke out of the zoo.

"Guilty or not guilty, let's get rid of these *niggers*."

I went on trial about nine o'clock in the morning. Within two hours the jury had come back with a conviction. I was convicted in their minds before I went on trial. I had no lawyers, no witnesses for me. All that spoke for me on that witness stand was my black skin—which didn't do so good. Judge Hawkins asked the jurymen: "Have you reached a verdict?"

"Yes."

"Have the clerk read it."

The clerk read it off: "We, the jurymen, find the defendant guilty as charged and fix his punishment as death."

If I recollect right the verdicts against us all were in in two days. All of us got the death sentence except Roy Wright. He looked so small and pitiful on the stand that one juryman held out for life imprisonment. They declared a mistrial for Roy.

No Negroes were allowed in Scottsboro during the entire time. I didn't see a Negro face except two farmers in jail for selling corn. One of the National Guards, he fired a shot through the courtroom window about noon of the day I was convicted. Later he said that was an accident.

On the night of the first day's trials we could hear a brass band outside. It played, "There'll Be a Hot Time in the Old Town Tonight" and "Dixie."

It was April 9 when eight of us—all but Roy Wright—were stood up before Judge Hawkins for sentencing. He asked us if we had anything to say before he gave sentence. I said:

"Yes, I have something to say. I'm not guilty of this charge."

He said, "The jury has found you guilty and it is up to me to pass sentence. I set the date for your execution July 10, 1931, at Kilby Prison. May the Lord have mercy on your soul."

The people in the court cheered and clapped after the judge gave out with that. I didn't like it, people feeling good because I was going to die, and I got ruffed.

I motioned to Solicitor Bailey with my finger.

He came over. I asked him if he knew when I was going to die.

He mentioned the date, like the judge gave it, and I said, "You're wrong. I'm going to die when you and those girls die for lying about me."

He asked me how I knew and I said that that was how I felt.

I looked around. That courtroom was one big smiling white face.

5. *A Nurse Visits a Charleston Slum, 1933*

. . . You may be sure that in the early years of my nursing career I worked more zealously, and for longer hours than many a white nurse. Racial prejudice was an obstacle that could be overcome only by unusual devotion to duty and outstanding success. My prayer was not to lose a single case. I have said I was fortunate in my professional contacts to have had work with cultured people. This was no snobbish feeling, but a realization that my success in these situations would give me a prestige valuable to my career. Then, too, I was able to acquire some of the gentler ways which my earlier underprivileged years had denied me.

Work in the horrible slums of historic Charleston was no less a privilege than the experience in the homes of the well-to-do. In the Negro quarters of the city I saw conditions that were much worse than any I had known. They quickened my sympathies and renewed my purpose to do something to help the people of my race.

Much of my work was in the obstetrical field. I remember the case of one wretched Negro woman whose common-law husband had deserted her and her five children ranging in age from one to six years. Another baby was expected within an hour. The doctor called me at twilight on Sunday and told me where to go and what to do. I felt sure that he would follow shortly.

When I entered the one-room apartment, I was amazed to see the mother sitting on a filthy ash-strewn floor, and huddled about her the five children, crying from terror and pangs of hunger. There was one stick of wood, but not a lump of coal in the house. How could I effect the necessary sterilization? While one of the neighbors rushed for the doctor, only to find him out, another hurried to the head nurse of the hospital, who sent me a lantern filled with kerosene and a bundle of newspapers. Cramming the latter into the open fireplace and striking a match, I contrived to raise a fire and heat some water. Then covering the filthy mattress with newspapers, I ordered my patient to get into bed.

"Ah no get into bed. I nebber libbers on de bed. I always libbers on de floor."

"Well, Auntie, you aren't going to 'libber' on 'de' floor this time," I replied.

But as it happened I was mistaken; for before I could get her onto the mattress where I felt only a miracle could prevent infection, a twelve-pound baby boy, black as ebony, bounced into the world to set up a wail as lusty as that of any year-old infant. Fortunately the delivery was normal. Bathing and applying antiseptic precaution and sterilized dressings to the mother, I proceeded to bathe the newcomer and wrap him in one of my underskirts, the only layette I could put my hands on. Then I cleaned the floor and put the wretched room into a semblance of order. When I took my departure, the mother was on the floor, reclining contently on an old coat.

The nurses at the hospital were so touched by this story that they made up an outfit for the baby and a flannelet gown for the mother, which I took with me the following day. The doctor came in during my visit; and upon examining the baby's eyes and navel cord, praised my work. He was sorry to have left me in the lurch, he explained, but Sundays were the only days he had with his family! . . .

6. Sam Mayhew Faces Job Discrimination, 1938–1939

. . . I can't tell you my real feelings, but I think I can give you an idea of what I mean. Take me: I have applied for work at the welfare office, tried hard to get work. All they had for me, they said, came under the unskilled head. I tried one of these jobs—digging ditches for the sanitary department of the board of health. With my artificial limb, I simply couldn't compete with the other men who were digging ditches. So the inspector said he couldn't use me. It wasn't fair to the other men to pay me what they were getting; as hard as the work was for me, I couldn't take any less. So I didn't last long at that. Then I applied again for work, for something in the skilled labor line. I had seen men overseeing groups of workers, keeping their time, and so forth, and this I knew I could do as well as anybody. They told me that only white men had these jobs, that I would have to take something in the unskilled classification or none. I'm just as needy—needier I expect—as the white men, and I can do the job as well. Because of my color, I must ditch or work on the road, in spite of my college training and in spite of physical handicaps from amputation and high blood pressure—sometimes I worked at the gin last fall with a blood pressure of 190. That leaves me helpless, for in this agricultural area there are no jobs open to day labor that I am able to do for a whole day at the time. Besides, there are tenants to do all the odd work on the farms. I asked Mr. Lee the other day to let me come work out his garden for him; he said he had more men idle on his place than he could give work to. There's nothing for me except relief, and what's $14.60 for three months and—seventeen grapefruits? Seventeen grapefruits!

The same thing is true of colored girls. Our high-school graduates need jobs just as much as the white girls. Go over yonder to the county office at the agriculture building. Not a single colored girl has a job there, when they could do the work as well and need it worse than the white girls. I don't think that discrimination is intended at Washington, but here in this county the colored race has no chance to get a job when it's a choice between color. I don't see much chance for our people to get anywhere when the color line instead of ability determines the opportunities to get ahead economically.

In private industry it's the same thing. Twice there has been an opening for skilled labor at the gin, a job in the office weighing and tagging cotton. In spite of my twenty-eight years' service, always on time and always having the interest of the gin at heart, nothing was said about letting me weigh and tag cotton; the job was given to a young high-school graduate that didn't know half the business I do, that hasn't a typewriter. My employers are good to me, generally speaking; one of them is. Oh, well, the other one does let me stay in his house without paying any rent or taxes, yes. They do furnish me in the summertime when I couldn't get rations, yes; but they take it out of my salary in the fall. How do I get to Jackson to get the relief food? Well, one of my employers takes me, yes. How did I get back and forth to see my wife when she was in the hospital? My employer took me, yes. Do I ever work their gardens, cut their grass for the favors they show me? Yes, yes I do. Yes, they pay me for it of course. It's one of the catch-up jobs I have to depend on to help with our expenses. One of my employers is paralyzed, and the other is in a bad state of health, can't drive far. But they have something; I don't. When I get in a tight, I sit down and type them a note asking for money. Sometimes I get it, but more often I don't. The traveling men that come by the gin are right good to me, often sending me boxes of clothes and hats after I've handed them one of my typed notes. I wrote a well-to-do man in Norfolk the other day, but so far he has sent me nothing. . . .

References

1. Booker T. Washington's Atlanta Address, 1895
   "The Atlanta Exposition Address," in Booker T. Washington, *Up from Slavery* (New York: Doubleday, Page & Co., 1901), pp. 218–225.

2. Richard Wright Recalls His Troubled Childhood, 1918
   Richard Wright, *Black Boy* (New York: Harper & Row, 1937), pp. 30–31, 83–86.

3. Ida B. Wells Crusades Against Lynching, 1892
   Alfreda M. Duster, ed., *Crusade for Justice: The Autobiography of Ida B. Wells* (Chicago: University of Chicago Press, 1970), pp. 62–64.

4. A Scottsboro Boy Stands Trial, 1931
   Haywood Patterson and Earl Conrad, *Scottsboro Boy* (Garden City: Doubleday and Company, 1950), pp. 22–25.

5. A Nurse Visits a Charleston Slum, 1933
   Jane Edna Hunter, *A Nickel and a Prayer* (Elli Kani Publishing Co., 1940), pp. 61–63.

6. Sam Mayhew Faces Job Discrimination, 1938–1939
   Tom E. Terrill and Jerrold Hirsch, eds., *Such as Us: Southern Voices of the Thirties* (Chapel Hill, North Carolina: University of North Carolina Press, 1978), pp. 277–278.

Further Reading

Ralph D. Bunche, *The Political Status of the Negro in the Age of FDR* (1973)

Allison Davis, *Deep South* (1941)

Allison Davis and John Dollard, *Children of Bondage: The Personality and Development of Negro Youth in the Urban South* (1940)

John Dollard, *Caste and Class in a Southern Town* (1937)

Gerald Gaither, *Blacks and the Populist Revolt* (1977)

William I. Hair, *Carnival of Fury: Robert Charles and the New Orleans Race Riot of 1900* (1976)

John Haley, *Charles N. Hunter and Race Relations in North Carolina* (1987)

Louis R. Harlan, *Booker T. Washington: The Making of a Black Leader, 1865–1901* (1972)

——, *Booker T. Washington: Wizard of Tuskegee, 1901–1915* (1983)

Gerald D. Jaynes, *Branches Without Roots: Genesis of the Black Working Class in the American South, 1862–1882* (1986)

Charles S. Johnson, *Growing up in the Black Belt: Negro Youth in the Rural South* (1941)

Hylan Lewis, *Blackways of Kent* (1955)

August Meier and Elliott Rudwick, *From Plantation to Ghetto* (1976)

John Rohrer and Munro Edmondson, *The Eighth Generation Grows Up: Cultures and Personalities of New Orleans Negroes* (1960)

Arnold H. Taylor, *Travail and Triumph: Black Life and Culture in the South Since the Civil War* (1976)

Edward L. Wheeler, *Uplifting the Race: The Black Minister in the New South, 1865–1902* (1986)

George Wright, *Life Behind a Veil: Blacks in Louisville, Kentucky, 1876–1930* (1985)

Robert L. Zangrando, *The NAACP Crusade Against Lynching, 1909–1950* (1980)

Document Set 14

The South Between the World Wars

Tradition and modernization met head to head in the South in the period between the two world wars. The intense conservatism so characteristic of southerners became a national trait as Americans demanded insulation and isolation from the events that had led to the carnage of the First World War and the rise of Bolshevism in eastern Europe. Nativism and calls for immigration restriction became synonymous with patriotism. The Ku Klux Klan, a phenomenon of the Reconstruction South, was reborn in Georgia and spread rapidly into the Midwest, where its devotees claimed to be the saviors of small-town, middle-class, Protestant America from blacks, Jews, Catholics, and the evils of rampant industrialism and big-city life.

In other ways the South remained different from the rest of the nation. An earlier generation of northerners, brought up on romantic tales of plantation life, had viewed the South as a quaintly distinctive region. This idealized picture faded, however, as tales of racial atrocities surfaced in the writings of northern journalists. The greatest critic of southern life and customs was H. L. Mencken, whose acerbic and widely read opinions antagonized southerners. Ironically, Mencken's assertions that the South was a cultural and intellectual desert forced some southerners into a critical appraisal of themselves and their section. Most, however, took solace in the belief that the simple agricultural way of life in the rural South was infinitely preferable to the unsettling changes associated with a rapidly modernizing world. For Mencken, the South might be backward and unsophisticated, but for southerners the region represented an oasis of shrinking tradition in an increasingly superficial, materialistic world.

The debate about southern culture and intellect became of secondary importance as economic depression engulfed the United States in the 1930s. The agricultural economy of the South, already suffering from a depleted cotton crop and low prices for farm products, was particularly hard hit. Southerners faced difficult choices during the Great Depression. Could fiercely independent-minded people retain their integrity while accepting government welfare? Could a region that abhorred federal intervention in its local affairs accept the massive infusion of financial aid offered by the New Deal?

The idea that the South was a culturally backward section of the nation gained tremendous impetus from the proceedings and coverage of a trial held in the town of Dayton, Tennessee, in the summer of 1925. In this so-called monkey trial, John T. Scopes, a young science teacher, was accused and convicted of breaking a state law by teaching Darwin's theory of evolution in the classroom. Although the anti-evolutionists, most of them strict fundamentalists, won the case, they were depicted by the national press as superstitious and unprogressive. In the first document, Scopes recounts the discussion that led to his decision to test the validity of the state law.

Education itself was a prerogative of the wealthy in southern society. In the second selection, Governor Huey Long of Louisiana describes the opposition to his plan of distributing free books to children in state schools and his successful maneuvering to overcome the objections. The third document, a survey conducted under the auspices of the New Deal's Works Project Administration (WPA) in 1936, reveals the prevalence of illiteracy in the southern states.

One area of the South that appeared to pros·

per during the 1920s was Florida, previously an underdeveloped and relatively isolated part of the nation. The get-rich-quick schemes of the kind featured in the fourth document proved an irresistible attraction to gullible speculators. The subsequent collapse of the nation's economy had especially severe repercussions in Florida.

New Deal legislation, especially the Agricultural Adjustment Act (AAA) and the creation of the Tennessee Valley Authority (TVA), helped southerners ward off the worst effects of the depression without attacking the structural reasons for southern poverty. After receiving an advisory report on conditions in the South, President Franklin D. Roosevelt, in a letter reproduced as the fifth doc-

ument, identified the section as the nation's greatest problem.

The New Deal dignified the worth of labor and led to a dramatic increase in labor-union membership in the United States. Southern businesspeople and industrialists were loath to accept changes in labor relations, however. The sixth document chronicles and laments the fate of nineteen-year-old union organizer Harry Simms. Fears that unionization would both undermine individual initiative and promote the idea of a biracial workplace effectively stifled class conflict in southern industry. The ability of the employer to present a paternalistic affection for his workers kept factory laborers quiet and submissive, as the final selection reveals.

Questions for Analysis

1. In comparison to the rest of the nation, how conservative was the South in the 1920s?

2. To what degree did Fundamental Protestantism reinforce traditional southern values?

3. Why did the southern states put so little emphasis on the value of education?

4. Per capita income for southern workers was significantly below the national average in the period between the world wars. Why, therefore, was class conflict absent in the South?

5. How did southerners react to criticism of their way of life? Did they unite in defense of their social values, or did they perceive the need for reform?

6. What impact did the New Deal have on the social and economic life of the South? Did the New Deal pave the way for fundamental changes in the South?

1. *Tennessee Teacher John T. Scopes on Breaking the Law, 1925*

. . . On a warm May afternoon, four days after the term was over, I was playing tennis on the old outdoor clay court at school with some of my students. Although the full blast of summer hadn't hit Dayton yet, it was already warm, and it didn't take much swinging and ball-swatting to work up a healthy sweat.

In the middle of our game, a little boy walked up and watched us smack the ball back and forth. He was waiting for me and when we had finished a point, he called, "Mr. Scopes?"

I nodded and trotted over to him.

"Mr. Robinson says, if it's convenient, for you to come down to the drugstore," he said. The boy didn't work at the drugstore. He had been summoned off the street to fetch me.

There was no urgency in the message. Fred E. Robinson, the owner of Robinson's Drugstore— "Doc," as we called him because of his profession as a pharmacist—also was chairman of the Rhea County school board, and I assumed he wanted to talk to me about school business. We finished the game. I was wearing a shirt and trousers and the shirt was stained with sweat. It was about three-quarters of a mile downtown to the drugstore, and I walked there dressed as I was.

Robinson's Drugstore was a social center for Dayton, where people would get together for a soda and stay to discuss any local issues or just to pass the time of day. Toward the back of the drugstore, near the fountain, there were wire-backed chairs arranged around wooden-topped tables. It was always a pleasant refuge from the outside heat.

That afternoon there was plenty of heat inside. Past the screened double doors at the front was the fountain and at a nearby table were half a dozen men in the midst of a warm discussion. In addition to Doc Robinson, there was Mr. Brady, who ran the town's other drugstore; Sue Hicks, the town's leading lawyer, who had been arguing for the Butler law; Wallace Haggard, another attorney, whose father owned the leading bank and was "Mr. Dayton"; a fellow who worked at the post office; and George Rappelyea.

Robinson offered me a chair and the boy who worked as a soda jerk brought me a fountain drink.

"John, we've been arguing," said Rappelyea, "and I said that nobody could teach biology without teaching evolution."

"That's right," I said, not sure what he was leading up to.

A copy of George William Hunter's *Civic Biology* lay on a nearby shelf. Robinson's Drugstore supplied Rhea County's textbooks. Hunter's was the text used in Tennessee for biology. It had been used since 1909. The state textbook commission had adopted it in 1919 and although the contract had expired in 1924, no other book had been adopted in the meantime. I got a copy of it and showed it to the men at the table.

"You have been teaching 'em this book?" Rappelyea said.

"Yes," I said. I explained that I had got the book out of stock and had used it for review purposes while filling in for the principal during his illness. He was the regular biology teacher. I opened the book and showed them the evolutionary chart and the explanation of evolution. "Rappelyea's right, that you can't teach biology without teaching evolution. This is the text and it explains evolution."

"Then you've been violating the law," Robinson said.

I didn't know, technically, whether I had violated the law or not. I knew of the Butler Act; I'd never worried about it. At the end of the term I had substituted in the classes of the principal while he was ill; I assumed that if anyone had broken the law it was more likely to have been Mr. Ferguson.

"So has every other teacher then," I said. "There's our text, provided by the state. I don't see how a teacher can teach biology without teaching evolution."

Robinson handed me a newspaper. It was the Chattanooga *News*, the afternoon paper, and he pointed to an advertisement, placed by the American Civil Liberties Union, which offered to pay the expenses of anyone willing to test the constitutionality of the Butler law forbidding the teaching of evolution in any public school.

"John, would you be willing to stand for a test case?" Robinson said. "Would you be willing to let your name be used?"

I realized that the best time to scotch the snake is when it starts to wiggle. The snake already had been wiggling a good long time.

I said, "If you can prove that I've taught evolution, and that I can qualify as a defendant, then I'll be willing to stand trial."

"You filled in as a biology teacher, didn't you?" Robinson said.

"Yes." I nodded. "When Mr. Ferguson was sick."

"Well, you taught biology then. Didn't you cover evolution?"

"We reviewed for final exams, as best I remember." To tell the truth, I wasn't sure I had taught evolution.

Robinson and the others apparently weren't concerned about this technicality. I had expressed willingness to stand trial. That was enough.

Robinson didn't indicate that my acquiescence would lead to an ordeal, and I didn't suspect it. Nor did he suggest that trouble might come out of the trial in any way. Instead, he walked over to the telephone and called the city desk of the Chattanooga *News*.

"This is F. E. Robinson in Dayton," he said. "I'm chairman of the school board here. We've just arrested a man for teaching evolution."

I drank the fountain drink that had been handed me and I went back to the high school to finish playing tennis with the kids. I assume everyone else in the drugstore went about his normal business too.

Afterward, Rappelyea wired the American Civil Liberties Union and got a promise to assist in my defense.

Rappelyea had argued with the townspeople over the Butler law before that afternoon. He would sit in Robinson's Drugstore and expound his views on evolution and the law. He said he had first got the idea of holding a test case in Dayton as he read the Chattanooga *Times* before dinner on Monday, May 4—the day before our encounter. An article stated that Superintendent of Schools Ziegler in Chattanooga had refused to sponsor a test case there. If Chattanooga backed down, then why not have the trial in Dayton? So Rappelyea had reasoned. The following afternoon, he precipitated the incident in the drugstore.

Rappelyea already knew me as an independent thinker, and he knew that I had subbed as biology teacher during that spring. He reasoned that, if Doc Robinson asked me, I would agree to become a defendant in a test case. Relying upon this analysis of my character, he convinced the businessmen of the town that the publicity of such a case would put Dayton on the map and benefit business. His was a convincing argument and the businessmen went along with it.

I don't know what Rappelyea's personal motives were. But I am convinced that he must have had a special reason for getting the case started. Possibly he hoped to open up the Tennessee coal business or win some new industry as a result. I didn't see how he could gain by the trial; at the same time I knew him well enough to realize he wouldn't have done the things he did if he hadn't had an angle.

As things turned out I had been tapped and trapped by the rush of events. That was all right with me. It appeared that Rappelyea and the businessmen of Dayton and I were entering the test case with different motives, and that was all right too, as long as we shared the goal of testing the constitutionality of the Butler law. I would lend my name, and possibly my reputation, to the case; they would handle the technicalities of my "arrest" and bond. I had no idea the undramatic drugstore scene would trigger the big news story that followed. I knew there would be a certain amount of publicity and that a great portion of our society would believe I had some kind of horns. At the same time, I knew that sooner or later someone would have to take a stand against the stifling of freedom that the Butler Act represented. It seemed still early enough to keep emotions from getting out of hand. Flare-ups are always probable in issues concerning religion, sex, and other intimate topics.

Evolution held great potential as a roiler of emotions. If the trend toward prohibiting the teaching of evolution could be stopped before the people's emotions flared up unreasonably, then we would be able to apply reason; therein lay my hope.

Logically, the principal should have stood trial instead of me. He was the regular biology teacher. He also was a married man with children and, when he had been asked, he wouldn't consent to participate in a test case. Who could blame him? He had something tangible to lose, and he felt first responsibility to his family, as he should have. After him, I was the next logical defendant. I was a bachelor. . . .

2. *Huey Long Passes an Unpopular Measure, 1928*

. . . The hope for free school books which had become a dream of the children of the State, particularly in the poor families, was at last a reality. Never in my life have I witnessed the pleasure to as many children and families. No accomplishment of my career has given me such satisfaction.

But in the Parish of Caddo, my home parish, the opposition was so furious that it would not relent even after the books were sent to them free.

"This is a rich section of the state," said Mayor Thomas of Shreveport. "We are not going to be humiliated or disgraced by having it advertised that our children had to be given the books free."

Their school board and public bodies pronounced the whole idea of free school books one of corruption and ordered suit. Even the church of which I was a member, holding a statewide convention in Shreveport, passed a resolution condemning the law.

At about that time, it so happened that an airport was to be built by the U.S. Government, the Third Attack Wing, immediately adjacent to the City of Shreveport. It was a fine and needed improvement for the City of Shreveport and Parish of Caddo. By some act of Providence, it developed that the State of Louisiana owned 80 acres of the ground needed for its construction. The Government would not finally award the airport unless the State would make a deed for that 80 acres to it. I was requested to make the deed.

"You have decided here," I sent word to the boards of Caddo, "that your children can't have free school books. People so well off don't need an airport. Whenever you get ready to allow these free school books to be handed out to the children, then I will be ready to talk to you about the State deeding 80 acres of land to the government."

The newspapers, with one voice, criticized such action on my part. Col. Ewing called me to New Orleans and stormed. I had no intention of relenting.

The Caddo Parish authorities finally consented to distribute free school books in their schools. I deeded the 80 acres to the Government. . . .

3. The WPA Surveys Southern Illiteracy, 1936

The Southeast still leads the country in illiteracy. The ratio of illiterates to total population 10 years of age and over ranged from nearly 15 percent in South Carolina to less than 1 percent in Iowa in 1930. . . . Of the seven States reporting 10 percent or more of illiteracy, five fell within the southeastern cotton region. Even more marked was the excessive ratio of illiterates 21 years of age and over, South Carolina again ranking highest with more than 18 percent, Mississippi and Louisiana following closely in line.

For rural areas alone the proportions were even higher. In the seven southeastern States the range in percent of illiteracy for the rural population 10 years of age and over was from 7.8 percent in Arkansas to 18.3 percent in Louisiana. The proportions for those 21 years of age and over ranged from 10.1 percent in Arkansas to 23.7 percent in Louisiana. Five of the seven States reported 15 percent or more of the rural adults as illiterate in 1930.

Since there are very few foreign-born persons in the southeastern cotton States, the Census definition of literacy means largely the ability to read and write English. Although Census enumerators were instructed not to return a person as literate simply because he could write his name, obviously a great many of those returned as literate were actually unqualified in the essentials of reading and writing. An intensive study in Alabama, covering more than 1,000 farm families receiving relief, showed that approximately one-third of the adults were essentially illiterate and an additional one-third were barely literate, having had the advantage of only a fourth, fifth, or sixth grade education. The fourth grade represented the modal school attainment for the entire group. Among the Negroes more than half of the adults were essentially illiterate. Obviously, this Alabama sample should not be considered as representative of all cotton farmers since it included only those who were on the relief rolls in December 1933. Yet the existence of such a relatively large group is sufficiently alarming to merit serious attention.

Not all illiterates in the Southeast were left over from the past generation. Besides high rates of illiteracy in the general population 21 years of age and over, all the cotton States showed more than 3 percent illiteracy among rural children 10 to 20 years of age in 1930—evidence of the persisting inadequate educational facilities of these States.

Relative Ranking of the States in Education, 1930

Illiteracy in the Population 10 Years Old and over, 1930

4. *Land for Sale in Florida, 1925*

We have the best of everything in

FLORIDA

Folks are actually buying property by wire.

What have you bought in Florida?

Palm Beach and West Palm Beach should be known as one place. Both are active, only a short bridge between.

We can show you property that will make a very large per cent for any money invested.

See Dixie and Okeechobee

See my Stewart Development

If you buy my ocean frontage at Boynton at the present price it will mean a fortune for you later on.

L. E. BRIGGS

—Service in Real Estate—

WEST PALM BEACH   FLORIDA

5. President Franklin D. Roosevelt Outlines the Southern Problem, 1938

To the Members of the Conference on Economic Conditions in the South:

No purpose is closer to my heart at this moment than that which caused me to call you to Washington. That purpose is to obtain a statement—or perhaps, I should say a restatement as of today—of the economic conditions of the South, a picture of the South in relation to the rest of the country, in order that we may do something about it; in order that we may not only carry forward the work that has been begun toward the rehabilitation of the South, but that the program of such work may be expanded in the directions that this new presentation shall indicate.

My intimate interest in all that concerns the South is, I believe, known to all of you; but this interest is far more than a sentimental attachment born of a considerable residence in your section and of close personal friendship for so many of your people. It proceeds even more from my feeling of responsibility toward the whole Nation. It is my conviction that the South presents right now the Nation's No. 1 economic problem—the Nation's problem, not merely the South's. For we have an economic unbalance in the Nation as a whole, due to this very condition of the South.

It is an unbalance that can and must be righted, for the sake of the South and of the Nation.

Without going into the long history of how this situation came to be—the long and ironic history of the despoiling of this truly American section of the country's population—suffice it for the immediate purpose to get a clear perspective of the task that is presented to us. That task embraces the wasted or neglected resources of land and water, the abuses suffered by the soil, the need for cheap fertilizer and cheap power; the problems presented by the population itself—a population still holding the great heritages of King's Mountain and Shiloh—the problems presented by the South's capital resources and the absentee ownership of those resources, and problems growing out of the new industrial era and, again, of absentee ownership of the new industries. There is the problem of labor and employment in the South and the related problem of protecting women and children in this field. There is the problem of farm ownership, of which farm tenantry is a part, and of farm income. There are questions of taxation, of education, of housing, and of health.

More and more definitely in recent years those in the South who have sought selflessly to evaluate the elements constituting the general problem, have come to agree on certain basic factors. I have asked Mr. Mellett to present for your consideration a statement of these factors as prepared by various departments of the Government. I ask you to consider this statement critically, in the light of your own general or specific knowledge, in order that it may be made representative of the South's own best thought and that it may be presented to Congress and the public as such.

I had hoped to attend your meeting and listen to your discussions. Unhappily, other pressing work makes this impossible. Please accept my sincere regret that I cannot be with you, and be assured that I anticipate with deep interest the result of your labors.

Franklin D. Roosevelt

The White House
Washington, D.C., July 5, 1938

6. The Murder of Harry Simms, 1932

Harry Simms was a young organizer who came into Kentucky when the miners were on strike. He was murdered on Brush Creek in 1932. He was a real good organizer—he was having a lot of influence, mainly among the young people.

A lot of people had been going up to New York to speak about the miners' plight. Aunt Molly Jackson had gone and was speaking and singing around at mass meetings. And these people didn't believe what was going on in Kentucky. A committee (the Dreiser Committee) came to investigate. They said, "We'll just go and see for ourselves what's going on there." They brought a truckload of food, milk, and clothes for the children.

We was going to form a demonstration to go and meet these people to welcome them to Kentucky. We had organizers to go into different sections—Straight Creek, parts of Harlan County. I was to lead them out of Clear Fork. There was a junction there where they could all come together. Harry Simms and Green Lawson was delegated to go and lead the miners out of Brush Creek.

There was two of these company gun men came along on one of these little cars that travel on the railroad tracks. When they saw Harry Simms and Green Lawson walking up the tracks, they stopped and got off and shot Harry Simms. They weren't interested in killing Green Lawson—they knew he was just a local boy. But Harry Simms was an outsider—as they're so fond of calling them.

I was on the committee to go and claim his body from the chief of police.

Tillman Cadle

The Murder of Harry Simms*

Come and listen to my story, come and listen to
    my song,
I'll tell you of a hero who now is dead and gone,
I'll tell you of a young lad, his age was just
    nineteen,
He was the bravest union man that I have ever
    seen.

Harry Simms was a pal of mine, we labored side
    by side,
Expecting to be shot on sight or taken for a ride
By the dirty coal-operator gun thugs that roamed
    from town to town
Shooting down the union men where'er they
    could be found.

Harry Simms and I were parted at 12 o'clock that
    day
Be careful, my dear comrade, to Harry I did say.
But I must do my duty, was his reply to me,
If I get killed by gun thugs, don't grieve after me.

Harry Simms was walking down the track that
    bright sunshiny day.
He was a youth of courage, his step was light
    and gay.
He did not know the gun thugs were hiding on
    the way
To kill our dear young comrade that bright sun-
    shiny day.

Harry Simms was killed on Brush Creek in 1932,
He organized the miners into the NMU,
He gave his life in struggle, it was all that he
    could do,
He died for the union, he died for me and you.

---

*Words and music by Jim Garland.   1947 by People's Songs, Inc.; assigned to Stormking Music, Inc., 1966.

7. *The Life and Labors of a Southern Factory Worker, 1939*

I like my work. I like working for Christian people. Mr. Pugh owns the shoe plant here in Hancock and he sure is a Christian man. Do you know why he's made such a big success in life? It's the Christian way he lives. They tell me he gives a tenth of all he makes to the church and the Lord made him successful. It makes you feel good to work for a Christian man like that.

My work is hard all right. It's hard on me because I ain't but only seventeen and ain't got my full growth yet. It's work down in the steam room which they call it that because it's always full of steam which sometimes when you go in it you can't hardly see. You steam leather down there and that steam soaks you clean to the skin. It makes me keep a cold most of the time because when I go out doors I'm sopping wet. Another thing that's hard about it is having so much standing up to do. My hours is from seven o'clock in the morning till four in the evening. And it's stand on my feet the whole time. When noon time comes and I'm off an hour, why I just find me somewheres to set and I sure set there. You couldn't pay me to stand up during lunch time.

I'm on piecework now and I can't seem to get my production up to where I make just a whole lot. You get paid by the production hour and it takes fifty pair of shoes to make that hour. You get forty-two cents for the hour. Highest I ever made in one week was eleven dollars and the lowest was seven dollars and forty-two cents. I usually hit in between and make eight or nine dollars.

Now and then somebody will say, "We ought to have us a union here of some sort." That kind of talk just makes me mad all over. Mr. Pugh is a Christian man. He brought his factory here to give us some work which we didn't have any before. We do pretty well, I think, to just stay away from that kind of talk. All but the sore-heads and trouble-makers is satisfied and glad to have work.

I don't blame Mr. Pugh a bit the way he feels about the unions. The plant manager knows Mr. Pugh mighty well and he told my foreman what Mr. Pugh said. Mr. Pugh said, "If the union ever comes in here and I have to operate my plant under a union, why I'll just close the plant down and move it away from Hancock so quickly it'll make your head swim." That's his word on it and I don't blame him none. I'd hate to see a union try here. No plant and no jobs for anybody. They just operate these unions out of Wall Street, anyhow, trying to ruin people like Mr. Pugh. Man told me that and he knows. He worked in Detroit during the War. Wall Street set some unions on Henry Ford and tried to put his back to the wall. But did they do it? Don't make me laugh!

Next to the unions, this new wages and hours business of the government's is bad, too. Some people that had been getting as high as thirty-five dollars a week was cut to only twenty-five which is about ten dollars a week less than they'd been getting before. They didn't like it because it meant their salary wasn't as much as it had been. Then some that hadn't got but five or six dollars got to getting as much as I get. They liked that, but it don't seem fair to me. Why should a man that's not worth as much to the plant as me get as much money as me?

My money has to go a long way. I've got to pay eight dollars a month rent and I have to buy coal and stove wood. I got to buy clothes for the family and something to eat for them. Then twice a month there's that five dollar ambulance bill which it's to take my brother that's got the T. B. to the City Hospital in Memphis where they take and drain his lungs. Sure charge you for an ambulance, don't they? Now, some people say if you just take one trip in an ambulance, the undertaker won't ask a cent for it. Figures he'll get your custom if you pass on. But they sure charge me for my brother.

Well, I'm always glad when it's quitting time. I like to work there, but you can't help getting tired. I go on home. I walk four blocks and I'm there. Usually I have to wait a while for supper so I just set at the window. I like to watch and see if maybe something will come along the street and I can watch it. Sometimes there's a new funny paper there and I will look it over—specially if it's Tarzan. That's the best thing in a funny paper, the Tarzan part. Nobody ever gets it over old Tarzan, do they? Most times, though, I like to just set there and watch.

That's one of the best things I liked about working in the filling station that time—always something to see. Cars coming in and out. I used to keep count of the out-of-the-state license plates and how many people wore straw hats. It was the first job I ever had. I waited on customers, such as selling gasoline and patching tires. I got a dollar ninety-eight a week there, but sometimes there were tips, and anyhow it was fun. I'd have worked for nothing almost if they'd let me.

Well, I got another job after that. My brother which he's my married brother is just about the best man to paper a house or give it a coat of paint in Hancock. They say around here that if you want a good job of painting or paper hanging, just call in the Sherrys. Lots of other men will work cheaper, but it's not a high-grade, A number-one, first-class job like my brother's. So I painted and papered a while. But I got to the place where the smell of paint didn't agree with me. I took painter's colic. I was afraid I'd get down sick like my other brother, so I quit and got a job in Pugh's shoe plant in the steam room which I'm still there in it after a year.

I work steady but I'm most always financially in need of money. It takes a lot to keep a family going. My little sister needs glasses but they cost too much. All of my family has weak eyes but we can't afford to wear glasses.

So I haven't the money for running around. I wouldn't if I had the money, either. The Bible is against running around and playing cards and seeing the moving pictures. People should study their Bible more and we'd have more Christian men like Mr. Pugh and more jobs. So me and a young lady I know of go to church and Sunday School instead of running around. My family belongs to the Baptist Church, but this certain young lady is a Nazarene and that's where we go.

You know, when you're blue and down at the mouth and don't see any use anyhow, a good sermon just lifts you up. You haven't got a thing to lose by living a Christian life. Take Mr. Pugh. He lives it and look where he is now. And if you don't make out that way, if you're poor all your life, then you get a high place in the Kingdom. Just do the best you know how and the Lord will take care of you either here or hereafter. It sure is a comfort.

References

1. Tennessee Teacher John T. Scopes on Breaking the Law, 1925
   John T. Scopes and James Presley, *Center of the Storm: Memoirs of John T. Scopes* (New York: Holt, Rinehart and Winston, 1967), pp. 57–62.

2. Huey Long Passes an Unpopular Measure, 1928
   T. Harry Williams, ed., *Every Man a King: The Autobiography of Huey P. Long* (Chicago: Quadrangle Paperbacks, 1964), pp. 114–115.

3. The WPA Surveys Southern Illiteracy, 1936
   T. J. Woofter, *Landlord and Tenant on the Cotton Plantation* (Washington, D.C.: WPA, 1936), pp. 126–128.

4. Land for Sale in Florida, 1925
   "The South of Yesterday, Today, and Tomorrow," in *Blue Book of Southern Progress* (Baltimore: Manufacturers' Record, 1925), p. 221.

5. President Franklin D. Roosevelt Outlines the Southern Problem, 1938
   "The President's Letter on Economic Conditions of the South," 1938.

6. The Murder of Harry Simms, 1932
   Guy and Candie Carawan, *Voices from the Mountain* (New York: Alfred A. Knopf, 1975), pp. 120–121.

7. The Life and Labors of a Southern Factory Worker, 1939
   These Are Our Lives: As Told by the People and Written by Members of the Federal Writers' Project of the Works Project Administration in North Carolina, Tennessee, and Georgia (Chapel Hill, North Carolina: University of North Carolina Press, 1939), pp. 231–235.

Further Reading

Edward H. Beardsley, *A History of Neglect: Health Care for Blacks and Mill Workers in the Twentieth-Century South* (1987)

Frank Freidel, *FDR and the South* (1965)

Ray Ginger, *Six Days or Forever: Tennessee v. John Thomas Scopes* (1958)

Nancy L. Grant, *TVA and Black Americans: Planning for the Status Quo* (1990)

Dewey Grantham, *Southern Progressivism: The Reconciliation of Progress and Tradition* (1983)

Donald H. Grubbs, *Cry from the Cotton: The Southern Tenant Farmers' Union and the New Deal* (1971)

James A. Hodges, *New Deal Labor Policy and the Southern Cotton Textile Industry, 1933–1941* (1986)

Preston J. Hubbard, *Origins of the TVA: The Muscle Shoals Controversy, 1920–1932* (1961)

Jack T. Kirby, *Rural Worlds Lost: The American South, 1920–1960* (1987)

Paul Mertz, *New Deal Policy and Southern Rural Poverty* (1978)

Michael O'Brien, *The Idea of the American South, 1920–1941* (1979)

Daniel J. Singal, *The War Within: From Victorian to Modernist Thought in the South, 1919–1945* (1982)

James J. Thompson, Jr., *Tried as by Fire: Southern Baptists and the Religious Controversies of the 1920s* (1982)

T. Harry Williams, *Huey Long* (1969)

Document Set 15

The Civil-Rights Movement

The seemingly impenetrable barrier of segregation showed signs of weakening in the late 1940s. The triumph of the Western democracies against fascist regimes in the Second World War highlighted a glaring contradiction in American life. African-Americans in the United States, and especially in the South, were free, but they were certainly not treated as the equals of white Americans. As foreign observers sought to discover the nature of a country that claimed to be the leader of the free world against communism, the U.S. government could no longer pass off the presence of racism as a fanciful invention of Soviet propaganda.

Black organizations seized the moment to escalate their campaign for change. The National Association for the Advancement of Colored People (NAACP) achieved important successes in its legal assaults on discrimination in higher education. The founding of the Congress of Racial Equality (CORE) in 1942 provided African-Americans with their first grassroots movement to fight segregation. Heavily influenced by spiritual leader Mahatma Gandhi's successful pacifist strategy against British rule in India, CORE leaders adopted a nonviolent approach designed to persuade people that segregation was a blight on all Americans, black and white alike.

The philosophy of nonviolent direct action is indelibly associated with Martin Luther King, Jr., a young Montgomery, Alabama, preacher who became the undisputed leader of the civil-rights movement. Under King's direction, the Southern Christian Leadership Conference (SCLC) and the Student Non-Violent Coordinating Committee (SNCC) channeled the energies of black people into nonviolent activities such as protest marches, boycotts of white-owned businesses, sit-ins at segregated lunch counters, and "freedom rides" on interstate buses.

White liberals from both the North and the South joined the civil-rights movement, helping to form a genuine biracial coalition to promote change in the South. Many white people welcomed the changes, which promised an end to the closed society that the segregated South had become, but others resolved to resist any movement toward racial equality. Segregationists dedicated to preserving the status quo joined citizens' councils whose primary purpose was to prevent the integration of the South's public-school system. The strength of the opposition and the commitment to a traditional way of life that white southerners had come to cherish highlight the problems facing the civil-rights movement.

King's vision for the future featured a society in which racial prejudice would be universally recognized and rejected as evil and intolerable. King partially realized his dream when Congress passed important legislation in the mid-1960s, outlawing segregationist practices and leading to the reenfranchisement of southern blacks. For those white southerners who remained solidly segregationist or who favored a gradual approach to integration, however, such federal intervention was anathema. The South, nursing a hurt that ran deep in its past, could now relieve its resentment by expressing outrage over the violation of the time-honored principle of states' rights.

For southern blacks, the achievements of the civil-rights movement represented the culmination of a long, hard struggle against racism. Perhaps more important to African-Americans than legislative remedies to rid the South of discriminatory laws was the knowledge and the comfort that they were establishing a better future for themselves. Strong feelings of pride and self-worth destroyed the stigma of inferiority that had haunted black people in the United States for centuries.

The Supreme Court, over which Earl Warren presided as chief justice, from 1953 to 1969, is widely acknowledged as the most liberal in American history. An Eisenhower appointee and an unlikely champion of American liberalism, Warren wrote the decision in the landmark case of *Brown* v. *Board of Education of Topeka, Kansas*, which permanently altered the course of events in the South. The first document is an extract from Warren's opinion; the second, the so-called Southern Manifesto, reflects the South's determination to resist the implementation of the Court's decision. In signing the manifesto, forty-eight members of Congress in effect accused the Supreme Court of judicial activism and of contravening the rights of individual states, a familiar refrain in southern history.

A single act of courageous defiance provided the spark that ignited the modern civil-rights movement. In December 1955 Rosa Parks, a member of the NAACP in Montgomery, Alabama, refused to give up her bus seat to a white passenger. Parks's arrest precipitated a year-long boycott that resulted in the desegregation of the city's bus line. In the third document, Parks provides her own account of the incident. The Montgomery bus boycott catapulted Martin Luther King, Jr., to national prominence. In the fourth document, a speech delivered to students at the University of California at Berkeley, King outlines his philosophy of nonviolent direct action.

The process of integrating public-school systems was slow everywhere and almost nonexistent in the Deep South. The city of Little Rock, Arkansas, became the symbol of southern resistance to desegregation. Governor Orval Faubus refused to allow nine black teenagers to enter Little Rock's Central High School. In the fifth selection, Elizabeth Eckford, a fifteen-year-old student in 1957, recounts the traumatic experience of her first attempt to enter Central High. In contrast to Little Rock, some southern cities desegregated their public-school systems quietly and responsibly. The sixth document provides insights into the methods of enforcing desegregation used by the city of Atlanta, Georgia, and the emotions of one schoolteacher in the early days of teaching an integrated class in an Atlanta high school.

King's famous "I Have a Dream" speech on the occasion of a civil-rights march to Washington, D.C., in 1963 is the subject of the seventh document. King's message conveys hope tinged with disappointment at the extremely slow improvement in race relations. The final selection is the commencement address at Howard University delivered by President Lyndon B. Johnson, whose strong commitment to civil rights was evident in his unswerving support for passage of the Civil Rights Act in 1964 and the Voting Rights Act a year later.

Questions for Analysis

1. Was nonviolent, direct action the most logical course for southern blacks to adopt in their fight against Jim Crow?

2. Were southern whites justified in branding federal interference in race relations in the South as a usurpation of states' rights?

3. Why did the Democratic party of the 1960s play such a leading role in promoting the passage of civil-rights legislation? How committed were presidents John F. Kennedy and Lyndon B. Johnson to the attainment of racial equality in the United States?

4. How effective was Martin Luther King, Jr., as leader of the civil-rights movement?

5. What role did liberal white Americans play in the civil-rights movement? Did they strengthen or weaken it?

6. What did southern blacks realistically expect the civil-rights movement to achieve—an end to racial discrimination or an end to racial prejudice?

1. *Brown* v. *Board of Education, 1954*

. . . In approaching this problem, we cannot turn the clock back to 1868 when the Amendment was adopted, or even to 1896 when *Plessy* v. *Ferguson* was written. We must consider public education in the light of its full development and its present place in American life throughout the nation. Only in this way can it be determined if segregation in public schools deprives these plaintiffs of the equal protection of the laws.

Today, education is perhaps the most important function of state and local governments. Compulsory school attendance laws and the great expenditures for education both demonstrate our recognition of the importance of education to our democratic society. It is required in the performance of our most basic public responsibilities, even service in the armed forces. It is the very foundation of good citizenship. Today it is a principal instrument in awakening the child to cultural values, in preparing him for later professional training, and in helping him to adjust normally to his environment. In these days, it is doubtful that any child may reasonably be expected to succeed in life if he is denied the opportunity of an education. Such an opportunity, where the state has undertaken to provide it, is a right which must be made available to all on equal terms.

We come then to the question presented: Does segregation of children in public schools solely on the basis of race, even though the physical facilities and other "tangible" factors may be equal, deprive the children of the minority group of equal educational opportunities? We believe that it does.

In *Sweatt* v. *Painter* (US) *supra*, in finding that a segregated law school for Negroes could not provide them equal educational opportunities, this Court relied in large part on "those qualities which are incapable of objective measurement but which make for greatness in a law school." In *McLaurin* v. *Oklahoma State Regents*, 339 US 637, 94 L ed 1149, 70 S Ct 851, *supra*, the Court, in requiring that a Negro admitted to a white graduate school be treated like all other students, again resorted to intangible considerations: ". . . his ability to study, to engage in discussions and exchange views with other students, and, in general, to learn his profession." Such considerations apply with added force to children in grade and high schools. To separate them from others of similar age and qualifications solely because of their race generates a feeling of inferiority as to their status in the community that may affect their hearts and minds in a way unlikely ever to be undone. The effect of this separation on their educational opportunities was well stated by a finding in the Kansas case by a court which nevertheless felt compelled to rule against the Negro plaintiffs:

Segregation of white and colored children in public schools has a detrimental effect upon the colored children. The impact is greater when it has the sanction of the law; for the policy of separating the races is usually interpreted as denoting the inferiority of the Negro group. A sense of inferiority affects the motivation of a child to learn. Segregation with the sanction of law, therefore, has a tendency to [retard] the educational and mental development of Negro children and to deprive them of some of the benefits they would receive in a racial[ly] integrated school system.

Whatever may have been the extent of psychological knowledge at the time of *Plessy* v. *Ferguson*, this finding is amply supported by modern authority. Any language in *Plessy* v. *Ferguson* contrary to this finding is rejected.

We conclude that in the field of public education the doctrine of "separate but equal" has no place. Separate educational facilities are inherently unequal. Therefore, we hold that the plaintiffs and others similarly situated for whom the actions have been brought are, by reason of the segregation complained of, deprived of the equal protection of the laws guaranteed by the Fourteenth Amendment. This disposition makes unnecessary any discussion whether such segregation also violates the Due Process Clause of the Fourteenth Amendment.

Because these are class actions, because of the wide applicability of this decision, and because of the great variety of local conditions, the formulation of decrees in these cases presents problems of considerable complexity. On reargument, the consideration of appropriate relief was necessarily subordinated to the primary question—the constitutionality of segregation in public education. We have now announced that such segregation is a denial of the equal protection of the laws. In order that we may have the full assistance of the parties in formulating decrees, the cases will be restored to the docket, and the parties are requested to present further argument . . . for the reargument this Term. The Attorney General of the United States is again invited to participate. The Attorneys General of the states requiring or permitting segregation in public education will also be permitted to appear as *amici curiae* upon request to do so by September 15, 1954, and submission of briefs by October 1, 1954.

It is so ordered.

2. *The Southern Manifesto, 1956*

Declaration of Constitutional Principles

The unwarranted decision of the Supreme Court in the public school cases is now bearing the fruit always produced when men substitute naked power for established law.

The Founding Fathers gave us a Constitution of checks and balances because they realized the inescapable lesson of history that no man or group of men can be safely entrusted with unlimited power. They framed this Constitution with its provisions for change by amendment in order to secure the fundamentals of government against the dangers of temporary popular passion or the personal predilections of public officeholders.

We regard the decision of the Supreme Court in the school cases as a clear abuse of judicial power. It climaxes a trend in the Federal Judiciary undertaking to legislate, in derogation of the authority of Congress and to encroach upon the reserved rights of the States and the people.

The original Constitution does not mention education. Neither does the 14th amendment nor any other amendment. The debates preceding the submission of the 14th amendment clearly show that there was no intent that it should affect the system of education maintained by the States.

The very Congress which proposed the amendment subsequently provided for segregated schools in the District of Columbia.

When the amendment was adopted in 1868, there were 37 States of the Union.

Every one of the 26 States that had any substantial racial differences among its people, either approved the operation of segregated schools already in existence or subsequently established such schools by action of the same law-making body which considered the 14th amendment.

As admitted by the Supreme Court in the public school case (*Brown* v. *Board of Education*), the doctrine of separate but equal schools "apparently originated in *Roberts* v. *City of Boston* (1849), upholding school segregation against attack as being violative of a State constitutional guarantee of equality." This constitutional doctrine began in the North, not in the South, and it was followed not only in Massachusetts, but in Connecticut, New York, Illinois, Indiana, Michigan, Minnesota, New Jersey, Ohio, Pennsylvania and other northern States until they, exercising their rights as States through the constitutional processes of local self-government, changed their school systems.

In the case of *Plessy* v. *Ferguson* in 1896 the Supreme Court expressly declared that under the 14th amendment no person was denied any of his rights if the States provided separate but equal public facilities. This decision has been followed in many other cases. It is notable that the Supreme Court, speaking through Chief Justice Taft, a former President of the United States, unanimously declared in 1927 in *Lum* v. *Rice* that the "separate but equal" principle is "within the discretion of the State in regulating its public schools and does not conflict with the 14th amendment."

This interpretation, restated time and again, became a part of the life of the people of many of the States and confirmed their habits, customs, traditions, and way of life. It is founded on elemental humanity and commonsense, for parents should not be deprived by Government of the right to direct the lives and education of their own children.

Though there has been no constitutional amendment or act of Congress changing this established legal principle almost a century old, the Supreme Court of the United States, with no legal basis for such action, undertook to exercise their naked judicial power and substituted their personal political and social ideas for the established law of the land.

This unwarranted exercise of power by the Court, contrary to the Constitution, is creating chaos and confusion in the States principally affected. It is destroying the amicable relations between the white and Negro races that have been created through 90 years of patient effort by the good people of both races. It has planted hatred and suspicion where there has been heretofore friendship and understanding.

Without regard to the consent of the governed, outside agitators are threatening immediate and revolutionary changes in our public-school systems. If done, this is certain to destroy the system of public education in some of the States.

With the gravest concern for the explosive and dangerous condition created by this decision and inflamed by outside meddlers:

We reaffirm our reliance on the Constitution as the fundamental law of the land.

We decry the Supreme Court's encroachments on rights reserved to the States and to the people, contrary to established law, and to the Constitution.

We commend the motives of those States which have declared the intention to resist forced integration by any lawful means.

We appeal to the States and people who are not directly affected by these decisions to consider the constitutional principles involved against the time when they too, on issues vital to them, may be the victims of judicial encroachment.

Even though we constitute a minority in the present Congress, we have full faith that a majority of the American people believe in the dual system of government which has enabled us to achieve our greatness and will in time demand that the reserved rights of the States and of the people be made secure against judicial usurpation.

We pledge ourselves to use all lawful means to bring about a reversal of this decision which is contrary to the Constitution and to prevent the use of force in its implementation.

In this trying period, as we all seek to right this wrong, we appeal to our people not to be provoked by the agitators and troublemakers invading our States and to scrupulously refrain from disorder and lawless acts.

3. *Rosa Parks Sits Down for Her Rights, 1955*

I had had problems with bus drivers over the years, because I didn't see fit to pay my money into the front and then go around to the back. Sometimes bus drivers wouldn't permit me to get on the bus, and I had been evicted from the bus. But as I say, there had been incidents over the years. One of the things that made this get so much publicity was the fact the police were called in and I was placed under arrest. See, if I had just been evicted from the bus and he hadn't placed me under arrest or had any charges brought against me, it probably could have been just another incident.

I had left my work at the men's alteration shop, a tailor shop in the Montgomery Fair department store, and as I left work, I crossed the street to a drugstore to pick up a few items instead of trying to go directly to the bus stop. And when I had finished this, I came across the street and looked for a Cleveland Avenue bus that apparently had some seats on it. At that time it was a little hard to get a seat on the bus. But when I did get to the entrance to the bus, I got in line with a number of other people who were getting on the same bus.

As I got up on the bus and walked to the seat I saw there was only one vacancy that was just back of where it was considered the white section. So this was the seat that I took, next to the aisle, and a man was sitting next to me. Across the aisle there were two women, and there were a few seats at this point in the very front of the bus that was called the white section. I went on to one stop and I didn't particularly notice who was getting on the bus, didn't particularly notice the other people getting on. And on the third stop there were some people getting on, and at this point all of the front seats were taken. Now in the beginning, at the very first stop I had got on the bus, the back of the bus was filled up with people standing in the aisle and I don't know why this one vacancy that I took was left, because there were quite a few people already standing toward the back of the bus. The third stop is when all the front seats were taken, and this one man was standing and when the driver looked around and saw he was standing, he asked the four of us, the man in the seat with me and the two women across the aisle, to let him have those front seats.

At his first request, didn't any of us move. Then he spoke again and said, "You'd better make it light on yourselves and let me have those seats." At this point, of course, the passenger who would have taken the seat hadn't said anything. In fact, he never did speak to my knowledge. When the three people, the man who was in the seat with me and the two women, stood up and moved into the aisle, I remained where I was. When the driver saw that I was still sitting there, he asked if I was going to stand up. I told him, no, I wasn't. He said, "Well, if you don't stand up, I'm going to have you arrested." I told him to go on and have me arrested.

He got off the bus and came back shortly. A few minutes later, two policemen got on the bus, and they approached me and asked if the driver had asked me to stand up, and I said yes, and they wanted to know why I didn't. I told them I didn't think I should have to stand up. After I had paid my fare and occupied a seat, I didn't think I should have to give it up. They placed me under arrest then and had me to get in the police car, and I was taken to jail and booked on suspicion, I believe. The questions were asked, the usual questions they ask a prisoner or somebody that's under arrest. They had to determine whether or not the driver wanted to press charges or swear out a warrant, which he did. Then they took me to jail and I was placed in a cell. In a little while I was taken from the cell, and my picture was made and finger-prints taken. I went back to the cell then, and a few minutes later I was called back again, and when this happened I found out that Mr. E. D. Nixon and Attorney and Mrs. Clifford Durr had come to make bond for me.

In the meantime before this, or course . . . I was given permission to make a telephone call after my picture was taken and fingerprints taken. I called my home and spoke to my mother on the telephone and told her what had happened, that I was in jail. She was quite upset and asked me had the police beaten me. I told her, no, I hadn't been physically injured, but I was being held in jail and I wanted my husband to come and get me out. . . . He didn't have a car at that time, so he had to get someone to bring him down. At the time when he got down, Mr. Nixon and the Durrs had just made bond for me, so we all met at the jail and we went home. . . .

4. Martin Luther King, Jr., Explains Nonviolence, 1957

From the very beginning there was a philosophy undergirding the Montgomery boycott, the philosophy of nonviolent resistance. There was always the problem of getting this method over because it didn't make sense to most of the people in the beginning. We had to use our mass meetings to explain nonviolence to a community of people who had never heard of the philosophy and in many instances were not sympathetic with it. We had meetings twice a week on Mondays and on Thursdays, and we had an institute on nonviolence and social change. We had to make it clear that nonviolent resistance is not a method of cowardice. It does resist. It is not a method of stagnant passivity and deadening complacency. The nonviolent resister is just as opposed to the evil that he is standing against as the violent resister but he resists without violence. This method is nonaggressive physically but strongly aggressive spiritually.

Not to Humiliate but to Win Over

Another thing that we had to get over was the fact that the nonviolent resister does not seek to humiliate or defeat the opponent but to win his friendship and understanding. This was always a cry that we had to set before people that our aim is not to defeat the white community, not to humiliate the white community, but to win the friendship of all of the persons who had perpetrated this system in the past. The end of violence or the aftermath of violence is bitterness. The aftermath of nonviolence is reconciliation and the creation of a beloved community. A boycott is never an end within itself. It is merely a means to awaken a sense of shame within the oppressor but the end is reconciliation, the end is redemption.

Then we had to make it clear also that the nonviolent resister seeks to attack the evil system rather than individuals who happen to be caught up in the system. And this is why I say from time to time that the struggle in the South is not so much the tension between white people and Negro people. The struggle is rather between justice and injustice, between the forces of light and the forces of darkness. And if there is a victory it will not be a victory merely for fifty thousand Negroes. But it will be a victory for justice, a victory for good will, a victory for democracy.

Another basic thing we had to get over is that nonviolent resistance is also an internal matter. It not only avoids external violence or external physical violence but also internal violence of spirit. And so at the center of our movement stood the philosophy of love. The attitude that the only way to ultimately change humanity and make for the society that we all long for is to keep love at the center of our lives. Now people used to ask me from the beginning what do you mean by love and how is it that you can tell us to love those persons who seek to defeat us and those persons who stand against us; how can you love such persons? And I had to make it clear all along that love in its highest sense is not a sentimental sort of thing, not even an affectionate sort of thing.

Agape Love

The Greek language uses three words for love. It talks about *eros*. *Eros* is a sort of aesthetic love.

It has come to us to be a sort of romantic love and it stands with all of its beauty. But when we speak of loving those who oppose us we're not talking about *eros*. The Greek language talks about *philia* and this is a sort of reciprocal love between personal friends. This is a vital, valuable love. But when we talk of loving those who oppose you and those who seek to defeat you we are not talking about *eros* or *philia*. The Greek language comes out with another word and it is *agape*. *Agape* is understanding, creative, redemptive good will for all men. Biblical theologians would say it is the love of God working in the minds of men. It is an overflowing love which seeks nothing in return. And when you come to love on this level you begin to love men not because they are likable, not because they do things that attract us, but because God loves them and here we love the person who does the evil deed while hating the deed that the person does. It is the type of love that stands at the center of the movement that we are trying to carry on in the Southland—*agape*.

Some Power in the Universe that Works for Justice

I am quite aware of the fact that there are persons who believe firmly in nonviolence who do not believe in a personal God, but I think every person who believes in nonviolent resistance believes somehow that the universe in some form is on the side of justice. That there is something unfolding in the universe whether one speaks of it as an unconscious process, or whether one speaks of it as some unmoved mover, or whether someone speaks of it as a personal God. There is something in the universe that unfolds for justice and so in Montgomery we felt somehow that as we struggled we had cosmic companionship. And this was one of the things that kept the people together, the belief that the universe is on the side of justice.

God grant that as men and women all over the world struggle against evil systems they will struggle with love in their hearts, with understanding good will. *Agape* says you must go on with wise restraint and calm reasonableness but

you must keep moving. We have a great opportunity in America to build here a great nation, a nation where all men live together as brothers and respect the dignity and worth of all human personality. We must keep moving toward the goal. I know that some people are saying we must slow up. They are writing letters to the North and they are appealing to white people of good will and to the Negroes saying slow up, you're pushing too fast. They are saying we must adopt a policy of moderation. Now if moderation means moving on with wise restraint and calm reasonableness, then moderation is a great virtue that all men of good will must seek to achieve in this tense period of transition. But if moderation means slowing up in the move for justice and capitulating to the whims and caprices of the guardians of the deadening status quo, then moderation is a tragic vice which all men of good will must condemn. We must continue to move on. Our self-respect is at stake; the prestige of our nation is at stake. Civil rights is an eternal moral issue which may well determine the destiny of our civilization in the ideological struggle with communism. We must keep moving with wise restraint and love and with proper discipline and dignity.

The Need to Be "Maladjusted"

Modern psychology has a word that is probably used more than any other word. It is the word "maladjusted." Now we all should seek to live a well adjusted life in order to avoid neurotic and schizophrenic personalities. But there are some things within our social order to which I am proud to be maladjusted and to which I call upon you to be maladjusted. I never intend to adjust myself to segregation and discrimination. I never intend to adjust myself to mob rule. I never intend to adjust myself to the tragic effects of the methods of physical violence and to tragic militarism. I call upon you to be maladjusted to such things. I call upon you to be as maladjusted as Amos who in the midst of the injustices of his day cried out in words that echo across the generations, "Let judgment run down like waters and righteousness like a mighty stream." As maladjusted as Abraham Lincoln who had the vision to see that this nation could not exist half slave and half free. As maladjusted as Jefferson, who in the midst of an age amazingly adjusted to slavery could cry out, "All men are created equal and are endowed by their Creator with certain inalienable rights and that among these are life, liberty and the pursuit of happiness." As maladjusted as Jesus of Nazareth who dreamed a dream of the fatherhood of God and the brotherhood of man. God grant that we will be so maladjusted that we will be able to go out and change our world and our civilization. And then we will be able to move from the bleak and desolate midnight of man's inhumanity to man to the bright and glittering daybreak of freedom and justice.

5. *Elizabeth Eckford Remembers Little Rock (1957), 1976*

That night I was so excited I couldn't sleep. The next morning I was about the first one up. While I was pressing my black-and-white dress—I had made it to wear on the first day of school—my little brother turned on the TV set. They started telling about a large crowd gathered at the school. The man on TV said he wondered if we were going to show up that morning. Mother called from the kitchen, where she was fixing breakfast, "Turn that TV off!" She was so upset and worried. I wanted to comfort her, so I said, "Mother, don't worry."

Dad was walking back and forth, from room to room, with a sad expression. He was chewing on his pipe and he had a cigar in his hand, but he didn't light either one. It would have been funny, only he was so nervous.

Before I left home Mother called us into the living room. She said we should have a word of prayer. Then I caught the bus and got off a block from the school. I saw a large crowd of people standing across the street from the soldiers guarding Central. As I walked on, the crowd suddenly got very quiet. Superintendent Blossom had told us to enter by the front door. I looked at all the people and thought, "Maybe I will be safer if I walk down the block to the front entrance behind the guards."

At the corner I tried to pass through the long line of guards around the school so as to enter the grounds behind them. One of the guards pointed across the street. So I pointed in the same direction and asked whether he meant for me to cross the street and walk down. He nodded "yes." So, I walked across the street conscious of the crowd that stood there, but they moved away from me.

For a moment all I could hear was the shuffling of their feet. Then someone shouted, "Here she comes, get ready!" I moved away from the crowd on the sidewalk and into the street. If the mob came at me I could then cross back over so the guards could protect me.

The crowd moved in closer and then began to follow me, calling me names. I still wasn't afraid. Just a little bit nervous. Then my knees started to shake all of a sudden and I wondered whether I could make it to the center entrance a block away. It was the longest block I ever walked in my whole life.

Even so, I still wasn't too scared because all the time I kept thinking that the guards would protect me.

When I got in front of the school, I went up to a guard again. But this time he just looked straight ahead and didn't move to let me pass him. I didn't know what to do. Then I looked and saw that the path leading to the front entrance was a little further ahead. So I walked until I was right in front of the path to the front door.

I stood looking at the school—it looked so big! Just then the guards let some white students through.

The crowd was quiet. I guess they were waiting to see what was going to happen. When I was able to steady my knees, I walked up to the guard who had let the white students in.

He too didn't move. When I tried to squeeze past him, he raised his bayonet and then the other guards moved in and they raised their bayonets.

They glared at me with a mean look and I was very frightened and didn't know what to do. I turned around and the crowd came toward me.

They moved closer and closer. Somebody started yelling, "Lynch her! Lynch her!"

I tried to see a friendly face somewhere in the mob—someone who maybe would help. I looked into the face of an old woman and it seemed a kind face, but when I looked at her again, she spat on me.

They came closer, shouting, "No nigger bitch is going to get in our school. Get out of here!"

I turned back to the guards but their faces told me I wouldn't get any help from them. Then I looked down the block and saw a bench at the bus stop. I thought, "If I can only get there I will be safe." I don't know why the bench seemed a safe place to me, but I started walking toward it. I tried to close my mind to what they were shouting, and kept saying to myself, "If I can only make it to the bench I will be safe."

When I finally got there, I don't think I could have gone another step. I sat down and the mob crowded up and began shouting all over again. Someone hollered, "Drag her over to this tree! Let's take care of that nigger." Just then a white man sat down beside me, put his arm around me and patted my shoulder. He raised my chin and said, "Don't let them see you cry."

6. *Atlanta Acts on Desegregation, 1961*

Policing Integration

When it became inevitable a year ago that Atlanta, Ga., would have to integrate four of its high schools this fall, the stage was set for great potential violence. Among the largest cities in the South and one which takes pride in being both cultured and cosmopolitan, Atlanta is still a deeply southern town. White segregationist feeling, fortified by a heavy influx of rural Georgians, runs high. One of the largest groups of the Ku Klux Klan is there too.

As the opening of school neared, the situation grew specifically threatening. Dynamite was stolen in metropolitan Atlanta, and there were known bombers in the city. Indeed, Atlanta in those critical days probably held the largest and most assorted congregation of racial cranks ever assembled in one place. The odds were excellent that there would be a hit-and-run sniping or bombing attempt.

It never took place. Nine Negro students entered formerly all-white high schools without any violence at all. And it came about through a dramatic, complex plan of prevention carried out by thousands of Atlantans who worked hard to save both their schools and their city's good name. In back of them was a resourceful, determined city government and police force. I watched the climactic moments of the highly skillful operation in a police car with two detectives who played important roles in the over-all plan.

The leading characters in Atlanta's plans were three city officials: mayor, school superintendent, chief of police. Once it was established last January that integration was certain, these men and their staffs started to work on the two main jobs ahead.

First it would be necessary to establish an environment of unqualified law and order. This would serve as fair warning to all troublemakers and at the same time reassure Atlanta's law-abiding citizens. The second job was to track down, identify and maintain surveillance on the group of twisted bigots who might commit overt acts of violence.

Mayor William Hartsfield gave strong, personal support to this preventive campaign. As no one else in Atlanta could, the mayor articulated the theme of law and order. One of his phrases became the campaign slogan: "Atlanta is too busy to hate."

Dr. John W. Letson, the Atlanta school superintendent, had already confronted racial violence when he was superintendent in Chattanooga, Tenn., in 1960. Letson's chief concern was the survival of public schools. Teachers, students, employees, the entire school system—all were alerted to the task of handling integration of the Negro students as efficiently and as kindly as possible.

But as the spring of 1961 passed into summer, more and more of the job fell on Police Chief Herbert Jenkins. He is a tall man with an easy manner who often wears loafers with his gold-braided uniform. He doesn't take himself too seriously. What he does take seriously is law enforcement. Jenkins created a security guard for each of the four Atlanta schools that were to be integrated. Each of these guards was made up of the best men in the uniformed divisions of the department. On the proper signal, 90% of the Atlanta police could turn out in 15 minutes to help them.

Putting the Fanatics Safely to Bed

The police studied the problem from every angle. They pored over blueprints of each floor of the schools, in case they should have to go inside to deal with trouble. The intelligence squad was given the critical undercover job of tracking down fanatics who might bomb the schools or attack the Negro students.

One evening not long before the opening of school, I met with two detectives on this squad, Lieutenant Clinton Chafin and Morris G. Redding, at police headquarters. They were to take me along on their special rounds.

We must have put every segregationist bomber in the southeastern United States to bed that night. We drove past a Ku Klux meeting hall. We went several times by the Grand Dragon's house. We stopped to talk with a man suspected of having taken part in past bombings, a man who told us he had been at the Montgomery bus terminal when the Freedom Riders arrived the first time.

But the department's first worry, my companions told me, was an organization that has never been mentioned in public.

It is called "Nacirema"—American spelled backward. "The people in it—they wear black masks and black robes—got out of the Klan because they were afraid they weren't going to get any action there," Lieutenant Chafin told me as we drove out past the city limits of Atlanta into Cobb County.

"What we do is come out here every Monday night when they meet and try to get some tag numbers," he said. "We really have no jurisdiction. The best we can do is try to nail them when they drive back into the city limits. Then at least we can stop them and make them identify themselves. We used to go up into the woods behind their clubhouse where they park their cars but they got onto that. They put cardboard over the tags and set out an armed sentry in the yard."

He pointed to a battered one-story concrete block building. A naked light bulb cast harsh shadows over the front and out onto the lawn. The shades were drawn. I could barely distinguish the shapes of four or five cars in the back.

"Not much crowd tonight," said Chafin to Redding.

"I think we're starting to have an effect on their membership," said Redding with evident pleasure.

We parked and sat silently, patiently. A faint noise, the city noise of Atlanta, was at our backs, like a whisper. This was a tribute in its way, I thought, that the law enforcement problem in Atlanta's school crisis had come down to this, to a few cranks meeting furtively, with two good policemen standing between them and the city they had sworn to protect.

"I believe we've got one," said Redding, as a car scratched off down the road, out of the driveway of the Nacirema clubhouse.

We beat him to the intersection, forced him to halt just long enough for Redding to get the number of his plate. He went on, looking at us snarlingly, a young man with deep-set eyes and high cheekbones.

Redding lifted the microphone, asked for the ownership of the car. We had not driven more than a half mile before he got the answer. We had not driven another mile before a call came notifying us that the young man had been stopped inside Atlanta.

Chafin took off at high speed. We found a group of detectives surrounding the young man. Chafin talked to him politely and in a way that seemed to me too cursory for the pains we had taken to get him.

"Oh, I know him," Chafin explained later. "That fella tried to buy dynamite last week."

That night we saw him to bed and later checked his house to make sure his car was there. We checked dozens of other houses the same way.

On the morning school opened I was back in the car again with Chafin and Redding. We drove out into a residential section of the city and stopped near a group of two-story units in a housing project.

On the seat between Chafin and Redding was a packet of pictures of known troublemakers, a seedy photographic catalogue of hatred and big-otry. Beside the pictures was a clipboard holding a list of license plates and descriptions of the cars these men owned.

At exactly 8:23 a 1956 Oldsmobile two-door hard-top, its green paint covered with a smudge of dust, came down the quiet street. The driver was a dapper-looking Negro in his late 30s. As he passed us, he looked aside at our car for a second, and without expression drove on.

The Quiet Start of a Historic Journey

The Oldsmobile parked about halfway down the hill. We pulled out, drove down toward him and parked illegally at a pedestrian crossing.

Almost at once a teen-age Negro girl came perkily along the concrete walk, cradling a stack of schoolbooks in her arms. She walked directly to the Olds and got in.

The driver was another detective on the Atlanta police force, and the Negro girl had just completed the first leg of her historic, possibly dangerous, journey to school.

The Oldsmobile drove a short distance and then stopped to pick up another Negro student before going on. As we approached the Henry Grady High School, both detectives in my car stiffened with apprehension. They looked intently at all the parked cars. Redding turned often to look behind us. At intersections he peered down every street. Finally we turned down the street that borders the school.

"It looks quiet," said Chafin with undisguised relief.

There were uniformed policemen and motor-cycle men all along the block. Up ahead, at the intersection at the front entrance of the school, we could see a clot of newsmen and TV photog-raphers, and the uniformed figure of Captain E. B. ("Bevo") Brooks who was in charge of the detail at Henry Grady.

Nodding toward him, Chafin said, "Well, they belong to Bevo now," and turned off on a side street. He halted momentarily to watch the Oldsmobile pull up to the school, see the two Negro children get out, watch the cameras flash.

It was precisely 8:45 A.M. School had started.

"By God," said Chafin proudly as he pulled away, "I don't see how we could have shaved it any finer."

Tension in the Classroom

. . . "We were as nervous as they were." I heard several teachers say the words almost as if they had all rehearsed them. Miss Lawrence described the first day of desegregation briefly: "You could hear a pin drop. Those children just sat there and they looked as if at any moment a frightful disaster, a tornado or something, might come upon them. It was obvious that none of them wanted to sit near the Negro child, and yet they were so curious you could read it all over their faces. I'll have to admit it, I was, too. How were we to know what might happen? After a while you realize that we *should* know, because we're the same old people, the same old teacher and children, in the same old room; some scattered dark faces don't make it any different. But you have to go through it to know it, or we did. No one else ever had in Georgia. . . .

The teachers talked to one another, compar-ing experiences and attitudes much as their stu-dents did. Miss Lawrence did this not only in her own school but with friends she had in other schools. All her friends agreed upon the need for outward calm and firm discipline, regardless of the turmoil in the students. Some wanted to go further, help bridge the silence and hesitation between dark and white students. Yet, any move in this direction required planning. The pulse of the class had to be carefully estimated day by day. The image was Miss Lawrence's and she continued it with the remark, "You can't treat a condition until you take stock of it.

"It's like anything else, what happens in the classroom will depend on us and the children both." She was evaluating the progress of desegregation, and emphasizing some of the variables. "I've been collecting stories this year, because each school is different, and even the classes in them." She gathered obvious pleasure from telling about teachers in one school peeking into a classroom during the first days. "I can just imagine what the parents or children would think if they saw that scene, a group of teachers behaving like children looking in a store window. Well, it was quite a novelty, and we're human like everyone else. Look at all those TV people who came around the first few days, and the reporters, too." Then she liked to mention the incident with the psychological facet to it: "I think you would be particularly interested in what happened to another English teacher. She was no integrationist, just a hard-working teacher. The first week she assigned a theme which was to be titled 'My First Week at School,' or something like that. She has been assigning that topic for years, and so have I. Would you believe that out of all her classes, with all those children, she received only a small handful of themes which even mentioned desegregation in connection with the first week of school? Imagine that, with all the police and the nationwide publicity, with all the coverage on television, those children were simply afraid to mention the subject. They ignored the most important thing to happen that week, or that year. It shows you what the mind can do. I've often wondered whether it was a deliberate thing, whether they were simply frightened, or whether it was unconscious and they really forgot. I suppose those children reflected the atmosphere around them: everyone was holding out on everyone else; no one really dared to say what he thought, or no one except a very few outspoken segregationists. Even they were quiet at first, at least in school itself. Those were crucial times, those first weeks. All kinds of attitudes were set, or for that matter prevented, by the policies we teachers adopted."

She felt that about her work generally, that teachers can do a lot. She was proud of her profession. "It all depends upon what you want, I mean what the teacher wants. The first thing, as I keep on saying, is that children must learn; nothing must be allowed to interrupt that. After that, it's almost a matter of what the teacher decides to do, of what her goals are. I know two history teachers who teach the same course. One of them sticks to facts and events; the other is concerned with ideas and ideals. Isn't that the same alternative that faces all of us in this situation, too? . . ."

7. *King's "I Have a Dream" Speech, 1963*

I am happy to join with you today in what will go down in history as the greatest demonstration for freedom in the history of our nation.

Fivescore years ago, a great American, in whose symbolic shadow we stand today, signed the Emancipation Proclamation. This momentous decree came as a great beacon light of hope to millions of Negro slaves who had been seared in the flames of withering injustice. It came as a joyous daybreak to end the long night of their captivity.

But one hundred years later, the Negro still is not free; one hundred years later, the life of the Negro is still sadly crippled by the manacles of segregation and the chains of discrimination; one hundred years later, the Negro lives on a lonely island of poverty in the midst of a vast ocean of material prosperity; one hundred years later, the Negro is still languished in the corners of American society and finds himself in exile in his own land.

So we've come here today to dramatize a shameful condition. In a sense we've come to our nation's capital to cash a check. When the architects of our republic wrote the magnificent words of the Constitution and the Declaration of Independence, they were signing a promissory note to which every American was to fall heir. This note was the promise that all men, yes, black men as well as white men, would be guaranteed the unalienable rights of life, liberty, and the pursuit of happiness.

It is obvious today that America has defaulted on this promissory note insofar as her citizens of color are concerned. Instead of honoring this sacred obligation, America has given the Negro people a bad check; a check which has come back marked "insufficient funds." We refuse to believe that there are insufficient funds in the great vaults of opportunity of this nation. And so we've come to cash this check, a check that will give us upon demand the riches of freedom and the security of justice.

We have also come to this hallowed spot to remind America of the fierce urgency of now. This is no time to engage in the luxury of cooling off or to take the tranquilizing drug of gradualism. Now is the time to make real the promises of democracy; now is the time to rise from the dark and desolate valley of segregation to the sunlit path of racial justice; now is the time to lift our nation from the quicksands of racial injustice to the solid rock of brotherhood; now is the time to make justice a reality for all God's children. It would be fatal for the nation to overlook the urgency of the moment. This sweltering summer of the Negro's legitimate discontent will not pass until there is an invigorating autumn of freedom and equality.

Nineteen sixty-three is not an end, but a beginning. And those who hope that the Negro needed to blow off steam and will now be content, will have a rude awakening if the nation returns to business as usual.

There will be neither rest nor tranquility in America until the Negro is granted his citizenship rights. The whirlwinds of revolt will continue to shake the foundations of our nation until the bright day of justice emerges.

But there is something that I must say to my people who stand on the warm threshold which leads into the palace of justice. In the process of gaining our rightful place we must not be guilty of wrongful deeds.

Let us not seek to satisfy our thirst for freedom by drinking from the cup of bitterness and hatred. We must forever conduct our struggle on the high plane of dignity and discipline. We must not allow our creative protest to degenerate into physical violence. Again and again we must rise to the majestic heights of meeting physical force with soul force.

The marvelous new militancy which has engulfed the Negro community must not lead us to a distrust of all white people, for many of our white brothers, as evidenced by their presence here today, have come to realize that their destiny is tied up with our destiny and they have come to realize that their freedom is inextricably bound to our freedom. This offense we share mounted to storm the battlements of injustice must be carried forth by a biracial army. We cannot walk alone.

And as we walk, we must make the pledge that we shall always march ahead. We cannot turn back. There are those who are asking the devotees of civil rights, "When will you be satisfied?" We can never be satisfied as long as the Negro is the victim of the unspeakable horrors of police brutality.

We can never be satisfied as long as our bodies, heavy with fatigue of travel, cannot gain lodging in the motels of the highways and the hotels of the cities. We cannot be satisfied as long as the Negro's basic mobility is from a smaller ghetto to a larger one.

We can never be satisfied as long as our children are stripped of their selfhood and robbed of their dignity by signs stating "for whites only." We cannot be satisfied as long as a Negro in Mississippi cannot vote and a Negro in New York believes he has nothing for which to vote. No, we are not satisfied, and we will not be satisfied until justice rolls down like waters and righteousness like a mighty stream.

I am not unmindful that some of you have come here out of excessive trials and tribulation. Some of you have come fresh from narrow jail cells. Some of you have come from areas where your quest for freedom left you battered by the storms of persecution and staggered by the winds of police brutality. You have been the veterans of creative suffering. Continue to work with the faith that unearned suffering is redemptive.

Go back to Mississippi; go back to Alabama; go back to South Carolina; go back to Georgia; go back to Louisiana; go back to the slums and ghettos of the northern cities, knowing that somehow this situation can, and will be changed. Let us not wallow in the valley of despair.

So I say to you, my friends, that even though we must face the difficulties of today and tomorrow, I still have a dream. It is a dream deeply rooted in the American dream that one day this nation will rise up and live out the true meaning of its creed—we hold these truths to be self-evident, that all men are created equal.

I have a dream that one day on the red hills of Georgia, sons of former slaves and sons of former slave-owners will be able to sit down together at the table of brotherhood.

I have a dream that one day, even the state of Mississippi, a state sweltering with the heat of injustice, sweltering with the heat of oppression, will be transformed into an oasis of freedom and justice.

I have a dream my four little children will one day live in a nation where they will not be judged by the color of their skin but by the content of their character. I have a dream today!

I have a dream that one day, down in Alabama, with its vicious racists, with its governor having his lips dripping with the words of interposition and nullification, that one day, right there in Alabama, little black boys and black girls will be able to join hands with little white boys and white girls as sisters and brothers. I have a dream today!

I have a dream that one day every valley shall be exalted, every hill and mountain shall be made low, the rough places shall be made plain, and the crooked places shall be made straight and the glory of the Lord will be revealed and all flesh shall see it together.

This is our hope. This is the faith that I go back to the South with.

With this faith we will be able to hear out of the mountain of despair a stone of hope. With this faith we will be able to transform the jangling discords of our nation into a beautiful symphony of brotherhood.

With this faith we will be able to work together, to pray together, to struggle together, to go to jail together, to stand up for freedom together, knowing that we will be free one day. This will be the day when all of God's children will be able to sing with new meaning—"my country 'tis of thee; sweet land of liberty; of thee I sing; land where my fathers died, land of the pilgrims' pride; from every mountain side, let freedom ring"—and if America is to be a great nation, this must become true.

So let freedom ring from the prodigious hilltops of New Hampshire.

Let freedom ring from the mighty mountains of New York.

Let freedom ring from the heightening Alleghenies of Pennsylvania.

Let freedom ring from the snow-capped Rockies of Colorado.

Let freedom ring from the curvaceous slopes of California.

But not only that.

Let freedom ring from Stone Mountain of Georgia

Let freedom ring from Lookout Mountain of Tennessee.

Let freedom ring from every hill and molehill of Mississippi, from every mountainside, let freedom ring.

And when we allow freedom to ring, when we let it ring from every village and hamlet, from every state and city, we will be able to speed up that day when all of God's children—black men and white men, Jews and Gentiles, Catholics and Protestants—will be able to join hands and to sing in the words of the old Negro spiritual,

"Free at last, free at last; thank God Almighty, we are free at last."

8. President Lyndon B. Johnson Makes a Commitment to Civil Rights, 1965

Dr. Nabrit, my fellow Americans:

I am delighted at the chance to speak at this important and this historic institution. Howard has long been an outstanding center for the education of Negro Americans. Its students are of every race and color and they come from many countries of the world. It is truly a working example of democratic excellence.

Our earth is the home of revolution. In every corner of every continent men charged with hope contend with ancient ways in the pursuit of justice. They reach for the newest of weapons to realize the oldest of dreams, that each may walk in freedom and pride, stretching his talents, enjoying the fruits of the earth.

Our enemies may occasionally seize the day of change, but it is the banner of our revolution they take. And our own future is linked to this process of swift and turbulent change in many lands in the world. But nothing in any country touches us more profoundly, and nothing is more freighted with meaning for our own destiny than the revolution of the Negro American.

In far too many ways American Negroes have been another nation: deprived of freedom, crippled by hatred, the doors of opportunity closed to hope.

In our time change has come to this Nation, too. The American Negro, acting with impressive restraint, has peacefully protested and marched, entered the courtrooms and the seats of government, demanding a justice that has long been denied. The voice of the Negro was the call to action. But it is a tribute to America that, once aroused, the courts and the Congress, the President and most of the people, have been the allies of progress.

Legal Protection for Human Rights

Thus we have seen the high court of the country declare that discrimination based on race was repugnant to the Constitution, and therefore void. We have seen in 1957, and 1960, and again in 1964, the first civil rights legislation in this Nation in almost an entire century.

As majority leader of the United States Senate, I helped to guide two of these bills through the Senate. And, as your President, I was proud to sign the third. And now very soon we will have the fourth—a new law guaranteeing every American the right to vote.

No act of my entire administration will give me greater satisfaction than the day when my signature makes this bill, too, the law of this land.

The voting rights bill will be the latest, and among the most important, in a long series of victories. But this victory—as Winston Churchill said of another triumph for freedom—"is not the end. It is not even the beginning of the end. But it is, perhaps, the end of the beginning."

That beginning is freedom; and the barriers to that freedom are tumbling down. Freedom is the right to share, share fully and equally, in American society—to vote, to hold a job, to enter a public place, to go to school. It is the right to be treated in every part of our national life as a person equal in dignity and promise to all others.

Freedom Is Not Enough

But freedom is not enough. You do not wipe away the scars of centuries by saying: Now you are free to go where you want, and do as you desire, and choose the leaders you please.

You do not take a person who, for years, has been hobbled by chains and liberate him, bring him up to the starting line of a race and then say, "you are free to compete with all the others," and still justly believe that you have been completely fair.

Thus it is not enough just to open the gates of opportunity. All our citizens must have the ability to walk through those gates.

This is the next and the more profound stage of the battle for civil rights. We seek not just freedom but opportunity. We seek not just legal equity but human ability, not just equality as a right and a theory but equality as a fact and equality as a result.

For the task is to give 20 million Negroes the same chance as every other American to learn and grow, to work and share in society, to develop their abilities—physical, mental and spiritual, and to pursue their individual happiness.

To this end equal opportunity is essential, but not enough, not enough. Men and women of all races are born with the same range of abilities. But ability is not just the product of birth. Ability is stretched or stunted by the family that you live with, and the neighborhood you live in—by the school you go to and the poverty or the richness of your surroundings. It is the product of a hundred unseen forces playing upon the little infant, the child, and finally the man. . . .

References

1. *Brown* v. *Board of Education*, 1954
   "*Oliver Brown et al.* v. *Board of Education of Topeka*, decided May 17, 1954," in Henry M. Christman, ed., *The Public Papers of Chief Justice Earl Warren* (New York: Simon and Schuster, 1959), pp. 120–122.

2. The Southern Manifesto, 1956
   "Declaration of Constitutional Principles, March 12, 1956," in *The Congressional Record*, 84th Congress, 2nd Session (Washington, D.C.: United States Government Printing Office, 1956), p. 4460.

3. Rosa Parks Sits Down for Her Rights, 1955
   Howell Raines, *My Soul Is Rested: Movement Days in the Deep South Remembered* (New York: Penguin Books, 1983), pp. 40–42.

4. Martin Luther King, Jr., Explains Nonviolence, 1957
   James M. Washington, ed., *A Testament of Hope: The Essential Writings of Martin Luther King, Jr.* (San Francisco: Harper & Row, 1986), pp. 12–15.

5. Elizabeth Eckford Remembers Little Rock (1957), 1976
   Elizabeth Eckford (with Daisy Bates), "The First Day: Little Rock, 1957," in Chris Mayfield, ed., *Growing Up Southern: Southern Exposure Looks at Childhood, Then and Now* (New York: Pantheon Books, 1976), pp. 258–261.

6. Atlanta Acts on Desegregation, 1961
   Policing Integration: George McMillan, "With the Police on an Integration Job," *Life*, September 15, 1961, pp. 35–36. Tension in the Classroom: Robert Coles, *Children of Crisis: A Study of Courage and Fear* (Boston: Little, Brown and Company, 1964), pp. 154, 157–158.

7. King's "I Have a Dream" Speech, 1963
   Washington, ed., *A Testament of Hope*, op. cit., pp. 217—220.

8. President Lyndon B. Johnson Makes a Commitment to Civil Rights, 1965
   Public Papers of the Presidents of the United States: Lyndon B. Johnson, 1965, Book II, June 1 to December 31, 1965 (Washington, D.C.: United States Government Printing Office, 1966), pp. 635—636.

Further Reading

Numan V. Bartley, *The Rise of Massive Resistance: Race and Politics in the South Since the 1960s* (1969)

Jack Bass, *Unlikely Heroes: The Southern Judges Who Made the Civil Rights Revolution* (1981)

Lerone N. Bennett, Jr., *What Manner of Man: A Biography of Martin Luther King, Jr., 1929—1968* (1968)

Taylor Branch, *Parting the Waters: America in the King Years, 1954—1963* (1988)

Carl M. Brauer, *John F. Kennedy and the Second Reconstruction* (1977)

Seth Cagin and Philip Dray, *We Are Not Afraid* (1989)

Clayborne Carson, *In Struggle: SNCC and the Black Awakening of the 1960s* (1981)

Adam Fairclough, *"To Redeem the Soul of America": The Southern Christian Leadership Conference and Martin Luther King, Jr.* (1987)

David Garrow, *Bearing the Cross: Martin Luther King, Jr., and the Southern Christian Leadership Conference* (1986)

———, *Protest at Selma: Martin Luther King, Jr., and the Voting Rights Act of 1965* (1978)

Elizabeth Huckaby, *Crisis at Central High: Little Rock, 1957—58* (1980)

Elizabeth Jacoway and David R. Colburn, eds., *Southern Businessmen and Desegregation* (1982)

Richard Kluger, *Simple Justice: The History of Brown v. Board of Education and Black America's Struggle for Equality* (1976)

David L. Lewis, *King: A Critical Biography* (1970)

Doug McAdam, *Freedom Summer* (1988)

Neil McMillen, *The Citizens' Council: Organized Resistance to the Second Reconstruction* (1971)

Harvard Sitkoff, *The Struggle for Black Equality, 1954—1980* (1980)

Robert Weisbrot, *Freedom Bound: A History of America's Civil Rights Movement* (1990)

Document Set 16

The Modernization of the South

World War II permanently changed the economic landscape of the South. To help build an effective war machine, President Franklin Roosevelt translated his concern about the lack of southern progress (see Document Set 14) into action by allocating billions of dollars to the establishment of industrial and military facilities in the South. The construction of shipyards, aircraft plants, and ordnance factories heralded a period of unprecedented economic growth for the southern states. Although this growth rate could not be sustained in the immediate postwar years, southern politicians and business leaders had become aware of the tremendous financial benefits that industrialization could bring to their hitherto predominantly agricultural region. State governments began to offer incentives that northern, and later overseas, investors found irresistible: inexpensive land, low tax rates, and a plentiful and cooperative labor force.

In the 1960s and 1970s, moreover, the South experienced a phenomenal rate of urbanization. A new readiness by southern farmers to accept mechanization led to a mass exodus of unskilled farm workers from the countryside. While many migrated to the North, others relocated to the towns and cities of the South in search of employment. The opportunity to learn new job skills, combined with the invention of the air conditioner, made factory work far more bearable than before. The modernization of the South has transformed outsiders' images of the region. In the mid-1970s, the national media used the term *Sunbelt* to denote a region of the South and Southwest where entrepreneurs could make lucrative investments and where thousands could spend their retirement years in a pleasant climate and a relaxing environment.

Modernization and industrial development have not provided all the answers for southern-ers. Workers in southern industry, discouraged by employers from joining labor unions, earn significantly less than do their counterparts in the rest of the nation. Many southerners who continue to work on the land live well below the national poverty level. A serious shortage of funds, caused in part by the reluctance of state governments to raise taxes on the private sector, continues to have an adverse effect on the quality of education in southern schools.

Industrial development has helped to rejuvenate many southern cities whose economic growth had stalled. One such city, Louisville, on the banks of the Ohio River in Kentucky, was the tenth largest urban center in the nation in 1850. By the 1960s, Louisville was a medium-sized city with a rather dilapidated appearance. As the first document shows, the revival of Louisville was due to a concerted effort in urban planning by community leaders.

Ethnic groups have contributed to and benefited from the South's modernization. The second selection outlines the progress made in Miami by the refugees who left Cuba in the aftermath of Fidel Castro's revolution. The blessings of prosperity bypassed other areas of the South: the third document highlights the deplorable social and economic conditions of life in remote parts of the southern countryside. In 1968 social researcher Tony Dunbar encountered the people of Louise, a small town in the Mississippi delta largely populated by low-paid blacks who worked on local plantations. Dunbar's harrowing account of life in Louise illustrates the almost complete absence of health care in some southern communities.

The vagaries of southern weather have made life unpleasantly unpredictable for workers on the land. Increasingly torrid summers, culminating in the sweltering heat of the summer of 1990, have forced southern farmers to experiment with planting less traditional crops than corn and soybeans. The fourth document reveals one Georgia farming family's efforts to cultivate heat- and drought-resistant crops. The hurricane season in late summer and autumn is a time of deep concern for southerners who live on the Atlantic and Gulf coasts. Occasionally, hurricanes of devastating fury wreak havoc on the southern coastline. The determination of southerners to rebuild and indeed improve their communities after a natural disaster is reflected in the fifth selection.

Tragically, human activity has bred some of the environmental catastrophes that have befallen the South. For example, in their efforts to attract investors to the region, southern state governments failed to enact effective legislation to regulate the discharge of industrial waste. The sixth and seventh documents reveal the extent of the pollution of two southern rivers. The *Newsweek* article reprinted as document 6 describes the damage caused by years of discharging chemical waste into the lower Mississippi; in the final selection, the gifted cartoonist Robert Ariail comments on procedures at the Savannah River Plant's nuclear waste storage facility.

Questions for Analysis

1. Is the process of industrialization in the South similar to or different from that in the rest of the nation?

2. Was the impetus for modernization in the South primarily a result of southern enterprise, outside influences, or both?

3. What effect has modernization had on agriculture in the South?

4. How has urban growth affected the character of southern towns and cities?

5. Have the working classes of the South made any substantial gains as a result of industrialization?

6. Have southern state governments jeopardized the environment by their concessions to outside investors?

1. A Journalist Examines the Transformation of Louisville, 1973

Revival Time for Louisville

Until a redevelopment effort led by business jelled four years ago, Louisville, Ky., had shared the experience of other medium-sized U.S. cities in watching its downtown deteriorate while suburbs absorbed new growth. "Louisville had always been long on antiques and old silver but short on risk-taking capital," explains lawyer Gordon B. Davidson, a former president of Louisville Central Area, Inc., a 12-year-old civic and business group whose rejuvenation efforts are now showing impressive results.

A five-year, $2-billion redevelopment plan combining public and private effort has left the worries over risk money mostly a memory. The plan for the city's downtown and Ohio River front has already given Louisville a new skyline, a reclaimed waterfront, and a growing reputation as a revived regional business center. The new look is drawing civic leaders from such cities as Memphis, Dayton, Birmingham, and Flint for a "how to" lesson in central city development.

Among the major projects at the heart of Louisville's revival:

A traffic-free shopping mall, lined with trees and outdoor cafes. The three-block retail hub is the nation's third largest pedestrian shopping mall. Its $1.5-million cost was financed by a special city tax on owners of property along the mall, at the suggestion of merchants and landlords themselves. Besides upgrading the quality of central city life, the mall is putting more dollars into store cash registers. In the two months since it opened, area retailers report a 15% sales increase over last year. New businesses are also coming to the mall. This fall, for instance, Ayr-Way Stores, Inc., a discount subsidiary of Associated Dry Goods Corp. that has four stores in suburban Louisville, will move into the mall with its first downtown outlet.

Plaza/Belvedere, a 7-acre, $13.5-million park, dedicated in May, on the riverfront. Beneath the complex of overlooks, landscaped courts, walks, and fountains is a 1,600-car municipal garage. The Plaza/Belvedere has been a catalyst for adjoining projects built on land reclaimed from auto wrecking yards and crumbling warehouses that once blighted the city's waterfront. Already the $6-million Louisville Trust Co. building, the $4-million American Life & Accident tower, and the $10.5-million, 29-story Galt House hotel have been built adjacent to the Plaza/Belvedere. More than $62 million in additional construction is planned for the waterfront. Among the projects are a Hilton hotel, two 30-floor apartment buildings, office buildings, and shops.

Also included is a $14-million complex containing county and city courts and public safety headquarters, now under construction. And a convention and exhibition center is planned to link the shopping mall with the riverfront. The state has guaranteed $25 million for the new convention facility.

The city's bankers, who provided interim financing for the Plaza/Belvedere three years ago when high interest rates discouraged selling of municipal bonds, have spurred the building boom with their own office towers. Along with Louisville Trust, the city's two largest banks have built high-rise corporate headquarters in the past five years. And the addition of more than 100 floors of modern office space to the city's rental stock has helped keep business from leaving the city. For example, Celanese Corp. was considering moving its downtown regional offices, but decided to stay after the new bank towers went up.

A Youth Movement

Louisville has never lacked plans for development—merely the push to bring them to fruition. The shopping mall, for example, was originally proposed in 1943, when Wilson Wyatt, Sr., was mayor. Now, 30 years later, the mall is a reality partly because of the efforts of 29-year old Wilson Wyatt, Jr., the former mayor's son and the current executive director of Louisville Central Area, Inc.

The talents of young civic and business leaders like Wyatt have been a key element in Louisville's new push. Says Maurice D. S. Johnson, chairman of Citizens Fidelity Bank & Trust Co. and a former resident of Kansas City, Mo.: "When I came to Louisville, I was struck by the fact that two nationally known companies, Kentucky Fried Chicken and Extendicare, were staffed by extremely young men. They were living examples that inspired a lot of young people as entrepreneurs."

The mix of youthful leaders and older, more established men gives the city what some Louisvilleans call their "unstructured power structure." Says lawyer Davidson: "There is no single power source. Consensus of just a few people can really make a project go."

Self-Help

Most urban planners see such collaborative effort as the key to redeveloping other medium-sized cities. Says Crawford C. Westbrook, vice-president of Victor Gruen Associates, the Los Angeles planning firm that helped Louisville update its downtown plan in 1969: "There was no Mayor Daley or Mayor Lindsay, and the federal government isn't playing Big Daddy any more. Redevelopment is almost exclusively a matter of leadership. And when a community like Louisville becomes self-reliant, it can always find the resources."

2. A Report on How Cubans Made Their Mark on Miami, 1971

How the Immigrants Made It in Miami

It seems to me remarkable that when you consider that these refugees arrived here with nothing but their skills and abilities, that 83% are fully self-supporting and only 17% require federal assistance.

—Howard H. Palmatier,
Director, Cuban Refugee Program,
Health, Education & Welfare Dept.

In the 10 years since Cubans began fleeing to the U.S. from Castro, they have made faster progress in their adopted country than has any other group of immigrants in this century. Almost overnight they have emerged from the deprived, refugee state and moved into the middle class, skipping lightly over—or never even touching—the lowest rung of the economic ladder that was a necessary first step for the Irish, the Jews, the Italians, and others. Today there are colonies of hardworking, prospering Cubans in the suburbs of New York and as deep into the Midwest as Chicago. Nowhere, though, has their imprint been felt more than in Miami, the original port of call for most of them.

Indeed, in the past decade, Miami has become a Latinized city. Of nearly 600,000 Cuban refugees believed to have entered the U.S. from 1960 to 1970 (about 410,000 are known to have arrived), more than 300,000 have settled in Dade County. The rapid staccato of Spanish is now commonplace in much of the City of Miami and is heard increasingly in Miami Beach. In many sections, signs printed in English have become the exception rather than the rule.

Cubans have avoided some usual immigrant problems. True, friction exists between Cubans and mainland whites and blacks. But the small percentage of Cubans receiving federal aid consists mostly of the young and elderly. The Cubans' crime rate is low; the rate at which they have learned to speak English is high. What is more, even their harshest critics acknowledge that the immigrants are resourceful, aggressive, and energetic. In fact, the Cubans have enjoyed an economic success that is spectacular.

Rags to Riches

Cubans operate 60% of all service stations in Miami, and companies that they own are putting up about 30% of all construction now underway in the city, including a $35-million, 40-story office building that will be the tallest in Florida when completed. Three presidents, 21 vice-presidents, and 200 officers of Cuban origin are in banking. Cubans operate 20 cigar manufacturers, 30 furniture factories, 10 garment plants, 45 bakeries, 12 private schools, 230 restaurants, 10 record-making plants, three radio stations, at least a dozen "giveaway" shopping guides printed in Spanish, and a daily newspaper, *Diarios Las Américas,* with 60,000 circulation.

There have been, of course, innumerable rags-to-riches stories. Probably the best known is that of David Egozi and Eugene Ramos, who parlayed $40,000 smuggled out of Cuba and $30,000 in borrowed capital into Suave Shoe Co., which makes low-priced, private label leisure footwear and had sales of $42.6 million last year.

Such enterprise has benefited Miami's entire Cuban population. First Research Co., which periodically surveys the Cuban community, estimates that the total annual income of Cubans in Dade County as of last Sept. 30 was nearly $588 million, an increase of $246 million since mid-1968. And the median income of Cuban families rose from $5,244 in 1967 to $7,200 last year, a 37% increase and well above the national average. In addition, nearly 90% of all Cuban families own more than one automobile.

To accomplish all this, the Cubans have borrowed liberally from neighborhood banks. Riverside Bank, for example, now has 18,000 Latin accounts worth $14 million, or 30% of total deposits. Current loans made by Cubans amount to $5½ million, or 19% of the bank's total.

"Their repayment record has been good," says Riverside President Tully F. Dunlap. "We find them industrious, conscientious, a definite asset to the bank." Tom Butler, district director of the Small Business Administration, reports that Dade County Cubans made 118 loans totaling $2.2 million in fiscal 1969, 75 loans totaling $1.1 million in fiscal 1970, and 147 loans totaling $2.1 million in the first eight months of fiscal 1971.

Assimilation

Because of the Cubans' economic success, a number of their leaders believe that the next five years will be more trying for the refugee population than were the last 10. Carlos Arboleya, president of Fidelity National Bank and a refugee himself, believes that the immigrants have done perhaps too well for themselves in too short a time. "The large majority of people in Miami used to look upon us as the 'poor Cuban refugee,' " he explains. "Now, suddenly, they don't see us as being so poor any longer. They see that we are a decisive force in the community socially, economically, and politically." As a result, he says, there is some envy, resentment, and jealousy on the part of the general public.

Many Miamians also see the Cubans as too clannish. Arboleya acknowledges that Cubans do stick together, especially while there is a language barrier. But he says: "I don't think this is true on the whole. The Cubans are a part of the community, from membership in the PTA to the Lions Club and other groups." And assimilation is moving forward. "I've had an opportunity to speak with civic leaders, with church leaders," says Palmatier, "and by and large they have only good things to say about the refugees—that they are ambitious, have strong family ties, and do not show up as a crime statistic, something of which we are especially proud."

Miami Police Chief Bernard Garmire confirms this last point. Cubans, he says, account for only 5% to 6% of the crime in the city while making up 30% of the population. Says Wilson Purdy, chief of the metropolitan Dade County police: "I think Cubans have made excellent citizens. While there has been some increases in narcotics violations among people with Spanish names, we can't say that it's a Cuban problem, but a problem of the community in general."

Both police departments have been actively recruiting Cubans, particularly because they need bilingual policemen. But they have had only limited success. "I think it has to do with their background," says Garmire. "Too many remember the police state in Cuba and don't want any part of police work."

Education

The Cubans, many of them highly skilled or with university degrees, have taken a more-than-usual interest in the schools, however. Thus, their children have not had the adjustment problem that some foresaw in the early 1960s. Says Paul W. Bell, executive director of the Dade County school system's division of instruction: "By and large, Cuban kids have had more of a positive than a negative impact. The concerns of many that academic standards would drop drastically because the Cubans didn't speak English and that they would drain resources from American pupils never materialized."

Bell believes that the vast majority of Cuban children adjusted well because they:
—Immediately began learning English as a second language (taught by American teachers with the assistance of Cuban aides).
—Attended classes with their American counterparts from the moment they entered school, and were concurrently taught the same subjects in their native language.

Because of this, the children have not fallen behind in their studies and take 1½ years, on average, to become proficient enough in English to end special instruction. "Keeping them with American students gave them maximum opportunity to learn English and use it on the outside while, at the same time, learning in their native tongue," says Bell. "There's no telling how long it might have taken had we kept the children apart—but it certainly would have been a lot longer."

Nationalization

Though the youngsters adjusted swiftly in school, their parents have not, to any degree, become involved in the American political system. Latest figures from the U.S. Immigration & Naturalization Service show that, while the number of exiles becoming citizens doubled to almost 21,000 between fiscal 1969 and fiscal 1970 (ending last June 30), less than 60,000 of the approximately 600,000 that have come to the U.S. since 1962 have become citizens. Fewer still have registered to vote, and Miami political experts doubt that as many as 10,000 cast ballots in last November's election.

Their involvement in Miami politics is just as lethargic. Miami Mayor David Kennedy offers this assessment: "They're more worried now about survival, reestablishing themselves socially and economically. The political adjustment comes last, but I believe we're seeing some signs of it."

Manual Suarez, who polled 8,141 to run fifth in the Dade County mayoralty race, points out: "When they do vote, as the figures show, they tend to vote in a bloc, but they're more interested now in Castro than in pollution."

Friction

Probably the biggest complaint against the refugees is that they are taking jobs that might otherwise go to native-born Americans, primarily blacks. Palmatier doubts that this occurs, except in isolated instances. Instead, he contends, Cubans created their own job opportunities as they expanded into a myriad of enterprises in retailing, wholesaling, and manufacturing. A good example, he says, would be Suave Shoe. Nonexistent before Egori and Ramos came to the U.S. it currently employs 1,900, more than 99% of them Cuban refugees.

Robert Sims, Dade County's community relations director and himself a black, argues the Cuban influx has hurt Negroes. He believes that when the Cubans began swarming into Miami in the early 1960s, members of his race were on the threshold of being "upgraded" into semiskilled clerical positions in department stores and offices.

"No," says Sims, "they didn't take away jobs. Instead, the jobs that were just about to go to blacks went to Latins, many of whom had the expertise, the know how, the drive to get going, and, in some cases, a willingness to work for less money." Then, says Sims, when the Cubans began creating jobs of their own, they gave them to later-arriving Cubans because of clannishness and language ties.

Sims describes Negro-Cuban relations as tense. "There is friction," he says, "not because they are Cubans but because they are recipients of favor from whites. The black community is not unlike an underdeveloped nation. There are tremendous problems, and it is looking to the developed nation, in this instance, white people, for help. And the blacks are upset because the Cubans have received a greater response." Dade County Mayor Steve Clark, who thinks the Cuban vote in the last election helped to beat his opponent, contends that "certain elements" are trying to create difficulty between blacks and Cubans. "If there was to be trouble," he says, "it should have happened eight years ago, when they first came to Miami.

Sims does not agree. He believes that, because of their growing numbers and their aggressiveness, Cubans will eventually become a major concern of the whites. "Suddenly, they're going to look around," he says, "and discover that Latins have taken over Miami, lock, stock, and barrel."

3. Tony Dunbar on Sickness and Poverty in the Mississippi Delta, 1968

The health of the people of Louise is incredibly poor. The community is ridden with sickness, disease, and chronic illness. While people's low income severely limits the medical care they may receive, many find themselves often living in the doctor's office. ("I'm just a doctor victim. I stays in the doctor's.") Barely a household is free of a case of high blood pressure, which shows itself in the swollen ankles of the women, results in a weakened heart, fainting spells, "nervous break-downs," and demands an abstinence from pork. Throughout the winter the children are plagued by colds that turn occasionally into pneumonia. Cases of asthma are not rare. Running sores and scabs dot the bodies of most children in the summer. While often a symptom of a dietary deficiency, they are caused in the main by unsanitary conditions which turn tiny cuts into painful infections. Diabetes is a common disease. Cases of tuberculosis and amoebic dysentery are not hard to find. Many children have a variety of internal parasites.

This baby right here; he'll cough and go out of breath, and you can't disturb him. He'll go out of breath. I don't seem to know what makes him do that. If you make him over-average mad, if he thinks you scold him some way or the other, he'll just go right out of breath. Sometimes it don't look like he'll get his breath back no way. That child there, she complains right smart about her stomach, and I taken her out to Belzoni to the doctor. Well the doctor said she might have worms and he gave me some worm medicine for her, but I don't know if she was taking it like she should have 'cause I was trying to go to school in order to pay him. . . . Sometimes they [sores] just break out all over in the sum-mertime. I've got another boy here who looked like he just never would get well of his sores.

People visit doctors most often for "high blood" pills and for cold medicine for the chil-

dren. For matters more or less serious than these, the expense of treatment is beyond the reach of the poor man; he would prefer to suffer through the illness or resort to home remedies. There is not in the Delta the hearty farm family of American folklore, living simply but comfort-ably and enjoying robust good health; instead there are people blighted by low income, inade-quate food, and disease.

There were many complaints in the interviews that people were unable to get doctors to come to their homes, even in the cities.

We ain't been checked by a doctor in so long I can't tell you what condition the family's in.

About 13 per cent of the black community in Louise has never seen a doctor. Also, about 49 per cent of the people have never seen a dentist. Due to the cost, people only see dentists when their teeth need to be pulled, and when that point is reached, many people choose to pull their own teeth.

How many of your children have ever seen a doctor?

I've got one in the family. It wasn't from sickness though. Had a little fat boy of mine. He went out to the outside bath-room one day. When he got ready to come back in, he went to zip up his pants, and he caught hisself in the zip. I taken him to the doctor. It was on a Wednesday; he takes Wednesday off, and you can't get him back to that office. So when I got to his office, he was gone. I never did try to go to his home to get him. We have a pretty favorable doctor up there in Midnight. He's real old; he'll practice till a certain hour in the evenin' and then he's through. Well, I went up there and his hours was up. Well I just kep' a goin' then. I went to Belzoni to take him to the hospital—I couldn't afford to wait because he's sufferin'—and they got it off.

There were numerous complaints about the federally supported hospital in Belzoni. The people said patients, even emergency cases, not able to produce cash have been denied admission to the hospital and directed to hospitals in Vicksburg and Jackson where some cost reductions are granted to indigent patients. Stories were told of suffering and death resulting from the drive to these cities, each seventy miles away.

I worked there at the hospital a long time. I worked over there about six or eight years. Now the hospital has changed a whole lot 'cause when I was over there we was gettin' $14 a week—go to work at seven, get off at five. . . . They take in black patients. Some, but it is so high over there that black people just can't pay it, and if you go in there and don't have the money, well, you have to go somewhere else. . . . I know a cousin of mine, on the Fourth of July, she had a miscarriage, and they carried her over there, and they wouldn't take her in. They had to rush her to Vicksburg and operate on her at once. Now, that could have been a life saved. At this hospital, you have to have money. . . . When I was there, they kept them [babies] separate. . . . The black babies stay in the nursery for a while, and then they bring them up and puts them in the diet kitchen, you know, on the colored side. Now that's what they were doing when I was there. I don't know what they're doing now.

As far as the wards are concerned, the hospital consists of, I think, thirty-four rooms that is used by patients, and eight of those rooms is used by black patients. . . . I wouldn't say they handle them any different, but it's seldom they handle any black patients. If you go to the hospital to have anything done, they will always refer you to another hospital—Jackson or Vicksburg.

The cost of medicine is one of those expenses that nags endlessly at a poor man. The shots or pills needed to check diabetes, the pills needed for high blood pressure, the nonprescription pills and syrups needed to fight the colds all winter are items which cut unbearable holes in the budget of the black man in the Delta. It is a bitter joke for a tenant farmer to pay ten dollars for an examination that shows he has "high blood" and must pay four dollars each month of his life for pills. The money is just not there. Rather than follow the doctor's instructions, he will buy, if he is able, a month's supply of pills and make them last six months.

Do you have to take medicine regularly for your sugar or high blood?

Sure does. Course I'm not able to buy the sugar pills. I take the shots or either take the sugar pills. And I'm not able to get the sugar pills. . . .

Because they're too expensive?

Too expensive. And the doctor put me in on health department sugar shots, and the lady wrote and told me to come up there, and said the government said I'd have to pay fifty cents a week to take this treatment. And I wasn't able to pay fifty cents a week. And I didn't ever go back, and that was last year. So I have to go to the doctor in Midnight, and I haven't been there in three, four months, near about four months, to get a sugar treatment 'cause I got light bills, burial club. . . . I get a little money and it goes.

Some people treat serious diseases with home remedies. They do so out of habit, certainly, but they are no more able to afford professional treatment now than when the practices began. Those who need medicine the most can afford it the least.

When they were babies, did either of them have large stomachs?

No sir. Well, you take that boy. When he was a baby he had a large navel, but he didn't have a large stomach.

You mean stuck way out?

Yeah, a navel you know would stick out way in front of him. Well, a lady gave my wife a remedy; told her to take a fifty-cent piece and bandage it, you know, tie it around him. That's when he was young, and it seems it went back in place.

How old was he then?

He's about eleven months old, I imagine.

Most babies in the black community of Louise are born in the home and are delivered by a midwife with the occasional assistance of a doctor. The number of miscarriages and infant deaths is startlingly large. (The infant death rate in 1964 in Humphreys County was 2,941 per 100,000 live births, compared to the national norm of 1,700.) Recent medical research indicates that it is during the second through the twelfth month of a child's infancy that his death may most characteristically be attributed to the fact that the nourishment which he received before and after his birth was insufficient to provide for his growth. When a woman is undernourished during pregnancy, her baby may be undernourished at birth. There have been 4 infant deaths for every 100 live births accounted for.

All of these children, were they born here at home or in a hospital?

Well, I got three was born in the hospital. The rest of 'em was born here in this house.

The ones born here in the house, were they brought in by a doctor or a midwife?

Well, I used to have trouble, and I needed a doctor's help.

Have you ever had any miscarriages?

I sure is. I've had twenty-six and I've only saved ten.

This is you?

And I only saved those with the doctor's help.

Husband: We lost a lot in one year like that.

Has your wife ever had any miscarriages?

Three.

Has she ever had any babies that didn't live?

Well, we had one that lived about three hours after she was born, then died.

So out of the five pregnancies you got the girl?

We got the girl.

Where were your children delivered?

All of mine was in the home.

By a doctor or midwife?

By a midwife.

Have you ever had any miscarriages?

Husband: Many of them.

How many have you had?

About five.

Many women in Louise eat cornstarch when they are pregnant. Some keep the habit and continue to eat as much as they can get after childbirth as a means of filling themselves up. The same is true of baking soda. And the same is true of clay. There was a time when most women in Louise ate clay and starch while they were pregnant. Now, one out of every four eats starch, and one out of every three eats clay. The best clay is said to come from the hill country around Canton or Yazoo City. Farmers passing through will pull off the roads and shovel the dirt into bags for their wives and friends. When a woman cannot get hill clay she may take a bagful out of the side of an irrigation ditch. She lets the clay dry out, or may bake or freeze it, and she will later break off little chunks to suck. Sometimes you can see a woman at work in the fields after mealtime pick a piece of dirt off the ground and pop it into her month.

At the hospital in Belzoni, there are beds for one out of every 534 people in the county. In Humphreys County, there are five doctors, one for every 3,740 people. There are two dentists, one for every 9,350 people. There are four nurses, one for every 4,675 people. Where the poverty of the people is so great, their health so poor, their ability to afford medical care so hampered, and the availability of medical services so limited, there is a crying need for public health programs. The Mississippi State Board of Health does not have the budget or the manpower to provide fully all of its designated services. For the eighteen counties in the Delta, there are only ten medical directors, i.e., doctors, for the county health departments. One doctor serves as the director for six separate health departments, and one of these serves two counties. The director of the Humphreys County Health Department also directs the Yazoo County department.

The Humphreys County department is staffed by two nurses and a sanitarian. In the areas that most directly benefit the poor, maternity and infant care and immunization against communicable diseases, much has yet to be done. It is estimated that 35 per cent (more than twice the national average) of the children in Mississippi from one day to nine years of age have not received basic immunizations, i.e., polio, diphtheria, smallpox, and typhoid fever. It can be inferred that the percentage is quite high in Humphreys County. One problem is that in Mississippi, where for ten years there has been no compulsory school attendance law, many children, especially those of poor families, miss getting their shots because they either do not attend school at all, or attend it very irregularly. Shots are given to all children in the Head Start centers.

Have any of your children been to see a doctor?

I know those she [a sister] left are going to have to go. They needs a check-up. . . . See she had tuberculosis and she left here about two weeks ago, and they was comin' around to check the kids, but they got on the wrong road.

In other words, they been lookin' for us, but they got throwed off and didn't find here. It was the Public Health Department that was lookin' for 'em, but they didn't find this place.

Maternity and child care services in Humphreys County barely exist. None of the people talked with in Louise could recall ever having heard of any lectures or courses being offered in child care. When medical problems arise during pregnancy or during a child's infancy that force a mother to go to the health department in Belzoni, she will be referred to a private physician for treatment that she often cannot afford. The department supervises 14 "granny" midwives in the county. Many mothers are assisted in their delivery by women who call themselves "midwives" but are under no supervision from the county. There are no nurse-midwives in the county.

What is desperately lacking in Humphreys County is free or inexpensive medical help and enough dentists, free or inexpensive hospital care and enough hospital beds, and free medicine. There are at this time no programs, federal or state, operating in the county aimed at fulfilling these needs.

4. Ambrose, Georgia, Farmers Fight Back Against Drought, 1990

Like many other longtime Coffee County farmers, Melvin Vickers and his son, Wayne, are plowing new ground in an effort to outsmart Mother Nature.

Instead of depending on traditional crops such as corn and soybeans, the Vickerses have switched to hogs and peanuts, a change that helped them weather this summer's devastating heat and drought.

About an inch of rain fell on their tiny northwest Coffee County community last week, prompting their peanut plants to bloom and dampening the choking dust in the hog pens, but the damage to the corn crop was already done.

"This has been the worst summer in 20 years," said Wayne Vickers, 41, who followed the footsteps of his father and grandfather into the farming business on land the family has owned here for generations. "If we were still depending on corn, we'd be in real trouble."

The Vickerses planted 42 acres of corn for hog feed and they've struggled to keep it alive.

"We've worked hard this year watering it, but it hasn't done a bit of good because of the heat," Wayne Vickers said.

While their hogs and peanuts also suffered, the corn was hit hardest of all, Mr. Vickers said.

"We usually get 125 bushels to the acre. This year, we'll be lucky to get 70," he said. "The hogs are what keep us going."

In cornfields all across south Georgia, the story is the same. Corn stalks are blackened and twisted, ears are shriveled and kernels are parched to hard little pebbles.

Coffee County agricultural agent Rick Reed said most farmers now realize that corn is not a good investment. It needs water, doesn't tolerate temperatures much above 95 degrees, and brings poor market prices, he said.

"This summer, we had three solid weeks of 100-degree temperatures and more than a month with no rain," he said. "But even in wet years, farmers don't make any money on corn. Most of them grow it only as animal feed or because it's a good rotation crop. A few do it because it's traditional. They've always grown corn and they'll grow it 'til they die."

George L. McKinnon, whose farmlands sprawl into neighboring Jeff Davis County, said he plants corn nowadays only for rotation purposes.

Mr. McKinnon, who has the biggest farm in the area and one of the largest in Georgia, tends 2,300 acres. His crop mix now is considerably different from what it was a decade ago, he said.

"I've got 235 acres in tobacco, 1,050 in peanuts, 700 in corn, 250 in wheat, 70 in cotton and the rest in soybeans," he said. "I've more than doubled my acreage of peanuts and tobacco and cut back on the beans."

Mr. McKinnon said the drought of 1986, which devastated his 1,500 acres of soybeans, taught him a lesson.

"I averaged about three bushels an acre, where I usually get 35 to 40 bushels," he said. "I probably lost half a million dollars that year."

Now, he puts his faith—and the bulk of his $1 million annual production loan—into tobacco and peanuts. Both crops are irrigated and both, he said, have the ability to bounce back from heat and drought.

"You just can't depend on corn or soybeans anymore," he said. "You've got to have something with price supports to fall back on."

Farm stabilization programs such as those for tobacco and peanuts guarantee farmers minimum prices for their crops, as long as production is limited to allotment acreage.

According to Mr. Reed, changing weather patterns prompted many Coffee County farmers to change their ways during the past decade, when drought has been the rule rather than the exception.

In 1976, he said, local farmers grew 76,000 acres of corn. This year, only about 25,000 of the county's farm acres are planted in corn, Mr. Reed said.

Farmers have also diversified from traditional row crops into hogs and poultry, according to Mr. Reed.

5. Gulf Coast Residents Recover from a Hurricane, 1979

The Gulf Coast is no stranger to storms, but the hurricane that hit Mississippi 10 years ago this month was unprecedented in size and fury. Now, a decade later, the Mississippi Coast has gone much further than rebuilding what it had; the resurrected Coast is a new creature.

"You couldn't say Hurricane Camille was a good thing," reflects Hudson Hamilton, assistant director at the Port of Gulfport. "But the fact is we're bigger and stronger than ever."

D. L. (Chick) Anderson, manager of the Mississippi Research & Development Center's Gulf

Coast Field Office, believes the substantial growth "would probably have come anyway, but it's happened a lot faster and more sensibly because of Camille. The hurricane pulled people together and got them moving."

The horror of that beautifully clear August morning after a night of fear was even worse than expected. The sky was bright blue, a Gulf breeze brought respite from the summer heat. But the beachfront scene for nearly 30 miles along "America's Riviera" was utter devastation.

Scenic U.S. Highway 90 was a shambles; the popular 26-mile sandy beach with its protecting seawall was virtually gone; 37,000 homes and 450 businesses were destroyed or damaged. Deer Island, offshore Biloxi, was cut in two; 150 vessels were sunk or grounded, including pleasure craft tossed like toys through buildings and three huge ocean-going vessels hard aground on the Gulfport beach.

Dollar damage would exceed one billion dollars. And the human tragedy was measureless: in her vicious sweep through the South, Camille killed 256 people and injured thousands. Two thirds of the storm's victims were on the Mississippi Gulf Coast.

In August 1979 scars remain on the Coast, both on the landscape and on the psyche. Steps leading nowhere in an empty lot mark where a "hurricane-proof" Gulfport home once stood. A huge weed-grown concrete slab at Pass Christian was once an elegant apartment building where 24 people attending a "hurricane-watch" party were killed. Gulfport's fashionable East Beach—where only six of 114 fine homes escaped with minor damage—has never returned to its former elegance.

But the tourist business is back and better than ever, says the evidence. The sand beach, seawall and scenic drive have been rebuilt and newly landscaped. New and elegant motels have risen (some were building literally in the wreckage of Camille). An imposing new Coast Coliseum dominates the landscape between Gulfport and Biloxi; in April, it was the setting for the "Miss USA" pageant, which drew invaluable national television publicity to the Coast.

And Baricev's is back on the beach. One of Biloxi's famous seafood restaurants, Baricev's—like everything facing the Gulf—was wiped out. Bob Baricev says the family had "no second thoughts at all" about rebuilding. The new restaurant, shiny and modern, lacks the well-worn charm of the old place but the food remains memorable and "we've been growing steadily every year," Baricev said.

The Friendship House admits to some problems, however. Manager Lou Soldo said the damaged landmark restaurant was open again three weeks after Camille. "Most places on the beach aren't doing as well as they used to," Soldo said, "except in the summer."

He blames the family-restaurant decline on the appearance of numerous fast-food chain outlets, plus the completion of Interstate 10 north of the city.

Tourism as a whole seems healthy. Retail tourist-related sales hit a record $74 million in 1977, up 10 percent from the year before and accounting for one third of Mississippi's total tourism business.

A novel "sky lift" being built at Biloxi's Fisherman's Wharf promises a unique new lure. The city bought a surplus ski lift and plans to hoist tourists a few hundred yards across the Sound to picnic and play on Deer Island.

Camille's damage to the seafood industry, another Coast mainstay, was unprecedented. The Gollott family, persistence personified, had to rebuild—for the third time.

Tommy Gollott, a state legislator, said, "Some of the businesses just couldn't afford to come back this time. Three hurricanes in 20 years, and Camille was the worst yet." Of the plants that were rebuilt, Gollott said, "I'd say 60 percent are busier than ever."

But the Coast's abundant oyster reefs, heart of the seafood business, were wrecked by Camille's vicious tides. The state is spending a million dollars to rebuild the offshore reefs, and federal funds have provided another million for reseeding.

Because of serious pollution problems on the Atlantic Coast, Gollott said, "The industry here is more important then ever. Pollution is our biggest problem too, but it's not as bad here as it is up east."

Mississippi is taking the long view, he said, in keeping the Sound clean now and anticipating future problems. "We're trying to create a regional sewage system for the whole Coast," he said. "We want to intercept the wastes and pump them back up to the forest lands north of here where they'd do some good and at the same time keep our water clean."

Such regional cooperation is a new experience for the Coast—and in large part is a result of Camille. The 50-mile-long Mississippi Coast is a study in contrasts: on the west the quiet old residential communities of Bay St. Louis and Pass Christian; on the east the burly industry of Pascagoula and Moss Point, including the giant Litton-Ingall's Shipyard, with 18,500 employees. In between, cheek-by-jowl, are soberly middle-class Gulfport, fun-loving and tourist-conscious Biloxi—and sprawling Keesler Air Force Base, a "city" of 25,000 by itself.

In the past, Tommy Munro said, Coast communities tended to go their separate ways. "But Camille changed all that. If any good came out of it, that hurricane brought us together."

Munro, president of the Biloxi Chamber of Commerce, was battalion commander with the Army National Guard during Camille's aftermath. An oil dealer, he also experienced the storm first-hand, losing five stations, a port terminal, and 15 station outlets. He estimates his replacement cost at $650,000.

William Bailey, executive director of the Gulfport Area Chamber of Commerce, agrees there is more unity now than before. "Our recovery slogan said it: 'Together we build.' We still have plenty of competitiveness," Bailey said, "but there's a real awareness here now that we are 'the Coast.' Separate entities, but each a part of the whole."

Cooperative ventures in the past few years, he noted, include the new Coliseum & Convention Center, a Gulfport-Biloxi Regional Airport Authority, chamber committees from different towns working jointly on common problems.

Camille spawned other positive fallout, broader than local cooperation. It helped force reassessment and redesign of flood insurance laws nationwide. According to Dr. Neal Frank, director of the National Hurricane Center in Miami, "After Camille and other storms of that period the federal laws were re-written, and the government now underwrites flood insurance. People just couldn't get it before."

The laws, plus building guidelines laid down by the Department of Housing and Urban Development, are admittedly controversial, Dr. Frank said, and are "probably going to be reworked by Congress" under legislation now pending.

Mississippi also tackled the flood-insurance problem after Camille, requiring companies doing business in the state to offer such policies.

Insurance companies did pay out an estimated $250 million in claims after Camille—but there was a lot of debate over wind-versus-water. The storm brought plenty of both: winds over 200 miles per hour, successive walls of tidal water 20 feet high.

A. L. Rainey, an institutional foods dealer in Gulfport, had a hassle on his hands. "When I got down to the warehouse Monday morning," he said, "the place looked pretty solid—on the outside. I opened the freezer doors and everything inside had collapsed. Ceilings, inside walls, everything."

An insurance adjuster from Orlando said he had no claim since it was obviously not wind damage. "I got on the phone and told the company to send me another adjuster, somebody from Kansas who knew something about wind."

Sure enough, the new adjuster allowed the claim. The peculiar nature of such storms is that a radical drop in barometric pressure (26.63 inches during Camille) caused the freezer walls to "breathe," to expand and contract enough to wreck the interior, Rainey explained.

Insurance payments, it is estimated, covered perhaps 20 percent of the hurricane's devastation. Another $750 million came in federal disaster relief funds, plus multiple millions and priceless services from individuals and groups nationwide and abroad.

To Coast residents, real heroes of the immediate recovery were the American Red Cross; the tireless National Guard, Navy Seabees, and airmen from Keesler; selfless volunteers from the Salvation Army, the Seventh Adventist and Mennonite-Amish churches; and countless others who cared.

Bob Hope led a fund-raising "We Care" telethon, and gifts and aid poured into the area—from school children's pennies to $100,000 donated by the St. Petersburg, Fla., business community.

"We owe this nation a debt we can never repay," said Wade Guice, Harrison County Civil Defense director.

The effects of Camille were measured in more than wind and water. A decade after the horrendous tragedy, civic leaders point out evidence of the Coast's comeback—a huge new Army Munitions plant in Pearl River County, to employ more than 1,500; a $200 million DuPont ilmenite plant at DeLisle; a burgeoning population up 26 percent in the past 10 years and a new boom in building and business.

Much of the growth would have come anyway, Chick Anderson believes. But Anderson adds that "Camille gave us a fresh start. What's happening here is happening with greater speed and a greater spirit because of Camille."

6. Newsweek *Exposes Environmental Catastrophe on the Mississippi, 1990*

When the sun sets on the Mississippi at La Place, La., a scarlet ribbon of smog lights the sky in the west. Between New Orleans and Baton Rouge, great streams of hydrocarbons spew from a hundred plants' smokestacks. Louisiana, which ranks 20th in population, falls third in an Environmental Protection Agency ranking of states by toxic air emissions. Twenty-five percent of the nation's chemical industry is in Louisiana. Most of it was built along this 150-mile stretch of the Mississippi, which had easy access to the offshore oilfields, plenty of fresh water—and, until recently, a state government that didn't look too closely into what Gov. Buddy Roemer calls "a deal with the Devil."

The urgent question of the day is whether the Devil's price was just the familiar irritations of smog and ozone, or something more sinister. The Greenpeace report called the area by its local nickname, the "cancer corridor." Compared to the rest of the Mississippi corridor, the 10 Louisiana parishes where the chemical industry is concentrated "consistently suffered some of the highest rates of mortality from all diseases, [and of] cancer deaths and infant deaths," according to Greenpeace. But the study admits that it cannot prove that these deaths were the result of breathing the air and drinking the water. Many other things could be responsible, such as poverty, high smoking rates and lifestyle factors. The culture of southeast Louisiana, to put it delicately, does not emphasize the virtues of postponing pleasure. "Greenpeace committed scientific malpractice," says Dan Borné, president of the Louisiana Chemical Association. Borné also asserts that the chemical industry actually returns water to the river "in better shape than when they got it out, in terms of pollution," so he may not be the most open-minded observer. But a disinterested authority, Dr. Joel L. Nitzkin of the Louisiana Office of Public Health, says that "air contamination just doesn't seem to be the answer. If there is a cancer problem related to industry, we believe it is relatively small."

Yes, but what do the people who live there believe? It's not always easy to tell, because the chemical industry keeps buying up the houses around them. The people suspect this is because that's the quickest and cheapest way to settle complaints. But the companies claim this is a responsible tactic to create buffer zones around potentially dangerous chemicals. Georgia Gulf bought out all 40 families who lived in Reveilletown, Iberville Parish, and settled a class-action lawsuit over alleged pollution. Dow Chemical is trying to buy the community of Morrisonville, near Baton Rouge. In 1982, after accidental emissions and 78 fires at the now defunct Good Hope Refinery, and numerous evacuations of the next-door elementary school, the oil company bought the school.

Among those who remain, suspicion is rampant. In 1987, Kay Gaudet, a pharmacist, reported to the state an unusually high rate of miscarriages in St. Gabriel. But a study by Luann White, associate dean of public health at Tulane, found that miscarriage rates in the parish were about the same as elsewhere in Louisiana. Oddly enough, this reassuring news was not well received in the community. "They were not really happy to hear this, because they were sure there had been an increase [in miscarriages] due to environmental problems," White says. "When you're dealing with the environment, there are emotional concerns, political concerns. Sometimes the concern taken least into account is science."

Terrebonne Parish

Past New Orleans, the Mississippi rushes on for another 115 miles to its triple outlet on the gulf. Between here and the mouth of the Atchafalaya, 110 miles to the west, lie the Cajun swamp parishes of Lafourche and Terrebonne. Here the land doesn't so much meet the sea as gradually shred into it. Cypress stand in clumps of real estate surrounded by water, brushing the ripples with their trails of Spanish moss. Inexorably the real estate is shrinking. Louisiana wetlands are disappearing at the rate of 50 square miles a year. An aerial photograph of Terrebonne Parish from, say, 30 years ago, would show a solid green carpet of marsh. Today, says Oliver Houck, professor of environmental law at Tulane University, "you see something that looks like a torn rag."

This is yet another environmental catastrophe perpetrated, in innocent pursuit of its congressionally mandated goals, by the Army Corps of Engineers. In its natural state, Terrebonne Parish was a shelf of silt just above sea level, continually compacting and sinking, but eternally renewed by the sediment in the floods that washed over it

every year. Now, as the river runs to the gulf between its formidable levees, the sinking goes on but there is nothing to rebuild with. "The Mississippi over the course of history wriggled across Louisiana like a hose, spraying all this life-giving stuff," says Houck. "When we decided to dedicate the river to navigation, we altered the balance. We have taken the hose and turned it off"—or, more precisely, directed it straight down a sewer, in the interest of efficiency.

Of course, the levees are not wholly to blame; how could there be an environmental catastrophe in Louisiana without the oil industry? To clear a route for drilling rigs, oil companies and the corps cut more than 10,000 miles of channels through the Louisiana marshes and swamps. These typically are built 100 feet or wider, but the destruction doesn't stop there; after the interlocking root systems of the marsh are severed, the canal banks may erode to three times their original width. This makes for a unique kind of wetland loss. Elsewhere on the North American coast, the shore is being washed back; here, the marsh is falling apart from within.

Ironically, the loss of swampland is accelerating just as its most characteristic inhabitant, the American alligator, is making a comeback. Hunting, banned for years, was reinstated in the early 1980s. Actually, most alligators are trapped on baited hooks left in the water overnight; that way they can be taken without damaging the skin, which has recently been bringing up to $58 a foot. "Alligator Annie" Miller, a tour-boat operator in Houma, now goes out just before hunting season with a boatload of chicken parts for her favorite animals—the ones who will come to the surface and entertain the tourists when called. Then they won't feel like feeding until the hunters have their limit of one alligator per 150 acres.

Louisiana, a poor, rural and conservative state, was slow to awaken to the ecological imperative. It is still very tough to take on the oil industry in the state legislature, but by referendum last year the people voted (by a 75–25 margin) to set aside a portion of oil and gas severance taxes to wetlands restoration. In line with President George Bush's declared national policy of "no net loss" of wetlands, Roemer has set the same goal for the state to achieve by 1992, although the oil-tax revenue, a maximum of $25 million a year, seems way inadequate to the job. All over the country people are uniting to save wetlands, one shopping center at a time, but 80 percent of America's wetland loss is occurring wholesale right here, home to nearly a third of the nation's seafood harvest. "If this were happening on Chesapeake Bay, it would be getting daily attention," says Bob Jones, the Terrebonne Parish engineer. "If we were losing 40 to 50 square miles a year to the Cubans, you know what kind of money we'd be spending on it."

The Gulf

With momentum gathered over 2,000 miles, the Mississippi falls off the Delta into the gulf, and the currents push it east to west, making a green-brown swirl in the blue waters. A continent's worth of nutrients drop into the sea and commence to make their way up the food chain in the direction of blackened redfish. Fishermen, shrimpers and oystermen all gather here for the wriggling bounty of the sea.

But sometimes what the river brings is death. Along the fishing villages of Mobile Bay, 130 miles from the Delta, there is a rare phenomenon the locals call "jubilee." It happens in the late summer months when the air is heavy and still and the gulf waters are as warm as blood. Then swarms of shrimp, crab and deep-sea fish may suddenly appear in the shallow water just off the beaches, swimming suicidally toward the shore—and the waiting nets, not to speak of the pots, of the lucky townspeople.

To biologists, these are not fish that are seeking to get eaten, but fish desperately searching for oxygen. The Mississippi, in its ceaseless fertilization of the continental shelf, can contribute to a condition known as hypoxia. Nitrogen from the river produces a bumper crop of algae, which sink to the ocean floor and decay, using up oxygen. When conditions are right, the fresh river water can settle like a blanket over the heavier salt water, trapping the fish in their asphyxiating bath. Farther from shore,

scientists have found "extensive, severe and long-lasting" hypoxic zones almost every year since 1985, covering areas up to 4,000 square miles, according to researcher Nancy Rabalais. Environmentalists, with their natural bent for drama, call this a "dead zone."

This may well be an entirely natural phenomenon. Or it may not; some evidence suggests that the area affected by dead zones is growing by as much as 19 percent a year. The "pregnant question," according to Donald Boesch, director of the Louisiana Universities Marine Consortium, "is whether man is doing something to intensify it." The nitrogen load of the river has been increasing more or less steadily since the 1950s. Nitrogen compounds are a ubiquitous industrial pollutant. Fertilizer runoff and sewage outflow are major sources. Burning fuel in cars and power plants creates nitrogen oxides, which precipitate out as one form of acid rain. A similar suffocation-by-algae has afflicted lakes, sometimes killing virtually everything in them. But this is the sea, swept by currents that dwarf even the mighty Mississippi. Could the same thing happen to *the entire Gulf of Mexico?* Are we seeing "a major change in our natural history," as R. Eugene Turner, chairman of marine sciences at Louisiana State University, puts it? Or is Texas A&M oceanographer Robert Presley right when he says, "I simply do not believe these horror stories that the Gulf of Mexico is being destroyed by man. It's just plain physically impossible."

The fishermen, for their part, go out with their nets and do their jobs; and if the catch is good, they thank God and the Mississippi, and if it's not, well, they'll have better luck another day. Here the river lies beyond the reach of the Corps of Engineers and the Minnesota-Wisconsin Boundary Area Commission and the yellow torrents of sewage. The rest of us have only the river we have made—a river that flows on command and runs where we tell it, whose water comes to us processed through the gates of 29 dams, every drop of it tainted and corrupted by civilization before being allowed to seek its solace in the sea. It carries with it the sorrows of a continent.

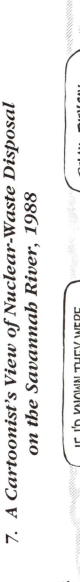

7. *A Cartoonist's View of Nuclear-Waste Disposal on the Savannah River, 1988*

References

1. A Journalist Examines the Transformation of Louisville, 1973
   "Revival Time for Louisville," *Business Week* (September 8, 1973), p. 52.

2. A Report on How Cubans Made Their Mark on Miami, 1971
   "How the Immigrants Made It in Miami," *Business Week* (May 1, 1971), pp. 88–89.

3. Tony Dunbar on Sickness and Poverty in the Mississippi Delta, 1968
   Tony Dunbar, *Our Land Too* (New York: Pantheon Books, 1971), pp. 49–57.

4. Ambrose, Georgia, Farmers Fight Back Against Drought, 1990
   "Farm Fresh: In Georgia, Tradition Bites the Dust," *Atlanta Journal and Constitution*, July 21, 1990.

5. Gulf Coast Residents Recover from a Hurricane, 1979
   Jerry DeLaughter, "Ten Years After Camille," *The South Magazine*, (July 1979), pp. 25–27.

6. *Newsweek* Exposes Environmental Catastrophe on the Mississippi, 1990
   Jerry Adler, "Troubled Waters," *Newsweek* (April 16, 1990), pp. 77–80.

7. A Cartoonist's View of Nuclear-Waste Disposal on the Savannah River, 1988
   Robert Ariail, *Ariail View* (South Carolina: The State, 1990).

Further Reading

Carl Abbott, *The New Urban America: Growth and Politics in the Sunbelt Cities* (1981)

Nelson M. Blake, *Land into Water—Water into Land: A History of Water Management in Florida* (1980)

Blaine A. Brownell and David R. Goldfield, eds., *The City in Southern History: The Growth of Urban Civilization in the South* (1977)

Thomas D. Clark, *The Greening of the South: The Recovery of Land and Forest* (1984)

James C. Cobb, *The Selling of the South: The Southern Crusade for Industrial Development, 1936–1980* (1982)

Albert E. Cowdrey, *This Land, This South: An Environmental History* (1983)

Ronald D. Eller, *Miners, Millhands, and Mountaineers: Industrialization of the Appalachian South* (1982)

Gilbert C. Fite, *Cotton Fields No More: Southern Agriculture, 1865–1980* (1984)

David R. Goldfield, *Promised Land: The South Since 1945* (1987)

Andrew Hamer, *Urban Atlanta: Redefining the Role of the City* (1980)

Robert G. Healy, *Competition for Land in the American South: Agriculture, Human Settlement, and the Environment* (1985)

E. Blaine Liner and Lawrence K. Lynch, eds., *The Economics of Southern Growth* (1977)

Randall M. Miller and George E. Pozzetta, eds., *Shades of the Sunbelt: Essays on Ethnicity, Race, and the Urban South* (1988)

Thomas H. Naylor and James Clotfeller, *Strategies for Change in the South* (1975)

Neal R. Peirce, *The Border South States* (1975)

———, *The Deep South States of America* (1972)

Bernard L. Weinstein and Robert E. Firestine, *Regional Growth and Decline in the United States: The Rise of the Sunbelt and the Decline of the Northeast* (1978)

Document Set 17

Race Relations in the Modern South

After gaining its greatest victories in the fight against racial discrimination in the South in the mid-1960s, the civil-rights movement entered a period of decline from which it has yet to recover. Pride in their successful efforts to improve conditions for themselves did not blind African-Americans to the fact that federally supervised desegregation was and would continue to be unpopular with white southerners. Abandoning the philosophy of nonviolent direct action, many southern blacks resorted to confrontation in their efforts to force the slow pace of change. Others, especially the increasingly restless students of SNCC (Student Non-Violent Coordinating Committee), took their lead from the militant black-nationalist leader Malcolm X, querying whether integration with white society was desirable at all.

It appeared that the white South was not ready for integration on anything but the most limited of scales. "White flight" from public schools to private institutions, a phenomenon of the 1960s and beyond, has undermined the effectiveness of desegregation in the southern states' public-school systems. Moreover, the attitude of some whites to blacks' advancement have hardened as affirmative action, busing, and the establishment of special scholarships reserved exclusively for racial minorities in higher education suggest to them that a reverse discrimination has taken effect. The credence that some whites give to the fallacious idea that African-Americans now possess equal opportunities for social progress and economic advancement but cannot take advantage of them reinforces old stereotypes of black laziness.

The reality is different. Despite affirmative-action programs, blacks still encounter barriers to achieving top positions in business and industry. At a lower level, African-Americans suffer because they cannot afford to pay the cost of training for jobs that require new technological skills. Black communities in the South, particularly in the bigger cities, experience higher levels of unemployment and poverty than white communities. Such problems, however, are not only regional but national. In 1980, according to the Bureau of the Census, the median black family income in the United States as a whole was $9,000 less than the median white family income.

In contrast, since the passage of the Voting Rights Act in 1965, African-Americans have made substantial political gains in the South as elsewhere in the nation. From small-town school-board member to state governor, southern blacks have enjoyed success in state and local elections. Presidential elections suggest that there remains, however, a racial dimension to voter behavior in the South. The white vote has turned strongly Republican since the Democratic party of Lyndon B. Johnson became the standard bearer for civil rights. Is it coincidence that Republican presidents from Richard Nixon to George Bush have acted to undermine the still elusive black quest for equality?

Blacks' frustration at the excruciatingly slow pace of racial change in both the South and the nation boiled over in 1965. Convinced that full integration could be carried out only on terms favorable to whites, some African-Americans embraced a concept known as Black Power, whose advocates urged black people to organize their own political programs in the fight to secure positive social change. In the first document, Stokely Carmichael, chairman of SNCC and a leader of the Black Power movement, and Charles Hamilton, a political scientist, explain why blacks should reject nonviolent direct action. By the end of the decade, ironically, Black Power meetings were little more than orthodox business conventions, with President Richard Nixon

223

redefining the movement as "black capitalism." The implications of Black Power frightened white people who had been prepared to cooperate with Dr. Martin Luther King, Jr.'s milder approach.

For some white southerners, however, equality for African-Americans was unthinkable. In rural Forsyth County, Georgia, white supremacy has hardly missed a beat, as the second selection reveals. Residents argue that racial strife is nonexistent there because of the almost total exclusion of blacks from the county. Traditionally, racial problems occur in communities with a sizable ethnic minority, as the third document illustrates. Although the utterance of racial slurs by prominent public figures has become mostly a thing of the past, thoughtless and insensitive remarks remain in evidence. In the fourth selection, Albert "Happy" Chandler, a former governor of Kentucky, defends a controversial comment that he made at a meeting of the University of Kentucky's Board of Trustees.

Controversy is no stranger to the careers of the Reverend Jesse Jackson of South Carolina and James Meredith, a prominent civil-rights activist from Mississippi. His unsuccessful efforts to capture the Democratic party's nomination for president of the United States in 1984 and 1988 notwithstanding, Jackson remains a charismatic national figure. In the fifth document, he declares his candidacy in the 1988 presidential election. Meredith's life has been nothing if not varied. The first African-American to gain admission to the University of Mississippi, Meredith confounded more conventional civil-rights activists in 1990 by joining the staff of North Carolina's Jesse Helms, the most conservative member of the United States Senate. The newspaper article featured in the sixth selection explains the reason behind Meredith's apparently strange decision.

The final document is a well-balanced analysis of African-American progress in the South today. Andrew Young did not win the Democratic party's gubernatorial nomination in Georgia, but history was made in Virginia, where Douglas Wilder was elected governor, albeit as a conservative Democrat.

Questions for Analysis

1. Are African-Americans still discriminated against in the South? If so, how?

2. Why did the influence of the civil-rights movement wane so quickly? Did southern blacks gain anything from adopting a more militant approach to race relations?

3. Is there any substance to white claims that affirmative action and the use of racial quotas constitute reverse discrimination?

4. Can racial prejudice account for the high incidence of poverty and unemployment in black southern communities?

5. How influential are African-Americans in southern politics?

6. How important is the issue of race in presidential and congressional elections in the South?

1. Black Power Advocates Challenge Nonviolence, 1967

. . . A key phrase in our buffer-zone days was non-violence. For years it has been thought that black people would not literally fight for their lives. Why this has been so is not entirely clear; neither the larger society nor black people are noted for passivity. The notion apparently stems from the years of marches and demonstrations and sit-ins where black people did not strike back and the violence always came from white mobs. There are many who still sincerely believe in that approach. From our viewpoint, rampaging white mobs and white night-riders must be made to understand that their days of free head-whipping are over. Black people should and must fight back. Nothing more quickly repels someone bent on destroying you than the unequivocal message: "O.K., fool, make your move, and run the same risk I run—of dying."

When the concept of Black Power is set forth, many people immediately conjure up notions of violence. The country's reaction to the Deacons for Defense and Justice, which originated in Louisiana, is instructive. Here is a group which realized that the "law" and law enforcement agencies would not protect people, so they had to do it themselves. If a nation fails to protect its citizens, then that nation cannot condemn those who take up the task themselves. The Deacons and all other blacks who resort to self-defense represent a simple answer to a simple question: what man would not defend his family and home from attack?

But this frightened some white people, because they knew that black people would now fight back. They knew that this was precisely what *they* would have long since done if *they* were subjected to the injustices and oppression heaped on blacks. Those of us who advocate Black Power are quite clear in our minds that a "non-violent" approach to civil rights is an approach black people cannot afford and a luxury white people do not deserve. It is crystal clear to us—and it must become so with the white society—*that there can be no social order without social justice*. White people must be made to understand that they must stop messing with black people, or the blacks *will* fight back!

Next, we must deal with the term "integration." According to its advocates, social justice will be accomplished by "integrating the Negro into the mainstream institutions of the society from which he has been traditionally excluded." This concept is based on the assumption that there is nothing of value in the black community and that little of value could be created among black people. The thing to do is siphon off the "acceptable" black people into the surrounding middle-class white community.

The goals of integrationists are middle-class goals, articulated primarily by a small group of Negroes with middle-class aspirations or status. Their kind of integration has meant that a few blacks "make it," leaving the black community, sapping it of leadership potential and know-how. . . . [T]hose token Negroes—absorbed into a white mass—are of no value to the remaining black masses. They became meaningless show-pieces for a conscience-soothed white society. Such people will state that they would prefer to be treated "only as individuals, not as Negroes"; that they "are not and should not be preoccupied with race." This is a totally unrealistic position. In the first place, black people have not suffered as individuals but as members of a group; therefore, their liberation lies in group action. This is why SNCC—and the concept of Black Power—affirms that helping *individual* black people to solve their problems on an *individual* basis does little to alleviate the mass of black people. Secondly, while color blindness *may* be a sound goal ultimately, we must realize that race is an overwhelming fact of life in this historical period. There is no black man in this country who can live "simply as a man." His blackness is an ever-present fact of this racist society, whether he recognizes it or not. It is unlikely that this or the next generation will witness the time when race will no longer be relevant in the conduct of public affairs and in public policy decision-making. To realize this and to attempt to deal with it does not make one a racist or overly preoccupied with race; it puts one in the forefront of a significant *struggle*. If there is no intense struggle today, there will be no meaningful results tomorrow.

"Integration" as a goal today speaks to the problem of blackness not only in an unrealistic way but also in a despicable way. It is based on complete acceptance of the fact that in order to have a decent house or education, black people must move into a white neighborhood or send their children to a white school. This reinforces, among both black and white, the idea that "white" is automatically superior and "black" is by definition inferior. For this reason, "integration" is a subterfuge for the maintenance of white supremacy. It allows the nation to focus on a handful of Southern black children who get into white schools at a great price, and to ignore the ninety-four percent who are left in unimproved all-black schools. Such situations will not change until black people become equal in a way that means something, and integration ceases to be a one-way street. Then integration does not mean draining skills and energies from the black ghetto into white neighborhoods. To sprinkle black children among white pupils in outlying schools is at best a stop-gap measure. The goal is not to take black children out of the black community and expose them to white middle-class values; the goal is to build and strengthen the black community.

"Integration" also means that black people must give up their identity, deny their heritage. We recall the conclusion of Killian and Grigg: "At the present time, integration as a solution to the race problem demands that the Negro foreswear his identify as a Negro." The fact is that integration, as traditionally articulated, would abolish the black community. The fact is that what must be abolished is not the black community, but the dependent colonial status that has been inflicted upon it.

The racial and cultural personality of the black community must be preserved and that community must win its freedom while preserving its cultural integrity. Integrity includes a pride—in the sense of self-acceptance, not chauvinism—in being black, in the historical attainments and contributions of black people. No person can be healthy, complete and mature if he must deny a part of himself; this is what "integration" has required thus far. This is the essential difference between integration as it is currently practiced and the concept of Black Power.

The idea of cultural integrity is so obvious that it seems almost simple-minded to spell things out at this length. Yet millions of Americans resist such truths when they are applied to black people. Again, that resistance is a comment on the fundamental racism in the society. Irish Catholics took care of their own first without a lot of apology for doing so, without any dubious language from timid leadership about guarding against "backlash." Everyone understood it to be a perfectly legitimate procedure. Of course, there would be "backlash." Organization begets counterorganization, but this was no reason to defer.

The so-called white backlash against black people is something else: the embedded traditions of institutional racism being brought into the open and calling forth overt manifestations of individual racism. . . .

2. *Confrontation in Forsyth County, 1987*

He stood alone on the gentle rise of land as thousands of tired marchers, all anxious to reach the safety of the buses, streamed below him on the two-lane asphalt road that links Cumming to the rest of the world. A crude sign suspended by a string hung from his neck. "I *live* here," it read. Over his mouth was plastered a strip of silver tape. It kept working loose and he kept raising his hand to push it back into place.

Behind him was the First Baptist Church. He was white and there was an unmistakable symbolism in the spot he had chosen. This was a House of God and the message of the solitary figure was that while he was harboring sympathy for the marchers' cause, his mouth was sealed. Was it fear? Was it survival instinct? It really didn't matter. An oasis is an oasis wherever you find it.

That simple act, performed in a sea of hate, took courage. The leaden January sky was growing darker, and after the 20,000 or more marchers, and the thousands of National Guardsmen, state troopers, deputy sheriffs, Georgia Bureau of Investigation, Justice Department and other security personnel left, the curtain of night would fall and he would still be in Forsyth County.

Walking into Forsyth County was returning to the dark past—to a time older people thought was behind them and younger people had never known. The racists, with the Ku Klux Klan in their front ranks, turned out 1,000 strong to curse and jeer the marchers who had come to protest the more than 75 years of exclusion of blacks from the county. Hate was in their voices, in their eyes and in the way their faces knotted up at the sight of the crowd. It was hard to judge who they hated the most—blacks or the whites who walked at their side.

And these were young people, many of them hardly past puberty. They repeated the same chant over and over again—"nigger go home, nigger go home." The intensity of their hate recalled the mobs that so many years ago lined the streets of Selma, Birmingham, Montgomery, Cicero; mobs in so many places that some of the names have faded from memory.

There were differences, however. Back then, you saw weatherbeaten older faces where the furrowed lines marked years of hard living and a lot of meanness. Now, the chanters were younger—the McDonald's generation, fast food, blue jeans and music videos. They came as young as five, and even at that age of innocence, they knew how to say "nigger."

The law had changed, too. Then, if you demonstrated for civil rights, you were never quite sure whether the police and/or the National Guard were going to protect you or let the wolves tear you apart. Now, with so many black National Guardsmen and such a scattering of black faces among the state troopers and other law enforcement officers, there was a sense of security on that score. The sight of a six-foot-three black National Guardsman dressed in green fatigues, a battle helmet, and caressing a four-foot long, well-seasoned wooden club tends to serve as something of a deterrent.

The faces of the demonstrators had changed as well. There were veterans of marches of more than 20 years ago, grown grayer and maybe a little stockier now, but most of the faces belonged to a new generation of whites and blacks, many of them on their first demonstration, many of them facing up close for the first time the naked and ugly force of racism.

Forsyth County has had a long time to live with its racism. In 1912, a black man was accused of raping a white woman. He was lynched. Two other blacks were given a swift trial and just as quickly hung. The rest of the black people in the county were forced to flee for their lives, leaving behind their homes, their land.

Blacks have never returned. The county has remained all white. When a small, mixed group attempted to stage a "Brotherhood March" to commemorate Martin Luther King's birthday, they were pelted with stones and other debris and forced to beat a hasty retreat out of town. A week later, that handful had grown to 20,000, drawn to Atlanta, the staging point, from as far away as San Francisco. Buses took them the 40 miles to the other world of Forsyth County and the county seat of Cumming with its 2,000 population. (The entire county has only 38,000.)

Over the 1¼ mile road that led from where the buses parked to the courthouse square where a brief rally took place, someone had hung a yellow banner, "Welcome to Forsyth County." It seemed ironic, but the business people and the governing officials did not want the county's image damaged any further. They were at the courthouse to greet the marchers while the racists, kept back by the show of force, vented their wrath. Along the route there were also some whites who encouraged the marchers and expressed shame at what was taking place in their county.

A black columnist, William Raspberry, writing in the *Washington Post*, reflected the view of those who saw the march as a futile gesture:

"A 1960's-style march through Georgia, no matter how much it looks like something King might have done, strikes me as a waste of courage, a purposeless exercise in nostalgia."

Most certainly, the one march, no matter how impressive, did not change a single thing in Forsyth County. But there are those times in the course of human events when not to respond to evilness is to acquiesce to it—by silence to give consent, thus, encouraging the spread of evilness. Forsyth was one of those times. . . .

3. *Florida Whites Express Concern About Cuban Migration, 1985*

South Florida's Melting Pot Is About to Boil

Miguel Pérez is used to waiting. He spent 15 years waiting to get out of Fidel Castro's Cuba, three of them in jail for trying to escape the island. Even after he got his wish—leaving Cuba for Miami with 125,000 other *Marielitos* in the 1980 boat lift from the Cuban port of Mariel—the slender meat cutter has had to wait. This time he is waiting for approval from Washington to apply for U.S. citizenship and for the right to send for his twin 11-year-old sons and the elderly parents he left behind.

Pérez's waiting days may finally be over. In November the Immigration & Naturalization Service announced that more than 120,000 Mariel refugees without criminal records could begin applying for legal residency in the U.S. Former political prisoners such as Pérez are likely to be included under the edict. Some could become eligible for citizenship as early as this summer. And Pérez may soon be able to send for his family. He will try to bring his father to the U.S. first. "He is old," says Pérez, "and he wants to die free."

Pérez's private dream, multiplied by the thousands of transplanted Cubans who share it, is viewed by some non-Latin Floridians as a potential nightmare. As a result, the ethnic and political pots are boiling in south Florida. Key to the tensions is a recent U.S.–Cuban agreement under which nearly 3,000 Mariel criminals and mental patients now held in U.S. prisons will be shipped back to Cuba. As part of the deal, normal immigration between Cuba and the U.S. will be restored. This means that once the *Marielitos* who remain in Florida are sworn in as citizens, they will have the right to send for an unrestricted number of husbands, wives, parents, and minor children—and the Castro government says it will not stand in the way.

Some south Florida residents fear the region cannot absorb tens of thousands—perhaps hundreds of thousands—more Cuban refugees. They warn that the state lacks the jobs, schools, and social services to cope with them. In the past, black leaders, edgy about outbreaks of racial violence in Miami's teeming slums, worried that blacks would be shoved aside by waves of Cuban immigrants. Now some whites are also concerned.

The charge that south Florida is already too Latinized—Latins constitute 44% of Dade County's population—is raising ugly passions. State and local politicians are treading a fine line between their Anglo constituents' fears and the reality of growing Latin political muscle. Some Republicans, encouraged by the predominantly pro-GOP sentiment among Cubans in Florida, see a new influx as a potential boon to their party. Democrats, sensing a threat to their dominance in the heavily Democratic state, are raising the specter of a GOP plot to tip the political balance.

Fueling Fears

Charges are flying that south Florida could be deluged with up to 300,000 Cuban newcomers. INS officials in Washington, however, sharply dispute these estimates—although they admit they don't yet know how many will immigrate. INS Commissioner Alan C. Nelson maintains that Florida leaders have "overreacted." He says: "It will not be 300,000, and it will not be tomorrow." In particular he points out: "Many of the people who came in 1980 came to be reunited with relatives. They're already here."

Nonetheless, in living rooms and political gatherings all over south Florida, anxious talk of another Mariel invasion is topic A. The public debate is being fueled by several Miami radio talk-show hosts who are conducting a campaign aimed at fanning resentment to large-scale Cuban immigration. Anxious listeners are jamming the stations' phone lines. Their biggest worry: being displaced by Cuban newcomers.

"The idea that these people are being assimilated is ridiculous. They are absorbing us, and not the other way around," talk-show host Al Rantel charged on a WNWS broadcast. Most of his callers agreed, pouring out their resentment over not finding a job or even being able to shop for groceries in Miami unless they speak Spanish. "It's like we're the foreigners here," complained one caller from South Miami.

Working with other radio personalities, Rantel has organized a write-in campaign to persuade Washington to reverse its decision on the *Marielitos*. The campaign, called Save Our South Florida, or S.O.S., has raised some $10,000 and mailed thousands of postcards protesting the INS policy to politicians in Tallahassee and Washington.

R. Ray Goode, president of the Babcock Co., a major Miami developer and homebuilder, says that more than just "the lunatic fringe" is concerned. He is particularly worried about who will pay. "The federal government must recognize that this is by no means a local problem," he declares. "It came about as the result of federal policies—or nonpolicies—and they [Washington] must subsidize the cost."

Governor Bob Graham agrees. He says he was not consulted on the deal with Castro or the decision to legalize the *Marielitos*, even though 80% of them have settled in south Florida. He claims Washington still owes state and local governments more than $150 million for services provided in the wake of the 1980 boat lift. "Immigration policy is a federal responsibility," Graham declares. "Washington must pay the cost." To which White House assistant Lee Verstanding counters: "Southwest states are facing the same problems [from other refugees]. We can't just single out one state."

Florida political observers suspect that Graham, a Democrat, has more than money on his mind. GOP sources admit that the addition of Cuban immigrants to voter rolls could dramatically boost Republicans' political power in Florida. And there is speculation that in 1986 Graham may challenge Republican Senator Paula Hawkins, a popular figure in the Cuban community. That challenge could be in jeopardy if the Cubans are registered en masse by the GOP.

Soul-Searching

Currently there is a 10-month wait in Miami between eligibility for citizenship and naturalization, but the Reagan Administration could shorten the waiting time if it chooses to. "President Ford's people sent 10 [federal immigration] lawyers down to Miami to speed things up before the 1976 elections," says an INS source. "The Reagan people did the same before last year's election. All they would have to do is put the Cubans in the Orange Bowl and swear 'em in."

While the politicians examine the angles, soul-searching over the new immigrants has extended to the heart of Miami's Cuban enclaves, where some established Cubans also worry about the cost of another wave. "We are not against people coming over from Cuba," insists Sergio Pereira, Dade County's assistant administrator and a Cuban refugee himself. "As a Cuban, I can tell you what will happen. The people come over [to Florida] on a Wednesday. Their families take off Thursday and Friday, and on Saturday they roast a pig. But by the time Monday comes around, they have to go back to work, and uncle needs a driver's license, and mother needs to go to a doctor. That," says Pereira, "is when they'll turn to us."

4. *"Happy" Chandler Makes a Statement, 1988*

. . . On April 5, 1988, I attended a meeting of the trustees investment committee in one of the little offices at the university. Four or five other board members were there and we took up the university's decision to dispose of its investments in South Africa.

The committee chairman was discussing in a general way how to get rid of our investments over there, and I said, just apropos of nothing: "The question of Zimbabwe [formerly Rhodesia] has arisen, and you know what's happened there. It's now all nigger. There are no white folks there anymore. The streets of Salisbury are boarded up. Grass is growing in the streets. And it's just changed."

There was a girl sitting in the back of the room I didn't know. She was a reporter for the *Lexington Herald-Leader*; she picked up on that remark, called it a racial slur and went to her supervisor at the newspaper and he said, "Print it!" Then they embarked on a campaign to make it stand up and make it a national issue.

My statement was not said in anger. It was not said in jest. It was just said. And not said to be offensive toward anybody living or dead. And as I told them later, I was born in a town of 800—400 white and 400 black—and we all called 'em niggers, and they didn't seem to mind, you understand. They answered me by saying that the blacks were afraid to remonstrate. I said I didn't believe that.

The Lexington paper was just nasty and low and mean. I've always insisted that criticism of public officials ought to be just and tempered and decent—but it ought to be just and tempered, it ought to be decent, and if it is not any of those things it ought not to be.

When the Lexington paper broke the story and quoted a group of U.K. students, and some others, as saying I should be punished by being forced to resign from the university board, Governor Wilkinson called me on the phone. He said he did not intend to ask me to resign, but suggested that I should make an apology.

"Governor," I said, "I do apologize for having said anything they construed to be offensive because I hadn't intended to be offensive." And I did make such a public apology—to anyone who might have been offended by my remark.

But that wasn't enough to satisfy the rabble-rousers. A militant campus group, virtually all black, and numbering about forty, according to the newspapers, said the word "nigger" was a terrible insult and demanded that I be forced off the university board.

These protestors waited on the president of U.K., David Roselle. He was weak at the start; the

newspapers quoted him as saying that "the university completely and totally repudiates what it is Governor Chandler says. Completely. We do not support his statement." He never showed me the courtesy of asking me about what I had said, or meant, and most assuredly never suggested personally to me that I should resign as a trustee. One student leader and a Lexington city councilman, both of whom are black, began fanning the flames and got the football players, who are also mainly black, stirred up so much they staged a one-day walkout of spring practice and threatened to boycott the annual Blue-White intrasquad game on April 23 or wear black arm bands as a symbol of defiance. Only my resignation, they asserted, would appease them. That was something I had no intention of doing.

To be honest, I was flabbergasted by this football squad walkout. Since the 1920s I have always maintained a healthy and close relationship with football players and coaches in Kentucky, especially at the university. Paul "Bear" Bryant and I were close; he called me "Skipper." I was frequently asked for counsel by coaches Blanton Collier and Fran Curci. Dr. Otis Singletary, during his time as U.K. president, insisted I serve on the athletic council. Of course, in later years I haven't shown up at Wildcat practice sessions like I used to, so my sports record probably is not so well known now to late-comers over there on the Lexington campus.

That present set of young men probably haven't the slightest concept of the Old South I grew up in when the word "nigger" was commonly used and was not necessarily a term of disrespect. I am proud of the strong political and personal friendships I have developed over the years with Negroes. . . . I have recounted many instances of going to bat for colored people because I believe they are entitled to equality under the law. And I have never deviated from that position in the slightest, and the record clearly shows that.

I am aware that the word "nigger" went out of style and became an offensive buzz word years ago. But even so, there was a period when the Negroes themselves could not settle on the terminology we were supposed to use. My son Ben reminded me that in a speech at the Wood-ford County Courthouse during the 1959 gubernatorial contest I remarked that I appreciated the help of the "black boys" in the current campaign. A black man, who still resides in our area, stood up and interrupted my speech by saying his people were "Negroes" and that they resented being called "black." Well, that was all right with me, but for quite a period of years there was a lot of confusion and indecision over whether they wanted to be known as "colored," "black," or "Negro." Now the preference seems to be "black."

Maybe I have lost touch with young black men like those trying to create a ruckus on the University of Kentucky football squad. I have to admit they dismayed me, seeing some with earrings and so forth in their noses and ears; I don't know what kind of people they are.

Naturally this was the kind of a furor that was picked up by news wires and was broadcast all over the country. And phone calls started flooding in on me at Versailles. My guess is that of the first 1,000, only three were negative. Baseball Commissioner Peter Ueberroth offered to fly down to Lexington and meet with football coach Jerry Claiborne and his players.

"Thank you, commissioner," I told Ueberroth, "but I believe Coach Claiborne will handle it all right." Actually I was not certain of it at the time; Claiborne seemed then to be just pussyfooting and not coming to grips with the situation.

Joe Morgan, one of the greatest black baseball players who ever lived, called wanting to help. We've been good friends since the days when he was the stellar second baseman for the Cincinnati Reds. Joe called the situation an "outrage" and said he would do what he could to stop it. I thanked him and told him not to worry, everything would settle down.

In retrospect, my *faux pas* was not a big deal, and certainly didn't deserve all the attention it received. It was one word, a racial slur, if you want to call it that, and spoken not in a public forum but in a small committee meeting and without any animosity or bad feeling. It was plain and simple my reversion to the language of my youth. Except for a reporter being present and deciding to turn it into a *cause célèbre*, the episode would never have created a ripple. . . .

5. *Jesse Jackson Seeks the Presidency, 1988*

My friends, we are here today in Raleigh, North Carolina, in the heart of the new South. I was born in Greenville, South Carolina, went to college in Greensboro, North Carolina, and got my first chance to serve politically in Raleigh, North Carolina, as head of the North Carolina Intercollegiate Council on Human Rights. We sought to end the laws of apartheid that wrecked this region culturally, economically, politically and spiritually.

Twenty-five years ago I was appointed to be a member of the delegation of young Democrats to Las Vegas, and the late Al House was elected their national president. Governor Terry Sanford gave me the opportunity to serve. I shall forever respect him for it.

It was clear then in national politics that a new South could arise, but we would have to rise together. Sons and daughters, locked away from each other by ancient and archaic customs, would have to find commonground. Once we found commonground we could become national political champions and elect Presidents, as well as national basketball, football and baseball champions. This region of rich soil and poor people can lead America to its loftiest and highest ideals.

We are here today at the dawn, early in the morning, of the new South. Early in the morning of our new possibilities. Early in the morning of our challenge to reach commonground; to end economic violence; and to assure economic justice to all of our people. We are early in the morning of the new South that elected new senators; the new South that defeated Judge Bork; and early in the morning of a new South characterized by humane priorities at home and human rights abroad.

The new South—where farmers and truck drivers, black and white, male and female, the very able and the disabled, the secure and the threatened—can come together and raise the standard of living for everybody.

I'm a son of the South. I've spent all of my adult life trying to build a new South. As the poor of the South are liberated, the South will become liberalized—with a commitment to liberal arts and science.

As a son of the new South, one who was born and bred here, developed in Chicago—urban America, the Midwest, the heartland of our nation—and one who has had the privilege to travel around the world to retrieve Americans from dungeons and foreign jails; as one who has had the privilege to meet the great leaders of the world; I can do no less than serve my country, offer my services, my skills, my energy, and my commitment to its ideals. My broadbased American experience—from the humblest of beginnings to the boardrooms of corporations, the picketline, negotiating sessions with workers, the Pope at the Vatican, heads of state—has made my appreciation and love for America a part of my blood, my bones, and my soul.

There is something wrong with our government today. The direction of its leadership, its priorities and its values are wrong. But there is nothing wrong with America. America is our land. America is God's country. America has been blessed, and God bless America.

My candidacy is a call to service. I have spent the last 25 years, not as a perfect servant, but as a public servant. My name has become known because I have served. That's why I want to be President—to serve the American people; to help to make their lives more purposeful and complete; to provide equal protection under the law for all; to improve the quality of life for all; and

to show that jobs, peace and justice are mutually re-enforcing goals.

I want to serve my country. The risk is great. The challenges are many. And the job is difficult. But we have an obligation to serve and I want to serve America.

I want to educate the children, make secure senior citizens, and enable its disabled. I want to serve America.

I want to stop drugs from flowing into America. I want to stop jobs from flowing out of America. I want to provide an affordable health care system. I want to house the American people. I want to stabilize the American family. I want to safeguard its liberties, its rights of privacy, and its public obligations. I want to serve America.

For its 650,000 farmers driven from their land; for its 38 million without health insurance; for its millions who lost their jobs to plant closings and leveraged buy-outs; for its millions who have lost their small business opportunities; for its millions who wake up America every morning and put America to bed each night; who grow its food; and whose shoulders energize our industries; whose sweat and blood fertilize our soil. I want to serve America.

I want to offer the highest and best service in our highest and most sensitive job. The job that has the most capacity to bring justice in our land, mitigate misery in the world and bring peace on earth—the office of President. Only in America is such a dream possible.

Today I offer my service to our country. I seek God's guidance and your prayers as we embark on this mission. Therefore, on this day, October 10, 1987, in Raleigh, North Carolina, I officially announce my candidacy to seek the nomination of the Democratic party for the office of President of the United States of America.

6. *Opposites Attract: James Meredith Joins Jesse Helms, 1990*

James Meredith, the civil rights hero who now shuns that title, is working on a project to rewrite U.S. social legislation as an assistant to Sen. Jesse Helms.

Meredith said he gave Helms, R-N.C., an 18-inch-tall stack of proposals when they discussed his joining the senator's staff last year.

"In a nutshell, this is what I told them I want to do: to rewrite domestic policy legislation on the order of the Great Society of Lyndon Johnson and of the New Deal of Franklin Roosevelt," Meredith said.

"To be quite frank, no one was willing to say I could do it. But Senator Helms was willing to let me try."

Meredith's journey from civil rights pioneer to the side of an archconservative senator isn't as surprising as it might appear.

Meredith, who broke the color barrier at the University of Mississippi, was an early loner in the civil rights movement, disillusioned by infighting and unwilling to work with its leaders, according to former colleagues and a biographer.

He surprised many in the movement five years ago when he described integration as a "con job" and even more when he went to work for conservative Helms last year. But Meredith said his behavior should not be a shock.

"I've been saying the same thing for many years. And they have been very much aware of my position," he said from Washington, D.C. "I operate on the principle that the real attraction to Senator Helms was his commitment to family and morality."

Meredith said last week that an elite group of powerful white men pull the strings of many black leaders. He issued a statement on Helms' Senate stationery accusing NAACP [National Association for the Advancement of Colored People] delegates of involvement in drugs.

Meredith said black leaders have been co-opted by white liberals whose programs are intended to reinforce control over blacks.

Benjamin Hooks, executive director of the National Association for the Advancement of Colored People, said Meredith's statements were irrational.

"I think he's had a difficult time keeping in touch with reality," Hooks said.

Helms is facing a re-election challenge by former Charlotte Mayor Harvey Gantt.

Gantt, a black Democrat, said Meredith's statements were a way for Helms to inject race into the campaign without having to personally "say anything that might be considered to be a racist remark."

Helms denied that, saying that Meredith has a right to speak for himself.

7. U.S. News and World Report *Analyzes Black Southern Progress, 1990*

On a July day, with the mercury hitting 97, Andrew Young wrapped himself in a suit, a tie and the mantle of the South. Surrounded by a Dixieland band and aides serving apple pie, Young had brought his gubernatorial campaign to Marietta, a Republican suburb of Atlanta. And he brought his stump speech extolling Dixie's virtues—a mix of the enlightened (" 'We Shall Overcome' is a Georgia hymn") and the technical ("The Dutch know they'll get a good return here").

For those who watched Young and his mentor, Martin Luther King, Jr., as they fought to pry the most basic rights from the white Establishment a scant generation ago, the sight of Young campaigning for governor—as a son of the South, no less—seems improbable. Yet this week he is almost certain to be among the top two finishers in Georgia's Democratic primary, making him eligible for an August runoff election and putting him one step closer to being his state's first black governor. In so doing, Young will try to join a growing cast of leaders who are breaking race barriers to statewide offices: Douglas Wilder, who was elected governor of Virginia last year; Harvey Gantt, Democratic nominee for the Senate from North Carolina. Theo Mitchell, Democratic nominee for governor of South Carolina; and Kenneth "Muskie" Harris, Republican nominee for lieutenant governor of Arkansas.

Do these breakthroughs signal the arrival of the "New South" that has been heralded for more than 100 years? The answer is no: The region is still some distance from such deliverance. The burdens of poverty and racism linger. And the rising fortunes of blacks in the Democratic Party have helped to spawn major white flight to Republican candidates. Today, though, blacks themselves offer tempered but encouraging signs about Southern life, from the skyline of Andy Young's Atlanta to the impoverished backwaters of the Mississippi Delta. . . . They claim that in some ways, the South has caught up with the North in race relations—and that in others, the South has pulled ahead. And beneath the headlines about pathbreaking politicians, there are quieter, more enduring signs of progress:

Reverse Migration

In a historic change, a significant number of blacks are returning to the South. Since 1980, more than 100,000 more blacks have moved into the South than have left. Census data show that between 1980 and 1990, the proportion of all American blacks living in the South increased—for the first time in the 20th century—from 52 to 56 percent. And some researchers predict brisker migration in the 1990s. The cultural and political implications could be profound. One scenario, suggests James Johnson, director of the Center for the Study of Urban Poverty, would be a shift of black political power out of Northern cities, creating a vacuum for newer immigrants.

Officeholders

More than two thirds of all black elected officials in the United States, 67.5 percent, are in the South. That's an amazing feat, considering that in 1940, racism kept all but 3 percent of Southern blacks from registering to vote. The rise of Southern-black elected officials is due, in part, to the greater number of blacks in the region. But blacks are also shooting for higher, more-visible offices in the South than elsewhere, and they are succeeding, because of white support. Their success holds greater promise of helping blacks because statewide offices are more powerful than local ones.

Attitudes

In 1958, 72 percent of Southern whites opposed sending their children to school with blacks; just 13 percent of Northerners said the same. By 1980s, only 5 percent of whites in both regions were opposed. And a Gallup Poll in June found Southerners slightly more optimistic than Northerners about race.

The differences between Southern and Northern cities seem more pronounced. There's not "the same explosive mix" of ethnicity and resentment in Southern cities, says Columbia University sociologist Jonathan Rieder, pointing to smoldering ethnic tensions in New York City that fueled the recent racial strife in Bensonhurst. Moreover, the South seems to have fewer provocateurs like New York's Rev. Al Sharpton. One reason why racial tensions aren't as pronounced in the South is that Southerners don't share the terror of black street crime that is common among Northern urban whites. Not surprisingly, a recent poll found 72 percent of black New Yorkers calling race relations "bad." A Georgia poll found the reverse: 64 percent of blacks described them as "good" or "very good."

That jibes with the experience of Lawrence Hanks, chairman of the political-science department at the historically black Tuskegee University in Tuskegee, Ala. When he received his Harvard Ph.D. in 1984, Hanks decided to return to the South. Born in Fort Gaines, Ga.—"a town that looks like the perfect backdrop for 'Mississippi Burning' "—he attended segregated schools until 10th grade, when the town's black and white high schools merged. Even though the integration was at times tense, he said there was genuine desire to make things go smoothly. When he went to supposedly liberal Boston in the midst of its 1970s busing crisis, he recalls, the contrast was striking: "For the first time in my life, I was told places I couldn't go without getting killed." Today, he is "a lot more hopeful" about the South than the North. Atlanta Congressman and civil-rights leader John Lewis agrees. He says small towns, like his native Troy, Ala., are warmer than the North: "You know each other better."

For other black professionals, the lure of the South is cities like Atlanta, which has the highest concentration of black business managers outside of Washington, D.C. Lawyer Michael Thornton, 30, moved there from Pittsburgh, drawn by a warmer climate, lower cost of living and a vibrant black culture. "Here, I would not be a fly in the buttermilk," he says.

These days, some of the most encouraging notes come from black leaders seeking high office. Significantly, Andrew Young argues that his color is a political advantage—an oddity that attracts the media but doesn't repel too many voters. "Georgians are tired of being called racist," says Young, who likens prejudice to acne, rather than a cancer on the body politic. . . .

References

1. Black Power Advocates Challenge Nonviolence, 1967
   Stokely Carmichael and Charles Hamilton, *Black Power: The Politics of Liberation in America* (New York: Random House, 1967), pp. 52−56.

2. Confrontation in Forsyth County, 1987
   James D. Williams, "The Long, Sad Road to Cumming, Georgia," *The Crisis* (March 1987), pp. 15−17.

3. Florida Whites Express Concern About Cuban Migration, 1985
   "South Florida's Melting Pot Is About to Boil," *Business Week* (February 4, 1985), pp. 86−87.

4. "Happy" Chandler Makes a Statement, 1988
   Albert B. Chandler with Vance H. Trimble, *Heroes, Plain Folks, and Skunks* (Chicago: Bonus Books, Inc., 1989), pp. 292−295.

5. Jesse Jackson Seeks the Presidency, 1988
   Jesse L. Jackson, "A Chance to Serve," *Black Scholar* (March/April 1988), pp. 22−23.

6. Opposites Attract: James Meredith Joins Jesse Helms, 1990
   "Civil Rights Pioneer Works on New Great Society," *The State* (South Carolina), July 24, 1990.

7. *U.S. News and World Report* Analyzes Black Southern Progress, 1990
   "Race and the South," *U.S. News and World Report* (July 23, 1990), pp. 22−24.

Further Reading

Floyd B. Barbour, ed., *The Black Power Revolt* (1968)

Thomas D. Boswell and James R. Curtis, *The Cuban-American Experience: Culture, Images and Perspectives* (1984)

David Colburn, *Racial Change and Community Crisis: St. Augustine, Florida, 1877–1980* (1985)

Margaret Edds, *Free at Last: What Really Happened When Civil Rights Came to Southern Politics* (1987)

David R. Goldfield, *Black, White, and Southern: Race Relations and Southern Culture, 1940 to the Present* (1990)

Elizabeth Jacoway and David Colburn, *Southern Business and Desegregation* (1982)

Theodore Kennedy, *You Gotta Deal with It: Black Family Relations in a Southern Community* (1980)

Ernest Lander and Richard Calhoun, eds., *Two Decades of Change: The South Since the Supreme Court Desegregation Decision* (1975)

Tom Landess, *Jesse Jackson and the Politics of Race* (1985)

Steven Lawson, *In Pursuit of Power: Southern Blacks and Electoral Politics, 1965–1982* (1982)

Michael V. Namorato, ed., *Have We Overcome? Race Relations Since Brown* (1979)

Eleanor M. Rogg, *The Assimilation of Cuban Exiles: The Role of Community and Class* (1974)

Harvard Sitkoff, *The Struggle for Black Equality, 1954–1980* (1981)

George B. Tindall, *The Ethnic Southerners* (1976)

Elizabeth Wheaton, *Codename Greenkil: The 1979 Greensboro Killings* (1987)

Raymond Wolters, *The Burden of Brown: Thirty Years of School Desegregation* (1984)

Document Set 18

The Enduring South

As a result of tremendous change in the South during the last four decades, contemporary scholars are constantly questioning whether or not the South has retained its unique regional distinctiveness. Certainly, the South can no longer be characterized by the features that once set it apart so obviously from the rest of the nation: intense commitment to the maintenance of racial segregation, a one-party political system, and hostility to the forces of modernization. The advent of industrialization and urbanization, the emergence of a two-party political system, and an atmosphere of greater racial tolerance have all steered the South closer to the mainstream of American economic, political, and social patterns of development. In addition, modernization has blurred the geographical boundaries of the South as northern influences have permeated the region. Conversely, southern influences can be perceived in areas outside the South.

Conscious of a need for a full examination of the effect of modernization on southern life and customs, Charles R. Wilson and William Ferris, the editors of a recently published, comprehensive anthology, define the South in a cultural context. The South, they insist, is a state of mind that exists both within and outside any geographical dimensions. In this sense, the South retains a distinctive cultural flavor. Another historian to wrestle with the question of enduring southern distinctiveness was the late David Potter, one of the most perceptive observers of the region. For Potter, southerners' ability to cherish and preserve their unique form of folk life will determine the durability of southern culture. Passed down through generations, traditions and customs provide southerners with a powerful sense of their heritage, reinforcing their relationships with God and nature. "Old-time religion," for example, emphasizing evangelicalism and fundamentalism, may be stronger in the South than anywhere in the Christian world. Family reunions stress the importance of kinship. Nowhere else in America are the skills of folk healers, herbalists, and root doctors given so much credence.

Perhaps more than anything, music epitomizes the feeling that southerners have for their region. From country music to jazz, from gospel to bluegrass, and from blues to beach music, the message is one of love, nostalgia, hope, faith, and camaraderie with others. The remarkable diversity of southern music is a product of the biracial origins of southern culture. Paradoxically, the forces that have helped to create the modern South have generated a fresh spirit of curiosity about the region's past. Future investigations into the nature of southern culture cannot afford to ignore the fusion of European and African influences that created the American South.

Southerners have always considered their customs and traditions in jeopardy from outside influences. In the late 1920s, a group of southern men of letters, calling themselves the Nashville Agrarians, collaborated on a book intended to serve as a warning to southerners that New South ideas of industrial progress threatened to extinguish their region's cherished agricultural heritage. The Agrarian critique of unchecked industrialism is outlined in the first document, an excerpt from the contribution by the poet John Crowe Ransom.

Southerners are identified easily by the way they talk. Tracing the origins of southern speech patterns, the literary critic Cleanth Brooks discusses in the second selection the chances of survival of a distinctive southern dialect. The South's unique brand of English received worldwide exposure in the mid-1970s when Jimmy Carter, a former Georgia governor and a peanut farmer, won the presidency of the United States. In the third document, *Newsweek* magazine analyzes the reasons for Carter's national appeal. During his term of office, President Carter was embarrassed frequently by the adventures and misadventures of his brother, Billy Carter, who made the rest of the nation keenly aware of the southern "good old boy." The "good old boy" and his close relative, the "redneck," are defined and dissected in the fourth document.

The essence of southern humor lies in its eccentricity, noted the essayist Mab Segrest. In *My Mama's Dead Squirrel*, she wrote, "Take a truth and stretch it as far as you can, take a story and sentence and load it down with as many details as possible without completely losing the point—and you have the Southern Baroque." Lem Griffis, a rural Georgian who lived near the Okefenokee Swamp, was a master of southern baroque, as the tall tales composing the fifth document reveal. If southern humor and music are distinctive, so are the numerous dance forms that the music has spawned. As the sixth selection demonstrates, the shag, native to just a handful of the states on the Atlantic seaboard, attracts a devoted core of followers.

Finally, defining the contemporary southerner is not an easy task. No one is more qualified to analyze the modern South and its people, however, than the sociologist John Shelton Reed, whose observations and personal views form the final document.

Questions for Analysis

1. What and where is the South? Is the South of today different from the South of the past?

2. How has modernization affected traditional southern culture?

3. Are southerners in danger of losing their distinctive cultural traits?

4. What patterns of behavior distinguish southerners from other Americans?

5. How have African influences shaped southern culture?

6. Why does southern religion retain its heavily evangelical flavor? Are southern religious practices substantially different from the religious practices of other Americans?

1. An Agrarian Condemns Industrialism, 1930

. . . And now the crisis in the South's decline has been reached.

Industrialism has arrived in the South. Already the local chambers of commerce exhibit the formidable data of Southern progress. A considerable party of Southern opinion, which might be called the New South party, is well pleased with the recent industrial accomplishments of the South and anxious for many more. Southerners of another school, who might be said to compose an Old South party, are apprehensive lest the section become completely and uncritically devoted to the industrial ideal precisely as the other sections of the Union are. But reconstruction is actually under way. Tied politically and economically to the Union, her borders wholly violable, the South now sees very well that she can restore her prosperity only within the competition of an industrial system.

After the war the Southern plantations were often broken up into small farms. These have yielded less and less of a living, and it [is] said that they will never yield a good living until once more they are integrated into large units. But these units will be industrial units, controlled by a board of directors or an executive rather than a squire, worked with machinery, and manned not by farmers living at home, but by "labor." Even so they will not, according to Mr. Henry Ford, support the population that wants to live on them. In the off seasons the laborers will have to work in factories, which henceforth are to be counted on as among the charming features of Southern landscape. The Southern problem is complicated, but at its center is the farmer's problem, and this problem is simply the most acute version of that general agrarian problem which inspires the despair of many thoughtful Americans today.

The agrarian discontent in America is deeply grounded in the love of the tiller for the soil, which is probably, it must be confessed, not peculiar to the Southern specimen, but one of the more ineradicable human attachments, be the tiller as progressive as he may. In proposing to wean men from this foolish attachment, industrialism sets itself against the most ancient and the most humane of all the modes of human livelihood. Do Mr. Hoover and the distinguished thinkers at Washington see how essential is the mutual hatred between the industrialists and the farmers, and how mortal is their conflict? The gentlemen at Washington are mostly preaching and legislating to secure the fabulous "blessings" of industrial progress; they are on the industrial side. The industrialists have a doctrine which is monstrous, but they are not monsters personally; they are forward-lookers with nice manners, and no American progressivist is against them. The farmers are boorish and inarticulate by comparison. Progressivism is against them in their fight, though their traditional status is still so strong that soft words are still spoken to them. All the solutions recommended for their difficulties are really enticements held out to them to become a little more coöperative, more mechanical, more mobile—in short, a little more industrialized. But the farmer who is not a mere laborer, even the farmer of the comparatively new places like Iowa and Nebraska, is necessarily among the more stable and less progressive elements of society. He refuses to mobilize himself and become a unit in the industrial army, because he does not approve of army life.

I will use some terms which are hardly in his vernacular. He identifies himself with a spot of ground, and this ground carries a good deal of meaning; it defines itself for him as nature. He would till it not too hurriedly and not too mechanically to observe in it the contingency and the infinitude of nature; and so his life acquires its philosophical and even its cosmic consciousness. A man can contemplate and explore, respect and love, an object as substantial as a farm or a native province. But he cannot contemplate nor explore, respect nor love, a mere turnover, such as an assemblage of "natural resources," a pile of money, a volume of produce, a market, or a credit system. It is into precisely these intangibles that industrialism would translate the farmer's farm. It means the dehumanization of his life.

However that may be, the South at last, looking defensively about her in all directions upon an industrial world, fingers the weapons of industrialism. There is one powerful voice in the South which, tired of a long status of disrepute, would see the South made at once into a section second to none in wealth, as that is statistically reckoned, and in progressiveness, as that might be estimated by the rapidity of the industrial turnover. This desire offends those who would still like to regard the South as, in the old sense, a home; but its expression is loud and insistent. The urban South, with its heavy importation of regular American ways and regular American citizens, has nearly capitulated to these novelties. It is the village South and the rural South which supply the resistance, and it is lucky for them that they represent a vast quantity of inertia.

Will the Southern establishment, the most substantial exhibit on this continent of a society of the European and historic order, be completely crumbled by the powerful acid of the Great Progressive Principle? Will there be no more looking backward but only looking forward? Is our New World to be dedicated forever to the doctrine of newness?

It is in the interest of America as a whole, as well as in the interest of the South, that these questions press for an answer. I will enter here the most important items of the situation as well as I can; doubtless they will appear a little oversharpened for the sake of exhibition.

1. The intention of Americans at large appears now to be what it was always in danger of becoming: an intention of being infinitely progressive. But this intention cannot permit of an established order of human existence, and of that leisure which conditions the life of intelligence and the arts.

2. The old South, if it must be defined in a word, practiced the contrary and European philosophy of establishment as the foundation of the life of the spirit. The ante-bellum Union possessed, to say the least, a wholesome variety of doctrine.

3. But the South was defeated by the Union on the battlefield with remarkable decisiveness, and the two consequences have been dire: the Southern tradition was physically impaired, and has ever since been unable to offer an attractive example of its philosophy in action; and the American progressive principle has developed into a pure industrialism without any check from a Southern minority whose voice ceased to make itself heard.

4. The further survival of the Southern tradition as a detached local remnant is now unlikely. It is agreed that the South must make contact again with the Union. And in adapting itself to the actual state of the Union, the Southern tradition will have to consent to a certain industrialization of its own.

5. The question at issue is whether the South will permit herself to be so industrialized as to lose entirely her historic identity, and to remove the last substantial barrier that has stood in the way of American progressivism; or will accept industrialism, but with a very bad grace, and will manage to maintain a good deal of her traditional philosophy.

. . . The hope which is inherent in the situation is evident from the terms in which it is stated. The South must be industrialized—but to a certain extent only, in moderation. The program which now engages the Southern leaders is to see how the South may handle this fire without being burnt badly. The South at least is to be physically reconstructed; but it will be fatal if the South should conceive it as her duty to be regenerated and get her spirit reborn with a totally different orientation toward life. . . .

2. Cleanth Brooks on the Language of the South, 1984

. . . The soul of a people is embodied in the language peculiar to them. Look at the way in which the Welsh still jealously cling to their own language even though for centuries Wales has been tied to England by the most powerful of political and economic connections. Consider the importance that the people of Quebec attach to their provincial French—not only in their everyday speech but even in their street signs, shop signs, and formal documents. Remember that a country as tiny as Belgium maintains two languages, French and Flemish.

The cases that I cite are, I grant, special and extreme. The difference between the language of the South and the English spoken in this country at large is not a difference of such magnitude. But more extreme cases may fairly be used to establish a point.

It is significant that peoples throughout history have often stubbornly held on to their native language or dialect because they regarded it as a badge of their identity and because they felt that only through it could they express their inner beings, their attitudes and emotions, and even their own concepts of reality.

Listen to James Joyce's Stephen Dedalus in *A Portrait of the Artist as a Young Man*: "The language in which we [Stephen and the dean of studies, an Englishman] are speaking is his before it is mine. How different are the words *home, Christ, ale, master* on his lips and on mine! I cannot speak or write these words without unrest of spirit. His language, so familiar and so foreign, will always be for me an acquired speech. I have not made or accepted its words. My voice holds them at bay. My soul frets in the shadow of his language."

That the South has its own idiom is tacitly conceded, I believe, by nearly everybody. Outsiders acknowledge that this is so by their amusement at what appears to them a very quaint English, or more emphatically by occasionally having to declare that they simply can't make out what is being said. But the most solid testimony to the individual quality is to be found in its literature and particularly in that rich outpouring of verse and prose during our own century.

Though I give proper credit to the individual literary talent manifested by those who have created this literature, I mean . . . to pay special tribute to the language itself—a language that they have inherited and which they have managed to use so well. It has proved to be a valuable and indeed indispensable resource.

Where did this language, or (if I must speak more cautiously) this idiom and dialect, come from? Is it a corruption of proper English? A discoloring of the clear waters issuing from the well of English pure and undefiled? An examination of the case will clearly reveal that no distortion or perversion has occurred, and indeed far less innovation has occurred than one might have supposed. The Southern dialect has perfectly sound historical roots.

I must warn you, however, that in what I shall be saying on this subject I cannot claim to be speaking as an expert. From the beginning, my basic training has been in literature. I am not by profession a language scholar. I am rather, in this field, an amateur, though an enthusiastic amateur. I am still trying to find out where the Southern dialect really came from.

Let me begin by making a few remarks about American pronunciation generally. In spite of our borrowings of words from other languages, French, Spanish, and German, for example, and in spite of our coinage of new words such as *OK*, *kodak*, and *razz-matazz*, American English

obviously derives from the English that was spoken in Great Britain several centuries ago. As far as pronunciation is concerned, we Americans speak an old-fashioned English. Contrary to what the layman assumes, in pronunciation it is the mother language that usually changes, not the daughter language. . . .

. . . [A] Southern language veritably exists and constitutes a rich resource for the writers of the South.

Obviously, the presence of even a rich and vital language will not make up for a user's lack of sensibility, intelligence, and imagination. The dull and awkward writer will remain so, with even the language of Shakespeare at his disposal. Nevertheless, a rich and expressive language counts for a great deal.

What is the future of the language of the South? Can it be said to have a future? In an increasingly urban, mobile, and industrialized society, can it survive? I'm not sure, but I have heard its death prophesied so often—as early as the 1920s with the advent of radio—that I have begun to take heart. It clearly has staying power.

I am confident, however, that I can identify its most dangerous enemy. It is not education properly understood, but miseducation: foolishly incorrect theories of what constitutes good English, an insistence on spelling pronunciations, and the propagation of bureaucratese, sociologese, and psychologese, which American business, politics, and academies seem to exude as a matter of course. The grave faults are not the occasional use of *ain't* but the bastard concoctions from a Latinized vocabulary produced by people who never studied Latin. Gobbledygook is a waste of everybody's time.

The great poet of our century, William Butler Yeats, years ago faced the problem as it manifested itself in Ireland. He rejoiced in the unwritten literature of the folk: the ballad, the folk song, and the folk tale. They were genuine art, and required no apology to anybody. He also revered the great tradition of written literature that has behind it Sophocles, Dante, and Shakespeare. The two literatures did not compete, but complemented each other.

Like Yeats's Ireland, the South has had a vigorous oral literature and, like Ireland again, a brilliant written literature, particularly in our present century. The great danger, as Yeats saw it, was that the mass of people would lose the virtues of the unwritten tradition without ever having achieved mastery of the great written tradition. They would thus be doubly losers: to have lost the ability to tell a good yarn or appreciate it when told, and yet not be able to read with understanding and delight the great literature of the past and present. Such loss is not made up for by sitting bemused, watching a situation comedy or even the best programs of our public television networks for four or five hours a day. If such losers do read at all, it's more often predigested fare that comes off the stands of the drugstore, not the shelves of a library or an honest-to-goodness bookstore.

Genuine literature is not a luxury commodity but neither is it an assembly-line product. It cannot be mass produced. It has to be hand made, fashioned by a genuine craftsman out of honest human emotions and experiences, in the making of which the indispensable material is our common language, in all its variety, complexity, and richness. Otherwise the literary craftsman has no way of expressing whatever penetrating insights into the human predicament he may possess—no way of setting forth for others his passionate feeling, his wit, or his wisdom.

3. *The Appeal of Jimmy Carter, 1976*

When Jimmy Carter sat down two years ago to write his biography for the 1976 Presidential campaign, he chose to introduce himself as "a Southerner and an American"—in that order. At the time, this dual citizenship looked like a curious credential to flaunt: scars as old as the Civil War and wounds as fresh as the civil-rights movement still seemed to exclude Dixie as a promising source of Presidents. But Carter avoided the worst bogs of the South's sometimes Gothic political tradition and adapted its best features brilliantly. His Southern mystique still puzzled and troubled a few unreconstructed Democrats in New York City this week. But his success left Southerners basking in a fine sense of political redemption. "We've got Carter," exulted Sen. Ernest F. Hollings, a South Carolina progressive. "Now we can rejoin the Union."

The reunion between the South and the rest of the Democratic Party was waiting to happen. "Everybody, black and white, now recognizes you don't have to be ashamed of turnip greens," grinned Carter's press secretary, Jody Powell. "Somebody else could have done what Jimmy did—if they'd gone to work for it." The truth seemed to be that the forces behind Carter's extraordinary accomplishment had been painfully at work for more than two decades. Freedom riders and court orders in the South, ghetto riots and school busing in the North shattered the myths of Southern white supremacy and Northern moral superiority that have divided the country and hamstrung the Presidential aspirations of Southern politicians ever since Reconstruction. Voters united in frustration over Vietnam, Watergate and Washington, as well as the race issue, chose to pay attention to Carter's "We're OK" politics—not to his accent.

Carter is an energetic, ambitious and driven politician of the new school of liberal Southern governors and senators who emerged during the turbulent '60s and '70s. He is a cool hand in a region that once reveled in hot, gallus-snapping demagogues—a man with Sunday-school manners and a naval officer's steely self-control. "I see Carter as a hard-as-nails idealist," said Reese Cleghorn, an editor on *The Charlotte Observer*. Where William Faulkner once mused darkly over "the courage and honor and hope and pride and compassion and pity and sacrifice" of an enduring South, struggling against centuries of racism, troubled conscience, bad blood and ignorance, Carter now uses the same cadences in his optimistic call for a national Administration "as honest and decent and open and compassionate" as the American people. "He is a Southerner without guilt," notes Donald Fowler, chief of South Carolina's Democratic Party. "It's a rarity."

The Georgia peanut farmer has skillfully applied and extended the South's traditional sense of place, family and community to national politics, in part from his own personal magnetism—and in part from the Americanization of the South's burden of history. "The South has come North," says Harvard's Dr. Robert Coles, a chronicler of both regions. "The nation is now struggling with the problems the South fought with for years. This is no regional stranger we are seeing in Jimmy Carter." What Carter has done is to engineer the beginnings of a new politics, Southern in accent and tactics, perhaps, but fully national in scope and goals. "If he's accused of being fuzzy—well, that's the way you talk to folks back home in order to change them," observes Eugene Patterson, editor of *The St. Petersburg Times*. "I call this duress with love." . . .

4. "Rednecks" and "Good Old Boys"—A Vanishing Species? 1989

Are we in the twilight of the Age of the Good Old Boy? Is the Era of the Redneck finally concluding down South?

Could be. There are signs everywhere. Too many women truck drivers are on the road. Pabst Blue Ribbon has all but disappeared. Nobody hangs around filling stations anymore. In fact, there aren't many filling stations left; they've been replaced by grocery stores with gas pumps.

Pool halls, the traditional nesting place for roughneck rednecks, are an endangered species. The Georgia Legislature considered a bill last winter declaring that billiard parlors no longer constitute public nuisances.

Everybody seems to be moving out of south Georgia, once the land of milk and honey for good old boys and rednecks alike. Long sections of U.S. 41, formerly the highway of dreams for GOBs and 'necks, have been abandoned. Famous love-nest motels along that path are boarded up, but a few have become halfway houses for ex-convicts and the mentally ill.

You don't see as many barbecue places as you used to. The kitchens are too clean in most of the ones that are left, and the pork that comes out of them looks like slices of Danish canned ham.

Sales of Thunderbirds and pickup trucks are not what they ought to be. Everybody wants a Mercedes or BMW. What good old boy a decade or so ago would have yearned for a German car?

Hardly anyone puts plastic Jesuses with sequins, or celluloid pink flamingos, in front yards these days.

In north Georgia, there are plans to build glass skyscrapers near Kennesaw and Acworth. Modernity is destroying the Paris and the Venice of the rednecks, and not a voice of protest is heard.

A six-lane highway now whizzes through the mountains, where Georgia moon is seldom sighted or sipped these days. The white liquor supply has dried up because the demand has disappeared. Most folks want bonded scotch now. Except the health freaks—they've quit drinking.

Oh, there's still a little liquid lightning around. But no self-respecting GOB or redneck would touch the stuff. It's got radiator lead and Clorox in it. Bootleggers don't take pride in their product anymore.

If you're a yuppie or a Yankee or both, we had better stop here to define our terms: Good Old Boy and Redneck.

A good old boy is a white Southern male, over 35, who has money, drives a good car, plays golf and poker, likes women and stock-car races (in that order), has a high school education or better, dislikes "Florida people," used to be Democrat and a smoker but has given up both Democrats and cigarettes, speaks lint-head Southern or better and can spit at least 10 feet. He drinks coffee every weekday morning in the local café or drugstore. If he works in an Atlanta office, his secretary brings him coffee. He's glad he's not a redneck.

A redneck, sometimes known as a 'neck, is a white Southern male, probably under 40, who owes a lot, drives a car that always needs a ring or a brake job, shoots pool, likes stock-car races and women (in that order), has a high school education or less, dislikes "Florida people," smokes, and always voted Republican. He lives in places like Woodstock and Tifton, and he drinks beer (not light and not dry). He wishes he were a good old boy.

Some good old boys you may have heard of: Agriculture Commissioner Tommy Irvin, chicken-and-eggs mogul Gene Sutherland, Public Service Commissioners Bobby Rowan and Bobby Pafford. Also Ted Turner, Zell Miller, Roy Barnes, Tom Murphy and Ron Hudspeth.

Humorist Lewis Grizzard, the Homer of the 'necks, is really a good old boy by virtue of his age, affluence and outlook.

Real rednecks you may have heard of: Gwinnett County Rep. Vinson Wall comes close.

You can tell GOBs and 'necks are disappearing, because when something goes wrong they are blamed. There are not enough of them left to defend themselves.

When the Atlanta banks, run mainly by GOBs, were accused of redlining to keep blacks from getting loans, nobody bothered to point out that Northern insurance companies were the real baddies. The insurance investors, mostly cold-eyed New Englanders, wouldn't buy any Atlanta bank loans made south of I-20. So naturally, the good-old-boy banks didn't make loans in that part of town. Otherwise, they would have violated one of the sacred tenets of banking: Never make a loan you can't sell to somebody else. (One other thing about GOBs: They're not into losing money, even for noble causes.)

When a big-time editor named Bill Kovach left the Atlanta newspapers, he blamed the good old boys. He said Southerners weren't ready for his no-holds-barred brand of journalism. In truth,

three non-Southern newspaper executives—a Hawaiian and two Ohioans—decided to let Kovach leave. None of the three qualifies as a Southern good old boy under any definition. Kovach must have figured no one in the North would understand if he reported being cashiered in Atlanta by non-Southerners. So he simplified the story. Why ruin a cliché?

When white supremacist David Duke was elected to the Louisiana Legislature, good old boys and 'necks were accused of putting him there. The truth: Lee Atwater, the national Republican Party chairman, tried his damnedest to beat Duke. Atwater is a cross between a good old boy and a redneck.

Duke is just a hater. That brings up another point. When most people think of rabid racism and the KKK, they also think of GOBs and rednecks. That may have been an accurate notion in the past. But not any more. No self-respecting Klansman of the '50s and '60s would have anything to do with these bozos of today. The old Klansmen, mean bigots though they were, thought of themselves as patriots. Today's Kluxers and skinheads are more than bigots; they are nuts. They detest their country as much as they despise Jews and blacks. Just listen to their rhetoric sometime if you don't believe me. There is not a true GOB or 'neck among them.

Imagine what the South would be like without rednecks and good old boys. The liberals would have no one to indict for racism. The gays would have no one to accuse of persecution. The feminists would have no one to fantasize about. There would be no market for bright-red condoms. Frederick's of Hollywood would have to start selling Fruit of the Loom.

Membership rolls of Kiwanis and Rotary would sag. Shriners and Jaycees would vanish, Sanford Stadium would be empty. Longhorn Steak House would go out of business. There would be no Varsity. Country-music radio stations would shut down. No one could qualify for the state patrol or to run for sheriff. Grizzard would be off the best-seller list. Miller, Barnes and Irwin would have to get out of politics and find honest work. Gun control might come into vogue.

And who would be left to fleece the Yankees?

5. *The Southern Humor of Lem Griffis*

Swamp 'Gators

Cothran: What about some of the animals in the swamp, Lem; what-all have you got out there?

Griffis: Well, we got many different kinds of animals hyer. I just motored 'long by an alligator a few days ago up here 'at was so long he was sweatin' in the face an' had frost on 'is tail.

Cothran: Hoo-ee.

Griffis: An' I have t' tell the lady-folks t' don't be afraid 'em alligators, because they're just man-eaters.

Cothran: That's comforting; I'm glad to know about that. What about snakes?

Cannibal Snakes

Griffis: Oh yeah, we have a good many snakes hyer. Y'know, snakes they're tur'ble 'bout fightin' they always fight until death, and when one kills the other he always do swaller' im; 'e never fails, always eats 'im.

I saw two of 'em run together for a fight, an' they caught each other by the tail an' went t' swall'in', an' they swallad an' they swallad 'til there wasn't anything but two heads there, an' gave one more swalla, an' 'twas no snake atall!

Jokes on Outsiders

These people comin' out here, s' many of 'em are fishin'. I tell 'em all kinda things. There's some fellers up here not long ago, four of 'em in a car, an' they rented a boat from me an' wanted t' go fishin'. They asked me how the fishin' was; I told 'em it wasn't good, that there's s' much water, 'til it was jus' like fishin' right out in the middle o' the Pacific Ocean.

One of 'em kinda strutched 'is eyes; don't think 'e'd ever been here before. Says, "My goodness, what will we do if the boat was t' sink?"

An' I told 'im, I said, "Go to the bottom, build up a fire, send up smoke signals, an' I'll go after ya."

One day I sat here in front o' this little store, an' station wagon drove up loaded down with people in the biggest kind of a hurry. The feller he slid the wheels an' stopped, the driver did, stuck 'is head out the winder an' said, "Hey, d' you have worms?"

I said, "Yes, why? Are you a doctor?"

You pull all kinda jokes on people comin' all day. A lot of 'em expectin' t' get here an' find people, y'know, that they cain't even converse with. They git down here an' listen at me go on for a while; they begin t' wonder then where in the worl' did such a guy as that ever originate at?

Cothran: Have you lived around here all your life?

Griffis: Not yet.

Cothran: Ohhhh. That's one on me!

Griffis: I was born hyer, in a log cabin I helped my father t' build.

Cothran (after pause): Now wai-i-t a minute! *That's* a *good* trick.

Another Joke on Outsiders

Cothran: What-all kinda jokes have you played on people that've come down here?

Griffis: Well, I useta be a lots worser'n I am now. There's some fellers down here from Texas one time, an' 'ey're a-tellin' about what big things they had in Texas. So one night, I slipped a turtle—oh, he'd a weighed about four or five pounds—under the cover, an' that feller went t' bed, an' found that thing in the bed, an' jumped out. He hollered, wanted t' know what that thing was. I told 'im that was just a common-size Georgia bedbug. Did 'e have anything in Texas that'd beat that?

6. *The Shag—A Distinctive Southern Dance, 1990*

Blonde, bubbly Doris Day strolled down the sidewalk singing "Que Sera." She bumped smack into Ruth Brown—black, rhythmic, with that squeal in her voice—wailing "Mama, He Treats Your Daughter Mean." Somehow, for some people, Brown won out. Music changed, dancing changed, life changed. The key word is "somehow."

Of course, that's not what happened, but the shag was born of music that appeared . . . somehow, from somewhere. Somehow people learned how to do it, whether they were taught by an older brother or a best friend or they taught themselves while partnering a bedpost, doorknob or refrigerator handle. And somehow, the dance spread, and endured. Within certain boundaries, that is.

"It never spread one inch beyond Virginia Beach or the South Carolina/Georgia line," says Phil Sawyer, a Columbia shagger and authority on the dance. "I attribute it to the fact that people elsewhere don't comprehend the subculture, the lifestyle, of shagging. But it's attractive to thousands in South Carolina, North Carolina, Georgia and Virginia."

The lifestyle, like the shag and its rhythm and blues music, is contradictory. It has to do with being cool when you're hot, with having fun but not planning it.

The dance never would have emerged without the music. Perry Como was a silly bubble compared to the gritty realism of The Midnighters. "If people think now that heavy metal music is bad for kids, it's nothing compared to what they thought rhythm and blues was in the '50s," says Del Roberts of Blythewood, former *Sandlapper* editor and a rhythm and blues lover. "They thought you were going straight to hell even thinking about playing this music and dancing to it."

Part of its lure was that it was hard to get. You had to find a record store that sold rhythm and blues—and that could be difficult—or locate a faraway radio station that scheduled regular R&B broadcasts. You could go to the beach and hang around a jukebox. But to hear it live, you had to go to a black dance. If you were white, that meant sitting in the balcony while the blacks danced below. It was in just such a situation at the Township Auditorium in Columbia that Carl Taylor proposed to Ellen Duncan, 31 years ago last May.

The song was "To Be Loved," the singer was Jackie Wilson and the moment was immortalized at the Taylors' 30th anniversary with a gold-framed copy of the 45rpm record.

The camaraderie continues among those early generations. But Ellen Taylor, a veritable godmother of shag, makes a point to dance with a young man on the beach and teach a young girl at a nightclub. "There will be new legends," she predicts, "and those people are going to create their own style of the shag. They may be a little more acrobatic, they may not be as smooth, or they may be smoother. But I think there'll always be a shag around as long as we've got a younger generation to do it."

While young shaggers add more bite and energy to the dance while listening to newer beach music—"Miss Grace" and "Carolina Girls"—the older ones bask in the old, heavy-on-the-saxophone R&B and recall when Elvis changed it all.

"After I heard black music, I despised Elvis Presley when he began recording the white version of that beat," Roberts says. "To me, he was just an imitator."

"He set music 20 years back," agrees Jo-Jo Putnam, a Columbia shagger.

Diehard white southerners who grew up next door to the blacks and learned to love their music, clung to the rhythm and blues. They stood fast, even while rock and roll steamrolled across the country. Their love for the music is why shaggers always dance to the very last note, says Raleigh dentist Steve Baker, a part-time deejay.

But why do people love the shag? Shagger Gretchen Giel hits on it in three easy words: "Because it's ours."

7. *John Shelton Reed Searches for the Southerner, 1990*

The woman was developing an orientation program for newcomers to the South, and she had come to see me because she'd heard I had written some books on the subject. "What does someone moving to the South need to know about the Southerner?" she asked. She waited expectantly.

I told her I couldn't possibly answer that question, that no one could say anything intelligent about "the Southerner." To begin with, I said, it matters where you're going in the South. Good advice for Tampa might not help at all in Austin, or Montgomery, or Hilton Head, or Bristol. W. J. Cash wrote 50 years ago in *The Mind of the South* that there are many Souths, and that may be even more true now. The South incorporates several different economies, many different landscapes. It has some of America's largest and fastest growing metropolitan areas and some of the country's wealthiest suburbs. It has some of the nation's poorest counties, which have been losing population for decades. It has university towns and military bases, elegant resorts and tacky ones. Even among its rural communities and small market towns there are obvious differences: The mountains aren't the Piedmont, and both of those are different from the Coastal Plains. The Southwest is something else again—and then there's Florida.

Consequently, I said there's no single "Southerner" for newcomers to know about. A Kentucky mountaineer, an old-family Charlestonian, a Texas wildcatter, an Alabama tenant farmer, an Atlanta businesswoman—what could all these people have in common? Many non-Southerners don't recognize what a diverse place the South is. (For that matter, neither do many Southerners.)

Even if someone's ideas about Southerners are accurate for some parts of the region, there will be a great many exceptions. And some images aren't accurate anywhere anymore because they don't reflect how fast the South has changed in the last generation. Some Americans really do still think of the South as a roman-tic land of moonlight and magnolias. If they come here, they're in for some surprises. So are those whose stereotypes run more to pellagra and Ku Kluxism. Neither image has much foundation in today's Southern reality, especially not in those parts where migrants are likely to be going.

I urged my visitor just to consider the changes of the last 25 years. Maybe by 1965 it was evident that the South's future would be that of an urban, industrial region, but it hadn't really sunk in. Now nearly three out of four Southerners live in urban areas, and—this is important—most have never lived anywhere else. As recently as two generations ago, farmers were half of the South's labor force. Now just 1 Southerner in 20 or so actually works on a farm, and most Southerners see farms only from the interstate. A sure sign of the South's development is that our birthrate is no longer at an agricultural society's high level. In fact, it's now lower than the national average.

To be sure, some parts of our region have been largely bypassed by the South's development, and they have the same problems they've always had. But most of the South now has the problems of a developed economy: problems of growth, not stagnation.

Changes in race relations have been even more astonishing. When the Voting Rights Act was passed in 1965, who would have guessed that anyone would soon be arguing that race relations were better in the South than elsewhere? But now many Southerners, both black and white, are doing just that, and they're not just whistling "Dixie." None of the many changes that the Voting Rights Act produced is more striking than the fact that more blacks now hold public office in the South than in any other region. Mississippi has more black elected officials than any other state. Meanwhile, average black incomes in the South have surpassed those in the Midwest, and they increased during the 1980s while declining elsewhere in the U.S. Perhaps the most persuasive testimony about the extent of these changes is that more blacks have moved to the South since the early 1970s than have left it, reversing a migration flow that in 1965 still seemed one of the unchangeable facts of American life.

These are only a few of the most obvious social and economic changes of the past few decades, I told my guest. Some changes were long awaited; others were completely unexpected, but most of them run counter to longstanding stereotypes. Consequently, I suggested, newcomers would be well advised to come with open minds and open eyes. They shouldn't think they know much about Southerners just because they've seen *Gone with the Wind*, "The Dukes of Hazzard," *Mississippi Burning*, or even "Designing Women." One thing few Southerners appreciate is being on the receiving end of uninformed stereotypes.

But, I said, we also don't appreciate hearing from newcomers that the South is no different from other parts of the country. That's because most Southerners believe the South is better. Indeed, most seem to believe they live in the best part of the South. Newcomers will find there's a lot of regional pride in the South and local pride, too. Country music's Tom T. Hall sings "Country is . . . loving your town." But bragging on your town isn't just a country trait. *Nobody* does more of it than Atlantans.

The woman asked me why Southerners think the South is such a good place to live.

Well, I told her, look at the very first issue of *Southern Living*. It said that Southerners "live better" because they can "use and enjoy the South's open country, its mild climate, long growing season, and relatively uncrowded highways." The highways may be more crowded than they were a quarter century ago, but there's still a lot of open country, and they can't take the climate away from us. Southerners still tell public opinion pollsters that the South offers superior living conditions.

Something else most Southerners say they like about the South is other Southerners. When you ask what we like about each other you get answers ranging from accents to values, but one thing in particular gets mentioned over and over again: Southerners describe each other as polite, courteous, friendly.

This business of Southern manners hasn't really been explored, but it's certainly something both natives and newcomers often notice and comment on. And I think they're right about that, I told my visitor. There are regional differences in manners—not good as opposed to bad, just Southern as opposed to 20th-century American in general.

Most of us find that Southern manners make life pretty pleasant, day to day, but they can confuse someone who doesn't understand them. Surely everyone knows that "Y'all come see us" doesn't mean you should actually drop in, but maybe not everyone understands that when repairmen don't show up as promised, it may be because they thought it would have been impolite to have told you they were just too busy to come.

In general, it seems to me that Southerners often go to some lengths to avoid disappointing people, and even more to avoid direct criticism and disagreement—that is, unless they mean to be offensive. (Excuse me for saying this, I told my visitor, but it follows that Southerners don't like to be criticized, even when critics mean to be helpful. Maybe newcomers ought to know that.)

"Why can't Southerners just say what they mean?" she asked.

But we do, I said. At least we usually understand each other. It's just a matter of how you say what you mean. You can see the same sort of roundabout approach in Southern humor. It isn't that Southerners can't be amused by Woody Allen or Rodney Dangerfield or Eddie Murphy, but there's also a peculiarly Southern form of humor that doesn't rely on one-liners or on wit. It's a matter of storytelling, where the humor is in the details and the style. As Jerry Clower once put it: "I don't tell funny stories. I tell stories funny." This takes some getting used to, and non-Southerners sometimes miss the point. Same with manners.

Some other Americans who like to think of themselves as straightforward, no-nonsense, and businesslike have been known to complain about Southern indirection. They wonder why Southerners can't just get to the point. But Southerners are likely to think that there are usually several points, one of them being to put the person you're dealing with at ease. So even in the business world there may be a tendency— just a tendency, that's all—to the sort of preliminary small talk and inquiries about family and so forth that are more common in Oriental bazaars than in the commerce of the Northeast.

The absence of those pleasantries can be misinterpreted, too, as when some Southerners complain about newcomers who order people around "like they owned them." Small talk can serve to make the point that just because you're paying someone doesn't mean you think you're better than he is. In this and other ways, Southern manners are egalitarian. I mentioned W. J. Cash again. In *The Mind of the South*, he wrote about the old-time Southern mill owner, mixing with the workers, slapping backs and knowing names, respecting them as human beings and Christians.

And speaking of religion, I said, something else that strikes many newcomers to the South is the part that churches play in the South's public and social life. They ought to be prepared for that. Certainly you'd be making a mistake to come to most parts of the South if you mind living in a place where most people are Baptists or Methodists. It would be like moving to Utah if you don't like Mormons, or Massachusetts if Roman Catholics get on your nerves.

You don't have to be Baptist or Methodist or even Protestant yourself; these days you can be whatever you want. But it helps if you're *something*. Belonging to a church and being more or less active in it is a taken-for-granted part of middle-class life in the South, in a way that it's not in many other parts of the country. Nearly everybody, rich or poor, urban or rural or suburban, black or white, has a church to go to. Even those Southerners who don't go to church at least know which one they're not going to.

Religion is tied in with race and social class, in complicated ways that Southerners understand but don't talk about much. In that, it's like hunting and fishing. Different folks do these things in different ways, according to how they were raised and what their circumstances encourage. Trout fishing is something like Episcopalianism—sort of the Anglicanism of angling, if you'll excuse the expression. Going after catfish with a cane pole and chicken innards may correspond to Holiness. Somewhere in between lies the market for bass boats and electronic fish-finders. Just so, some Southerners hunt quail, while others hunt squirrel, and coon-hunters are different from the Ducks. Unlimited crowd. But they're all hunters. You don't have to hunt and fish if you live in the South, but if you don't like hunters, you might be happier somewhere else. Same with religion.

And that reminds me of sports, I said. There is something almost religious about Southerners' attachment to their teams. In small towns, going to the high school game on Friday night is almost on a par with going to church on Sunday. It's the same with college sports. Where else would a magazine like *Southern Living* pick an all-star football team each fall? But it makes sense: A great deal of Southern social life does seem to revolve around tailgate parties.

Newcomers might want to pick a team and follow it. It doesn't greatly matter which one—it's like religion that way, too. Again, you don't have to be interested in sports to live in the South, but life may be easier if you are, or can pretend to be. Even in the business world, much of that small talk I mentioned earlier has to do with sports. A newcomer who doesn't know the New Orleans Saints from the Macon Whoopees might find it a good investment (if nothing else) to learn.

Of course, much of this is just speculation, I told my visitor, and even if all of it's true it may be changing. One constant in the South has been change. That's a paradox, isn't it?

I looked at the time and realized I had another appointment. So I said I'm sorry, but there's really no way to say what people moving to the South ought to know about Southerners. You can't begin to generalize, and even if you could I wouldn't do it. Southerners don't much like folks generalizing about them.

References

1. An Agrarian Condemns Industrialism, 1930
   John Crowe Ransom, "Reconstructed but Unregenerate," in Twelve Southerners, *I'll Take My Stand: The South and the Agrarian Tradition* (Baton Rouge: Louisiana University Press, 1962), pp. 17–22.

2. Cleanth Brooks on the Language of the South, 1984
   Cleanth Brooks, *The Language of the South* (Athens, Georgia: University of Georgia Press, 1985), pp. 2–4, 52–54.

3. The Appeal of Jimmy Carter, 1976
   "The Southern Mystique," *Newsweek* (July 19, 1976), p. 30.

4. "Rednecks" and "Good Old Boys"—A Vanishing Species? 1989
   Bill Shipp, "Rednecks in the Sunset," *Atlanta Magazine* (May 1989), pp. 43–44.

5. The Southern Humor of Lem Griffis
   John A. Burrison ed., *Storytellers: Folktales and Legends from the South* (Athens, Georgia: University of Georgia Press, 1989), pp. 116–117, 119, 121.

6. The Shag—A Distinctive Southern Dance, 1990
   Aïda Rogers, "The Mysterious Shag Lifestyle: Being Cool When You're Hot," *Sandlapper* (July/August 1990), pp. 16–17.

7. John Shelton Reed Searches for the Southerner, 1990
   John Shelton Reed, "In Search of the Elusive Southerner," *Southern Living* (June 1990), pp. 92–94.

Further Reading

H. Brandt Ayers and Thomas H. Naylor, eds., *You Can't Eat Magnolias* (1972)

Kenneth K. Bailey, *Southern White Protestantism in the Twentieth Century* (1964)

Wilbur J. Cash, *The Mind of the South* (1941)

Richard N. Current, *Northernizing the South* (1983)

James M. Dabbs, *Haunted by God: The Cultural and Religious Experience of the South* (1972)

Carl N. Degler, *Place over Time: The Continuity of Southern Distinctiveness* (1977)

John Egerton, *The Americanization of Dixie: The Southernization of America* (1974)

Fifteen Southerners, *Why the South Will Survive* (1981)

Walter J. Fraser, Jr., and Winfred B. Moore, Jr., *The Southern Enigma: Essays on Race, Class and Folk Culture* (1983)

Robert L. Hall and Carol B. Stack, eds., *Holding on to the Land and the Lord: Kinship, Ritual, Land Tenure, and Social Policy in the Rural South* (1982)

Paul Hemphill, *The Good Old Boys* (1974)

Fred C. Hobson, Jr., *Tell About the South: The Southern Rage to Explain* (1983)

Florence King, *Southern Ladies and Gentlemen* (1975)

Bill C. Malone, *Southern Music: American Music* (1979)

John Shelton Reed, *The Enduring South* (1972)

Francis B. Simkins, *The Everlasting South* (1963)

Robert P. Steed, Lawrence W. Moreland, and Tod A. Baker, *The Disappearing South? Studies in Regional Change and Continuity* (1990)

Charles R. Wilson and William Ferris, eds., *Encyclopedia of Southern Culture* (1989)

Howard Zinn, *The Southern Mystique* (1964)

Credits

pp. 10–11 "A Letter from Eliza Lucas Pinckney" in H. Roy Merrens, ed., *The Colonial South Carolina Scene: Contemporary Views, 1697–1774*, 1977. Reprinted by permission of The University of South Carolina Press.

p. 59 Reprinted by permission of Louisiana State University Press from *William Johnson's Natchez: The Antebellum Diary of a Free Negro*, edited by William R. Hogan and Edwin A. Davis. Copyright © 1951 by Louisiana State University Press.

pp. 60–61 From *Bullwhip Days: The Slaves Remember*, edited by James Mellon. Copyright © 1988 by James Mellon. Used by permission of Grove Press, Inc.

pp. 66–67 Entries for Oct. 24, Nov. 5, 1850, and March 17, 1851, in Theodore Rosengarten, *Tombee: Portrait of a Cotton Planter* (New York: William Morrow and Company, 1986), pp. 506, 508, 526. Reprinted by permission.

p. 68 Letters from Ann Elizabeth Middleton to Nathaniel Middleton, July 25, August 6 and 9, 1852 from the Nathaniel Middleton Papers from the Southern Historical Collection, Library of the University of North Carolina at Chapel Hill.

p. 98 "Circular of the 1860 Association" in Archibald Rutledge Papers from the Southern Historical Collection, Library of the University of North Carolina at Chapel Hill.

p. 108 Reprinted from *Fighting for the Confederacy: The Personal Recollections of General Edward Porter Alexander*, edited by Gary W. Gallagher. Copyright © 1989 by The University of North Carolina Press.

p. 139 From *All God's Dangers: The Life of Nate Shaw* by Theodore Rosengarten. Copyright © 1974 by Theodore Rosengarten. Reprinted by permission of Alfred A. Knopf Inc.

p. 153 From Melton McLaurin, *Separate Pasts: Growing Up White in the Segregated South*, 1987. Copyright © 1987 by The University of Georgia Press. Used by permission.

pp. 163–165 Excerpts from *Black Boy* by Richard Wright. Copyright © 1937, 1942, 1944, 1945 by Richard Wright. Reprinted by permission of HarperCollins Publishers.

pp. 165–166 From Alfreda M. Duster, ed., *Crusade for Justice: The Autobiography of Ida B. Wells*. Copyright © 1970. Reprinted by permission of The University of Chicago Press.

pp. 166–167 Text from Haywood Patterson and Earl Conrad, *Scottsboro Boy*, Doubleday, 1950. Reprinted by permission.

pp. 168–169 From *Such as Us: Southern Voices of the Thirties*, edited by Tom E. Terrill and Jerrold Hirsch. Copyright © 1987 by The University of North Carolina Press. Reprinted by permission.

pp. 213−215 Jerry DeLaughter, "Ten Years After Camille," *The South Magazine* (July 1979).

pp. 215−218 Jerry Adler "Troubled Waters" from *Newsweek* (April 16, 1990). Copyright © 1990, Newsweek, Inc. All rights reserved. Reprinted by permission.

p. 219 Cartoon by Robert Ariail, 1988. Reprinted by permission of *The State*.

pp. 224−226 From *Black Power: The Politics of Liberation in America* by Stokely Carmichael and Charles Hamilton. Copyright©1967 by Stokely Carmichael and Charles Hamilton. Reprinted by permission of Random House, Inc.

pp. 226−227 James D. Williams, "The Long, Sad Road to Cumming, Georgia," *The Crisis* (March 1987). Reprinted with permission of the Crisis Publishing Company.

pp. 228−229 "South Florida's Melting Pot Is About to Boil" Reprinted from February 4, 1985 issue of *Business Week* by special permission. Copyright © 1985 by McGraw-Hill, Inc.

pp. 229−231 Reprinted, by permission, from *Heroes, Plain Folks, and Skunks* by Albert B. Chandler with Vance Trimble (Bonus Books, Inc., Chicago). Copyright©1989 by Albert B. Chandler.

pp. 231−232 "A Chance to Serve" by Jesse Jackson (March/April 1988) from *The Black Scholar*. Reprinted by permission of the publisher.

pp. 232−233 "Civil Rights Pioneer Works on New Great Society," *The State* (July 24, 1990).

pp. 233−234 "Race and the South," Copyright © July 23, 1990. Reprinted by permission of *U.S. News and World Report*.

pp. 238−240 Reprinted by permission of Louisiana State University Press from *I'll Take My Stand: The South and the Agrarian Tradition* by Twelve Southerners. Copyright © 1930 by Harper and Brothers. Copyright renewed 1958 by Donald Davidson.

pp. 240−242 From Cleanth Brooks, *The Language of the South*. Copyright © 1985 by The University of Georgia Press. Used by permission.

pp. 242−243 "The Southern Mystique." *Newsweek* (July 19, 1976). Copyright © 1976, Newsweek, Inc. All rights reserved. Reprinted by permission.

pp. 243−244 Reprinted with permission from *Atlanta Magazine*, May 1989, pp. 43−44. " 'Rednecks' and 'Good Old Boys'—A Vanishing Species,' " by Bill Shipp.

p. 245 From John A. Burrison, ed. *Storytellers: Folktales and Legends from the South*. Copyright©1989, 1991 by The University of Georgia Press. Used by permission.

p. 246 From Aida Rogers, "The Mysterious Shag Lifestyle: Being Cool When You're Hot," *Sandlapper* (July/August 1990). Copyright © 1990 RPW Publishing Corp. Reprinted with permission from *Sandlapper,* ®The Magazine of South Carolina.

pp. 247–249 "In Search of the Elusive Southerner," by John Shelton Reed. First published: June 1990, *Southern Living*. Reprinted by permission of the author.